WITH THE
GRAIN

WITH THE GRAIN

ELLEN HODGSON BROWN

Carroll & Graf Publishers, Inc.
New York

Copyright © 1990 by Ellen Hodgson Brown
All rights reserved

First Carroll & Graf edition 1990

Carroll & Graf Publishers, Inc
260 Fifth Avenue
New York, NY 10001

Library of Congress Cataloging-in-Publication Data

Brown, Ellen Hodgson.
    With the grain / Ellen Hodgson Brown. — 1st Carroll & Graf ed.
        p.   cm.
    Includes bibliographical references and index.
    ISBN: 0-88184-573-6
    1. Vegetarianism.   I. Title.
RM236.B69   1990
613.2'62—dc20   90-31725
                                                                      CIP

Manufactured in the United States of America

Table of Contents

Preface

"Take nothing on its looks. Take everything on evidence."
                              —*Great Expectations*
                              Charles Dickens

I didn't intend to write a diet book when I started researching. I was just concerned about what to feed my children. I had replaced animal foods with plant foods as an experiment in my own diet—and lost weight, and had more energy.

It's one thing to experiment with my health, quite another to experiment with that of the children. What would my mother say when their legs started to bow and pernicious anemia set in? Is a vegetarian diet safe for children? Would they fare better in the long run with or without meat? What about milk products and eggs? Those concerns were what first took me to the bookshelves.

Few of the books in health food stores answered my questions in a way that inspired confidence. They tended to reach contradictory conclusions without citing the evidence on which they were based. If they did cite studies, it was in a general way. I couldn't tell what the actual findings were. I'm a lawyer by profession, trained in painstaking research and skeptical of claims that are unsupported by evidence. Most popular nutrition books required a leap of faith I wasn't prepared to make.

I ventured into the University of California Medical Library to see if the latest in medical science could answer my nutritional questions.

Three years later, I'd read enough studies to satisfy myself. A grain-based diet without meat fulfills nutritional needs, even for children. These needs can be met not only without meat, but without animal products at all. If your children

1

aren't allergic to milk or eggs, it's easier to plan a nutritionally sound diet with these foods than without them; but
healthy children have been raised entirely on plant foods.
Adults need animal foods even less than children do. Adults
are finished forming new muscle and bone. They can handle more bulky foods, in more quantity, than children.

Researchers disagree about your need for milk. It's a
particularly good source of calcium, but it provides this
nutrient along with certain undesirable substances not found
in plant sources. These substances include saturated fat and
cholesterol, which are hard on the arteries and fattening;
lactose (milk sugar), which many people lack the enzymes
to digest; and certain milk proteins that can also provoke
allergic reactions.

If you are allergic to milk, it can't be replaced by meat,
which is a very poor source of calcium. Plant foods are
better options. Tofu, or soybean curd, is a high-protein
Oriental milk alternative that is an excellent source not only
of the calcium lacking in meat, but of the iron lacking in
milk. While "bean curd" may sound unpalatable, it can
actually form the basis of tasty dishes even children enjoy.
(See Recipes.)

Although I wasn't researching weight loss, I also came
across studies explaining the twenty pounds I'd lost—without
trying—when I switched from meat and salad without bread
(the standard dieter's fare) to bread and salad without meat.
Other studies explained why my stamina and endurance
increased when I substituted grains for meat, which I once
thought was an athlete's most important food.

Then there was the ominous body of evidence linking a
diet of animal products to the twentieth-century epidemic of
chronic diseases—heart disease, stroke, osteoporosis, kidney disease, cancer, diabetes, and obesity—and noting
their peculiar absence in populations whose diets centered
around grains instead of meat. Other data attested that the
world food crisis could be alleviated by using land to feed
people rather than livestock.

These studies form the basis of this book. They are both
epidemiological (involving compilations of data from studies
of different populations), and experimental (based on care-
fully designed and controlled laboratory research with animals and people). The summary presented here is heavily

footnoted. You can look up any studies that strike you as dubious.

Since researchers often disagree, I paid particular attention to contradictory studies and tried to reconcile them into a consistent theory supported by all the evidence. If your goal is simply to lose weight and improve your health, you may not care to read closely reasoned analyses of contradictory studies; so I've put them in the footnotes for those who like in-depth study. Within the text, details of research are indented and blocked off.

Chapter 1 previews the issues covered in depth in this book. Its basic message is that if you replace meat, cheese, and eggs with vegetables and grains, you will lose weight and live longer. But you don't have to become a strict vegetarian to achieve these results. Simply make this switch to whatever extent suits your taste and temperament, and you should notice improvements in your medical checkups and on the scales.

Introduction
by John Robbins

Something deep within the human psyche is shifting in our times. Everywhere people are exploring all kinds of alternatives to the established and conventional ways of living. Vegetarianism is on the rise. A few decades ago the average American mother would have been more upset to discover that her son or daughter had become a vegetarian than to learn that he or she had taken up smoking. But today, as increasing numbers of us partake of the advantages of a more vegetarian lifestyle, the average American mother is becoming ever more willing to consider the possibility, not only for her children, but also for her husband and herself.

For most of us, the transition towards vegetarianism is done in stages, gradually substituting chicken and fish for red meat, and then weaning away from flesh foods while retaining eggs and milk as staples. But there is always a leading edge to every social movement, and today more and more people are experimenting with a "vegan" diet—not only going meatless, but also eggless and dairyless.

Raised believing that the "Basic Four Food Groups" are the foundations of a proper diet, I would never have believed that a vegan diet could adequately support our health, much less be nutritionally superior. But as Ellen Hodgson Brown shows, with careful and complete attention to detail, such is actually the case.

Her presentation is particularly persuasive, and a pleasure to consider, because she doesn't preach or make us feel guilty. She simply presents the facts, clearly derived from scrupulous scientific research, and lets us decide for ourselves to what extent we wish to change, and bring our lives into accord with what has now been learned.

For those of us who have maintained our psychic loyalty to the Basic Four Food Groups, it might be helpful to realize that these groups did not come down from Mt. Sinai. Nor are they actually the products of scientific concern for our well-being. They are rather the result of extensive lobbying pressure in Washington, paid for and exerted on behalf of the meat, dairy and egg industries—what the Center for Science in the Public Interest calls the "fat lobby." There used to be seven food groups; before that there were twelve.

It is hard to overestimate the power of the programming we have all been subjected to which convinces us that animal products are necessary for our health. Few of us realize to just what an extent this conditioning has been the deliberate work of the meat, dairy and egg industries. The National Dairy Council is actually the leading supplier of the "nutritional education" materials used in our public schools. And the Dairy Council is not a council of elders, generously bestowing us with wisdom on behalf of health. The Dairy Council is actually a trade lobby, whose purpose is to promote the sale of dairy products.

The slick advertising campaigns bombarding us from the meat, dairy and egg industries take a toll on our sanity. It becomes hard to objectively consider the merits and demerits of various food choices. And that is precisely why exhaustive and painstaking scientific investigations are in order, so that our lives and health are not at the complete mercy of commercial interests.

What Ellen Hodgson Brown has done in *With the Grain* is to clearly present a fully documented argument in favor of a vegan diet. If you want to be trim and healthy, she says, try the vegan way. And she is correct. Your body will thank you for the rest of your life.

What she doesn't say is that so also will the animals thank you, who are spared the terrible suffering of today's merciless factory farms. And so also future generations, because the less meat we eat today, the more natural resources will be left for tomorrow. She just appeals directly and rationally to our desire for personal health, and doesn't bring in the ethical and environmental argument that so many of us find so moving.

With the Grain will appeal to people who want to know what medical science is telling us today about the pros and cons of a totally vegetarian diet. However close to the leading edge we decide to live, however radical a statement we feel called to make with our lives, it helps to know the facts. Ellen Hodgson Brown has done us a great service in presenting these to us simply and straightforwardly. Her book is well written, well organized, and points us in the most important direction we could possibly move today.

She has done her job. It is up to us whether we take heed.

February 1990

Section I

THE PLANT-CENTERED DIET

Chapter 1

An Old Diet with a New Name

"Pythagoras . . . entirely abstained from wine and animal food, and still prior to these from voracity, and confined himself to such nutriments as was slender and easy of digestion. In consequence of this, his sleep was short, and his soul vigilant, and pure, and his body confirmed in a state of perfect and invariable health."[1]

Animal products compose two of the four basic food groups. They also contribute two-thirds of the fat to the American diet.[2] The idea that you can not only survive but thrive without them is a revolutionary one. But the essentially-plant-foods diet is far from new. It was the original diet of man.[3] And it's still the diet of the gorilla, our nearest relative in the animal world.

It's also the diet of most of the world's poor, not out of religious principle but from necessity. Their protein comes from beans and grains (wheat, rice, and corn) rather than meat. Not only have they survived on this diet, they have escaped the chronic diseases that have been called "twentieth-century epidemics" and "the black plague of affluence."[4]

"Veganism" is so new in this country that the initiated can't even agree on how to pronounce it. Is it the generic "vedj"—as in "vegetable"—or the exotic "veeg," as cultists prefer?

Never mind how you pronounce it. What is it? The vegan diet consists of foods that grow in the earth—grains, beans, nuts, seeds, vegetables, and fruits. It excludes animal products—meat, poultry, fish, milk, cheese, and eggs. While traditional vegetarians replace meat with cheese and eggs that are equally high in fat and cholesterol, vegans replace meat with plant foods.

At least that's the scrupulously-vegan diet. This book is

about the essentially-vegan or "plant-centered" diet. Grains, beans, and greens are the focus of the daily fare. But a pat of butter on your bread, an egg to hold your casserole together, or a piece of fish when there's nothing like nut loaf on the menu are still okay. Animal products shrink from the slab of steak in the center of your plate to the bits of shrimp in your chop suey. Animal products *can* be dispensed with altogether. But for the not-so-Spartan, token amounts won't substantially alter either your waistline or your lifeline.

Don't Third World populations have shorter life spans than we do?

It's true that people in developing countries don't live any longer, on the average, than heart-attack-prone Western meat-eaters. But the diseases their flesh is heir to are of the infectious variety. One problem is their bacteria-ridden water. Another is lack of food. It's hard to keep up your resistance when you're starving. Yet people who do manage to survive past the age of sixty remain relatively free of the chronic diseases that plague Western countries. And the symptomless forms of chronic disease seen in America's young people are absent from Third World youths.[5]

Vegetarians in industrialized countries, who aren't troubled with infectious disease, not only have a lower incidence of chronic disease than meat-eaters they also live an extra decade or so. The difference in life expectancy is nine years for women and twelve years for men.[6] Studies show that in any given period, significantly fewer vegetarians die than meat-eaters—not only from cardiovascular disease (the number one killer), but *from any cause.*

A West German study reported in 1988 followed 1,904 vegetarians for five years. Observed deaths from all causes were only thirty-seven percent as great as expected based on national mortality statistics. Heart disease deaths were only twenty percent as great as expected, and cancer deaths were only fifty-six percent as great as expected.[7]

An American study reported twenty-one years of follow-up on 27,530 Seventh Day Adventists (SDAs), a religious group that advocates a vegetarian diet. All the participants' lifestyles were similarly abstemious, except that some of them ate meat. The researchers found that deaths from all causes were twenty percent greater for SDAs who ate meat at least five times a week as for those who ate it less than once a week.[8]

One reason for the greater longevity of people who avoid animal products is their tendency to remain thin. How much you weigh is directly related both to your risk of chronic disease and to how long you will live.[9] Obesity is rare not only among Third World essentially-vegan populations (who simply may not get enough food), but also among vegans in industrialized countries (who can afford all the bread they can eat.)[10]

In fact, a strange phenomenon has been documented among vegans in industrialized countries. They weigh an average of twenty pounds less than other people *who eat the same number of calories.*[11] It seems that *calories count less* for vegans than for meat-eaters (or for egg- and cheese-eating vegetarians).

Why would calories count less for vegans?

This question has been answered by recent medical studies that explode the time honored calorie-counting theory of weight loss. These studies, which are investigated in Chapter 2, show that carbohydrate calories are actually *less fattening* than *the same number* of calories from fat. They show that body fat comes mainly from dietary fat. You'd have trouble getting fat on complex carbohydrates even if you stuffed yourself with them.

Most of the calories in grains, beans, and greens come from carbohydrate, while most of the calories in meat, cheese, and eggs come from fat. Meat is about half fat and half protein by weight, but a gram of fat contains more than twice as many calories as a gram of protein. Most meats contain *no* carbohydrate and grains contain almost no fat.[12]

It appears we are physiologically adapted to the diet of our tree-swinging forebears, who lived on the carbohydrate- and fiber-rich foods of the earth. Carbohydrate metabolism is regulated by the body—as you eat more, you burn more. But no such mechanism steps in when you eat fat, which stays around making you fatter. We haven't evolved mechanisms to regulate the metabolism of the fat-rich foods of the flesh.

That doesn't mean you have to become a vegan, or any other kind of vegetarian, to lose weight. But the more you substitute complex carbohydrates for fat in your diet, the more weight you will lose. And according to the United States Department of Agriculture (USDA), *meat is the largest single source of fat in the American diet.*[13] The more flesh you can keep off your plate, the more of it you'll keep off your hips.

An appealing advantage of this diet is that you don't have to reduce your food intake to reduce your waistline. Simply substitute grains, greens, and beans for meat, cheese, and eggs. These plant foods can be more satisfying than your basic slab of meat, as we'll see in the next chapter and in the Recipes section of this book.

What about milk?

Dairy products have certain well-recognized nutritional virtues. But they're high in saturated fat and cholesterol, and many people don't digest these foods well.

We'll look at recent research dispelling the myth that if you don't eat meat, you have to double up on milk products and eggs to get enough protein and other nutrients. If you're allergic to milk—or if you're trying to lose weight, or are worried about your cholesterol level—you can do without milk as well as meat.

If you're not any of these things, a little milk won't hurt. But you won't lower your weight or your cholesterol much by replacing the slab of meat on your plate with a cheese omelette of the same size. The idea is to *tend* toward the vegan, while allowing yourself enough in the way of animal products to keep from feeling fanatical, or cheated, or bored.

Can I have my bread and my butter too?

If you want to drop 20 pounds in a month, you have to take your grains and greens without grease. But if you just want a gradual, painless weight loss—or if you'd like to eat as much as you want of enjoyable food without *gaining* weight—you can certainly indulge in enough butter to make your plant foods appealing. (Later, we'll examine evidence suggesting that butter is no worse for you than margarine, and may actually be better, despite its animal origins.)

Consider these little-known facts, also verified by the USDA:

Butter is *not* a major contributor to American fat cells. Our average annual intake of butter is only 5 pounds a head.[19] Compare this to our intake of fat-rich meats. In 1984 the average American ate:

Beef	78.6 pounds
Pork	61.7 pounds
Chicken	55.7 pounds
Seafood	13.6 pounds
Turkey	11.4 pounds
Veal	1.8 pounds
Lamb/mutton	1.5 pounds
TOTAL	224.3 POUNDS[14]

Over a lifetime, this works out to something like 2,000 whole chickens, 500 fish, 40 pigs, and 20 cows![15]

A quick look at these figures suggests how you can salvage the joys of butter for your monk's fare of bread: simply slash your intake of meat and other animal foods. You can afford a little butter if it's all the animal fat you eat.

I eat butter. But I don't eat meat, and I rarely eat cheese or eggs. At age 41 (the last time I had a checkup), my serum cholesterol level was 120 milligrams per deciliter—100 mg/dl below the national average—and my blood pressure was 100/70. I haven't put on a pound in 20 years, except when I was pregnant.

Yet my husband, who is 6'3" and weighed 230 pounds when he was eating the ordinary American diet, used to complain that I ate more than he did. And in college, when I was eating dormitory food, I was 20 pounds overweight. I'm not the naturally-thin, high-metabolism type. Inside this slender body is a fat person struggling to get out. I've kept the demon at bay by passing up meat, cheese, and eggs; and by seducing it with loads of vegetables, made delicious with bread and a bit of butter. (You could achieve the same result with rice or potatoes. I just happen to crave bread and butter.)

My husband, when he switched to an essentially-vegan diet, dropped fifteen pounds in six weeks. His serum cholesterol also dropped more than twenty percent, from 230 to 180 mg/dl. During that time, he ate as much food as he wanted. But he *didn't* eat meat, cheese, or eggs—or butter and margarine.

That's fine for six weeks. But once you've lost the weight, you aren't going to maintain your diet unless you can enjoy eating it for the rest of your life. The best thing to be said for butter (or the odd bit of cheese or egg) is that it makes vegetables and grains tastier. You need your vegetable and grains, which supply not only vitamins, minerals, and protein, but what the American diet lacks most—complex carbohydrates and fiber.

What's so good about fiber? Isn't it the indigestible part of the plant we intentionally refine away?

It is. We've spent thousands of years figuring out how to get rid of this integral plant component in order to make a smoother, whiter product, only to discover that fiber is vital to health.

Fiber makes bulky stools. Fiberless animal foods, on the other hand, can make small stools that cause muscles to strain, blood vessels to rupture, and intestinal walls to weaken. These are the symptoms of a condition so common in this country that we spend more than $400 million a year just for over-the-counter remedies. Constipation contributes to hemorrhoids, varicose veins, and diverticular disease. These problems are virtually unheard of among people subsisting on high-fiber plant foods.[16]

A low-fiber, high-animal-foods diet is associated with lower blood pressure and serum cholesterol levels, the two major risk factors for heart disease; and with cancer, especially of the colon and breast.

Why? One reason is that our intestinal tracts evolved to handle the high amounts of fiber in the primate diet. Where meat-eating dogs and cats have very short, smooth intestinal tracts that allow for the quick evacuation of their rapidly-digested prey, we have very long, convoluted intestines with tiny pockets where meat can get trapped. If the food is high in fiber, it acts as a broom to sweep out these pockets, and to move the intestinal contents along. But if the food is fiberless meat, it collects in these pockets, where it undergoes putrefaction (rotting) by intestinal bacteria. Some of the end-products of this process are known carcinogens.[17]

High-fiber grains are now prescribed for diabetics, who have traditionally avoided carbohydrates; and for ulcer patients, whose diets were formerly limited to the smooth and the bland.[18] The surprising success of these diets is attributed to fiber's ability to slow the absorption of food, which helps to regulate blood sugar and delay the emptying of the stomach's contents into the duodenum.

Certain plant fibers also have antitoxic effects. Drugs, chemicals, and food additives that are highly toxic to rats and mice on low-fiber diets have no adverse effects when given with diets that are high in these types of fiber.[19]

Instead of changing my diet, can't I just take wheat bran along with it?

This expedient might have the desired effect on intestinal function, but it won't give you the other benefits of whole plant foods. Their antitoxic effects are greater than can be accounted for by their fiber content alone.[20] Nor will wheat bran lower your cholesterol level. Serum cholesterol is lowered by some types of fiber, but wheat bran doesn't seem to be one of them. If you're adding fiber for this purpose, try pectin, which is found in fruit; or psyllium, which is found in Metamucil; or oat bran.

Fiber doesn't fully account for the cholesterol-lowering effects of grains and greens. Soybeans have a substantial cholesterol-lowering effect. But soybean *fiber*, taken alone, does not. Neither does wheat fiber. Yet when people substantially increase their intake of bread, their serum cholesterol levels drop dramatically.

Phytosterol may also explain these cholesterol-lowering effects. This is what the plant manufactures in place of cholesterol, and it is structurally similar to it. Phytosterol interferes with the absorption of cholesterol, reducing the amount of cholesterol in the blood. But you don't get much phytosterol in bran, the outer husk of the grain. You need to eat the whole plant.[21]

There is another problem with *adding* bran to your diet. The bran of wheat is where most of its phytic acid is carried. Phytic acid is a phosphorus compound that has the property of combining with minerals—especially calcium, iron, and zinc—to form insoluble compounds that are eliminated through the bowels. The result is that valuable minerals are lost from the body.

Vegetarians accustomed to high-fiber whole grain foods don't seem to have these problems. But for people unaccustomed even to whole wheat flour, adding *extra* bran can lead to trouble. Besides its detrimental effects on mineral absorption, wheat bran is a wood-like fiber that is indigestible and can produce gas and bloating.[22]

Moreover, by simply adding bran, you can't avoid the long-term effects of a high-meat diet. These effects are associated not only with the fiber meat lacks, but with other harmful properties it contains. While meat is a good source of many nutrients, it provides them along with certain toxic waste products that clog up the system and contribute to its ultimate breakdown. Meat's high nitrogen, sulfur, and phosphorus content are implicated in bone disease, and in kidney and liver failure. Its nitrogen content is linked to kidney stones and gout, and its high phosphorus content to the pathological calcification of normally-soft tissues and organs. Its high content of the higher-chain fatty acids is linked to cancer. Its saturated fat and cholesterol are linked to cardiovascular disease, diabetes, and obesity; and even its protein may be linked to elevated blood cholesterol levels, independently of its fat content.

These associations, which we'll look at in detail, help explain why the chronic diseases are rare among populations too poor to afford meat. Chronic diseases are distinguished from infectious ones in that they develop gradually from a lifetime of use and abuse. They have reached epidemic proportions in this country. Less "well-nourished" populations that eat grain-based, essentially-vegan diets are strangely resistant to them.[23]

Aren't too much fat and too little fiber the culprits in chronic disease?

They are; and both reflect the same shift in dietary focus: from wheat to meat.

According to the USDA, not only is meat our largest single source of fat, but wheat is our largest single source of fiber.[41] If two-thirds of our fat intake comes from animal foods, *all* of our fiber comes from plant foods.[24]

Grains are the major source of food for about 1.5 to 2 billion people in the world today. Bread alone accounts for 70–80 percent of the food eaten in the Near East, 60–70 percent in some parts of Africa, and 75 percent in the Middle East and Far East. A Turkish soldier may eat three loaves of bread in a day. The average American woman eats less than two slices in the same period. Only 18 percent of our national caloric intake comes from wheat, and only 24 percent from grains in general—compared to 70 percent, or more, in much of the rest of the world. It has been estimated that we eat only a fifth as much fiber as either the rural African native today, or the average American in the mid-nineteenth century.[25]

What our diet lacks in fiber-rich grain products is made up for in fat-rich animal products—meat, poultry, fish, dairy products, and eggs. These animal foods are the source of not only most of our dietary fat, but all of our dietary cholesterol. *Plants do not manufacture cholesterol*, which is contained only in animal tissues.[26] Cholesterol is a recognized villain in cardiovascular disease, and cardiovascular disease is the number one killer in this country. The disease is rare, on the other hand, among Third World populations on grain-based diets.

Isn't meat necessary for protein and certain minerals?

No. This is another area in which recent medical research has corrected old nutritional myths.

Studies show that *nearly all plant foods provide enough protein to satisfy your needs*. Some fruits are an exception, but they can be balanced against other plant foods—such as beans and nuts—that provide protein well in excess of your needs.[27]

Minerals, too, are adequately supplied by plant foods. Long-term vegetarians have normal blood mineral levels, although they get their minerals from grains and greens. Vegetarians also seem to have better bones in old age than meat-eaters. This is true even of essentially-vegan Third World populations who don't drink milk, the "ideal" calcium source.[28]

If these results are hard to believe, read on. Studies show you can easily get along on a diet that is mainly—or even wholly—made up of foods from the earth. At the same time, you can shrink your waistline and stretch your lifetime, while eating all the good food you want.

Chapter 2

Wheat vs. Meat:
All Calories Are Not Equal

"O truly happy life, which . . . hast so improved and per-
fected my body, that now I have a better relish for plain
bead, than formerly I had for the most exquisite dainties! In
fact I find such sweetness in it, . . . that I should be afraid of
sinning against temperance, were I not convinced of the
absolute necessity for it, and knowing that pure bread is,
above all things, man's best food. . . ."[1]
—Luigi Cornaro, 16th-century centenarian

Many conscientious dieters have eaten the hamburger
and left the bun, following established nutritional guidelines
that bread is fattening. But as any farmer knows, you can't
fatten a pig only on wheat, which is very low in fat. Dieting
fads change, and in Germany the current one is to actually
load up on bread. This fad is based on a study done at the
Institute of Nutrition Science in West Germany, in which
moderately overweight men and women eating eight to ten
slices of bread daily lost an average of thirteen pounds in
four weeks.

These results were confirmed in a University of Michigan
study, in which overweight college men eating 12 slices daily
of high-fiber bread lost nearly twenty pounds in ten weeks.
During that time, the men voluntarily reduced their caloric
intake by an average of 1,225 calories a day. But there was
a difference between this diet and the ordinary low-calorie
version: the dieters weren't suffering. They never got hungry.[2]

One reason for the weight loss resulting from a high-
bread diet is that bread fills you up more, calorie-for-calorie,
than concentrated foods like meat and sugar. After you've
finished your three or four slices of bread a meal, you don't
feel like eating much else.

21

But a more revolutionary principle is also at work: calories from fat and protein are *more fattening* than those from carbohydrates. A 1988 study reported in the *American Journal of Clinical Nutrition* found that obese women who claimed they ate fewer calories than thin women actually did. What they ate more of was fat—especially saturated fat—and protein. Thin women, by contrast, ate more carbohydrates and fiber.[3]

Most saturated fat comes from animal foods. Most carbohydrates, and *all* fiber, come from plant foods. No animal foods contain fiber, while virtually all plant foods do, at least when they're plucked from the tree. Juices, oils, and other refined derivatives lack fiber only because it's been removed by human ingenuity. Most meats lack carbohydrates entirely, while milk (which contains milk sugar) is only about 5 percent carbohydrate by weight. That means that animal foods are generally fattening, and plant foods are generally slimming.

Why is fat more fattening than carbohydrate?

Certain physiological mechanisms step in to regulate the metabolism of carbohydrate, burning it up as fast as it comes in; but no such mechanism regulates the metabolism of fat—or of *excess* protein, which our bodies convert to fat.

Weight loss principle #1: Plant foods fill you up with fewer calories.

Studies show that high-bulk, high-fiber carbohydrate foods (like bread) trigger your appetite-control mechanisms. Low-fiber, concentrated energy foods (like meat, cheese, and ice cream) don't have this effect.

The difference in the satiety value of carbohydrates and fats was demonstrated in a study in which people were allowed to eat as much as they wanted of two different diets. One was high in carbohydrate and bulk (fresh fruits, vegetables, whole grains, and beans), while the other was low in bulk and high in concentrated calorie foods (meat, fats, and desserts). The participants reported that both diets were equally satisfying. Yet those on the concentrated energy diet had a tendency to eat *beyond* comfortable fullness. Apparently their appetite-control mechanisms weren't triggered by the low-fiber, concentrated foods, so they didn't feel satisfied when they had "enough." Result: they ate *twice* as many calories as the people in the high-bulk group.[4]

Carbohydrates also stimulate insulin, while fat doesn't. Insulin seems to serve as the body's signal that it's been fed. When insulin is injected into the brains of baboons, the animals eat less and lose weight.[5]

In addition, carbohydrates trigger the release of serotonin, a nerve transmitter that apparently tells the brain when the body is full. This signal lessens the urge to binge. When animals are fed diets that reduce the amount of serotonin in their brains, they respond by binging on carbohydrates. Serotonin decreases pain sensitivity and increases drowsiness, which may explain why dieters who avoid carbohydrates often have trouble falling asleep.[6]

Animal studies suggest that if you deprive yourself of carbohydrates today, you'll crave them tomorrow. Fat deprivation won't have this effect. Daily changes in the carbohydrate intakes of animals strongly influence their carbohydrate intake the next day. Changes in fat intake don't significantly affect later fat intake. The reason is probably that the body's carbohydrate stores are limited, while fat is overstocked. The amount of carbohydrates eaten in a day is approximately equal to the amount stored in the body. The amount of fat eaten is less than 1 percent of stored body fat.[7] You could go without fat for 100 days before you'd use up your body stores, but you could go for only one day without carbohydrate.

Despite their reputation for "sticking to the ribs," fatty foods will leave you hungry sooner than the same number of calories from carbohydrates. Fat gives you that heavy, full feeling faster because it slows the emptying of the stomach more than carbohydrates do. Fat increases your caloric intake more than it slows gastric emptying. Nine grams of carbohydrate contain the same number of calories as only four grams of fat. That means that if you substitute the same weight of fat for carbohydrate, you'll more than double your caloric intake. This substitution, however, falls far short of halving the rate at which your stomach is emptied after you eat the fat meal.[8]

A four-ounce hamburger patty is about the same size as an English muffin, and the hamburger will make you feel as if you've eaten more. Why? Because you have. The hamburger patty contains nearly three times as many calories as the English muffin. *Three* English muffins (or two with a pat of butter on each of the four halves) will give you the same number of calories as the hamburger patty, and will fill you up more.

Fiber encourages you to throw in the napkin after fewer calories.

Your appetite control mechanisms are triggered not only by the carbohydrate in plant foods but by their fiber content. Dietary fiber absorbs water and fills the intestines, leaving a large residue of undigested material that increases the feeling of fullness.[9]

It's quite possible to consume hundreds of ice cream calories before feeling sated. A salad meal rarely has this effect. The problem with the ice cream is that it goes down too easily. Fiber gives you the satisfaction of chewing. It also makes your meal last long enough for some of it to reach the small intestine before all of it has disappeared from your plate. Apparently, tension receptors in the intestinal wall then activate satiety signals that prevent overeating.[10]

Fiber also alters the absorption of carbohydrates. It flattens the blood glucose response and lowers serum insulin, probably by slowing the absorption of glucose so it is spread out along a greater length of intestine. The uptake of glucose by the tissues is thus able to keep pace with its absorption.[11] This blood sugar regulation helps to keep you from thinking about food. When your blood sugar drops, you feel weak and tired—a sensation generally equated with hunger.

The importance of fiber in satisfying hunger was demonstrated in a study in which men and women were fed whole meals of either apple juice, apple puree, or whole apples. Although each meal contained the same number of calories, the participants reported that the fiber-free juice was significantly less satisfying than the pulpier puree, and the puree significantly less satisfying than the whole apple. The participants' blood sugar levels rose the same amount after all three meals, but they dropped much faster after the juice meal than after the whole apple meal, with an intermediate drop for the puree meal.[12]

Fiber also alters the absorption of fat, reducing the amount of it you absorb from your food. Fat absorption from whole wheat bread, for example, is much lower than from animal foods. Apparently the fiber binds with dietary fat so some of it passes through undigested. Tripling your fiber intake can increase your fat excretion by 50 percent. Fiber also reduces the absorption of calories in general.[13] Some calories don't count because they are excreted along with the indigestible fiber.

Weight loss principle #2: Carbohydrate calories are less fattening than fat calories.

Not only do high-fiber, high-carbohydrate plant foods make you feel satisfied with fewer calories; those calories are actually *less fattening* than the calories in carbohydrate-free animal foods. One researcher estimates that before a significant portion of your carbohydrate calories would turn into fat, you'd have to eat about 4,000 calories just in carbohydrates. That's double the average daily caloric intake in carbohydrates alone.[14]

This surprising finding has brought about a radical change in dietary theory. It's no longer *how much*, but *what* you eat that counts. And it's the high-fat high-protein animal foods— *not* the high-carbohydrate, high-fiber plant foods—that tip the scales.

What evidence is there that carbohydrate calories don't count?

This phenomenon is clearly shown in rats. Rats allowed to eat as much as they want of a high-fat diet become obese, while those allowed to eat as much as they want of grains stay slim. This isn't because rats like fatty foods better than grains and eat more of them. Rats also retain twice as many calories from fats as from grains *per thousand calories eaten.*[15]

Too much protein does the same thing to rats as too much fat. Full-grown rats on a high-protein diet wind up weighing nearly twice as much as rats eating *the same number of calories* in the form of carbohydrates. They also have nearly twice as much body fat.[16] Since the length of these rats stays the same, this extra weight doesn't represent extra growth. It represents extra girth: obesity.

Only those rats on high-carbohydrate diets can eat all they want and stay slim. Diets high either in fat or in protein fail to stimulate the animal's body to burn off its excess energy, which is packed away as fat.

What about in humans?

Clinical studies demonstrate similar effects in us. These studies show that body fat comes mainly from dietary fat. You can eat carbohydrate with impunity without gaining weight.[17]

In a study showing the effects of fat, thin people gained weight easily when their extra calories came from fat. But they had trouble gaining weight even when they overate on a mixed diet that was high in carbohydrates.[18]

That protein has similar effects was shown in a study in which overweight people lost weight when they were restricted to low-protein foods, although they could eat all they wanted of these foods. In another study, men gained weight when they were switched from a low-protein to a high-protein diet, although their caloric intakes were unchanged.[19]

The effects of carbohydrates were shown in a study in which men lost weight, although they literally stuffed themselves with bread. At one sitting, they ate an average of ten slices covered with two tablespoons of jam. In the next ten hours, only 2 percent of this bread meal was converted to body fat—and at the same time the men burned up, or oxidized, body fat. Net result: they *lost* fat.[20]

Researchers conclude that dietary fat is a much greater threat to maintaining body weight than dietary carbohydrates, and that the popular practice of cutting down on carbohydrates to lose weight is actually counterproductive. It encourages bypassing starches in favor of foods with a low carbohydrate content (like meat and dairy products) that are much higher in fat.

Calories do count, if they come from fat. But if they come from carbohydrates, your intake would have to reach about 4,000 calories a day before any significant portion of them would turn into body fat.[21]

Why is fat more fattening than carbohydrates?

One reason fat is more fattening is that it's converted to body fat and stored more efficiently. It takes energy to convert carbohydrates to fat, so you burn up calories in the process. But fat is already fat. It can go straight to the hips with little metabolic intervention.

The amount of energy used in converting food fat to body fat is equal to only 3 percent of the calories eaten. The amount used in converting carbohydrate to body fat is equal to 23 percent of the calories eaten.[22] If you're a compulsive calorie-counter, that means you can reduce the count by 20 percent for high-carbohydrate foods.

Carbohydrates are converted by the body not only to fat but to glycogen, the form in which carbohydrates are stored in the liver and muscles. This conversion burns up only 7 percent of the calorie intake. But the body's ability, to expand its glycogen stores is limited. We store only about a half-pound to a pound of it in our livers and muscles. Most excess weight is stored instead in adipose tissue (body fat). These fat stores can be expanded almost indefinitely.[23]

Fat is more fattening than carbohydrates for another reason. Carbohydrate balance is *regulated* by the body, while fat balance isn't. As you eat more carbohydrates, your metabolism speeds up so you burn more of it. Your heart rate speeds up, your temperature rises, your thyroid increases your metabolic rate, and you get a burst of energy. The effect is similar to what happens when you exercise: your metabolism burns calories at a higher rate, not only while you're working out but for several hours afterwards. That's why both exercise and high-carbohydrate diets are so effective for burning up unwanted pounds.[24]

This built-in mechanism for regulating carbohydrate metabolism explains why a bread binge won't show up on the scales. It also helps explain the virtual absence of obesity among native Africans when their diets were predominantly whole carbohydrate foods, and its emergence when Western-style diets became common.[25]

It seems that we are physiologically adapted to handle high-carbohydrate, high-fiber, low-fat plant foods. We're ill-adapted for the high-fat, low-carbohydrate, low-fiber animal foods around which the affluent diet is centered.

What kind of bread?

On the other hand, we may not be physiologically adapted to handle the carbohydrates in commercial white bread either. It differs from the bread eaten in less industrialized countries in important ways. Commercial white bread has had most of the fiber and vitamins refined out of it, and it contains iodate and bromate, additives that inhibit the thyroid and can make you feel sluggish.[26]

White bread isn't all bad. Unlike refined sugar, it doesn't adversely effect blood sugar and insulin levels. Moreover, a diet in which white bread is the main source of protein can actually meet protein needs. But for losing weight, wholemeal bread remains your best bet. Studies comparing the satiety value of different breads show the more refined the bread is, the more of it that must be eaten to feel satisfied. Wholemeal bread fills you up with less.[27]

In the Michigan study reported earlier, the participants were
divided into two groups. One ate a specially-made high-fiber
bread, while the other ate ordinary white bread. The higher-
fiber group not only reduced their caloric intake more and
lost more weight than the white bread group, but they got
less hungry in the process.[28]

Look for stone-ground whole wheat bread without additives. Sprouted whole wheat bread is better yet. Sprouting
increases the nutrient content of wheat. It also releases
phosphates from their storage form as phytic acid, which
detrimentally affects mineral absorption. Sprouting may also
help if you're allergic to wheat, since it inhibits allergic
reactions to gluten, wheat's main storage protein.[29]

Another alternative for the allergy prone is to switch to
rice or potatoes. If you ate nothing but potatoes, you could
eat *twenty* medium-sized ones in a day and you'd have
consumed only 1,700 calories. With two pats of butter on
each, eleven potatoes would give you the same total.

On paper, potatoes are low in protein. Yet certain populations get nearly all their protein from this source and remain
in remarkably good health.

In a Polish experiment, a man and woman ate nothing for six
months except potatoes with butter or pork fat, and a few
apples and pears. On this diet, they maintained nitrogen
equilibrium; that is, they met their protein needs. They also
reported that they felt great, did not tire of the diet, and had
no craving for change.[30]

*Isn't a high-protein, low-carbohydrate diet the fastest
way to lose weight?*

Possibly, but the pounds are unlikely to stay off, because
most of the weight lost on a low-carbohydrate diet is water.
This weight shows up again on the scales as soon as you
return to your normal eating habits.[31]

Worse, the loss of water reflects an unhealthy condition in
your body. When the body runs out of carbohydrates, it
burns fat and protein for fuel. But unlike carbohydrates, fat
and protein leave unwanted byproducts that create an acid

condition in the blood. Acids produce hydrogen ions in the body. The kidneys correct this metabolic acidosis by increasing the rate of hydrogen ion excretion, which means they increase urine formation. You lose pounds of water, but with it go valuable minerals you can't afford to lose. Many deaths have been reported from liquid protein diets due to a sudden stopping of the heart probably caused by these mineral losses.[32]

The idea behind the high-protein, low-carbohydrate diet was to prevent muscle atrophy by supplying dietary protein. The theory fails, however, at intakes below 900 calories a day, because the dietary protein never makes it to the muscles. The body's first need is for fuel. If none is supplied in the form of carbohydrates, the body breaks down the protein and burns it for fuel instead.

You're better off eating your 900 calories as carbohydrates, which is a cheaper and cleaner burning fuel. In place of your 300-calorie allotment in liquid protein, try a baked potato with two tablespoons of sour cream and a heaping plate of steamed vegetables. This meal not only is lower in calories, but is more satisfying and takes longer to eat.

Better yet, eat 1,200 calories or more. You may lose weight more slowly, but you will preserve your muscles and your mineral balance in the process.

How often can I eat?

This question has prompted some interesting studies with rats. When forced to eat their daily allotment in two one-hour periods, rats gain substantially more weight than when allowed to nibble all day long, although the number of calories they eat is the same. Rats eat more food when allowed to eat all they want—nibbling all day—than if they eat only during a single hour in the day. But they don't gain additional weight.[33]

People seem to respond in the same way to infrequent meals. The less often they eat, the more they weigh. Gorging on the same number of calories in fewer meals can also adversely affect your glucose tolerance (predisposing you to diabetes) and your blood lipid levels (predisposing you to heart disease).[34]

It is best, therefore, to spread your calories out over many small meals, rather than a few large ones. Apparently the body can burn up only a certain amount of food at a sitting, and the rest gets stored as fat.

Chapter 3

Bread vs. Sugar: All Carbohydrates Are Not Equal

"Things sweet to taste prove in digestion sour."
—Shakespeare[1]

Simple sugar is pure carbohydrate. Can it, like whole-grain bread, be eaten with impunity without gaining weight?

The answer, of course, is no. But why not? How do the carbohydrates in sugar differ from those in bread and other whole plant foods?

Sugar differs in three important ways: (1) it lacks the accessory nutrients necessary for its metabolism; (2) its carbohydrate molecules have already been reduced to their simplest form; and (3) it lacks fiber.

The combustion of carbohydrates requires small but essential amounts of vitamins, minerals, fat, and protein. These are stripped in the refining process from sugar and other processed foods. When you eat these foods, you go in the nutritional red. Since you're short of something, you crave more food. You also feel tired because you can't properly burn up the sugar you just ate. You're too tired to exercise to burn it off, so it gets packed away as fat.[2]

In addition, the refining process removes fiber, which suppresses hunger by keeping the small intestine full. Fiber also helps to regulate blood sugar, apparently by acting as a barrier to the diffusion of nutrients into the stomach. Their absorption is slowed and spread out through the entire length of the small intestine.

Both complex carbohydrates (grains and other whole plant foods) and simple carbohydrates (sugar) cause your blood sugar to go up. The rise after you eat sugar, however, is followed by a precipitous plunge. When your blood sugar drops, your energy level drops along with it, and you reach for food to get back your strength. High-fiber, complex-carbohydrate foods produce a much slower drop.[3]

Why do complex carbohydrates keep blood sugar elevated longer than simple carbohydrates?

Because they're digested more slowly. Sugar is already in its simplest form. But complex carbohydrates are made up of many sugar links that are broken down and released gradually over a long period. Some 10–20 percent of the carbohydrates in bread may make it all the way to the colon before it gets absorbed. When digestion is slow, sugar is continuously being released into the bloodstream, and your blood sugar stays level.

Protein and fat are also digested slowly; and sugar contains neither of these components. Whole grains contain both. Beans are digested even more slowly because they contain even more protein and fat, along with certain non-food factors that inhibit digestion.[4]

Wouldn't animal products, which are higher in protein and fat, work better yet?

This logical assumption was the basis of the high-protein, high-fat, low-carbohydrate diet traditionally prescribed for diabetics and hypoglycemics. Recent medical opinion, however, has changed radically in this area.

Both diabetes (too much sugar in the blood) and hypoglycemica (too little sugar in the blood) result from faulty insulin activity. Insulin is the hormone that regulates blood sugar levels. Its job is to remove excess sugar from the bloodstream into the cells, where it is either burned or stored as fat. This sugar is the cells' food source. Without it they starve, and the brain eventually lapses into a coma. When the pancreas makes too little insulin, or when the insulin it does make isn't used properly, the result is diabetes. When the pancreas overreacts by producing too much insulin, the result is hypoglycemia.

The problem with treating these conditions with a meat-centered, high-fat diet is that excess fat, like excess sugar, actually interferes with insulin activity.[5]

The traditional diabetic diet also lacks fiber, which helps regulate blood sugar levels. Worse yet, it is high in saturated fat and cholesterol. This is of particular concern to diabetics, who are already *twice* as likely as other people to succumb to a heart attack.

The latest in diets for diabetics stresses bread, beans, and other complex carbohydrates in place of high-fat animal foods. Whole grains and beans are slowly digested like animal foods, but rather than raising serum cholesterol and triglycerides they actually lower these risk factors.[6]

Aren't diabetics supposed to avoid carbohydrates?

Not any more. In 1979 the Food and Nutrition Committee of the American Diabetes Association recommended that carbohydrates be increased to 50–60 percent of the total calories of insulin-dependent diabetics. This recommendation was motivated in part by the increased threat to diabetics of cardiovascular disease on a high-fat, animal-products diet. It also followed the discovery that whole grains and other plant foods, far from being dangerous to diabetics, actually aid in the control of their condition.[7]

> In a landmark study, the carbohydrate intake of diabetics was nearly doubled by substituting high-fiber complex carbohydrates for animal foods. On this diet, diabetics on high doses of insulin substantially reduced their prescriptions, and those on low doses abandoned their syringes altogether.[8]

While benefits have resulted with either complex carbohydrates alone or fiber alone, the best effects have come when these elements were combined.[9] Again, this means bread, beans, and other whole plant foods. Sugar won't work because it contains neither complex carbohydrates nor fiber.

Sugar also won't lower serum cholesterol and triglycerides. In fact, it has the opposite effect.

In one study, substituting sucrose for cooked wheat starch in the diets of normal people increased serum cholesterol an average of 7.4 percent and triglycerides an average of 33 percent.[10]

Some researchers go so far as to blame sugar for the modern-day epidemic of cardiovascular disease. U.S. sugar consumption has doubled since 1900. It now provides 15–25 percent of our total calories. Complex carbohydrate consumption dropped by 50 percent during the same period.[11]

Both diabetes and cardiovascular disease are virtually unknown in countries where the diet is low in high-fat, fiberless animal foods and high in complex carbohydrates. The emergence of these diseases in underdeveloped countries is associated with three dietary changes: less fiber, more fat, and more sugar.[12]

Isn't diabetes genetic?

A reduced ability to handle sugar can be genetic. But glucose tolerance is improved by a proper diet and made worse by an improper one, even in normal people. Glucose tolerance is substantially better after a few weeks on a high-bread diet than after either a high-sugar or a high-fat diet. A high-sugar diet also produces elevated insulin levels in normal people. Elevated insulin levels in response to a sugar load are considered one of the first detectable symptoms of diabetes.[13]

In a study comparing the effects on blood sugar and blood insulin levels of a diet high in sugar and one consisting mainly of whole grains and beans, the diets produced similar rises in blood sugar. But blood *insulin* levels were *twice* as high on the high-sugar diet as on the high-fiber diet. In other words, the cost in insulin to maintain normal blood sugar was twice as great when the diet was high in sugar.[14]

In another study, the two carbohydrates tested were sugar and fiberless wheat starch. Again, blood sugar reached equivalent levels, but the cost in insulin was much greater when the carbohydrate was sugar.[15]

Excess insulin secretion also occurs at some stage in all cases of obesity—a disease clearly of dietary origin. Four out of five diabetic adults either are or have been obese.[16]

Insulin activity is impaired not only by sugar but by fat. The consumption of meat, which is high in fat, is also linked to diabetes. Diabetes is very common in beef-eating populations. Moreover, blood glucose, like serum cholesterol, goes up as meat consumption goes up.[17]

A 21-year study was reported in 1985 involving over 25,000 Seventh Day Adventists, about half of whom were vegetarians. Their collective risk of death from diabetes was found to be only half that for all whites in the United States. More significant, the risk for vegetarian SDAs was substantially lower than for non-vegetarian SDAs. The association with meat remained after correcting for weight, exercise, and other dietary factors.[18]

So sugar is bad, but what about other natural sweeteners, such as honey and maple syrup?

These sweeteners also cause sudden rises and falls in blood sugar, although probably less severe than those caused by refined sugar. For a natural sweetener that produces more stable blood sugar levels, try fructose (fruit sugar). It can be purchased as a refined white powder, but the more natural alternatives for cooking are the fruit juice concentrates. (See Recipes.)

Honey and pure maple syrup are nevertheless better for you than table sugar, because they contain certain essential trace elements that refined sugar lacks. One of these is chromium, which seems to function as a glucose tolerance factor necessary for optimum insulin activity. A deficiency of chromium results in disturbances in carbohydrate metabolism. Maple syrup contains twice as much chromium as ordinary table sugar; honey contains nearly 4 times as much; and molasses contain 15 times as much. Superfine white sugar contains only ¼ the chromium of ordinary table sugar.[19]

What about artificial sweeteners?

The most widely used sugar substitute is aspartame (Nutrasweet or Equal). Unlike other artificial sweeteners, it has never been definitely linked to cancer in laboratory animals. Its safety, however, still hasn't been established. Some people are allergic to it; and high levels of phenylalanine, its chief ingredient, can have irreversible toxic effects on the brains of the unborn. That means you should avoid Nutrasweet, *at least* during pregnancy.[20]

These risks aside, artificial sweeteners can be a boon if you're a dieter with a sweet tooth. Their virtue is that they can fool your taste buds without fooling your pancreas. In one study, obese patients secretly given foods sweetened with aspartame unwittingly reduced their caloric intake by 25 percent.[21] Artificial sweeteners don't create the erratic swings in blood sugar that real sugar does.[22] They are good not only for diabetics and hypoglycemics, but for dieters who want to avoid the post-sugar hunger that results from plunging blood sugar levels.

Serious health advocates contend that if you give up sweets altogether, you'll lose the taste for them; and that artificial sweeteners simply prolong your craving. But Nutrasweet and Equal can be useful expedients while you're trying to lose those extra twenty pounds.

Soft drinks, however, have nothing to recommend them, whether sweetened with sugar or Nutrasweet. Not only are all their calories empty ones; they are also high in phosphate additives that are hard on your bones.[23]

If you can't live without caffeine, coffee is better than a cola drink. For some people, coffee may even have certain virtues. It activates the thyroid, a gland that tends to be sluggish in people with weight problems. Roasted coffee can also supply the minimum daily requirement of vitamin B1, along with about 20 percent of the daily requirements of manganese and niacin. Despite rumors to the contrary, it hasn't *yet* been definitely linked to cardiovascular disease or cancer.[24]

As always, moderation is the key.

Chapter 4

Salvaging the Joys of
Butter for Your Bread

"It was the *best* butter, the March Hare meekly replied."
—*Alice's Adventures in Wonderland*

For nutritional purposes, we don't actually need more fat than is provided by nature in whole foods. The only excuse for *adding* fat to our foods is that it improves the taste. The reason for this has been explained scientifically. Most of a food's flavors are carried in its aromas, and most odor molecules dissolve only in fat.[1] To make the fruits of the earth more satisfying, we grease them up a bit.

This isn't a biological necessity, even for flavor. Gorillas live on fresh green leaves, without butter or other dressing. (Contrary to popular opinion, most of the gorilla's diet consists of leaves, not fruit. Gorillas don't eat meat at all—or milk either after weaning. The diet of the gorilla and the biological proximity of this great ape to man are discussed in Chapter 7.)

But we have jaded our taste buds—probably by over-stimulating them from birth with salt, sugar, and other concentrated flavors—so they remain unimpressed by the taste of leaves just plucked from the plant. We feel cheated without some fat dripping over our leaves, grasses, and roots. Dieters without this pleasure tend to get depressed and to go off their diets.

As was observed in Chapter 1, if you need to lose twenty pounds in a month, your best bet is to take your grains and greens without grease. If your goal is a gradual, painless weight loss—or if it's to eat as much as you want without *gaining* weight—you can enjoy your bread, potatoes, and cooked vegetables dressed with a bit of butter. Even with this normally forbidden spread, if you omit other animal products, you'll be substantially reducing your fat intake.

The average thirty-year-old American male gets 71 of his daily 115 grams of fat from animal products.[2] That's enough fat to butter *eighteen* slices of bread.[3] If he buttered only four slices in a day and cut out other animal products, he'd have cut his fat intake in half.

Isn't margarine healthier than butter?

The jury is still out on this question, but margarine isn't found in nature, and it's been added to our diets so recently that our systems are unlikely to have adapted to it.

Margarine is normally made from polyunsaturated oils. In most studies, polyunsaturated oils have lowered serum cholesterol, thus reducing the risk of heart disease.[4]

These studies, however, can't be applied to margarine, because *it isn't really polyunsaturated*. It starts out that way, but in order to make it solid at room temperature (so it looks and spreads like butter), it has to be hydrogenated. That means the unlinked—or unsaturated—carbon atoms in the vegetable oils are saturated with hydrogen. The result is a type of fat that not only *is* saturated but *isn't* commonly found in nature. These fats are called *trans* fatty acids, because they contain *trans* double bonds in place of the natural *cis* double bonds.[5]

Trans fatty acids are incorporated into human cells and can be found in many tissues in humans and animals. Their nutritional safety hasn't yet been established. Some studies suggest they *increase* serum cholesterol and are linked to both heart disease and cancer.[6] One study found that people who died of heart disease ate more hydrogenated fats and had significantly higher concentrations of *trans* unsaturated fatty acids in the blood than comparable controls.[7] A 1988 review of the literature concluded that after thirty years of research, the role of hydrogenated fats in the causation of disease is still uncertain.[8]

Trans fatty acids inhibit the metabolism of essential fatty acids (EFAs), the polyunsatured fats that can't be manufactured by the body but must be obtained from food. EFAs are protective against heart disease. In animal studies, when the diet has been low in EFAs, *trans* fats have raised serum cholesterol more than butterfat. They also produced significantly more atherosclerotic lesions. This problem is overcome experimentally by providing sufficient EFAs in the diet. The trouble is that *trans* fats tend to increase the need for EFAs; and in the normal human diet, they're likely to be deficient.[9]

What about liquid vegetable oils?

These are easier on the arteries than margarine. Polyunsaturated vegetable oils generally lower serum cholesterol. Unfortunately, in animal studies they've also been linked to cancer—but this link is found *only* when the diet also contains substantial amounts of cholesterol. Researchers postulate that the way polyunsaturated fat lowers blood cholesterol may be to drive it out of the blood and into the bowel, where it can act as a carcinogen.[10] If so, you could escape any potential cancer risk by avoiding animal products altogether, because you wouldn't be eating cholesterol along with polyunsaturated fat. A similar theory is given by macrobiotic experts, who assert cancer growth is stimulated by animal fat and other dietary toxins and won't occur in their absence. As evidence, they cite the fact that people in tropical societies who eat a balanced diet of grains and other plant foods don't get skin cancer, no matter how long they're out in the sun.[11]

But there's another explanation for the apparent link between polyunsaturated fat and cancer. Under this theory, you may be better off with butter. It seems polyunsaturated oils are particularly susceptible to free radical formation. Free radicals are chemically reactive molecules that can damage proteins, fats, and nucleic acids (DNA and RNA). The fact that the carbon chains in liquid vegetable oils are unsaturated, or unlinked, means they contain open spaces that are free to hook up with oxygen. This oxidation is what makes oil go rancid, and it contributes to cell damage and aging.[12] Under this theory, the only really safe way to eat vegetable oil may be to leave it in the plant, where its carbon chains can't react with hydrogen *or* oxygen.

The second safest alternative is to buy oil cold-pressed, because it's not heated during processing. And don't deep-fat fry in it. Free radical formation is particularly rapid when oil is heated. In animal studies, heated vegetable oil has also been associated with the hardening of the arteries that leads to heart disease.[13]

A third alternative is to switch to monounsaturated oils. These include olive oil, peanut oil, rapeseed oil ("canola"), and avocado oil. They're safer for cooking, because the link with cancer seems to be only with polyunsaturated oils (like corn and safflower oil). Monounsaturated oils are more stable and less easily oxidized by heat. They've also been shown to lower serum cholesterol and blood pressure levels.[14] The one proviso is for peanut oil. It significantly *increases* atherosclerosis in monkeys, when fed as the sole food fat in a cholesterol-rich diet. The reason isn't clear, and neither is the significance of this finding for humans, since human diets that are high in peanut oil are usually low in cholesterol.[15]

A fourth alternative has been recommended by some authorities. This is to buy only vegetable oils that are heavily laced with BHT and other antioxidants.[16] Conclusive evidence of BHT's safety, however, has yet to be produced. In 1958, the British Food Standards Committee recommended that it be taken off the list of permitted antioxidants. This recommendation wasn't acted on because of industry protests. More recent studies implicate BHT in the development of cancer. It has been shown to cause spreading lesions in the stomachs of rats, and to activate mutagens.[17] If you're into antioxidants, your best bets are fresh fruits and vegetables, which perform the same function naturally.[18]

Fortunately, the concern about polyunsaturated fat and cancer may be more theoretical than real. Despite what it does to laboratory rats, polyunsaturated fat hasn't been established as a risk factor for humans. A high intake of polyunsaturated fatty acids is common in vegetarians, and they have a lower than average risk of developing cancer.[19]

How do butter and margarine compare?

Butter's carbon linkages are already saturated with hydrogen; they can't link up with oxygen and contribute to free radical formation. But butter contains cholesterol, which is also easily oxidized, particularly during cooking.[20] That means it can also contribute to free radical formation. The Indian solution is ghee, a butter derivative from which the easily-oxidized parts have been removed.

Margarine doesn't contain cholesterol; and its carbon linkages are saturated like butter's. They aren't subject to oxidation. But in margarine these bonds are in the unnatural *trans* form associated with cancer and cardiovascular disease.

Butter has certain other advantages over margarine. It promotes the absorption of calcium,[21] and it's a good *natural* source of vitamin A. Margarine also contains vitamin A, but not naturally. It's added in.

It's hard to say in theory whether butter or margarine poses the greater risk. We have to look at epidemiological studies, and the results of these to date are far from clear.[22]

The deciding factor may be the taste. Most people think butter tastes better.

Doesn't butter raise serum cholesterol and contribute to heart disease?

In large amounts, it probably would. But you can butter *seven* slices of bread with the cholesterol you'd get in one hamburger patty.[23]

Cholesterol and saturated fat are major suspects in cardiovascular disease. They're also principal constituents of butter. The studies linking these variables, however, generally haven't distinguished between meat and milk as sources of animal fat. People who get their saturated fat and cholesterol mainly from butter have lower blood pressures, lower serum cholesterol levels, and less heart disease than people who get them from meat. (In this case, "meat" excludes fish, which contains oils that lower serum cholesterol.)

The Yemenite Jews in Yemen use a lot of butter, but they don't drink milk. They are reported to be free of arteriosclerotic heart disease. They also eat large amounts of bread. In studies reproducing their diets experimentally, bread has lowered serum cholesterol.[24]

A second group of people who have very little heart disease despite a high intake of butterfat are the African Masai.

This primitive nomadic tribe inhabits Southern Kenya and Northern Tanzania. They live almost exclusively on raw milk, supplemented occasionally with blood and meat. In the rainy season, their milk intake averages a *gallon* daily, typically eaten in a fermented form resembling yogurt. Their saturated fat and cholesterol intakes are unusually high, but their serum cholesterol remains low.

> In a study of 254 Masai, the average serum cholesterol level was only 135 mg/dl, nearly 100 mg/dl below America's national average. Autopsy examinations showed atherosclerosis and coronary heart disease were rare.[25]

People in North India also have low blood pressures and a low incidence of heart disease, although they eat large amounts of butterfat and are heavy consumers of salt and cigarettes.

> In a study that compared railway clerks in North and South India, the North Indian clerks had substantially lower blood pressures, less than half as much hypertension, and only 1/15th as many deaths from heart disease as the South Indian clerks. Yet the North Indian clerks ate nearly *twice* as much salt as the South Indian clerks, smoked *three times* as much, and ate *nine times* as much fat—mainly butter. The South Indians, on the other hand, ate *six times* as much meat—mainly from beef—and substantially less plant fiber. The critical variables seemed to be meat and fiber. Butterfat and salt either didn't affect blood pressure or lowered it.[26]

Why would butterfat be easier on the arteries than beef?

The evidence for this is only circumstantial. Assuming butter is better, it may be due to differences in the length of their carbon chains. Butter's are shorter. Shorter means more liquid and, presumably, less clogging. Beef tallow is so hard that candles can be made from it. Butter melts at room temperature.[27]

Although recent studies show that stearic acid, a saturated fat found in beef and coconut oil, actually lowers serum cholesterol, the net effect of these foods is to make serum cholesterol go up.[28] Cholesterol only drops with *pure* stearic acid. Beef and coconut oil also contain palmitic acid, which raises serum cholesterol.

A 1988 study suggested that butter may be better than meat fat for weight control. In animal studies, obese rats fed medium-chain triglycerides (the kind found in butter) gained less weight than those fed the long-chain triglcyerides found in beef fat. The reason seems to be that medium-chain triglycerides are more satisfying. When medium-chain triglycerides were fed to humans thirty minutes before lunch, they ate fewer calories at lunch than when long-chain triglycerides were fed first.[29]

Butterfat has the advantage that it aids in the absorption of calcium, which seems to protect against heart disease. In fact, some authorities contend milk *with* fat is healthier than milk without it. They cite studies in which rats fed non-fat dry milk developed atherosclerotic lesions, but those fed the same milk with added cream did not. The Masai eat their milk products whole (and raw).[30]

Butter contains virtually no protein, but for some people that's an advantage. Animal proteins, like animal fats, have been associated with cardiovascular disease. The protein in milk is what's primarily responsible for milk allergies, which are also associated with cardiovascular disease. Milk sugar (lactose) is another popular milk allergen that is nearly absent from butter.[31]

Butter won't provoke an allergic reaction as fast as milk, or clog your arteries as fast as eggs.[32] It will clog them faster than cold-pressed vegetable oil, but you can't spread vegetable oil on bread. You need enough spread to make the bread appealing that makes your nutritious salad of dark mixed greens appealing. While the jury is out, you might as well treat yourself to some butter. But you'll still want to paint it on sparingly. The staple in your bread-and-butter diet should be the bread.

Chapter 5

Protein: Enough Beats a Feast

"[I]t is difficult to obtain a mixed vegetable diet which will produce an appreciable loss of nitrogen [an essential element of protein] without resorting to high levels of sugar, jams, and jellies, and other essentially protein-free foods."
—Dr. D. M. Hegsted, et al.
Harvard School of Public Health[1]

It's no news that bacon, steak, and eggs put you on the fast track to a heart attack. But can you get enough protein without them? Or are saturated fat and cholesterol necessary concomitants of a high-protein diet?

The answer is yes to both questions. A diet high in protein means a diet high in animal foods. But you can get enough protein *without* eating a high-protein diet. *Nearly all* whole plant foods supply enough of this over-emphasized nutrient to satisfy your needs.

The National Research Council sets the recommended daily allowance for protein at 44 grams for women and 56 grams for men. That's only about half our actual national intake. These estimates are high because they include a wide margin of safety. Other authorities put the minimum requirement at 25–40 grams a day.[2] All of these amounts are easily supplied by a diet solely of plant foods.

Averaging the figures in various studies, the protein intake of vegetarians who eat milk products and eggs is about 70 grams a day. For those who eat no animal products at all, it's about 60 grams a day.[3] Both intakes are well above minimum requirements.

The average daily protein intake in this country is around 100 grams—twice the recommended allowance and as

45

much as four times the minimum requirement.[4] We could cut this protein intake in half without jeopardizing protein needs.

Don't these minimum requirements apply only to a mixed diet that includes liberal amounts of animal proteins?

That used to be the rule. However, recent studies show protein requirements are equally low on a diet that includes *no* animal protein, but is made up simply of a variety of plant foods.[5] The plant proteins complement each other, resulting in proteins that are as complete and usable as animal proteins.

You could satisfy your protein needs if your only protein source were a *single* grain—bread, or rice, or potatoes. You'd need more of this single protein than if you were eating a mixed diet, but not much more. The minimum protein requirement for an average-sized man is estimated at 27.6 grams when half of it comes from animal foods. When the protein comes only from mixed vegetable sources, the requirement is 32.4 grams—not much higher. And when the protein comes only from white flour, it's 42.1 grams—still less than the RDA.[6]

But does excess protein do any harm?

Unfortunately, it does. Any excess over the body's needs is either converted to fat or burned for fuel. If it's stored as fat, it contributes to obesity, heart disease, cancer, and other chronic problems. If it's burned for fuel, it leaves certain toxic residues that force the kidneys to work harder, precipitating their eventual breakdown. The toxins the kidneys normally filter out of the body then back up and poison it.[7]

The problem is that protein isn't a "clean-burning" fuel. Only carbohydrate falls into that category. Carbohydrate consists of carbon, oxygen, and hydrogen. As carbohydrate is burned (or oxidized) by the body, these elements are converted to carbon dioxide—which is exhaled with the breath—and water.

Protein contains an added element—nitrogen—that can't be oxidized by the body. When you eat more protein than you need, its carbon, oxygen, and hydrogen components are converted to fat and sugar (the simplest form of carbohydrate). But its nitrogen is converted to ammonia, a toxic waste product that must be excreted in the urine as urea. This means extra work for the kidneys, which must form excess urine. With the loss of this liquid, the body becomes dehydrated and vital minerals are lost—including potassium, magnesium, and calcium. The loss of calcium is particularly troublesome because it contributes to osteoporosis (bone loss).[8]

Another metabolic end-product of meat digestion is uric acid. It results from the breakdown of purines, substances found predominantly in meat. When the kidneys are unable to dispose of this uric acid properly, it can collect in the joints, producing a form of arthritis known as gout. It can also settle in the kidneys, producing kidney stones. Elevated blood levels of uric acid characterize several other chronic diseases, including heart disease, hypertension, and obesity. Both uric acid production and kidney stones occur more often as meat consumption increases.[9]

For your kidneys, the lower protein content of plant foods is a distinct advantage. Whole grains and greens provide enough protein for your needs without burdening your kidneys with nitrogenous waste products, or your arteries with fat and cholesterol.

What percentage of the diet should be protein?

The Protein-Calorie Advisory Group of the United Nations suggests that protein should make up 5 percent to 5.5 percent of your calories.[10]

A gram of protein contains 4 calories. To satisfy this guideline, you need only 25 grams of protein in an average 2,000-calorie day. That amount of protein is supplied by four whole wheat English muffins, or four bowls of oatmeal.

The United States RDA, which averages 50 grams/day, is about twice as high as the U.N. recommendation. The National Academy of Sciences/National Research Council recommends that protein make up 7.6 percent of the calories an adult man consumes. The Food and Agriculture Organization (FAO) recommendation is 7 percent of the total calories consumed. Using any of these figures, the diets of even poor populations exceed the requirement. The populations of most countries, independent of income, select a diet containing approximately 11–13 percent of their calories as protein. The American diet is about 16 percent protein— three times the U.N. requirement, and more than twice the FAO and National Research Council recommendations.[11]

People living at starvation levels on grains and roots do suffer from protein malnutrition, but it's not because their diets supply too little protein. It's because they supply *too few calories*. The first need of the body is for fuel for energy. If the diet is lacking in carbohydrates, protein will be burned in its place. The result will be protein deficiency,30 even though protein intake is adequate. These people don't need more concentrated protein foods. They just need more food.[12]

What percentage of ordinary plant foods is protein?

All whole vegetables and grains are more than 5 percent protein, and most are more than 10 percent. Fruits average about 4 percent.[13]

To get 25 grams of protein for every 2,000 calories of food, you need only one gram of protein for every 80 calories you eat. To get 50 grams of protein, you need one gram of protein for every 40 calories. The number of calories required to furnish one gram of protein for some typical grains and greens are listed below, rounded to whole numbers and listed from best to worst:[14]

Spinach, alfalfa sprouts, broccoli	8
Tofu (bean curd)	9
Cauliflower	10
Mushrooms	11
Soybeans	12
Lettuce, lentils, peas	14
Kidney, black, navy beans	15
Green beans	17

Celery, summer squash, garbanzo beans	18
Eggplant, tomato	21
Whole wheat pancakes	22
Whole wheat bread	23
Oatmeal	24
Corn	26
White bread	31
Shredded wheat	32
Potato	36
Corn tortilla	42
Granola	44
Brown rice, corn flakes, crackers	48
Sweet potato	67

All of these foods easily meet the 1:80 U.N. requirement. Only the sweet potato is significantly below even the 1:40 U.S. RDA, and its protein deficiency may be merely theoretical. Certain New Guinea natives manage to stay in robust health, although they get nearly all their protein from this source.[15]

The fruits and other plant foods that don't meet the 1:40 RDA can easily be balanced by high-protein plant foods—the greens, beans, and nuts that provide well over 1 gram of protein for every 40 calories.

Harder to balance are the "empty" calories—sugar and fats—that contain no protein at all. Two-thirds of the calories in the American diet now come from these sources (24 percent from sugar and 42 percent from fat).[16] The remaining calories (600 in the average 2,000-calorie diet) have to supply one gram of protein for every 15 calories to meet the U.S. RDA. If you eat this type of diet, you may have to resort to meat to make up for the protein deficit in your other foods.

There is a healthier alternative. You can raise your protein/calorie ratio by cutting down on sugar and added fats. Vegetarians tend to do just that. Their diets contain substantially fewer "empty" calories than the national average. This may be because of a preoccupation with health, or it may be because vegetarians on high-carbohydrate diets simply don't crave sweets.

I noticed that myself. When I was trying to lose weight by eating meat and salad and excluding carbohydrates, I had a

serious sweet tooth. When I satisfied my craving for bread
and gave up meat instead, I no longer cared about dessert.

Macrobiotic vegetarians have an explanation for this phenomenon. The macrobiotic dietary philosophy is based on
the Oriental principle of balancing opposites ("yin" and
"yang"). Meat is considered a very contractive food, while
sweets are very expansive. To counteract the contractive
effects of meat, we are drawn to expansive foods, such as
sugar. We are also drawn to alcohol, cigarettes, and mood-
altering substances. Conversely, a craving for expansive
substances is curbed by cutting down on meat consumption.
There are no Western medical studies to support this theory, but it's interesting that Americans are among the world's
largest consumers not only of meat but of sugar.[17]

Aren't plant proteins incomplete proteins?

No. It used to be thought that only animal proteins adequately supplied the essential amino acids—those that can't
be produced by the body, but must be obtained from food.
This theory, however, was based on studies involving rats,
which are now known to need up to five times as much
protein per calorie as we do. Even human milk, which
contains only one-tenth as much protein as rat milk, is seriously deficient when tested on rats. But it's obviously sufficient for human infants, who grow much more slowly than
baby rats.[18]

Egg protein is used by rats with 100 percent efficiency,
while wheat protein is used only about half as efficiently.
From this observation, it was concluded that eggs had the
ideal amino acid structure and wheat was an inferior protein source. Later studies, however, demonstrated that at
low levels of protein intake, egg protein and wheat protein
are used by *people* with equal efficiency. The proteins in
wheat, rice, potatoes, and other plants satisfy human protein requirements without supplementation from other
sources, animal or plant.[19]

Analysis has shown that the diets of vegetarians provide
from twice to many times the minimum requirements for all
essential amino acids. This seems to be true even for vegans, who eat no animal products at all.[20]

There is some dispute about taurine, an amino acid traditionally considered non-essential because of our ability to synthesize it from methionine. Some researchers now question whether this ability is adequate to meet the body's needs.[21] Yet vegan mothers manage to produce about thirty times as much taurine in their breast milk as cows do; and the growth and development of vegan children has been shown to be normal.[22]

The relative proportions of the amino acids in the vegan diet closely resemble those in human milk. And human milk presents the ideal pattern—at least for babies. The amino acid profile in the omnivore diet more closely resembles that in cow's milk. The vegan diet is also closer than the omnivore diet to the FAO reference pattern, the amino acid pattern of the ideal protein based on estimated human requirements.[23]

Vegans eating grain-based diets actually *need* less protein than people eating meat-based diets. This is because of the protein-sparing-effect of carbohydrates. The efficiency of protein utilization varies with the non-protein calories in the diet. When these calories are about half carbohydrate and half fat, as in the usual Western diet, protein utilization isn't as good as when more of the calories come from carbohydrate. When the diet contains twice as much carbohydrate as fat, protein utilization is increased by about 13 percent; and it's increased as much as 50 percent at very low intakes of protein and calories (as on very low-calorie diets).[24]

Don't vegetarians have to worry about balancing complementary proteins?

Not really. Bread, rice, and potatoes contain all the essential amino acids and will supply complete proteins if eaten alone. You'll meet your protein requirement faster if you throw in some other plant foods to round out the amino acid profile of your grains, but you don't have to consult nutritional tables to figure out which ones. Just go for variety.

The traditional diet of certain Middle Eastern populations is 85–95 percent bread. Clinical tests have shown that this diet is adequate to meet protein needs, supplemented with only 5–10 percent ordinary vegetables and fruits.

Nitrogen balance was maintained in men over a 50-day period on a diet in which 90–95 percent of the protein was provided in the form of bread made from *white* flour. The other 5–10 percent was supplied by vegetables and fruits. Nitrogen balance started out severely negative, but by the end of the study the men had recouped all (and slightly more) of their nitrogen losses. When their endurance was measured on a motor-driven treadmill, it was as good as, or better than, at the beginning of the study. The men also had to eat an extra 800 calories a day to maintain their weight— further evidence that you can eat extra calories without gaining weight by switching to a high-carbohydrate diet.[25]

Lysine is the amino acid in which wheat is the shortest. Theoretically, adding lysine to bread, either directly or by combining it with high-lysine complementary foods, should improve its protein value. But this effect hasn't been observed experimentally.[26]

In a two-month study, college men ate a bread diet in which 75 percent of the protein came from wheat and the rest from ordinary plant foods like potatoes and fruit. Although the diet provided only 46 grams of protein a day, nitrogen balance was maintained, showing protein needs were being met. Then 20 percent of the bread was replaced with either peanut butter, rice, or beans. These foods should have "complemented" the bread by supplying additional lysine. They failed, however, to improve the protein value of the diet.[27]

Soybeans don't need to be combined with anything else, because their amino acid content is close to ideal. But even rice, which is less than ideal, can maintain nitrogen balance when used as the sole source of protein. A diet in which 75 percent of the protein comes from rice and 25 percent from wheat can maintain protein balance as well as one in which half the protein comes from animal sources.[28]

Potatoes, too, can satisfy your protein requirements without help from other foods. In fact, people have lived for long periods on nothing but potatoes.[29]

That doesn't mean you should try to live on only one food, or only a few foods. The more restricted your diet, the more you risk deficiencies in other essentials, like vitamins and minerals. Moreover, when foods with poor amino acid patterns are eaten alone, the amino acids that can't be used have to be burned like carbohydrates for fuel. What is left are amine waste products that burden the kidneys and liver, just as excess meat protein does.[30] For people with healthy eliminatory organs, this isn't a major problem. But if your kidneys are slowing up, it's worth watching your amino acid combinations. Combining complementary proteins also becomes more important for pregnant women, nursing mothers, and children, who need proportionately more of their calories in the form of protein.

What's important is that ordinary mixtures of foods will do the job, without particular care and planning. The combining rules are simple. You probably combine your foods properly without even thinking about it. You just need to eat (1) legumes (beans and peas) with grains or dairy products; and (2) nuts and seeds with legumes or dairy products. (Contrary to popular belief, the peanut butter sandwich isn't a great protein combination because peanut butter and wheat are deficient in similar amino acids.) The ideal proportions of these combinations vary, but generally they should be heavy on the grains and light on the beans. This is how traditional societies on grain-based diets have combined their proteins for thousands of years.[31]

Diets centered around a single grain can maintain robust health. The rural Iranian diet is 85–95 percent bread. The diet of the Tarahumara Indians is 80 percent corn. The diet of certain New Guinea natives is 80–90 percent sweet potatoes. By accepted standards, these diets are inadequate to meet nutritional needs. New Guinea sweet potatoes, for example, are only about 4 percent protein. The total protein intake of natives living on them averages only about 20 grams a day. Yet these New Guineans continue to impress tourists by their splendid physiques.[32] Judging by their blood pressure and serum cholesterol levels—and by their athletic abilities—these vegans are healthier than we are.[33] The athletic prowess of the Tarahumara Indians is extraordinary, as we'll see in the next chapter. We'll also see that athletes *aren't* among those people who have increased protein needs.

Chapter 6

Meat or Wheat: Which is the Breakfast of Champions?

"In the fall of 1963, a party of American 'river runners' attempted to conquer the twisting, boulder-strewn Barranca del Cobre, a gigantic canyon of the Sierra Madre Occidentale of North-Central Mexico. Unable to cover more than a few miles a day . . . they ran dangerously low on food and were forced to abandon most of their equipment. . . . Their lives may have been saved only because of the help and guidance they received from some Indians chancing to cross their path. In describing the climb up the canyon wall, one of the party stated: 'Each one of us carried a canteen, but nothing else. For five miles we climbed that trail, which seemed designed only for goats. At one point, as we toiled upwards, the Indians passed us, each carrying a 60-pound pack of our gear. Suddenly, I realized it was their third trip of the day.' "[1]

This excerpt from the *American Journal of Physical Anthropology* describes an incident with the Tarahumara Indians of Mexico. They subsist on a diet that is 80 percent corn and 10 percent beans. The only animal food they eat with any regularity is eggs (averaging two per week). Meat is eaten solely on holidays.[2]

By Western standards, this diet is entirely inadequate to meet nutritional needs. Yet these Indians are exceptionally strong and healthy. Their anthropological literature records feats of physical endurance unequaled by Western athletes. One anthropologist described a young Tarahumara who carried a 100-pound burden for a distance of 110 miles in 70 hours. Another, serving as a messenger, made a round trip of nearly 500 miles in five days. Other anthropologists noted that the Tarahumara successfully competed with mules: they could be hired for 25 *centavos* a day to carry 50-pound loads at least twice as far as mules. Mexican ranchers also hired Tarahumara Indians to chase and capture wild horses.[3]

The feat the Tarahamura are most famous for are their kickball races—lasting up to two days, non-stop. A small wooden ball is propelled by the players' feet over twisting routes involving steep climbs and descents, for a distance of *100 to 200 miles*. Researchers conclude that "the reported performances of the Tarahumara require a revision of our physiological concepts of maximum work tolerance."[4]

They also require a revision of our concepts of the protein needs of athletes. The belief that heavy muscular exercise requires large amounts of protein—particularly meat protein— has persisted for hundreds of years.

Early in this century, however, an American physiologist named Chittenden, experimenting on himself and on soldiers and athletes with low protein intakes, found that 40–55 grams of protein a day were sufficient for athletic performance. Stamina actually increased at these lower intakes. Chittenden concluded that lower protein intakes were healthier than higher ones, due to the extra work the unnecessary protein imposed on the kidneys.[5]

Other studies show that people with a low protein consumption can undertake strenuous exercise without showing a significant increase in protein metabolism. Muscular efficiency is either no worse, or actually better, on low-protein than on high-protein diets.[6]

Increased physical activity does increase your need for energy. For this purpose, grains work better than meat. On high-carbohydrate diets, long-distance cyclists ride farther, long-distance cross-country skiers race faster, long-distance canoeists paddle faster, and soccer players score more late-in-the-match goals. Athletes have set world records and won national competitions with *no* meat—or other animal foods—in their diets. The first men to run a mile under four minutes were vegetarians.[7]

*If meat isn't necessary for athletic prowess, why do I
feel weaker without it?*

Meat can give you a *feeling* of energy. This sensation, however, doesn't reflect actual muscular strength, which studies
show is no greater for meat-eaters than for vegetarians.[8]

One doctor's explanation is that meat, like coffee, acts as a
stimulant. Both speed up the endocrine glands to deal with
toxins that must be eliminated. In coffee, the toxin is caffeine. In meat, the toxins are ammonia and other end-
products of its metabolism. The abstaining meat-eater, like
the abstaining coffee addict, may experience a feeling of
tiredness when he withdraws from these stimulants.[9] The
feeling is temporary.

Another doctor notes that the cholesterol supplied by meat
is the core molecule of several adrenal hormones, including
adrenalin (epinephrine) and cortisone. Eating cholesterol-
rich foods stimulates the adrenal glands to produce more of
these hormones, which give a feeling of energy and euphoria.

The adrenal glands are bean-sized glands located on the
top of the kidneys. Their functions include the release of
hormones that convert glycogen (the storage form of carbohydrates) to glucose (the form in which carbohdyrates are
burned for energy). Adrenal hormones also raise blood pressure, creating a "rush."

The feeling of power that results is expensive. High blood
pressure is a major risk factor for heart disease. Both high
blood pressure and heart disease are conditions to which
meat-eaters are particularly prone.[10]

There's another reason why you may feel tired when you
first abandon animal foods: It takes time to adapt to changes
in diet. You can't tell in the beginning how you're going to
feel in the end.

The ability of the body to meet its protein needs is determined by nitrogen balance studies. Nitrogen is the critical
element distinguishing protein from carbohydrates and fat.
When the amount of nitrogen that goes in equals the amount
that goes out, the body is said to be in nitrogen balance.

When grains are substituted for meat as the sole source of
protein, nitrogen balance begins in the negative. This means
that the body can't initially meet its protein needs from

grains alone. But after about ten days, nitrogen balance turns positive, and it becomes more positive for the next couple of weeks. It takes about thirty days to reach nitrogen equilibrium on a reduced protein intake.[11]

It also takes time for your digestive enzymes and intestinal microorganisms to adapt to different types of protein, it takes time for them to adapt to smaller amounts of it, regardless of source. The higher your protein intake to start with, the longer it takes to reach nitrogen equilibrium on a reduced-protein diet.[12]

The solution to this problem is to avoid radical changes in diet. Replace meat, cheese, and eggs with grains, greens, and beans gradually, over a period of six months or so. This is also the key to maintaining mineral balance, as we'll see in a later chapter.

Won't meat sustain athletic performance longer than grains?

No. What athletes need most is glycogen. When glycogen runs out, they experience muscular fatigue. Glycogen is the storage form of carbohydrate. There's no carbohydrate in meat, which consists solely of protein and fat. Protein is burned for fuel only if the diet is low in carbohdyrates. Fat, too, seems to be unable to maintain performance at high intensities.[13]

The superiority of carbohdyrates over fat as a fuel is proven in studies comparing the effects on athletic performance of high-carbohydrate and high-fat diets. Heavy exercise is sustained *twice* as long on a high-carbohydrate diet as on a high-fat diet, even when protein intake is the same.[14]

When you aren't exercising, your energy demands are met mainly by fat. During exercise, an increasing amount of energy must come from carbohydrates; and carbohydrate storage is much more limited than fat storage. At least fifty times as much fat as carbohydrate is stored in the body. Glycogen is found almost exclusively in the muscles and liver, which have a limited storage capacity. Fat is stored in fat cells everywhere in the body.

High-carbohdyrate diets replenish the glycogen stores of athletes. They can increase glycogen stores to beyond their original capacity. This phenomenon is the basis of carbohdyrate loading, a strategy that has recently become popular for prolonging endurance exercise.

Doesn't carbohydrate loading mean going for a period of time without carbohydrates?

Originally it did. Carbohydrate loading involved depleting muscle glycogen stores by heavy exercise, followed by a low-carbohydrate diet for three days, followed by a high-carbohydrate diet. The exercise caused the muscles to supercompensate for the glycogen loss by increasing their stores to beyond their initial capacity. The low-carbohdyrate diet was thought to further this process. Recent studies, however, show that supercompensation is achieved better without this intermediate step, which seems to slow the process down and impair performance. So the latest strategy for carbohydrate loading is exhaustive exercise followed directly by a diet high in complex carbohydrates.[15]

Won't sugar work as well as bread for carbohydrate loading?

At first, glycogen stores are replaced as well by simple sugar as by complex carbohydrate. But after about two days, glycogen stores are significantly higher if the carbohydrate comes from starch.

During exercise, on the other hand, simple sugar is as good as complex carbohydrate for prolonging endurance.[16]

Don't athletes need more protein than office workers?

Not according to the Protein-Calorie Advisory Board of the United Nations. It recommends a diet of 5 to 5.5% protein for a person with "moderate activity." For a person engaged in "heavy activity," requiring a greater calorie intake, a *lower* percentage of calories from protein is recommended. In other words, if you exercise heavily, you need more calories but not more protein; so the protein percentage of your diet actually goes *down*.[17]

A contrary position was taken recently by researchers at Kent State University. They suggested that if you engage in *very* heavy exercise, like weight-lifting, you need twice the amount of protein recommended for sedentary people.[24] Even so, if you spend four hours a day pumping iron, you're going to have to *eat* twice as much as the clerk working at his desk to get enough fuel for your energy needs. You'll be doubling your protein intake automatically, as long as you don't fill up on junk food.

Another researcher calculated the total protein requirement for athletes at only 47 grams per day, even during the active phase of muscle building. This is less than the 56-gram RDA for an adult man. The calculation was based on the FAO/WHO value of 25 grams for the average-sized man, rounded up by 30 percent to insure that it covered the requirements of virtually the entire population; plus 7.5 grams of protein to replace what would be lost in sweat during four hours of strenuous exercise; plus another 7 grams to increase muscle mass. This researcher concluded that the "evidence causes skepticism" about any requirement of protein of much more than 1 gram per kilogram of body weight per day.[19]

One gram per kilogram is about twice the athlete's daily 47-gram requirement. A 220-pound weight lifter weighs 100 kilograms. To get one gram of protein for each kilogram he weighs, he needs to eat 100 grams of protein a day.

Again, if he's hoisting weights for four hours a day, he's going to have to eat about 4,000 calories a day just to meet his energy requirements. This is twice the calorie intake of the average desk worker. The weight lifter's 100-gram protein requirement is the same, measured by the calorie, as for the 2,000-calorie-a-day secretary: 1 gram for every 4 calories.

The Kent State team proposes a daily requirement as high as 2 grams of protein per kilogram of body weight. They concede, however, that the amount by which exercise increases protein requirements, if it does at all, hasn't been determined. They warn:

"[T]here is little evidence to suggest that the massive quantities of protein routinely consumed by [weight lifters] are either necessary or beneficial. . . . [T]oo much protein will not only be converted to fat and stored (with the associated detrimental effects, i.e. heart disease, appearance, etc.), but it will also place excessive demands on the kidneys and could result in significant losses of body water."

At least one world-class body builder has not only sustained but improved his performance by eating a low-protein vegetarian diet. Swedish-born Andreas Cahling is a professional body builder who got his start in Greco-Roman wrestling and power lifting. He now follows a Tarahumara-like diet with no animal foods except the occasional egg. He has surpassed his achievements on a high-meat diet. He won the title of "Mr. International" and placed fifth in the professional body-building world championship. The proof is in the performance.

Section II

OUR ROOTS IN THE TREES

Chapter 7

The Gorilla in Your Business Suit

"The Siamiadae then branched off into two great stems, the New World and Old World monkeys; and from the latter at a remote period, Man, the wonder and glory of the universe, proceeded."

—Charles Darwin[1]

We've seen you can survive without animal foods, and drop pounds painlessly by replacing them with plant foods; but why bother, if you're not worried about your waistline?

The answer, of course, is that you can also extend your life. A diet high in complex carbohydrates and fiber, and low in cholesterol and saturated fat, can ward off the chronic diseases that are our national bane. Complex carbohydrates and fiber are found only in plant foods. Cholesterol is found only—and saturated fat is found mainly—in animal foods.

Our bodies are evolutionarily designed to regulate carbohydrate intake, while they are unequipped to regulate fat intake. Thus, as carbohydrate intake increases, oxidation increases along with it, and carbohydrate balance remains constant. But fat intake isn't metabolically regulated. Any excess results in deposits of fat in the tissues and arteries.[2]

This physiological anomaly, however, is more serious than just excess pounds. Deposits of arterial fat also characterize atherosclerosis, the underlying cause of death for over half the American population. Atherosclerosis and the cardiovascular diseases it spawns are so common in Western countries that we think of them as inevitable concomitants of old age. They are rare, however, among people in underdeveloped nations who eat grain-based, essentially-vegan diets.[3]

Why is it that animal foods make us put on weight, while we can eat plant foods to our heart's content and stay slim?

63

Why does animal fat cause fatty deposits to build up in our arteries, while it doesn't have this effect in dogs and cats? Why do we need fiber for proper intestinal function, while carnivores can get along without it?

The answers are suggested by a study of comparative physiology, which shows that man has the same physiological structure as the essentially-vegan leaf-eating and fruit-eating primates. The primate digestive system has been modified by evolution to enable it to extract nutrients from high-fiber, high-carbohydrate, low-protein plant foods. These evolutionary modifications have made the human digestive organs poorly suited to a meat-rich diet. The unrelenting stress imposed on these organs by a diet low in fiber and carbohydrates, and high in animal protein and fat, underlies the twentieth-century epidemic of chronic diseases.

What evidence is there that we're physiological vegans?

The first clue is the internal and external design of our bodies. Physiologically, man bears a greater resemblance to two other primates—the gorilla and the chimpanzee—than to any other species. The immunological, alimentary, skeletal, nerve, and blood protein structures of these three primates are remarkably similar. So are the parasites that inhabit our intestines. Many parasites require very specialized physiological conditions to survive and reproduce. Man shares a greater percentage of them with the gorilla and the chimpanzee than with any other animal. Even closer similarities are seen in the chromosomes by which we and our fellow primates are genetically programmed. Certain fluorescent dyes produce patterns on the Y chromosomes of man and the gorilla that are produced on those of no other mammal.[4]

What do gorillas and chimpanzees eat?

The gorilla is a folivore, or leaf-eater. Its diet is basically salad. It varies in different areas, but greens—vines, herbs, leaves, bark, stems, and roots—are always the major constituent.

The chimpanzee is also a tree-food animal, but it goes for

the fruit more than the leaves. Classified as a frugivore, or fruit-eater, its native diet is more than two-thirds fruit and less than one-third leaves.[5]

The vegetables and fruits favored by these great apes are also the foods their digestive systems (and ours) are structurally adapted to process.

Don't gorillas and chimpanzees eat meat?

Not gorillas. In the wild, they generally avoid eating other animals even when they have the chance. They will occasionally eat snails and insect larvae, but these animal foods make up only a marginal part of their diet.[6]

Wild chimpanzees aren't above eating meat, but they're faced with the problem of having to catch it first. Nature didn't equip them for the pursuit.

The diet of the chimpanzees studied by one researcher was only 4 percent animal food. For us, this would be equal to about two hamburgers *a week*. This is only one-tenth the amount of animal food in the American diet, which is nearly half composed of it.[7]

Anthropologist Jane Goodall observed wild chimpanzees eating meat in cycles, limiting their kills to about twelve a year. Then they would lose interest, partly because it was too much trouble.[8]

Unlike true carnivores, neither chimpanzees nor humans are biologically equipped for hunting. To kill, we need weapons. To remove the flesh from the bones and reduce it to bite-sized morsels, we use knives. Carnivores have powerful teeth and jaws adapted to killing prey and slicing flesh from bone with a scissor-like action. We have teeth better designed for chewing up leaves and fruit, and grinding nuts and seeds. Carnivores have claws that are formidable weapons in prey capture. We have fingers for picking and pulling apart greens, fruits, and nuts.

Arguably, our long-fingered, grasping hands developed from swinging in trees rather than plucking fruit, but the evolutionary implications are the same. What attracted our primate ancestors to the trees were their fruit and green leaves. Tree leaves are a major food source that is found worldwide. Yet primates are among the few vertebrates that actually use them for food. Apparently other verte-brates aren't structurally adapted to process this food source.[9]

In any case, our hands have evolved beyond their tree-swinging functions. Our fingers are less like those of tree-swinging apes, such as the orangutan, than those of the gorilla, which walks on the ground like we do. The formidable look-ing gorilla is very fussy about his food. He holds his meal in his hands and eats daintily. The fingers of the orangutan are very long. The gorillas' fingers are short and broad, with a short but opposable thumb, allowing him to make the precise movements necessary to get at the most tasty parts of plants.[10]

Aren't our canine teeth for tearing flesh?

This argument has been made, but our canines are vestig-ial at best. They are small and inefficient compared to the awesome weapons of the tiger and the cat, and simply won't do what theirs will do—kill, pull apart, and devour whole, live game. We have tiny canines, flattened molars, and mobile jaws. These structures are less like those of the true flesh-eaters than like herbivorous animals', whose jaws allow only vertical movement and permit little or no chewing or grinding.[11]

Aren't our canines at least evidence that we evolved from meat-eaters?

They are, but they don't represent a recent evolutionary trend. They go back to the dinosaurs. Large canines ap-peared in the earliest stages of the evolution of mammals and are actually a very primitive trait.

The earliest vertebrates were carnivores. Mammals evolved from mammal-like, meat-eating reptiles that had simple cone-shaped teeth separated in front and back by a greatly en-larged and obvious canine tooth. These reptile-like teeth were designed only for grasping. The early placental mam-mals retained canine teeth that were pointed, projecting, and definitely larger than the incisors. In man, the canines have shrunk and have merged with the incisors. Even the vegetarian gorilla has canines that are larger than ours.[12]

Why did these early carnivores evolve into plant-eaters?

The carnivorous diet had its limitations. Without prey, the carnivore is surrounded by great quantities of energy-containing plant compounds it can't use. The energy is locked up in cellulose and other fibrous substances that make up a large proportion of plant material. This plant material is impervious to all known vertebrate digestive enzymes.

While highly-evolved animals lack the enzymes to break these woody parts down, certain microorganisms do not. Herbivores solved the problem by developing digestive systems that could house and nurture a wide variety of these microorganisms. The microorganisms break down structural carbohdyrates by fermentation, exposing the energy-containing material locked inside to the animal's digestive enzymes.

This new breed of plant-eating vertebrates included the leaf- and fruit-eating primates. It also included man's predecessors, the early Miocene hominoids. The dental structures of these pre-human apes indicate they picked their food from the trees of the tropical jungle. Five million years ago our diet was exclusively fruit.[14]

What prompted our hominoid predecessors to become meat-eaters?

Easy access to fruit was apparently ended by the Ice Age and migrations to colder climates. Snow and drought forced them to hunt other animals for a living.

We didn't succeed as hunters because we were biologically equipped for the pursuit. Rather, it was through the use of weapons created by our intellectual ingenuity. The same ingenuity later allowed us to domesticate animals, enormously increasing the availability of animal foods. Our superior intellects also prompted us to alter the chemical structure of our food by cooking it; to alter its chemical balance by salting and preserving it; and to alter its fat content by breeding animals and injecting them with hormones.

The problem is that physiological evolution hasn't kept pace with the dietary revolution our intellects have devised.

All the major chronic diseases have been linked to overloading our digestive systems with substances they're ill-equipped to handle—including refined and processed foods, sugar and salt, pasteurized milk, and domestic meat.[15]

Man has been eating meat for several million years. Isn't that long enough to evolve a digestive system capable of disposing of it properly?

Possibly, but not necessarily. The rate of evolution is variable. The dolphin has a digestive tract adapted to eating meat, but it also has a four-chambered stomach, indicating it was at one time a herbivore. That evolutionary change, however, has taken 25 million years and still isn't finished.[16] The 5-million-year span between us and our fruit-eating hominoid predecessors is short by comparison.

Even if the human digestive system has had time to adapt to the wild game eaten by Stone Age man (and by certain healthy primitive populations today), it hasn't had time to adapt to the substantially different product found at the supermarket.

Recent breeding and feeding practices have drastically altered the composition of meat. Its fat content has increased from the modest 3.9 percent found in wild game to 25–30 percent or more. Its polyunsaturated fat content has decreased to only one-fifth the amount found in wild game. Its omega-3 polyunsaturated fatty acids have decreased to almost nothing. Polyunsaturated fatty acids—particularly those of the omega-3 variety—tend to reduce the risk of heart disease, while saturated fat increases it.[17]

Not only are we eating a different animal than the Neanderthals did; we're eating it much more often. For them, as for primitive people today, abundance alternated with scarcity. They suffered periods of involuntary fasting that let the digestive organs rest. The continual supply of meat today puts a continual stress on our kidneys, the organs whose job it is to dispose of the waste products of protein digestion. There is evidence that *sustained* excesses of protein predispose even healthy people to the progressive deterioration of those organs.[18]

Even in times of plenty, it isn't easy snagging passing game with rocks and spears. Unlimited access to meat came only when man learned to domesticate animals. That drastically altered the natural limitations to the amount of meat in his diet. He had a ready and abundant supply. It also increased the fat content of his meat, since domesticated animals have a steadier food supply and get less exercise than wild animals. Animal domestication took place in the past 5,000 to 10,000 years, during which our genes have changed minimally.[19]

The availability of meat in a cheap, cleaned, wrapped and even cooked form is a luxury limited to Western civilization in this century. A hundred years ago, you had to butcher a pig yourself. Twenty years ago the retailer got a carcass. Today retailers receive packages of brand name pork chops ready for the consumer. There are now fresh meat entrees that can sit on a supermarket shelf for eighteen months without the need for freezing.[20] The dietary revolution brought about by the Industrial Revolution, agribusiness, and modern food-processing techniques has occurred too recently to have had any impact on the evolution of the human digestive organs.

Don't our digestive organs resemble a cat's more than a cow's?

We aren't ruminants.[21] We don't have four-chambered stomachs, and we can't digest straw and hay. But we aren't carnivores either. We are most like gorillas, who consume very large amounts of vegetation and virtually no animal products.[22] Gorillas are leaf-eating vegans.

Doesn't our digestive machinery at least work for animal food?

It does, but not as well as a carnivore's. It gets overworked and breaks down. Different conditions are required for the digestion of plant and animal matter. The problem is that the plant-digesting adaptations of the human digestive organs actually interfere with the efficiency of their meat-digesting capabilities.[23]

Plant cell walls are made up of fibrous substances that are impervious to vertebrate digestive enzymes. Plant-eating animals responded by developing enlarged stomach areas that harbor bacteria capable of degrading structural carbohdyrates by fermentation. Because these microbes are important for the digestion of plant foods, the conditions necessary for their growth are essential to plant-eating animals. These conditions include an environment sufficiently alkaline for bacteria to survive in it, and a digestive tract large and slow moving enough for large quantities of food to be retained during microbial action.

For meat digestion, on the other hand, it's better that conditions favorable to bacterial growth *not* be present. The bacteria that readily multiply in dead meat might otherwise infect the eater.

The plant-eater has a long, convoluted intestinal tract, in which bacteria complete the digestive processes that are begun in its stomach. The carnivore has a short intestinal tract that allows for the quick evacuation of the waste products of meat digestion, which its own digestive enzymes complete with little microbial intervention. Unlike plant-eaters, carnivores are also equipped with proteases (protein-digesting enzymes) that are powerful enough to digest prey without further processing; and with uricase, an enzyme that breaks down uric acid, a potentially toxic end-product of meat metabolism.

In the plant-eater, conditions favorable to bacterial survival prevail. The carnivore's digestive system is too strongly acidic for bacteria to survive in it. The mouth of the carnivorous snake contains an acid venom that is so strong a bactericidal that it sterilizes the gut contents of its prey, permitting the snake to swallow mice and other relatively large animals whole and live, without regurgitation. Without this initial sterilization, putrefaction (the breakdown of meat by bacteria) would dominate digestion and result in poisoning. In plant-eaters, by contrast, the saliva is alkaline to facilitate starch digestion. Starch digestion is initiated in the mouth by an alkaline enzyme called ptyalin. Ptyalin is scant or lacking in the saliva of carnivores, whose diets contain few carbohydrates.[24]

How does the human digestive system compare to the carnivore's?

The digestive tract of a meat-eating animal is usually only three times the length of its torso, measuring from mouth to anus. The human digestive tract has a very long, convoluted small intestine followed by a large, smoother one. It's about twelve times the length of the torso—four times as long as a carnivore's, and one-fourth longer than most herbivores'.

Human saliva, which breaks down food in the mouth, is more alkaline than a carnivore's and contains ptyalin for starch digestion. A lower acidity is also found in the human stomach, which favors the digestion of carbohydrates more than of proteins. When you eat starch and protein together, about 8 times as much of the starch as the protein is digested in your stomach before the whole meal is expelled into the intestines.

We also have weaker proteases than carnivores. Protein digestion must be completed in our intestines by enzymes secreted by bacteria, rather than by endogenous enzymes secreted by our own digestive organs. We also lack the enzyme uricase, so our blood has a higher concentration of uric acid than other animals'.[25]

Comparative physiology suggests that our digestive organs are peculiarly adapted for processing plant foods. The same conclusion follows from an investigation of the chronic diseases that result when those organs break down.

Chapter 8

Dead Meat: You Are What You Eat

"Without beef on the table, is it really a meal?"
—The Iowa Beef Council

The tendency of affluent Western populations to develop a variety of chronic diseases indicates our digestive systems aren't designed for their civilized contents. Cardiovascular heart disease, hypertension, and some types of cancer have emerged as dominant health problems only in the past century. These diseases, which account for a majority of Western deaths, are significantly less common in countries too poor to construct their meals around animal foods. Moreover, these diseases can be induced in laboratory animals by feeding them diets that simulate affluent Western man's.[1]

Abnormalities characterizing the chronic diseases include elevated serum cholesterol levels, elevated blood urea and uric acid levels, loss of calcium from the bones and teeth, and unnatural deposits of insoluble calcium salts in normally soft tissues of the body.[2] All are linked in some manner to our limited ability to handle meat.[3] They don't trouble true carnivores eating their natural diets. And they rarely trouble other primates, even in captivity. Chronic disease is common *only* in laboratory animals fed simulated human diets.[4]

What causes elevated serum cholesterol levels, and why don't carnivores face this problem?

Cholesterol is a waxy, fat-like compound found only in animal tissues. It's actually an indispensable substance in the bodies of animals, comprising an essential component of the structural membranes of all cells and a major compo-

72

nent of brain and nerve cells. Cholesterol is manufactured in the liver and intestines, where a central regulatory mechanism maintains equilibrium between its synthesis and destruction, and assures that serum cholesterol remains at the proper level.

In humans, this regulation is limited. Indulgence in cholesterol-rich food tends to cause serum cholesterol to rise and atherosclerotic lesions to form in the arteries. These lesions are responsible for most heart attacks and many strokes.[5] Again, *"cholesterol-rich food" means food derived from animals—meat, milk products, and eggs.* Plants don't manufacture cholesterol.

In other plant-eating animals—including apes, rabbits, and pigs—cholesterol produces lesions like those formed in man. But in meat-eating animals, more efficient regulatory mechanisms operate, so a cholesterol-rich diet doesn't result in these lesions.[6]

Dogs and rats are protected by a mechanism by which they convert large amounts of cholesterol into bile acids. Bile acids are a component of bile, a fluid secreted by the liver. Bile is stored in the gallbladder, from which it is ejected periodically into the small intestine to help emulsify fats and cholesterol for digestion. Bile acids are converted to bile salts, which are used as emulsifying agents.

The mass conversion of cholesterol into bile acids prevents excess dietary cholesterol from accumulating in the arteries of meat-eating animals. It also protects them from gallstones.

We lack this mechanism. While we are protected by other regulatory feedback mechanisms, they are less effective than the large increases in bile acid secretion that protect the dog and the rat. We are susceptible both to cholesterol build-up in the arteries and to gallstone formation.[7]

What are gallstones?

Gallstones are hard masses consisting of cholesterol, bile pigments, and calcium salts. They form when an increase in the amount of cholesterol in bile overwhelms the bile salts' ability to dissolve it.

Gallstones are very rare in wild animals, and almost as

rare in non-industrialized countries. They're common, however, among civilized people. They've been found at autopsy in approximately 15 percent of adults.[8]

This association seems to be environmental rather than hereditary. The condition is common, for example, among American blacks, but rare among their West African relatives. Meat consumption seems to be a critical variable. Gallstones are only half as frequent among vegetarians as non-vegetarians, even in industrialized countries. In hamsters, when soy protein is substituted for milk protein in the diet, gallstone incidence drops by 75 percent.[9]

What if I stick to lean meat, from which most of the cholesterol has been removed?

This is the popular solution to the cholesterol problem, but studies with animals show blood cholesterol is raised even by meat from which *all* the cholesterol has been removed. And in some human studies, eliminating animal protein has been more effective than eliminating animal fat in lowering serum cholesterol levels.[10]

What about fish?

Fish is unique among the flesh foods normally sold in the supermarket, because its composition hasn't been appreciably altered since the Stone Age. It hasn't been shot with hormones and antibiotics, or confined in small cages. Its fat content remains unchanged.

As a general rule, heart disease incidence is correlated directly with meat consumption, but fish is an exception to this rule. In fact, a recent study showed that men who eat 7 ounces of fish a week are 50 percent *less* likely to die of heart disease than those who eat none.[11] The low rate of heart disease among Eskimos, despite a high intake of saturated fat and cholesterol, is attributed to their heavy fish consumption.

Fish actually has a high fat content, but its fat is unique in that it contains large quantities of long-chain, highly-polyunsaturated omega-3 fatty acids. The fatty acids in most flesh foods are of the saturated variety that raise serum cholesterol levels. Polyunsaturated fatty acids generally lower them. Omega-3 fatty acids lower serum cholesterol by "thinning the blood"—reducing the tendency of blood platelets to aggregate, or clump together. In fish, they seem to serve as a sort of antifreeze that prevents the blood from thickening in cold water.

Another advantage of fish over other flesh foods is that it lives on seaweeds and sea vegetables, which are higher in minerals than the land vegetables other animals eat. Minerals are continually being washed from the land into the sea. Cod liver oil, for example, is rich in nutrients because the cod stores the vitamins and minerals it obtains from sea vegetables in its liver.

But as macrobiotic vegetarians point out, you can skip the middleman and go straight to the source: the seaweeds themselves. This approach is actually safer, since fish oils have an alarmingly high cholesterol content. Cod liver oil provides a whopping 570 mg of cholesterol per 100 grams (about a tablespoon). This is nearly twice the 300-mg cholesterol limit recommended by the American Heart Association *for an entire day.* Other fish oils are even worse.

Certain plant foods also supply generous quantities of omega-3 fatty acids, without the cholesterol that accompanies fish oil. Good plant sources include walnut oil and walnuts, wheat germ oil, rapeseed oil, soybean lecithin, soybeans, tofu, beans, butternuts, and seaweed.[23] The richest known plant source is purslane, a vegetable used in soups and salads in Greece and Lebanon—countries where the incidence of heart disease and cancer is low.[12]

Are there other risks associated with fish consumption?

There are, and we'll take a closer look at them in Chapter 20.

Today, fish and other flesh foods are likely to contain environmental contaminants, including industrial chemicals and pesticide residues. Flesh foods are at the top of the food chain; that is, humans eat animals that eat smaller animals that eat plants. Environmental contaminants are more concentrated as you move up in this progression. Fish are particularly susceptible to contamination. They accumulate some toxic chemicals to *more than 100,000 times* the level present in water. Meat, fish, and poultry contain about 13 times as much pesticide residue as vegetables and grains, and 2½ times as much as dairy products. Fiber-rich fruits, vegetables, and grains, on the other hand, are not only low in pesticide residues; they actually help get toxic chemicals out of the body.[13]

The higher levels of contaminants in meat mean higher levels of contaminants in meat-eaters. These high contaminant levels are suspected in cancer and other toxin-induced illnesses. A 1962 study found that the level of DDT in the bodies of meat-eaters was double that in vegetarians. The use of DDT has now been banned, but it has often been replaced by other toxic substances. And the total use of pesticides has increased.[14]

A study reported in the *New England Journal of Medicine* investigated the pollutants in the breast milk of vegetarian and non-vegetarian mothers. The pollutant level in the milk of women who had been vegetarians for more than a year was only ⅕₀th *to* ⅟₁₀₀th as high as in non-vegetarian mothers.[15]

Another problem linked to the consumption of meat can't be avoided by replacing it with fish. This is osteoporosis, or bone loss, a disease to which the Eskimos are particularly susceptible. Eskimos have an earlier and greater bone loss than any other people in the world. The phenomenon is attributed to their heavy consumption of meat and fish.[16]

Is the high rate of bone loss among Eskimos due to too much meat or merely too little calcium?

It isn't from too little calcium. The average calcium intake of Eskimos is actually higher than in this country—and is several times that of non-milk-drinking vegetarian populations, who are less troubled by osteoporosis than we are.

A correlation between osteoporosis and flesh foods, rather than calcium, is corroborated by studies comparing the bone mineral content of elderly vegetarians and meat-eaters in Western countries. In some studies, the rate of bone loss of vegetarians has been only *half* that for meat-eaters, although their calcium intakes were comparable.[17]

How would meat consumption cause bone loss?

Two constituents in meat—protein and phosphorus—seem to pull calcium from the bones. Many studies show that as protein intake increases, the calcium lost in the urine increases along with it. And because calcium is the major component of bone, calcium loss means bone loss. These studies show dietary protein has a greater effect even than dietary calcium on calcium balance (the net retention of calcium). The calcium loss resulting from a high protein intake can't be corrected by increasing calcium intake, because the body's ability to absorb calcium at higher levels of intake falls off dramatically.[18]

Does phosphorus have the same effect as protein on urinary calcium?

No. Increasing dietary phosphorus actually *decreases* the amount of calcium lost in the urine. This favorable effect has led some researchers to conclude that phosphorus has no deleterious effects on human bone.

But animal studies show that when phosphorus exceeds calcium in the diet, calcium is pulled from the bones into the blood, even when urinary calcium is reduced. There is evidence that the same effect occurs in humans.

In the typical Western omnivorous diet, phosphorus exceeds calcium by something like 3 to 1. Nearly half the phosphorus comes from meat.[19]

If phosphorus pulls calcium from the bones but isn't excreted in the urine, where does it go?

Good question. In animals, it goes to the soft tissues—particularly the kidneys, heart, and lungs—where it contributes to the pathological calcification of those tissues.[20] Whether this also happens in humans remains controversial, but substantial circumstantial evidence suggests it does. This whole subject, which is very complicated, is explored in Chapter 15.

Don't all meat-eating animals at least face the problem of bone loss?

No, not on their natural diets. Bone disease seems to be a man-made condition. It's found only in humans and in the animals we feed.[21]

Other meat-eating animals have a compensatory mechanism that maintains bone integrity over a wide range of protein loads. In rats, when protein intake is increased, calcium absorption increases along with it. We lack this compensatory mechanism. A high-protein diet leads to a serious loss of bone calcium in humans.[22]

Even this compensatory mechanism, however, won't protect carnivores from excess phosphorus. Bone loss occurs in domesticated carnivorous animals when their diets contain more phosphorus than calcium. In the muscle meats we give our pets as table scraps, phosphorus outweighs calcium by about 20 to 1.[23] Dog-food processors correct this problem by adding bone meal to their products; but no one adds calcium to our burgers.

How do wild carnivorous animals that live mainly on meat preserve a favorable calcium/phosphorus ratio?

The bodies of animals actually contain nearly twice as much calcium as phosphorus, but 99 percent of this calcium is stored in the bones and teeth. Muscle meat contains very little.[24] Wild carnivores, lacking knives and forks to separate the bones from the flesh, wind up eating substantial amounts of bone along with the muscles and organs of their prey.

Why does meat appeal so much to our taste buds, if our stomachs aren't designed to handle it?

Actually, our taste buds are evidence of our innate vegetarianism. Unlike lions and wolves, few people are instinctively aroused by the smell of bleeding flesh. Few carnivores, on the other hand, sniff twice at ripe fruit. Only after cooking, tenderizing, grinding, salting, and seasoning does meat acquire appeal equal to that of the fruits and nuts that are the staples of our gorilla forebears.

Unfortunately, the cooking that renders meat palatable also renders it mutagenic, or potentially cancer-producing. The link between animal products and cancer is investigated in the following chapter.

Chapter 9

The Cancer Connection

"In ancient times, lack of food gave languishing bodies to death. Now, on the contrary, it is abundance that buries them."
—T. Lucretius Caro,
De Rerum Natura, 55 B.C.

"So far the most likely culprit [in food-related cancer] is the high-animal fat diet. . . ."
—R. Lee Clark, President of the
American Cancer Society[1]

No disease is more terrifying than cancer. The sufferer faces excision of his cancer by the surgeon or bombardment with poisonous chemicals in the hope that the tumor will succumb before the patient does. It would be better to treat the cause, and mounting evidence points to dietary factors. Studies linking cancer to a diet high in animal foods suggest that this disease is again rooted in our attempt to force animal foods into digestive organs designed for leaves and fruit.

Cancer is an uncontrollable growth of cells. For some reason, the normal mechanisms that stop protein synthesis and cell multiplication are lost, and protein accumulates until cell division is forced. This uncontrolled growth has been linked to the growth-stimulating components in our national diet— fat, protein, calories, and hormones. These are the same components that make us grow taller and heavier, on the average, than Third World populations; that make Oriental children on Westernized diets grow taller and heavier than their parents; and that make American girls menstruate earlier than girls in essentially-vegan Third World countries. Fat, protein, calories, and hormones are largely supplied by animal products.[2]

Cancer is rare in essentially-vegan populations. In Western societies, by contrast, it's the second leading cause of death, preceded only by coronary heart disease. Not only are the offspring of American immigrants taller than their forebears, their cancer rates are significantly higher.[3]

Epidemiological studies show vegetarians are less likely to develop cancer than meat-eaters. Colorectal cancer is the leading cancer in this country among men and women, and breast cancer is the leader among women. The incidence of both colorectal cancer and breast cancer increases along with the consumption of animal protein and fat (especially pork and beef fat).[4] Bowel cancer incidence is 2–6 times as high in the United States as in countries where the diet is essentially vegetarian. Breast cancer incidence is 5–6 times as high.[5]

A 1989 study showed that a certain hormonal pattern, characterized by high total and non-protein bound androgens and low sex-hormone-binding globulin, is accentuated in women with breast cancer. This hormonal pattern is associated with a Western-type diet, rich in proteins and fat, and poor in complex carbohydrates and fiber.[8]

Isn't cancer caused primarily by environmental and chemical carcinogens?

About 50 percent of all cancers can be traced to environmental contaminants unrelated to diet. They include tobacco, occupational chemicals, medical drugs, and ultraviolet light. No such link, however, has been demonstrated for the other 50 percent. Cancers having no apparent environmental cause include those of the colon, breast, uterus, and prostate. What these cancers have been linked to is diet—specifically a diet high in fat-rich animal foods and low in fiber-rich plant foods.[7]

Even where environmental factors are involved, they merely *initiate* cancer growth. Initiation involves a brief and irreversible interaction between a carcinogen and genetic material. A second stage, called promotion, is necessary for cancer development. In this stage, promoter substances cause transformed cells to proliferate and form a tumor. Substances called anti-promoters have the opposite effect.

You can probably guess which is which. At present, the substance most clearly established as a promoter is dietary fat.[12] Possible anti-promoters include fiber, the cruciferous vegetables (including broccoli, cabbage and cauliflower), the protease inhibitors in beans and seeds, and certain vitamins and minerals. All of these are found in plant foods.[8]

The protective effect of vegetables was shown in a Japanese study in which cancer deaths among 122,000 older men were recorded over a 16-year period. Deaths among men who ate meat, smoked, drank, and ate vegetables were only two-thirds as great as among men whose habits differed only in that they did not eat vegetables. And among men who not only ate vegetables but also avoided meat, alcohol and cigarettes, deaths were only two-fifths as great.[9]

People in tropical societies eating a balanced diet of plant foods don't get skin cancer, no matter how long they're exposed to the sun. The initiator is there (the sun), but the promoter is lacking.[10]

Epidemiologically, meat consumption is clearly linked to cancer of the large bowel. Yet this cancer occurs no more frequently in meat-eating Mormons than in vegetarian SDAs. One factor thought to protect Mormons from cancer is their higher than average intake of natural fibrous plant foods, particularly stone-ground whole wheat. On the other hand, Mormons do have significantly higher blood pressure and serum cholesterol levels, putting them at greater risk for heart disease.[11]

Researchers again point to our Stone Age physiology, which is adapted to high-fiber, low-fat plant foods. Anthropologists estimate that the diet of prehistoric people in warm climates was only about 20 percent fat, compared to our 40 percent. It also included about 45 grams of fiber a day, compared to our 15 grams.[12]

Colon cancer has been linked not only to the consumption of fat but to the consumption of meat—especially red meat.

Whether these correlations are independent of each other is unclear, since meat is also our primary source of fat.[13] The popular emphasis is on fat as the chief offender, but there is some evidence that too much meat, accompanied by too little fiber, is an even more important factor.

> Colon cancer rates in Kuopio, Finland, are among the lowest in developed countries, and are only one-fourth those in nearby Copenhagen. In a study comparing the diets of people in these two cities, the low-risk Finns were found to eat *more* fat (largely from dairy products) than the Danes. But the Finns ate only two-thirds as much meat. They also consumed twice as much fiber and four times as much milk as the Danes.[14]

> Bowel cancer is many times more prevalent among southern than northern Indians, although the northern Indians eat *nine times* as much fat. The southern Indians eat sixteen times as much meat and substantially less fiber.[15]

How is the meat/cancer connection explained? Many theories have been proposed. They're based on (1) the carcinogenic compounds produced from the metabolic end-products of animal foods by intestinal bacteria; (2) the lack of fiber in a meat-centered diet; (3) mutagens formed in the cooking of meat; (4) the higher-chain fatty acids found only in meat; and (5) the stimulation of hormone production by growth promoters in animal foods. These associations, which we'll look at here in turn, are all traced to our evolutionary predisposition for fibrous plant foods, and our evolutionary inability to handle large quantities of animal foods.

1. Carcinogenic compounds are produced from meat by intestinal bacteria.

The nature of the diet affects the nature of the intestinal bacteria. These bacteria are believed to have evolved along with their host. But on an evolutionary scale, human diets containing large amounts of animal protein and fat are recent. These diets produce a biochemical environment in the intestines in which microbes can produce chemical compounds that are harmful to the host, since it hasn't had a long-term evolutionary association with them. These compounds have been suspected in the origins of colon cancer, breast cancer, stomach cancer, bladder cancer, diverticular disease, appendicitis, hemorrhoids, and ulcerative colitis.[16]

Suspect compounds resulting from the degradation of meat proteins include ammonia, which is thought to be produced in the metabolism of urea by colonic microflora; phenols, which are produced from the bacterial degradation of tyrosine, an amino acid in meat; amines, which are produced from the bacterial metabolism of tryptophan, another amino acid in meat; and nitrosamines, which are produced by bacteria from nitrate and nitrite in meat. Amines have been implicated in the origins of bladder cancer. Phenols promote tumor growth in mice. Ammonia also has tumor producing potential. Nitrosamines are known carcinogens.[17]

Other suspect compounds result from the digestion of fat and cholesterol by bile acids. Population studies show that large bowel cancer is most common in populations having high concentrations of bile acids in their stools. Case studies show that patients with large bowel cancer have higher levels of fecal bile acids than matched controls do. Heart disease patients treated with drugs to lower serum cholesterol have an increased risk of large bowel cancer, apparently from the greater exposure of their colons to bile acids produced when the cholesterol removed from their arteries is metabolized and excreted. In rats exposed to carcinogens, dietary cholesterol is a known promoter of cancer.[18]

The increased secretion of bile acids with a high fat intake alters the bacterial content of the bowel. The result is enhanced conversion of primary bile acids to secondary bile acids by bacterial action in the gut. These secondary bile acids are the real suspects. They're structurally similar to known carcinogens. They've been implicated as promoters of colon tumors in mice.[19] The colons of meat-eaters are exposed to more of these harmful secondary bile acids than lacto-ovo-vegetarians, and lacto-ovo-vegetarians are exposed to more than vegans.

One study compared fecal bile acids in SDA vegans, SDA lacto-ovo-vegetarians, SDA non-vegetarians, and non-SDA non-vegetarians. All lived in the Los Angeles area, where

SDAs have a substantially lower risk of bowel cancer than the general population. When stool weights, body weights, and fat intakes were taken into account, total fecal bile acids were similar. Their composition, however, was significantly different. The ratio of secondary to primary bile acids in the stools of SDAs who ate animal products (milk or meat) was twice that for vegans; and for general population non-vegetarians, the ratio was 5-6 times as great.[20]

In the colons of people at high risk for colon cancer, flora have been found that have an increased capacity to transform bile acids into potential carcinogens. More of these flora are found in the colons of meat-eaters than of vegetarians.[21]

2. The fiber theory

Besides excreting fewer secondary bile acids, low-risk populations also eat more plant fiber; and plant fiber seems to be protective against colon cancer. Fiber decreases the content of bile acids in the colon. It may do this by increasing fecal bulk (thus diluting bile acid concentration); or it may promote the removal of bile acids from the bowel into the circulation; or it may reduce the time bile acids remain in the colon and expose it to harmful compounds.[22]

Like the meat link, the fiber link can be traced to the evolution of the human digestive system. The intestinal tracts of both ruminants and primates evolved to process the high amounts of fiber in their diets. Some 30–50 percent of the leaves that are the gorilla's chief food may be made of cell wall material. The fruit favored by the chimpanzee is also high in indigestible material. The evolutionary response to this problem was a delicate symbiotic relationship between the animal and certain intestinal microorganisms that could break this fiber down by fermentation.

It has long been known that cows need a high-fiber diet for proper intestinal function. The reason is that the slow rate of fiber digestion by the fiber-digesting bacteria prevents the end-products of digestion from accumulating faster than they can be eliminated. When cows are fed low-fiber diets, this regulatory mechanism is disrupted, and the cows develop a condition called rumen acidosis from the toxic accumulation of metabolic waste products.[23]

But the importance of fiber for the proper functioning of the human intestinal tract has only recently been recognized. Diets that are low in fiber have now been linked epidemiologically with cancer of the colon, atherosclerosis, diverticular disease, and diabetes. These "Western" diseases are several times as prevalent in meat-eaters as in vegetarians. The proposed explanation is that the low fiber content of the Western diet slows intestinal transit time. This leads to changes in the composition of the bacteria in the gut, which then produce substances that are harmful to the host.[24] While cancer of the colon is common in humans, it is rare in dogs and cats, apparently because they have shorter intestinal tracts and shorter intestinal transit times.[25]

The shorter intestinal tracts and higher levels of bactericidal acids in carnivores also protect them from food-borne infections. The long journey meat must make through the convoluted human intestines provides a fertile environment for these infections, which result when microorganisms contaminating the meat penetrate the mucus membranes coating the intestines and multiply in the tissues.[26] This problem is prevented to some extent by cooking, which kills many food-borne bacteria. But cooking meat introduces other hazards, and one of them is an even greater risk of cancer.

3. *The link with mutagens formed in the cooking of meat*

Cancer begins when genetic mutations occur in chromosomal DNA. Substances that induce genetic mutations in animals are called mutagens. Significant levels of them are found in cooked, but not raw, meat. They're also found in the stools of humans after, but not before, they eat cooked meat. Vegetarians, who have a low risk of cancer, also have low levels of these fecal mutagens. Cancer was rare among the primitive meat-eating Eskimos, but only when they ate the meat raw.[27]

Mutagens have been traced particularly to the cooking of protein. Foods that are higher in fat and lower in protein produce fewer mutagens when cooked than those with the opposite composition. Fried bacon, for example, is actually less mutagenic than fried chicken, apparently because it is lower in protein.

While all cooked food shows some mutagen formation, cooked meat is by far the worst. Vegetarian protein sources—including milk, cheese, beans, and tofu—show only negligible mutagen formation under normal cooking conditions. Various starches are only 3–10% as mutagenic as beef when similarly cooked.

The mutagen level varies not only with the food but with the temperature and the cooking time. Less heat for less time is better. The level of mutagens produced by cooking plant foods doesn't approach those produced in the cooking of beef, even when the temperatures are higher and the cooking periods are longer.

Chicken, like beef, produces significant mutagenicity even at moderate cooking temperatures and times. Eggs don't, except under severe cooking conditions. Milk, cheese, beans, and tofu, like eggs, develop mutagenic activity only under the most severe cooking conditions.[28]

What is the safest way to cook meat?

To keep the mutagen level low in ground beef, it should be cooked for less than 10 minutes on a side at a temperature below 300 degrees. In theory, frying on the low-medium setting of your range will accomplish this. Unfortunately, few ranges actually give accurate control of temperature. In practice, these settings can result in temperatures well within the mutagen-producing range.

If you're worried about cancer, the worst thing you can do to a steak is to broil it, and the best is to microwave it. But don't use the browning element. Mutagenicity increases with charring. Next to microwaving, the safest cooking methods are stewing, poaching, and boiling (although extended boiling of beef stock can produce significant mutagen formation). Next to broiling, the worst method is frying.[29]

In Japan, broiling is currently the most popular method of preparing fish (the most popular flesh food). In a 1983 study, Japanese who ate broiled fish twice or more weekly were nearly twice as likely to get stomach cancer as those who ate it less often. And they were 30 percent more likely to get cancer of any type.[30]

Besides the level of mutagens, a critical variable is whether the food is accompanied by anti-promoters that inhibit cancer growth, including vegetables, fiber, and certain plant proteins.[31]

What is the best way to cook plant foods?

Cooking plant foods by any method doesn't seem to do much harm, because their levels of mutagens remain low. An exception is fried potatoes, which have been linked to breast and ovarian cancers in vegetarian women.[32]

Stir-frying involves less oil, lower temperatures, and shorter cooking times than deep-fat frying. For vegetables, it may actually be preferable to boiling. Among the vegetarian Japanese and northern Indian Punjabis, colon cancer incidence is extremely low.[33] Both groups eat their vegetables stir-fried. (For the Indian and Oriental stir-fry methods, see Recipes.)

The anti-cancer properties of vegetables are attributed in part to their vitamins. When vegetables are boiled, vitamins that may serve as anti-promoters are lost in the water. Stir-frying coats the vegetables so their vitamins are retained. Your boiled vegetables won't necessarily be lower in fat anyway, since you'll probably coat them with butter to make them tastier.

Both vitamin C and vitamin A are lost when vegetables are boiled.[34] Vitamin A is the one most strongly linked to lower cancer rates. One of its major functions is to control cell differentiation. Loss of cell differentiation is a basic feature of cancer. Vitamin A is found in both plant and animal foods. However, studies provide stronger support for a protective effect of the plant form of the vitamin (beta carotene). Vitamin C may also have anti-cancer properties, but the evidence here is less clear.

In any case, cooking does less damage to plant foods than to animal foods. Applied to meat, heat treatment reduces digestibility and amino acid availability. Applied to plant foods, moderate heating actually improves digestibility.[35]

In fact, for plant foods cooking was a landmark evolutionary advance. It made plant starch, a universally available food source, accessible to vertebrate digestion. Fruits and meats can be digested uncooked, but raw plant starches are highly indigestible because they're surrounded by an indigestible cellulose wall. Cooking causes the starch to swell, which breaks down this wall and exposes the starch to the action of digestive enzymes. Cooking also destroys certain substances in plants that inhibit their digestion. Raw beans, for example, contain a substance that inhibits the digestive enzyme trypsin; but this trypsin inhibitor is easily destroyed by heat. Cooking made beans available as an important source of protein for much of the world's population.[36]

The difference between cooking plant foods and cooking animal foods is that plant foods are primarily starch, which isn't materially altered or damaged by heat. Animal foods are primarily fat and protein, which are damaged by the process.[37]

4. The higher-chain fatty acid hypothesis

The lower incidence of cancer in vegetarians has also been linked to the absence of higher-chain fatty acids in plant foods.

There are four families of fatty acids, and two of them—linoleic acid and linolenic acid—are considered essential. Humans can't make them from other substances in the body but must get them in their diets. The essential fatty acids are abundant in plant foods.

Higher-chain fatty acids are those containing long chains of carbon molecules. They are found in meat. The higher-chain fatty acids are necessary for proper cell membrane fluidity, but you don't have to get them from food. Normal human cells contain enzymes that form higher-chain fatty acids from essential fatty acids. Here we differ from many carnivorous animals, which lack these enzymes. Apparently, they *must* eat animal fat to obtain the higher-chain fatty acids.

Many cancer cells have the same limitation. Cancer cells are primitive cells similar to the rapidly multiplying ones

forming the human embryo. Many lack the enzymes necessary to convert essential fatty acids to higher-chain fatty
acids. It's been postulated that when a diet lacks animal fat,
cancer cells can't get the higher-chain fatty acids they need
for proper cell membrane fluidity. They either fail to reproduce normally, or are more susceptible to attack by the
body's immune system. A diet that lacks the higher-chain
fatty acids provided by animal fat inhibits cancer growth.[38]

The fatty acids in milk are shorter than those in meat,
which may explain why milk drinkers are less susceptible to
colon cancer than meat-eaters are.[39] But milk is suspect in
another way. It contains high levels of hormones, and these
link it to the hormone-dependent cancers, especially cancer
of the breast.

5. *The link between cancer and the growth-stimulating components of our national diet*

The hormone-dependent cancers include those of the
breast, ovary, testis, prostate, and uterus. They occur ten
times as frequently in this country as in Japan, and five times
as frequently as in India and Central Europe.[40] Epidemiological and laboratory studies link them to fat, protein, calories, and hormones. These growth stimulating components
are all generously supplied by animal products.

Americans mature early, indicating we have high blood
levels of sex hormones—estrogens, androgens, and prolac-
tin. High serum hormone levels are linked to certain dietary
components: fat, protein, and calories. As intakes of these
components go up, blood hormone levels go up. The incidence of hormone-dependent cancer rises with them.[41]

Cancer incidence is also linked to obesity. This too-common
American affliction comes from excess fat and excess calories. In cancer-prone animals, when the intake either of fat
or of calories is significantly reduced, so is their incidence of
cancer. Obesity also elevates estrogen levels, and studies
show that human tumor cell growth is stimulated by physiological doses of this hormone.[42]

Protein has a similar effect. Cancer incidence is reduced
in mice when their protein intake is limited, even if their
caloric intake is unchanged. In rats exposed to carcinogens,

tumor incidence is significantly higher when their diets are high in protein. The reason seems to be that malignant tumors have greater protein requirements than normal tissues. Limiting a single amino acid in the diet has successfully limited tumor growth.[43]

In women, the leading hormone-dependent cancer is breast cancer. In men, it's prostate cancer. Internationally, these two cancers are correlated with the same foods that are correlated with bowel cancer—mainly meat and animal fat.[44]

Prostate cancer is directly related to obesity—and to intakes of milk, cheese, eggs, and meat. It's also directly related to high serum levels of testosterone and estrogen. Vegetarian SDA men, who have a low risk of prostate cancer, also have low plasma levels of these hormones.[45]

In black South African men whose usual diets were essentially vegan, urinary excretion of androgens and estrogens decreased on a Western diet, suggesting that higher levels of these hormones were being retained in their bodies. Conversely, in white North American men fed a vegetarian diet, urinary excretion of these hormones increased.[46]

In a clinical study of serum estradiol levels in men, this most potent of human estrogens dropped by 50 percent after only three weeks on a high-carbohydrate, low-fat, high-fiber diet.[47]

Breast cancer is also correlated highly with estrogen levels. Vegetarian SDA women, who have a low incidence of breast cancer, excrete greater amounts of this hormone than meat-eating women; and they have lower levels of it in their blood.[48]

In a study comparing vegetarian and meat-eating women, the meat-eaters' intakes of animal protein and animal fat were three times the vegetarians. The serum level of estrogens associated with cancer was also 50 percent higher in the meat-eaters.[49]

The hormonal effect of meat was shown in a study in which a Western diet was fed to black South African women. Their menstrual cycles increased from an average of 27 to 30 days. A vegetarian diet fed to Western women had the opposite effect. Soy protein, by contrast, had no effect on the length of the menstrual cycle.[50]

In the United States and England, particularly high correlations have been found between breast cancer incidence and milk consumption. In one British study investigating the link between fat and breast cancer, a positive association was found *only* with dairy fat. With other kinds of fat, the correlation was a negative one.[51]

Hormones aren't limited, however, to milk. Hormonal substances used as growth promoters can also be detected in meat. This may explain why in Japan, where milk is not a major item in the diet, breast cancer incidence is 8.5 times as high among women who eat meat daily as among those who do not.[52]

In terms of breast cancer risk, milk is clearly not an ideal food. But it's still considered the ideal calcium source. American women, who are also at high risk for osteoporosis, are urged to drink even more of it. We'll investigate that paradox after we look at the impact of the modern diet on our kidneys.

Chapter 10

Kidneys on Strike

"Why is renal disease inexorably progressive? Insight into [this question becomes] readily apparent when consideration is given to the possibility of a fundamental mismatch between the evolutionary design characteristics of the human kidney and the functional burden imposed by modern ad libitum eating habits. Sustained rather than intermittent excesses of protein . . . impose similarly sustained increases in renal blood flow and glomerular filtration rates, . . . predispos[ing] even healthy people to progressive glomerular sclerosis and deterioration of renal function."
—*New England Journal of Medicine*[1]

Kidney disease is another devastating condition that is on the rise. About 65,000 Americans must undergo regular dialysis treatments to filter waste products from their blood. Kidney dialysis and transplants are so expensive that the federal government now assumes much of their cost. Together, these treatments impose an annual burden on United States taxpayers of several billion dollars.[2]

Kidney disease has been linked to the unrelenting burden imposed by a high-meat diet on organs designed for grains and greens. Reviewing sixty years of research, a 1988 report in the *American Journal of Clinical Nutrition* concluded that excess protein can have a harmful effect on kidney function, and that a reduction in protein intake can relieve many of the symptoms of kidney toxicity.[3]

The kidneys function to rid the blood of toxic waste products. Meat produces substantially more of these toxins than plant foods do. All kidney disease involves the inadequate excretion of urea, creatinine, and uric acid; and all of these substances are nitrogen-containing products of meat metabolism.

Other chronic conditions are also associated with the toxic buildup of meat metabolism wastes. Elevated uric acid levels have been found in patients with hypertension, heart disease, obesity, and diabetes. Uric acid buildup can also be responsible for arthritis, rheumatism, and kidney stones.[4]

How can protein, an essential nutrient, be harmful?

Protein, of course, is good. It's only *excess* protein that leads to trouble. You're more likely to get excess protein from a diet that's heavy in animal foods.

We've seen that protein differs from carbohdyrates in that it consists not only of carbon, oxygen, and hydrogen— which are burned by the body for fuel—but also nitrogen, which can't be oxidized by the body. The nitrogen is converted to ammonia, a potential toxin. Ammonia must be converted by the kidneys to urea and excreted in the urine. When the kidneys have trouble excreting urea properly, the blood level rises. The blood urea nitrogen or BUN level (the urea level expressed in terms of the nitrogen it contains) is widely used to screen for kidney malfunction.[5]

Both animal and vegetable protein contain nitrogen that the body must dispose of as urea. Yet what elevates BUN levels seems to be *meat* protein specifically, not just protein in general. Thus, BUN levels are markedly reduced on a diet in which the protein comes from bread, even when the *amount* of protein is the same as in a comparable diet containing animal protein.

Healthy college men were fed a diet for ten weeks limited to 70 grams of protein a day. For the first three weeks, approximately 40 percent of their protein came from animal sources. For the following seven weeks, none of it did. During the latter period, 90–95 percent of the protein came from wheat, almost exclusively in the form of white flour. During the bread period, the BUN level dropped to approximately half what it was at the end of the meat period.[6]

The BUN levels of lacto-ovo-vegetarians, who eat animal protein in the form of milk and eggs but not meat, are only about half those of non-vegetarians eating the same amount of protein. Milk- and egg-eating vegetarians also have lower blood and urinary levels of creatinine, and lower urinary levels of uric acid.[8] Uric acid comes from the metabolism of purines, and meat is their major dietary source. Creatinine comes from creatine, an amino acid normally found in muscle tissue. When the kidneys fail, serum creatinine inexorably rises, making it another reliable indicator of the progress of kidney failure.[7]

Other substances that must be disposed of by the body result from the putrefaction of meat by intestinal bacteria. They include ammonia, phenols, phenolic ethanol, and amines. (Appropriately, two of these foul-smelling amines are named cadaverine and putrescine.)[8]

The first organ to work on these substances is the liver. In the healthy human, the liver is capable of detoxifying metabolic waste products before they circulate in the bloodstream. But when the liver can no longer handle its load of wastes, they can reach toxic levels. The result is an often-fatal condition called hepatic coma. This condition can be provoked in patients with advanced liver disease by giving them dietary protein.[9] They improve somewhat when their protein source is switched from meat to milk and cheese.[10] But they show the most dramatic improvement when their protein is changed from animal to vegetable. This happens even when the *amount* of protein is as much as doubled.[11]

After the liver has done its work, it sends its waste products to the kidneys for excretion. The functional unit of the kidney is the nephron. Each kidney contains about a million of them—far more than it needs under ordinary circumstances. The nephrons separate the solid components and proteins of the blood from its fluid element, then move the desirable components back into the blood. The undesirable components go into the urine.

Kidney disease results when the kidneys aren't removing these waste products properly. Some types are reversible. but nephrons may be permanently lost. As more and more losses occur, existing nephrons can increase in size in an apparent attempt to filter more fluid. Their rate of filtration (called the glomerual filtration rate, or GFR) can also increase. But these adaptations can't compensate completely. Deterioration continues, with lost nephrons being replaced by scar tissue.

Progressive loss of kidney function results in the accumulation of waste products. Most of these come from the metabolism of protein, particularly meat protein. Their build-up in the blood results in a toxic condition called uremia. At this stage, the underlying disease is usually unresponsive to treatment. Radical therapeutic intervention is required.[12]

The filtration rate increases in both animals and humans after a meal of meat. A large fish meal can increase the GFR of a seal by 150 percent. In animals (who eat only intermittently), the GFR presumably then returns to baseline levels. But in modern man, who eats animal proteins continually, the GFR remains elevated. The reserve nephrons intended merely for intermittent overloads are constantly overworked. Eventually they fail.

That's the theory of the researchers quoted at the beginning of this chapter. They hypothesize that the progressive loss of kidney function that characterizes normal old age is the result of the heavy and unrelenting workload imposed by the end-products of a meat-rich diet. Kidney function declines over time even in healthy adults. By eighty years of age, it's only one-half to two-thirds as great as in young adults. These researchers suggest animal protein can play a leading, rather than merely supporting, role in the process.[13]

Evidence for the theory comes, in part, from clinical studies of diabetics. They're especially susceptible to kidney failure. It seems that hyperfiltration by the kidneys precedes rather than follows the loss of nephrons in diabetics. The implication is that the kidneys break down because they are overworked, rather than being overworked because they've broken down. Other evidence comes from studies linking certain types of kidney disease to an allergic reaction to animal proteins.[14]

Researchers writing in the *Archives of Internal Medicine* in 1989 questioned the theory, since they found that creatinine clearance was no worse in people accustomed to high-protein diets than in those accustomed to low-protein diets.[15] But other researchers have shown that the mean GFR is significantly lower in vegans than in omnivores, and that creatinine clearance is poorly related to GFR. They warned that studies using only creatinine clearance to compare the GFR of meat-eaters and vegetarians must be interpreted with caution.[16]

The progressive loss of kidney function poses a serious problem only for people with kidney disease from some other cause. The kidneys have a large reserve capacity. Humans can operate with less than a third of their kidney function intact. The problem is that you can't tell ahead of time if you're going to be one of the victims. Like heart disease, kidney disease is a silent killer. The patient doesn't usually seek help until the condition is irreversible.[17]

Whether or not a low-protein vegetarian diet can delay the onset of kidney failure, there is no dispute that it can delay the progress of the disease once initiated. In fact, this diet can halt the normally inexorable progress of kidney failure altogether.[18]

In a study reported in the *New England Journal of Medicine* in 1984, 24 patients with chronic renal failure were treated with a low-protein, low-phosphorus diet supplemented with amino acids and keto acids. The diet slowed or halted the progression of kidney failure in a majority of cases, while maintaining the patients in nutritional health. The accumulated postponement of dialysis was an estimated thirteen years, saving taxpayers an estimated $400,000.[19]

For patients with kidney failure, a vegan diet can be a godsend, because the medical alternatives can be a nightmare.

What's wrong with the medical alternatives?

The options are hemodialysis and kidney transplantation. The transplant is the most radical and perilous alternative. It's hard to find a donor, and the transplanted kidney may be recognized as foreign by the patient's immune system and be rejected. To prevent this, drugs or irradiation techniques are used to suppress the immune response. This can be particularly hazardous because the immune system is the body's chief means of defense against invading microorganisms. The most common cause of death associated with a kidney transplant isn't rejection of the kidney. It's infection following immune suppression.

The less radical alternative is hemodialysis. It involves hooking up an exposed artery and vein to an artificial kidney, generally for several hours a day, several days a week. The machine removes waste products and uremic toxins, and corrects electrolyte imbalances.

But hemodialysis can't keep the disease from progressively deteriorating the kidneys. Eventually, their function is entirely destroyed. There is little doctors can do to slow or halt this process. Not only does hemodialysis fail to reverse the problem, but it's expensive, inconvenient, and discouraging to the patient.[20]

Hemodialysis and kidney transplantation fail to correct another serious problem associated with kidney failure: skeletal degeneration and the buildup of calcium deposits in the soft tissues (the kidneys, heart, arteries, and lungs). These deposits can severely impair the functioning of the calcified organs. If the patient is kept alive by kidney dialysis, progressive skeletal degeneration may be what keeps his condition from improving.

The incidence of atherosclerotic heart disease in patients with kidney disease is many times that in the normal population. Atherosclerotic heart disease is the leading cause of death in hemodialysis patients and the second leading cause of death in transplant patients after infection. Arterial calcification is the major villain in atherosclerosis. Calcium is what causes the hardening (sclerosis) of the arteries. In patients with kidney disease, this calcification is accelerated. Even if kidney function is reestablished by a transplant, existing extra-skeletal calcium deposits won't dissolve; and new ones may continue to form.[21]

As we'll see in the next section, skeletal degeneration and extra-skeletal calcification are two sides of the same coin: calcium is pulled from the bones and settles in the soft tissues. The process has been linked to excess protein and excess phosphorus; and both of these are contributed to the diet primarily by meat. Studies show an essentially-vegan diet can delay the progress, not only of kidney failure, but of the bone disease inevitably accompanying it.[22]

What does meat have to do with kidney stones?

Meat is the major dietary source of purines, which metabolize to uric acid. When the kidneys can't excrete enough uric acid through the urine, it may accumulate in the tissues and joints and crystallize. The result is pain, swelling, and stiffness. If uric acid and other metabolic waste products settle in the joints, the disease is called arthritis. If they accumulate in the nerves, the illness is known as neuritis or neuralgia. If they attack the soft parts of the body, it's called rheumatism. If they accumulate in the kidneys, the result is kidney stones.[23]

Gout, or gouty arthritis, is a singularly painful condition resulting from the inability of the kidneys to excrete uric acid as fast as it builds up in the blood stream. It occurs particularly in men fond of rich meats and drink. Some of its more famous victims included Henry VIII, Dr. Samuel Johnson, and Alexander the Great. The dietary prescription for gout is to reduce alcohol consumption and purine intake, and again that means reducing meat intake.[24]

Urinary stone disease is another agonizing condition linked to uric acid buildup. Like gout, urinary stones are more likely to occur in men than in women. Stones usually form in the kidneys, but they can be lodged anywhere in the urinary tract, including the kidneys, ureter, or bladder. If they get trapped in the ureter and block urine flow, the pain can be excruciating.

Urinary stones are a disease of affluence. Their incidence is directly related to the average annual protein intake of the population. In the United States, hospitalization for kidney stones is sixteen times as great as in India and Thailand; and it's 160 times as great as among the essentially-vegan black South African Bantu. Heredity won't explain these differences, since American blacks have about the same risk of stones as American whites.[25]

Animal protein is the *only* dietary variable consistently correlated with urinary stones. This correlation is established by studies not only of large populations, but of the eating habits of people with a tendency to form stones.[26]

In a British study, a 45 percent increase in stone incidence between 1958 and 1969 was correlated specifically with animal protein and, more specifically, with flesh protein.[27]

Vegetarians are more likely to escape this excruciating condition. Stone prevalence among vegetarians is only about half what it is among meat-eaters.[28]

Why would meat consumption be correlated with urinary stones?

Urinary stones consist of four major components—calcium, phosphorus, uric acid, and oxalate. A diet high in flesh protein increases the urinary excretion of all of them.[29]

> In a British clinical study, when 34 grams of protein in the form of fish were added to the diets of normal people, urinary calcium, oxalate, and uric acid all went up significantly. The effect was to increase their probability of forming stones by an estimated 250 percent. It also increased their protein intake from the average in Great Britain to that in the United States, where stone incidence is more than five times as great as among the British.[30]

The most common type of stone is the calcium-containing stone, which accounts for 50–80 percent of stone incidence worldwide. Almost half of these stones are pure calcium oxalate. The rest are a mixture of calcium oxalate and calcium phosphate. Uric acid stones comprise 5–20 percent of the stones in industrialized countries.[42] Although this is a relatively small proportion of all stones, there is evidence that increased urinary uric acid also increases the risk of calcium oxalate stones.[31]

As we'll see in the next section, one reason calcium gets into the urine is that it's pulled from the bones to buffer excess dietary protein. Kidney stones are only part of this problem. More pervasive is the accompanying calcium loss from the skeleton, which produces the hunched backs, fractured hips, and lost teeth of old age.[32]

The second major stone component is oxalate. It, too, comes primarily from meat digestion. Although oxalate is a constituent of plant foods, dietary oxalate accounts for only 5–10 percent of urinary oxalate. The rest comes from metabolism. Particularly, it comes from the metabolism of animal protein, which has a high content of tyrosine, tryptophan, and phenylalanine. Portions of these amino acids are metabolized to oxalate.

The third stone component, uric acid, comes from the metabolism of purines. Purines are also derived mainly from meat; and purine excretion is directly correlated with purine intake. Those who suffer a recurrence of stones have been shown to eat nearly twice as much purine as healthy people. Victims of gout, another disease of purine excess, often have crystals of uric acid in their urine. They may also pass uric acid stones.[33]

The fourth major stone component is phosphorus. Again, meat is its largest single dietary source. Phosphorus is also found in plant foods; but in plants it comes in the organic form of phytic acid, which actually seems to *inhibit* stone development.[34]

Shouldn't stone formers reduce their calcium intake?

That's the logical approach, but changes in calcium intake have only a small effect on urinary calcium. A much greater effect results from reducing protein intake, particularly animal protein intake.[35]

An Australian study compared meat-eating Mormons and vegetarian Seventh-Day Adventists. Their diets were similar except for meat intake. The intake of calcium was not significantly correlated with urinary calcium excretion, but the intake of protein (both total and animal) was. Urinary calcium was significantly higher in the Mormons.[36]

In a 1988 study, urinary calcium excretion was found to be 50 percent greater on a diet containing animal protein than on one containing vegetable protein. This was true although protein and calcium intakes were the same on both diets.[37]

Researchers conclude that rather than reducing their intake of calcium, recurrent stone formers should reduce their intake of meat.

Section III

THE ENIGMA
OF OSTEOPOROSIS

Chapter 11

Bone Loss: Too Little
Calcium or Too Much Meat?

"Toothlessness is for me chief in the range of cosmic insults heaped upon man . . . and in the long strategic retreat called life, I'll always see myself as backing toward my grave tooth by tooth. . . ."[1]

Lost teeth and fragile bones are nearly universal in old age. The progressive erosion of the bones and teeth is due to a gradual leaching of calcium. Loss of calcium from the teeth results in gum disease, the chief cause of tooth loss. Loss of calcium from the bones results in osteoporosis, or bone decalcification, causing the high incidence of broken hips and fractured vertebrae common to senior citizens.[2]

But low calcium *intake* is not—or is not alone—the culprit. Many people with very low intakes manage to maintain bone integrity well into old age, while many people with adequate or high intakes do not.[3]

One suspect that's been implicated is meat consumption. In a landmark study comparing 1,500 vegetarian women with 1,500 meat-eaters from the same region, bone loss in the older vegetarians was only half as great as in the older meat-eaters.[4] Their calcium intakes were comparable, and so were their intakes of other essential nutrients. The only significant variable was meat intake.

Not that vegetarians take in more calcium; they excrete less of it. A 1988 study reported in the *Journal of Clinical Endocrinology and Metabolism* found that people eating a vegan diet lost only two-thirds as much urinary calcium as on a similar diet that included meat, although the calcium and protein contents of the diets were the same.

A series of three diets was fed to fifteen normal adults (eight women and seven men). Each diet lasted twelve days. The diets contained similar amounts of calcium, phosphorus, and sodium; and of total fat, carbohydrates and protein (75 grams per day). In the first diet, protein came from meat and cheese. In the second, it came from soy protein and eggs. In the third, it came from soy protein alone. Average daily calcium losses were only 103 mg/day on the vegan (soy) diet. They rose to 150 mg/day on the meat and cheese diet, with the ovo-vegetarian diet showing intermediate values.[5]

This chapter documents the lower incidence of osteoporosis in vegetarians. The following chapters attempt to explain it.

What is osteoporosis, and why should I be worried about it?

Osteoporosis isn't a disease. It results from the gradual thinning and increased porosity of the skeleton. As the bones thin and weaken, they are less able to withstand the physical stresses of everyday living. At the extreme, bones that started out with the consistency of wood end up like cardboard. Hips subjected to the surgeon's drill in replacement operations shatter like powder.

Women, particularly after menopause, are more prone to bone loss than men. Seventy to 80 percent of hip fractures occur in women. According to a recent report sponsored by the National Institutes of Health, osteoporosis affects as many as 15–20 million Americans. In fact, most Americans over fifty probably have it. They just haven't sustained the fracture that will place them in that category.[6] The condition is difficult to detect clinically before 30–50 percent of the bone mass is already gone.

A recent X-ray study of older people in central Kentucky revealed that 92 percent of elderly whites and 68 percent of elderly blacks had some degree of osteoporosis.[7]

When osteoporosis strikes, the vertebrae, or bones of the spine, are usually the first to go. Among Caucasians in the

United States over the age of sixty, 25 percent of women and 6 percent of men have osteoporosis severe enough to involve vertebral fracture.[8] These fractures may occur spontaneously, or they may happen during everyday activities, such as lifting groceries or making a bed. As the bones become weaker and more porous, the vertebrae can no longer support their load. They simply collapse under the weight of the body. The result is acute pain and physical deformity. An inch or more in height can go with the collapse of each vertebra, up to a total of as much as eight inches. The rib cage tilts downward in a "dowager's hump," the spine curves in and the abdomen curves out.

The most serious consequence, however, is hip fracture. If you're a woman and you live to be ninety, your chances of breaking a hip are 1 in 3; and if you're a man, they're 1 in 6.[10] Hip fractures are the twelfth leading cause of death in America. Falls are the leading cause of accidental death in elderly white women. It's not clear, however, whether the fall causes the hip to break—or the hip simply collapses, causing the fall. The statistics for women who suffer hip fractures are alarming: 15 percent die shortly after, and nearly 30 percent die within a year. Fewer than half regain normal function, and those who do are twenty times more likely than other women to develop a hip fracture on the other side.[9]

These tragedies aren't inevitable. In certain cultures, they're very rare.[10] These populations do *not* have higher intakes of calcium. In fact, their calcium intakes would be considered insufficient by Western standards. Heredity also won't explain the phenomenon. Diet, however, may. The diets of these solid-boned populations are low in protein. It seems that protein, when eaten in excess, seriously impairs calcium balance.

We'll get to the clinical evidence for that connection in the next chapter. First, let's look at the epidemiological evidence, which shows that essentially-vegan populations have better bones in old age, despite calcium intakes that are lower than ours.

How is calcium intake related to bone loss?

Epidemiologically, it isn't.

The average daily intake of calcium varies from a high of 1,000–1,400 mg per day in Western countries to a low of 200–500 mg in many developing countries. In the West, calcium is derived mainly from milk, milk products, and flour fortified with calcium. In developing countries, vegetables are usually the main source of calcium.[11]

Many population studies of communities with different levels of calcium intake have been carried out. They show that the quality of bones and teeth is equally good in populations in which dietary calcium is low. Osteoporosis and dental cavities are often *less* common there than in affluent, milk-drinking, high-calcium-intake populations.[12]

The Bantu are a tribe populating practically all of the lower half of Africa and numbering over 50 million people. The Bantu sustain only *one-twentieth* as many hip fractures as Americans. Other solid-hipped peoples are the Malaysians in Singapore, who sustain only a fifth as many fractures; and the Chinese in Hong Kong, who sustain only a third as many. These figures are age- and sex-adjusted, so the results can't be attributed to differences in life expectancy.[13] Heredity won't explain them either, as we'll see shortly. And calcium intake certainly won't explain them. The average American calcium intake is 500–850 mg per day, while the Bantu intake averages only 200–400 mg, and the Malaysian intake averages only 134 mg.[14]

Most studies have found no correlation between calcium intake and bone density, even among people in the United States. One of these studies included over 2,000 women. Studies conducted in Guatemala, Costa Rica, El Salvador, Nicaragua, Panama, and Honduras actually found skeletal mass to be *inversely* related to national calcium intakes. The *less* calcium in the diet, the *thicker* the skeleton.[15]

It seems that people on low-calcium diets succeed in absorbing more calcium from their food.

In studies using Peruvian prison inmates, intestinal absorption of calcium was adequate to maintain positive calcium balance even when the diet contained as little as 100–200 mg of calcium daily. After about a week on a reduced calcium intake, the men adapted to the diet so that the amount of calcium they lost by elimination was still no greater than the amount taken in.[16]

Adaptation to a low-calcium diet, however, is unlikely if the diet is also high in protein, as we'll see in the next chapter.

Are the low calcium intakes of Third World populations sufficient even for pregnant women and growing children?

Calcium balance studies show modest amounts of calcium are enough even for people in these high-growth categories.[17] But again, these populations are on low-protein diets.

> In women in India, calcium retention has been shown to be adequate to satisfy the needs of both mother and fetus, although daily calcium consumption is limited to between 260 and 420 mg.[18]

> A study comparing American children in Surinam consuming Western diets and urban Creole children consuming calcium-poor diets showed that their cortical (or outer) bones were equally thick. So were the cortical bones of poor Javanese school children, as compared to those of Javanese children at boarding school who received thirteen times as much milk.[19]

Most women are in positive calcium balance in late pregnancy, regardless of the amount of calcium in their diets.[20] Like the Peruvian prisoners, they adapt to the amount of calcium consumed: the less taken in, the less excreted.

A substantial drain on skeletal calcium is imposed on women in Third World countries by multiple pregnancies and extended nursing periods. Bantu women average six to eight pregnancies each and nurse each infant for two to three years. Their white neighbors in Cape Town and Johannesburg, by contrast, have an average of only two pregnancies, and in many cases don't nurse their infants at all. The white women also consume 800–1,200 mg of calcium a

day. The older Bantu women should have poorly mineralized bones compared to their white counterparts. But autopsy bone specimens indicate that Bantu women have thick
cortices that are well mineralized even after the age of
seventy. South African white women, on the other hand,
have the same high incidence of osteoporosis as women in
Western countries.

Meat plays a prominent role in the diets of South African
white women. The Bantu diet is essentially vegan. If Bantu
women receive meat or other animal proteins at all, their
weekly intake is likely to be limited to twenty grams—or
less than that in one hamburger patty.[21]

In Western countries, women have a much higher incidence of osteoporosis than men, but this isn't true in
essentially-vegan populations. The higher incidence among
women in industrialized countries is attributed to the postmenopausal loss of estrogens secreted by the ovaries.[22] Good
in theory, except that Bantu women in Africa and Chinese
women in Hong Kong have the same very low rates of
fracture as the men in their countries. This is true although
they reach menopause at the same age as American women.[23]

American men consume up to twice as much calcium as
American women.[24] But this variable also won't explain the
stronger bones of Bantu and Chinese women, who consume
substantially *less* calcium than American women.[25]

Again, the critical variable appears to be meat consumption, which is at least fifteen times as great in the United
States as among the African Bantu and East Asians.[26] Not
only do elderly American meat-eating women suffer greater
bone loss than women in these essentially-vegan populations, they lose more bone than vegetarian women *in the
United States.*[27] Significant differences have also been demonstrated in estrogen levels between Asians and Caucasians, and between vegetarian and meat-eating Caucasians.[28]

Could the stronger bones of the Bantu and the Chinese be hereditary?

This theory has been proposed, based on evidence that
blacks, even in the United States, sustain fewer fractures
than American whites from the same region. Meat-eating

American blacks, however, have five to ten times as many fractures as their vegetarian Bantu relatives in Africa. Environment clearly plays a major role. Nutritional differences might explain bone differences between whites and blacks even in this country. Meat is the food of the affluent, who tend to be white.

Although older blacks in industrialized countries may have thicker bones than older whites,[29] the bones of elderly native Bantu women are no thicker than elderly English women's. And the bones of black Bantu *children* are actually *less* dense than those of Caucasian children.[30]

The Chinese have less compact bone than Caucasians *at all ages*. This is true whether they were born in the United States or abroad. The lighter skeletons of the Chinese have been thought to indicate an increased bone loss due to an inferior diet.[31] But the theory is belied by the lower fracture incidence of elderly Chinese as compared to better-fed Caucasians.

Heredity therefore won't explain the lower fracture incidence of either the Bantu or the Chinese, who are actually *born* with *thinner* bones.

Could the stronger bones of vegetarians be due to greater physical activity?

Bone loss can result from lack of exercise. But this variable won't explain the bone differences in American vegetarians and non-vegetarians, because their activity levels are the same.[32] It also won't explain the frail bones of Eskimos, whose senior citizens tend to remain quite active.[33]

What's wrong with the bones of Eskimos?

They're in the worst shape of any population group. Eskimos over the age of forty have 10 to 15 percent less bone than comparable whites. During their seventies, Eskimo females have almost 30 percent less bone than white females, whose bones are already frail compared to those of the Bantu and the Chinese. Even Eskimo males have 15 percent less bone at this age than white males.

In white females, bone loss begins in their forties; and in white males, it begins in their fifties. Eskimos, of both sexes, first lose bones in their late thirties. Osteoporosis generally isn't diagnosed in white women until their seventies, but Eskimo women reach this state of demineralization in their sixties. In white women, bone loss levels off after that; but in Eskimo women, it just continues to get worse.[34]

Eskimos have not only the greatest bone loss but also the highest meat intake of any population group. Caribou, sea mammals, fish, and birds are their staple foods.

Could the Eskimos' high rate of bone loss be due to an insufficient calcium intake?

No. Their daily calcium intakes range from 500 to 2,500 mg—equivalent to those in this country, and well above those of the native Bantu and Chinese.[35]

Another proposed explanation is that the Eskimos' ability to absorb calcium is impaired by a deficiency of vitamin D. Eskimos don't get much sunshine in the winter. However, researchers haven't been able to substantiate this theory— probably because Eskimos get plenty of sunshine in the summer, along with dietary vitamin D from fish oils.[36]

What about heredity?

If the fragile bones of elderly Eskimos are an inherited trait, younger Eskimos should have thinner bones than their Western counterparts. Yet no significant differences in mineral mass have been found between these younger groups.[37]

The genetic theory is also dispelled by comparative studies of Caucasian vegetarians and meat-eaters. In some studies, the bones of elderly vegetarians have been as much as 50 percent thicker than elderly meat-eaters, and their rate of bone loss as much as 50 percent lower.

British researchers studied 25 lacto-ovo-vegetarians aged 53–79, who had abstained from meat for 10–77 years. They were compared to a control group of 25 meat-eaters matched for age and sex. X-ray and laboratory examination showed that the bone densities of the vegetarians were 50 percent greater than the meat-eaters'. Bone density decreased in both groups with age, but it decreased less in the vegetarians. Moreover, it seemed to stop at about age 69, so that the vegetarians aged 70–79 actually had denser bones than the meat-eaters aged 50–59.[38]

The largest of these studies was designed to investigate anecdotal reports that vegetarian SDA women don't get osteoporosis. The study showed that after the age of 50 the rate of bone loss in SDA women was 40–50 percent less than in meat-eating women. This was true although their genes, calcium intakes, and levels of physical activity were the same.

The bones of 1,500 vegetarian SDA women were compared with those of meat-eating women of similar racial stock from the same Michigan locale matched for age, socioeconomic status, and reported physical activity. No significant differences in calcium intake were found between the two groups. Bone mineral content was determined by passing beams of gamma rays through the women's left forearms. An increased mineralization with age occurred in both groups until about age 20. From that age until about 55, when menopause normally occurs, there was no change in either group. But differences then became increasingly apparent. Between ages 50 and 89, the average decrease in bone mineral mass for the omnivores was 35 percent, while for the vegetarians it was only 18 percent. This means that the older vegetarian women lost only half as much bone as the matched meat-eating women.[38]

A 1980 follow-up comparing younger women in these two groups eliminated heredity as a variable. No significant differences in bone mineral mass were found between these younger groups.[40]

Most studies have confirmed the lower bone loss of American vegetarians.[41] In a follow-up study reported in 1988, the bone mineral densities of 304 older women from all over the continental United States were found to closely parallel those from the earlier Michigan studies. Dietary analyses revealed that the diets of the lacto-ovo-vegetarian women did not

differ significantly from meat-eating women's in any essential components. Intakes of calcium, protein, energy, fat,
and fiber were equivalent. What did differ were certain
nutrient relationships: the calcium/phosphorus ratio, and the
excess of acid or base in the diet.[42]

Both of these relationships are tied to the consumption of
meat. Meat is high in phosphorus, and it turns the urine
acid. We'll look at the significance of these factors in the
following chapters.

Chapter 12

Excess Protein: The Calcium Drain

"[P]rotein intake has a far greater effect on urinary calcium than does calcium intake."
—R. Walker, H. Linkswiler
University of Wisconsin[1]

Standard nutritional texts recommend a high-protein diet as good for the bones, on the theory that protein aids calcium absorption.[2] The premise, however, is based on studies showing only that *too little* protein impairs calcium absorption.[3] If some is good, more isn't necessarily better. Other studies show that when protein intake is increased above about 50 grams per day (the approximate RDA for protein), calcium absorption is also impaired. The result is a net loss of calcium from the body.[4] Bone loss results when protein intake is *either* too high or too low.

Too high doesn't mean as compared to the national average, which is itself too high. It means more than the RDA, which is already twice the minimum requirement—and only half the average intake in this country. Fifty grams of protein (the RDA) is less than that supplied by one chicken breast, or by one 6-ounce steak.[5]

How much does added protein increase calcium loss?

All other things being equal, urinary calcium increases as protein intake increases. A 100 percent increase in dietary protein generally results in a 50 percent increase in urinary calcium. A 200 percent increase in dietary protein results in a 100 percent increase in urinary calcium.[6] If you double your protein intake, you increase your calcium requirement by 50 percent.

115

The evidence comes from calcium balance studies, which are based on the premise that what goes in must either stay in, or come out. If the calcium coming out exceeds the calcium going in, the body is in negative calcium balance. A negative calcium balance means a net loss of bone because nearly all the body's calcium is stored in the bones.

Calcium balance studies show that protein intake has a far greater effect than calcium intake on calcium balance.[7]

When daily protein intake was varied from zero to nearly 562 grams, and calcium was varied from 100 to over 2,000 mg, urinary calcium loss was eight times as great on the highest as on the lowest protein intake, *regardless of calcium intake.*[8]

What happens to calcium balance at normal extremes of intake?

Normal parameters were tested by comparing diets containing 48 and 141 grams of protein daily. These amounts approach the normal upper and lower limits in the American diet, which averages about 100 grams daily.[9] The higher intake in this study was actually the *minimum* recommended for lactating mothers by Adelle Davis, a popular nutritional writer of the sixties—not that more accredited authorities agree with her; but she represents one extreme.[10] In the study, healthy young men on the low-protein diet retained calcium. On the high-protein diet, they lost about 84 mg a day.[11]

Measured by the day, a calcium loss of this amount isn't much; but maintained for a year, it would produce a skeletal loss of 2–3 percent.[12] That works out to 20–30 percent per decade, or *total skeletal disintegration in about forty years.*

When protein intakes are proportionately higher, calcium loss is, too. This is true even when calcium intake is increased at the same time. When the protein intakes compared were 75 and 225 grams daily, the difference in urinary calcium loss in healthy young men was 137 mg/day, although calcium intake on the high-protein diet was increased to nearly double the RDA. At that rate (about 50 grams a year), the entire skeleton would be gone in 25 years.[13]

Aren't these greater rates of bone loss than are found in normal people?

They are, but these rates are seen in patients with osteoporosis, who sometimes lose 90 mg of calcium a day.[14] This represents about 20–30 percent of the entire skeleton in just ten years.

In normal women immediately after menopause, bone loss reaches a high 6 percent per year.[15] If that rate of loss were maintained, the entire skeleton would have dissolved in seventeen years.

Over a lifetime, bone loss obviously isn't this great. But it's still enough to do serious damage. By the time the average American woman is ready to retire at 62, 40 percent of her skeleton has already dissolved.[16]

What portion of normal bone loss is due to excess protein?

This question was investigated in a study of 168 middle-aged Roman Catholic nuns eating the usual omnivorous diet. The study was particularly important because it tested calcium balances on normal diets.

The daily intakes of the nuns averaged 68 grams for protein, 660 mg for calcium, and 1,145 mg for phosphorus. Their average urinary calcium loss was 22 mg. But nuns whose protein intake averaged 102 grams (the average U.S. national intake) lost 54 mg of calcium a day—more than twice as much. Calcium loss more than doubled with an increase in protein intake of only 50 percent.[17]

The difference in daily calcium loss between these two extremes was 32 mg.—again, not much each day, but enough to increase skeletal loss by 1 percent a year, or 30 percent in 30 years. Interestingly, this is the rate of bone loss actually found in American women over 35.[18]

If the average American protein intake were cut by a third, calcium loss would be cut by more than half, and so would the daily calcium requirement. This finding helps explain why Third World populations eating plant-centered, low-protein diets maintain healthy bones on calcium intakes only half as great as ours.

How much could I cut my calcium losses by switching from a high-protein to a low-protein diet?

If your normal protein intake were in the upper ranges recommended by Adelle Davis, you could reduce calcium loss by as much as *90 percent*. This was the result of a study comparing women on otherwise equivalent diets containing 123 grams and 46 grams of protein a day.[19] On the high-protein diet, the daily average calcium loss was 121 mg. If that rate of loss were continued, the whole skeleton would be gone in about 30 years. On the low-protein diet, the average loss was only 14 mg. That's 90 percent less than on the high-protein diet. It's also about 75 percent less than on the average American diet.[20]

This 14-mg loss was within the range that can be eliminated by a modest increase in calcium intake. Rates of calcium absorption vary, from about 10 percent to 50 percent.[21] At a rate even as low as 10 percent, however, an additional 140 mg of calcium will easily eliminate a 14-mg loss. This amount of calcium is supplied by 6 ounces of tofu, a cup of broccoli, or a half cup of milk.

Isn't this the solution—to increase calcium intake?

Unfortunately, that works only when calcium intake is low to start with. Urinary calcium loss can't be corrected by increasing calcium, if it's already within the range considered adequate; that is, between 800 and 1,400 mg a day. At higher intakes, the body's ability to absorb calcium drops off dramatically.

This problem was illustrated in a study testing two diets that were identical except for their protein content. One contained 47 grams and the other contained 141 grams of protein—again the approximate upper and lower limits of what is considered normal in the American diet. The high-protein diet increased urinary calcium loss by about 200 mg a day. This loss wasn't corrected, although calcium intake was raised from 800 to 1,400 mg, adding *three times* as much calcium as was lost inthe urine. Daily calcium loss dropped by only

65 mg, leaving a net loss of 135 mg. That rate of loss is enough to dissolve 4 percent of the skeleton in a year, or 40 percent of it in ten years. These losses occurred although the participants were young men whose absorption rates should have been good.[22]

The problem is compounded for the elderly because the body's ability to absorb calcium declines with age. On a diet that includes 95 grams of protein and 700–800 mg of calcium, younger men absorb about 38 percent of the calcium. Older men absorb only about 15 percent.[23]

The secret for improving calcium balance isn't to add calcium. It's to subtract protein. The best calcium balances in these studies resulted at daily protein intakes of about 50 grams. That's low by American standards, but it's enough to meet the RDA and maintain protein needs.

Can bone loss be reversed by increasing calcium intake?

This has worked in some studies, to some extent. But the patients were generally older women with longer prior histories of low calcium intakes.[24]

In a landmark study, twelve elderly women with habitually low calcium intakes were given daily supplements supplying 750 mg of calcium and 375 units of vitamin D. (Vitamin D promotes the absorption of calcium.) Their average daily protein intake was 59 grams; low enough not to have affected calcium balance. Seventeen other women on similar diets weren't given supplements. At the end of the three-year study, bone densities of the women receiving supplements had increased by 6 percent, while the other women's had decreased by 7 percent.[25]

In other patients, supplementing the diet with calcium hasn't been successful.[26] People with already high intakes who aren't helped by more are losing calcium somewhere else. The likely suspect is a too-high protein intake. Their calcium losses can't be corrected by increasing calcium intake, because the elderly have trouble absorbing calcium at higher intakes. They aren't likely to *retain* calcium unless they alter the other critical variable, protein intake.

Why does excess protein increase urinary calcium loss?

Protein reduces the rate at which calcium is reabsorbed by the kidney tubules. The calcium that isn't reabsorbed is excreted in the urine.[27] Nobody knows exactly why, but several theories have been proposed.

One is that calcium is drawn from the bones into the blood to neutralize excess acid. Calcium plays a role in regulating the acid/base balance, or pH, of the blood. When the acidity of the blood is too high, calcium is lost in the urine, producing demineralization of the bones. When the blood is made more alkaline, as with alkaline buffers like sodium bicarbonate, urinary calcium loss is reduced. The proposed explanation is that the body buffers blood acidity with calcium, an alkaline-forming element. Since most of the body's calcium is stored in the bones, and since bone calcium is more readily mobilized than any other bodily source of calcium, increased blood acidity results in decreased bone calcium.[28]

That would explain why the urine of meat-eaters is generally acid, while that of vegetarians is generally alkaline.[29]

Is meat more acid-forming than vegetable protein?

It is. Protein isn't the only thing that increases blood acidity. Sulfur (which metabolizes to sulfuric acid) and purines (which metabolize to uric acid) also have this effect. Meat is high in both.

Predominant among the sulfur-containing amino acids is methionine. Meat contains about twice as much methionine as grain protein, and five times as much as bean protein. In one experiment, adding methionine to the diet caused calcium excretion to triple.[30]

Sulfur induces urinary calcium loss in another way. It combines with calcium carbonate, the form in which calcium is released from the bones as a buffer. The result is a complex molecule the tiny kidney tubules have trouble reabsorbing. The calcium that isn't reabsorbed is lost in the urine.[31]

Then there is the problem of phosphorus. It's another mineral that increases blood acidity; and meat is high in it. In animal studies, excess phosphorus has caused bone loss independent of dietary protein.[32]

But phosphorus has an anomalous effect on calcium balance. While the bones of phosphorus-fed animals are disintegrating, their urinary calcium loss *goes down*. Phosphorus causes calcium to be lost from the bones, but not the body.

Is this retained calcium helping the bones? Or is it merely contributing to the pathological calcification of tissues and organs that is the bane of the elderly? This complicated question remains unsettled.

Chapter 13

Phosphorus: The Calcium Antagonist

"Most studies have failed to support a relationship between calcium consumption and osteoporosis in man. If animal studies are indicative, phosphorus intake may be a more significant parameter than calcium intake with respect to the effect of diet on this disease."

—G. Anderson, H. Draper
University of Illinois[1]

The American diet contains several times as much phosphorus as calcium. Meat is its major source. In rats, rabbits, horses, dogs, and cats, when phosphorus exceeds calcium in the diet, serious bone loss results in a matter of months.

Does the same thing happen in humans? Teenagers raised on phosphate-laden hot dogs and soft drinks have healthy bones. A few months, or even a few years, are insufficient to demonstrate bone loss from a calcium/phosphorus imbalance in people. Our bones don't turn brittle until after about fifty years of dietary abuse, and that's too long for controlled experiments.

Whether or not the high phosphorus content of meat contributes to human osteoporosis remains unsettled. The issue is clouded by the experimental finding that phosphorus actually *improves* calcium balance. That is, when it's added to a high-protein diet, urinary calcium loss *goes down*.

Adding *meat* to the diet doesn't actually improve calcium balance, but in some studies, it hasn't hurt calcium balance either. Some researchers think the high phosphorus content of meat actually protects the bones against the calcium loss that would otherwise result from its high-protein content.[2]

Then why aren't the bones of Eskimos protected by the phosphorus in their high-meat diet?

Good question. And why are the bones of elderly meat-eaters in worse shape than those of elderly vegetarians, whose protein sources contain less phosphorus than meat does? Why is urinary calcium loss substantially higher in meat-eating Mormons than in vegetarian SDAs?[3]

Other researchers contend that any phosphorus-induced improvement in calcium balance merely points up a defect in calcium balance studies: They measure only calcium lost from the body, *not* calcium lost from the bones. When an investigation is made of the bones themselves, excess phosphorus clearly *increases* skeletal loss, at the same time that it reduces urinary calcium loss. This effect has been demonstrated in both animals and humans.[4]

Aging rats whose bones had been injected with radioactive calcium were fed diets containing the concentration of calcium recommended for growing rats and known to prevent bone loss in adult mice. Phosphorus was varied so that the Ca/P (calcium/phosphorus) ratio ranged from 2:1 to 1:3. The phosphorus dosage of the group receiving three times as much phosphorus as calcium was high for rats. But it was comparable to the upper end of the human phosphorus intake, which is also three times the recommended allowance for calcium. After six months on these diets, bone loss was determined by measuring the calcium and phosphorus in the bones, the total weight of the bones, and the radioactive calcium lost by elimination. Bone loss was clearly seen in all rats except the controls. Yet in the high-phosphorus groups, the total amount of calcium lost in the urine was *50 percent less* than in the low-phosphorus control group. Calcium was being pulled from the bones, but it wasn't being excreted.[5]

What happens to the calcium lost from the skeleton, if it isn't lost from the body?

In animals, the calcium lost from the bones has been traced to the soft tissues—the heart, lungs, kidneys, and blood vessels.[6] These extra-skeletal calcium deposits are like those that cause the arteries to harden in atherosclerosis, and that characterize many other diseases of old age.

> In the same rat study, the lost bone calcium was traced by killing the animals and measuring the amount of mineral in their kidneys and hearts. In the kidneys of the rats fed three times as much phosphorus as calcium, the calcium concentration was more than ten times as great as in the controls; and in one of these experimental animals, it was nearly 100 times as great. The kidneys of the experimental animals were yellow and granular and their calcification was apparent to the eye. The calcium contents of their hearts had also increased significantly. In the rats receiving twice as much phosphorus as calcium, kidney calcium was greater than in the controls by 50 percent. And even the kidneys of the rats receiving *equal* amounts of calcium and phosphorus contained 13 percent more calcium than the controls.[7]

What about carnivorous animals accustomed to a high-meat diet?

Even the bones of carnivores disintegrate when they eat a diet composed exclusively of muscle meat.[8] If they were to eat the entire carcass with its bones, they'd get more calcium than phosphorus; but phosphorus is highly concentrated in muscle, while calcium is sparse.

> Cats were fed nothing but water and unsupplemented raw beef heart, having a Ca/P ratio of 1:20. Within 6–8 weeks they developed osteoporosis, indicated on X-ray examination by a visible thinning of the skeleton. They also developed compression fractures of the lumbar vertebrae (fractures resulting from the collapse of the spine). Adding enough cal-

cium to bring the Ca/P ratio to 1:1 prevented these problems. But adding only enough to bring it to 1:2 did not. The same condition resulted when the raw beef heart was supplemented with vitamins.[9]

A similar condition was reversed in a tiger after 6 weeks on a diet in which enough calcium was added to bring the Ca/P ratio to 2:1.[10]

Excess phosphorus also causes bone loss in dogs, although urinary calcium loss is unaffected.

Phosphate was added in increasing levels to the diets of adult female dogs. The diet at the highest level of phosphorus supplementation contained the same amount of calcium as regular laboratory chow, but its phosphorus content was increased until its Ca/P ratio was about 1:3—a ratio typical of the American diet. After only 5 months, X-ray examination revealed a fourfold increase in the number of holes in the dogs' bones. Although calcium was clearly being lost from the bones, the amount lost in the urine remained the same on both diets.[11]

What about in humans?

Humans are harder to study than rats or cats; but there is some evidence that we're similarly affected. Phosphorus suppresses urinary calcium loss in humans, but it doesn't suppress bone loss—and may increase it.

Seven postmenopausal women with osteoporosis were given daily supplements containing one gram (1,000 mg) of phosphorus, in an attempt to increase bone formation. At each visit to the clinic, bone biopsies were taken.[12] The bone surfaces on which new bone was being formed were compared before and after phosphate treatment with the bone surfaces on which calcium was being drawn from the bones into the blood, a process called bone resorption. The phosphate supplements did not cause the desired increase in bone formation. To the contrary, the bone forming surface *decreased*, and the bone resorbing surface *increased*. This effect correlated directly with total phosphorus intake. Yet calcium balance was *improved*. Phosphorus decreased urinary calcium loss while it increased bone loss.[13]

Five healthy young volunteers were subjected to 24–30 weeks of continuous bed rest to induce "disuse osteoporosis"—bone loss caused by immobilization. Treatment with potassium phosphate did not prevent this problem, but it did prevent the increased urinary calcium loss that usually accompanies bed rest. Again, calcium was being lost from the bones but not the body.[14]

Has the amount of phosphorus that induces bone loss been established for humans?

No. It has for animals, but the experiments by which these determinations are made can't be performed on humans.

In animals, mineral requirements are determined by looking at their direct effects on the bones. Nutrients are fed at different levels and in various proportions. Then portions of bone are removed and examined under the microscope and in the test tube. Only when these tests reveal normal bones are the optimum proportions of calcium and phosphorus established. These determinations must be made indirectly for humans, by measuring mineral losses from the kidneys, intestines, and skin. Since dietary phosphorus *reduces* calcium losses as measured by these means, many authorities conclude that excess phosphorus has no detrimental effects on human bone.

Yet why our bones should react differently from those of every other animal species hasn't been explained. There is reason to suspect that the optimum Ca/P ratio is actually higher for humans than for other animals. A comparison of the milk of cows, horses, sheep, and humans reveals that human milk has the highest ratio among these species. It contains more than twice as much calcium as phosphorus.[15]

A high dietary Ca/P ratio is clearly essential to the health of a human infant. When babies are fed large amounts of cow's milk, they can develop a condition called neonatal tetany, a syndrome of convulsions occurring in otherwise healthy babies who are artificially fed. These infants have significantly higher serum phosphorus levels and lower serum calcium levels than breastfed infants. Why? Because the phosphorus concentration in cow's milk is six times that in human milk.[16]

What is the Ca/P ratio in the average American diet?

The calcium intake of the average milk-drinking omnivorous human is placed by different authorities at between 400 mg and 850 mg per day, while his average phosphorus intake from natural sources is placed at between 1,500 and 2,000 mg. A USDA survey in 1960 showed the Ca/P ratio was approximately 1:2.8. Since then, our diets have changed. We now drink less milk and eat more high-phosphorus foods. Particularly on the increase are foods that contain phosphate additives, which are widely used in food processing. (Phosphate is the form in which phosphorus is used by the body. In its pure form, phosphorus is poisonous.) This addition to our phosphate intake hasn't been accurately documented but may increase it by as much as 500 mg daily. That would bring the total to 2,000–2,500 mg, versus a mere 400–850 mg for calcium. That means Western diets with a Ca/P ratio of 1:4 may not be unusual.[18]

How much of this phosphorus comes from meat?

The phosphorus in meat outweighs its calcium content by about 20 to 1. In chicken breast the ratio is 23 to 1; in ground beef, 16 to 1; in calves' liver, 51 to 1; in pork chops, 19 to 1; in halibut, 16 to 1; in canned tuna, 48 to 1.[19]

The average phosphorus intake from meat, fish, and poultry in this country is about 800 mg a day, or about half the daily total from natural sources.[20]

How do these ratios compare to vegetarian protein sources?

The major protein source for lacto-ovo-vegetarians is milk, which contains slightly more calcium than phosphorus. The ratio is 1.2 to 1. Macrobiotic vegetarians replace milk with soy products. Soybean curd, or tofu, has a Ca/P ratio equivalent to that in milk.[21] Even better ratios are found in seaweeds, which are popular in Japanese macrobiotic cooking. Their calcium outweighs their phosphorus content by as much as 40 to 1.[22]

The ratios in other vegetarian staples are less impressive, but they're still substantially better than in meat. Cream of wheat and corn tortillas contain as much phosphorus as calcium. Whole wheat bread contains twice as much. White rice contains four times as much. Brown rice contains 7 times as much.[23]

Fruits and vegetables vary in their calcium and phosphorus contents, but on the average they contain about equal amounts of each. Green vegetables with particularly good ratios, that are good sources of calcium, include collards (4:1), kale (3:1), Swiss chard (3:1), and parsley (3:1). The ratios in these greens are substantially better than in milk, which contains almost as much phosphorus as calcium. Processed cheese has so much phosphate added that it contains *more* phosphorus than calcium.[24]

What is the Ca/P ratio in the typical vegetarian diet?

For milk-drinking vegetarians, it's about 1:1. For vegans, it's about 1:2—not as good, but better than the 1:3 or 1:4 for omnivores.[25]

Can't a high phosphorus intake be counteracted by taking megadoses of calcium?

No, for the same reason you can't counteract a high protein intake with huge doses of calcium. Calcium absorption falls off at higher intakes, while phosphorus absorption doesn't.

The problem was illustrated in an experiment in which equal amounts of calcium and phosphorus were given at increasing levels to aging rats. No bone loss occurred at low intakes. But when the concentrations of both minerals were increased, the result was a progressive increase in bone loss, although the amounts of calcium and phosphorus were the same at each level.[26]

A vegan diet containing a Ca/P ratio of 1:2 at low levels of intake is easier on the bones than an omnivore diet contain-double the amounts in the same ratio. In the low-level vegan diet, more of the calcium will be absorbed.

The Bantu diet has a Ca/P ratio that isn't much better than ours, mainly because the Bantu calcium intake is so low.[27] But at their low intake levels, nearly all the calcium is absorbed. Another difference between their dietary phosphorus and ours is that theirs comes mainly in the organic phytate form found in plant foods. We'll look at that distinction later.

At the high intake levels typical of the American diet (say, 1,200 mg of calcium and 2,400 mg of phosphorus), a Ca/P ratio of 1:2 can result in a ratio of minerals *retained* that is as low as 1:12. This is because the calcium may be only 15 percent absorbed. Even at the relatively modest level of 800 mg a day, older people absorb calcium at a rate of only 15 percent.[28]

The young absorb more calcium. However, they also need more because their skeletons are still developing. A Ca/P ratio of 1:1 will preserve the bones of old rats, but young rats need twice as much calcium as phosphorus.[29]

People of all ages have trouble getting enough calcium to keep up with their phosphorus intakes. Phosphorus is essential to the body, but it's amply supplied by most foods.[30] It's easy to get enough, and hard not to get too much.

What happens to animals when they're fed amounts of phosphorus equivalent to those in the American diet?

In rabbits, their bones turn porous in a matter of months.

Rabbits were fed an experimental diet containing the same amount of phosphorus per pound of bodyweight as is normally found in the human diet. Its Ca/P ratio was 1:2—better than in the diets of many humans. The control animals were fed the same diet except that enough calcium was added to bring the Ca/P ratio to 1:1. At the end of the 6-month study, the bones of the animals fed the experimental diet had 6 to 12 times as many holes per X-ray cross-section as those of the control animals.[31]

But rabbits may not be comparable to humans. What about monkeys and other primates?

Monkeys react more like we do in that their bone loss is slow to develop.[32] They are, however, prone to a form of bone loss; and it resembles human osteoporosis. This condition, called simian bone disease, is ranked the third most common disease among domesticated monkeys. It doesn't occur in monkeys in the wild. It strikes only those animals fed by humans.[33] It's been seen in baboons in a zoo on a diet with a Ca/P ratio of 1:3.6, and in a spider monkey in a pet store living on a diet of high-phosphorus human foods.[34]

The skeletal lesions seen in simian bone disease are similar to those found in dogs and humans suffering from secondary hyperparathyroidism. This condition, which we'll look at in the next chapter, is strikingly similar to osteoporosis; and it results from a Ca/P imbalance in the diet. In monkeys with simian bone disease, the diagnosis of hyperparathyroidism is confirmed by the presence of overactive parathyroid glands.[35]

Chapter 14

How Meat Stresses Your Parathyroids

"A lifelong [high-meat] diet may promote negative calcium balance and deplete skeletal mineral . . . from the low-grade stimulation of the parathyroid glands which must exist to counteract the chronic losses of urinary calcium. To what degree this diet-induced hyperparathyroidism contributes to human skeletal disease is not known. It certainly is a real phenomenon in experimental studies with animals."
—A. Licata, M.D.
University of Rochester School of Medicine[1]

The body contains only half as much phosphorus as calcium. The blood contains only a third as much. The American diet contains these elements in the reverse proportions or worse. The problem is that excess phosphorus can squeeze calcium out of the blood. The blood can hold only a certain amount of these two minerals together in solution at one time. When it gets oversaturated, calcium and phosphorus are lost as calcium phosphate salts. In animals studies, these salts wind up in the soft tissues—the heart, lungs, kidneys, and blood vessels—where they contribute to the pathological calcification of those tissues.[2]

This isn't bad just for the soft tissues. It's also bad for the bones. Blood calcium must be kept above a certain level; and when it falls, calcium is pulled from the bones into the blood to bring it back to normal. The result is bone loss.

Keeping blood calcium up is the job of the endocrine glands known as the parathyroids. When serum calcium falls, the parathyroids release their hormone, called parathyroid hormone, or PTH. PTH pulls calcium from the bones into the blood to correct the imbalance. This process is called bone resorption.[3]

"Hyperparathyroidism" is the condition that results when

the parathyroids secrete too much PTH. It results in bone loss (osteoporosis), and in the buildup of unnatural calcium deposits in the soft tissues. Elevated levels of PTH are also found in the blood of people eating a diet high in phosphorus.[4] Based on these observations, some researchers attribute the bone loss of elderly Westerners to a low-grade nutritional hyperparathyroidism produced by the high phosphorus content of their diets.[5] Bone loss is once again traceable to meat, our major dietary source of this mineral.

What evidence is there that the chronic stimulation of the parathyroids results in bone loss?

The role of the parathyroids is shown in animal studies in which those glands have been removed. Excess phosphorus induces bone loss in normal animals, but it doesn't in those without parathyroids.[6]

Overactivity of the parathyroids is stimulated in animals by injecting them with PTH. Examination of the bones twelve hours later shows a decrease in the number of osteoblasts (the cells that form new bone), and a marked increase in the number of osteoclasts (the cells that break down or resorb bone). At the same time, the bone marrow is replaced by uncalcified connective tissue. The result is the beginning of osteoporosis.

Clinically, the same results are produced in humans suffering from chronic overstimulation of the parathyroids—the condition known as hyperparathyroidism. The bones of these patients fracture easily and present the same X-ray picture as the bones of PTH-injected rats. These X-rays show the extensive formation of immature new bone, which is characteristic of rapid bone formation. But this new bone, which replaces the compact bone, is spongy and often remains uncalcified. The result is an increase in bone formation, but a decrease in its rigidity.[7]

This type of spongy, uncalcified bone is also characteristic of osteoporosis. The symptoms of osteoporosis and hyperparathyroidism are strikingly similar. Both are characterized by loss of calcium from the bones, spontaneous fractures, and vertebral collapse, as well as by calcium deposits in the kidneys and kidney stones. The X-ray pictures presented by the bone-forming and bone-resorbing surfaces are also similar. The amount of bone-resorbing surface is increased to well above normal in both conditions. The levels of PTH circulating in the blood of many patients with osteoporosis, like those with hyperparathyroidism, are also higher than normal.[8]

The close similarities between these two conditions suggest that osteoporosis is simply a low-grade nutritional secondary hyperparathyroidism. It may be caused either by too little dietary calcium, or by sufficient calcium but excess phosphorus. In either case, PTH is released into the bloodstream, causing calcium to be resorbed from the bones into the blood.[9]

What is secondary hyperparathyroidism?

When the parathyroid glands secrete too much PTH although blood calcium is normal—that is, when there's an abnormality in the glands themselves, as from a tumor—the condition is called primary hyperparathyroidism. When the parathyroids become overactive from a Ca/P imbalance, the condition is called secondary hyperparathyroidism.

The most common cause of secondary hyperparathyroidism is kidney failure. When the kidneys don't function properly, phosphorus isn't excreted properly. It accumulates in the body, causing blood phosphate to rise at the expense of blood calcium. To prevent blood calcium from dropping to dangerously low levels, a sensor mechanism in the blood signals the parathyroids. They increase blood calcium by secreting PTH, which draws calcium from the bones into the blood. Serum calcium then returns to normal. But the PTH level can't return to normal, or the cycle recurs. So it stabilizes in a higher range. With each successive wave of nephron destruction, this cycle repeats itself. The PTH level increases, and with it the detrimental effects of PTH on the bones—and on the soft tissues, where the calcium settles.[10]

In kidney failure, as in primary hyperparathyroidism, bone disease and extra-skeletal calcification are serious complications. If a patient with chronic kidney disease survives his illness long enough, skeletal deterioration is almost inevitable. Again, calcium is lost from the bones, but not the body.

Skeletal degeneration occurs although calcium balance remains either normal or only modestly negative. As in animals, this lost bone calcium is accompanied by a substantial increase in soft-tissue calcium. And the soft-tissue calcium is accompanied by high circulating levels of PTH.[11]

When the kidneys fail, urea and other breakdown products of protein metabolism build up in the blood. This condition is called uremia. It is typically accompanied by skin- and soft-tissue calcification, which can be reversed by removing the parathyroid glands.[12] In severe uremics, secondary hyperparathyroidism is an almost universal symptom. The standard low-protein diet given to patients with early renal failure won't reverse this condition. A vegan diet that is very low not only in protein but in phosphorus, will. No other treatment has successfully achieved this without other serious complications.[13]

The same effect has been demonstrated in animals. A higher concentration of calcium is found in the soft tissues of rats with experimentally-induced uremia than in non-uremic animals. This calcification can be prevented either by removing the parathyroids, or by depriving the animals of phosphorus before inducing the disease. Even normal rats have lower soft tissue calcium concentrations when they're deprived of phosphorus than control rats given their normal diets.[14]

Hyperparathyroidism is also associated with arthritis, kidney stones, and other forms of extra-skeletal calcification. The presence of calcium phosphate crystals in the joints of patients with arthritis is a condition sometimes called pseudo-gout. Its cause is unknown, but in a study of the abnormalities and disease associations of patients with this condition, a clear link was established with hyperparathyroidism.[15]

What does this have to do with diet?

In kidney disease, phosphorus builds up in the blood because the kidneys can't get rid of it. But there is another condition in which the parathyroids are stimulated, although kidney function is normal. This condition results from too much phosphorus in the diet. It's called nutritional secondary hyperparathyroidism, and it's characterized by skeletal degeneration like that seen in primary hyperparathyroidism and kidney failure. It may also be characterized by extra-skeletal calcification, a subject we'll look at in the next chapter.

In animals—including horses, cows, goats, dogs, cats, ti-gers, and monkeys—nutritional secondary hyperparathyroi-dism has been induced by diets that are either too low in calcium, or that contain optimum calcium and higher amounts of phosphorus. Bone lesions result that are similar to those seen in osteoporosis. Another symptom is periodontal dis-ease, a disease of the supporting structures of the teeth that can end in their detachment. This is also seen in people with osteoporosis. The dietary Ca/P ratios of patients with periodontal disease are similar to those producing second-ary hyperparathyroidism in adult experimental animals.[16]

Periodontal disease involves the loss of tooth-bearing bone, and eventually, it means lost teeth. Twenty years ago, half the population was toothless by the age of sixty. Higher-income groups didn't fare better in this respect, although their intake of calcium from milk products was substantially higher. The reason may have been that they not only drank twice as much milk but ate twice as much meat. Since milk improves the Ca/P ratio only slightly, their Ca/P balance remained little better than in lower-income populations.[17]

Is the amount of phosphorus contributed by meat to the American diet enough to stimulate PTH secretion?

It is. Studies show that the release of PTH can be trig-gered in humans by an extra gram (1,000 mg) of phosphorus daily. That's a little more phosphorus than is supplied by meat in the ordinary diet, and a little less than is supplied by meat and additives together.

The decrease in serum calcium is enough to cause bone loss in rats.[18] It's also nearly the same drop that is produced in humans by a diet providing an additional gram of phos-phorus from ordinary foods containing phosphate additives.

A four-week study tested the effects of two diets, one with and one without additive-containing foods. The no-additive diet had a Ca/P ratio of 1 to 1.4 and contained 1,000 mg of phosphorus. The high-additive diet had a Ca/P ratio of 1 to 2.8 and contained 2,100 mg of phosphorus—1.1 gram more than the low-additive diet. Protein and calcium were similar (95 grams and 700 mg, respectively). On the high-phosphate diet, serum calcium decreased by 0.35 mg/dl—within the range found to stimulate PTH secretion in humans and to cause bone loss in rats. The other diet did not have this effect.[19]

This drop in serum calcium isn't merely temporary. Serum calcium remains significantly depressed three hours after a high-phosphorus meal, and it doesn't return to normal by the next meal. As much as eighteen hours may be required to reach a normal calcium level after a heavy dose of phosphate. Since mealtimes aren't this far apart, it appears a daily diet containing an extra gram of phosphorus from meat and additives must produce a chronic low-grade parathyroid stimulation in humans.

In the next chapter, we'll look at evidence that the chronic stimulation of the parathyroids caused by a dietary calcium/phosphorus imbalance leads to extra-skeletal calcification; and that this, in turn, causes the hardening of the arteries and internal organs endemic to old age. We'll also look at different theories explaining this pervasive symptom of aging.

Chapter 15

Speculating About Pathological Calcification

"Calcification can proceed to the point where, in advanced atherosclerosis, cutting through the aorta at autopsy is accompanied by an audible crunching sound."[1]

Extra-skeletal calcification (or pathological calcification) is the deposit of bits of calcium in normally-soft tissues. It characterizes most chronic diseases. In coronary heart disease, bone-like matter is deposited in the vital arteries feeding the heart. In hypertension, calcium deposits clog the tiny capillaries in the extremities, preventing the free flow of blood. In the kidneys, they occur as kidney stones; and when the kidneys fail, they appear throughout the arteries and internal organs. In arthritis, the deposits occur in bone joints. In bursitis, they occur in the bursae. In scleroderma, calcified patches appear on the skin. In cancer, mineral deposits tend to be localized in the region of the tumor. In tuberculosis, calcium is deposited in the lungs. In the eyes, they produce cataracts.[2]

Atherosclerosis means hardened fat. In its early stages, it's characterized by a soft, fatty buildup resembling toothpaste. Calcium is what turns these reversible fatty streaks into irreversible atherosclerotic lesions. The mixture of calcium and fat converts the toothpaste into cement.[3]

Where does this calcium come from?

The medical answer is that calcium is released by cells when they're lethally injured. Precipitated calcium phosphate salts have been called "the gravestones of cells."[4]

But that explanation, while no doubt true, leaves some questions unanswered. If arterial calcification resulting from the death of cells is inevitable in old age, why is it substantially worse in elderly Westerners than in elderly vegan Bantu natives? And why is the incidence of atherosclerotic heart disease among Bantus only about one-tenth that among whites in the United States of equal age?[5]

Researchers determined the degree of calcification in the aortas of 70 South African Bantus and 58 Johannesburg whites who had died and been autopsied. Calcium in the aortas of the Bantus had barely doubled between the ages of 50 and 80, while in the whites it had increased sixfold—a difference of 300 percent. Whites in the 65–74 and 75 + age ranges had three times as much calcium in their aortas as Bantus of equal age. None of the Bantus had severe atherosclerosis, while ten of the whites did.[6]

The difference has been attributed to heredity, but there is no evidence that Africans actually possess a racial immunity to coronary heart disease. Prosperous Africans frequently fall victim to this condition when they adopt American or European ways of life.[7]

What other possible sources of calcification are there?

In metastatic calcification and in calcinosis universalis (the kinds that spread), no evidence of cell death or previous tissue damage has been found. These calcifications result from a Ca/P imbalance in the blood.[8] There is evidence that both the calcium in extra-skeletal calcium deposits and the matrix necessary for them to crystallize come from the resorption of bone. And bone resorption, as we've seen, results from an excess of phosphorus in the blood.[9] Atherosclerotic calcium phosphate deposits also have the same composition as bone. Their X-ray diffraction patterns are indistinguishable from apatite, one of the two mineral constituents of bones and teeth.[10] This evidence suggests that some of the calcium precipitating in our arteries and organs comes from the resorption of bone. Bone resorption, in turn, can come from excess phosphorus in the diet.

There is also evidence that the *kind* of phosphorus in the

diet affects the tendency to form extra-skeletal calcium deposits.

Kidney stones are extra-skeletal deposits of calcium, phosphorus, and other substances. South African blacks seldom get them. Yet their phosphorus intakes are similar to those of South African whites, who have the same high incidence of kidney stones as whites in other Western communities. The distinction seems to be in the kind of phosphorus eaten. For the whites, it's primarily inorganic phosphorus from animal sources. For the blacks, it comes mainly from phytate, the organic form in which phosphorus is found in plant foods. Phytate contains components that are shown experimentally to *retard* the formation of hydroxyapatite crystals.[11]

This may explain why osteoporosis, arterial calcification, and atherosclerosis are so much rarer among the South African Bantu than among Americans, although the Ca/P ratio of their diet is no better than ours. Their dietary phosphorus is mainly in the organic form that comes from plants.

What evidence is there that excess phosphorus causes extra-skeletal calcification?

This effect is clearly seen in rats. When phosphorus is added to their diets at 5–8 times the normal dosage, their kidneys grow to a remarkable size and weight and develop pathological lesions apparent to the eye. Giant epithelial cells appear and spread, and the kidneys become extremely calcified. These changes take only fifteen days to develop.[12]

When rats receive smaller amounts of phosphorus, kidney calcification is less evident but still detectable. It's seen even in rats on their usual commercial diets, in which the Ca/P ratio is an apparently favorable 1:1.2—much better than in the average human diet.[13] When the Ca/P ratio is reduced to that in human diets, the effects on the kidneys of rats are quite dramatic. Their calcium contents increase by anywhere from 10 to a 100 times.[14]

In rabbits, as in rats, soft-tissue calcium increases when their diets contain an amount of phosphorus equivalent to that in the human omnivorous diet.[15] The same thing happens even to dogs, although meat is their natural diet. When the Ca/P ratio of their laboratory food is increased from the usual 1:1 to 1:3, detectable bone loss occurs after about ten months. Microscopic examination of the organs at autopsy reveals extra-skeletal calcification in the kidneys, tendons, thoracic aortas, and hearts.[16]

Does excess phosphorus have the same effect on humans?

It's harder to tell with people. Our diets can't be controlled from birth, and our organs can't be removed for laboratory analysis. The same effect probably does occur, although the experiments necessary for its detection can't be performed on us.

In both animals and man, soft-tissue calcification evident to the eye is seen when large amounts of phosphorus are ingested. Extra-skeletal calcification has been found at autopsy in patients given substantial amounts of phosphate, and calcium deposits in phosphate-injected veins have been noted on X-ray examination.[17]

In patients given moderate amounts of supplementary phosphorus—normally one gram (1,000 mg) per day—extra-skeletal calcification hasn't been detected.[18] But these patients haven't been typical of the normal human situation. They were given phosphorus to counteract hypercalcemia—*too much* calcium in the blood. Since their blood was already overloaded with calcium, added phosphorus wouldn't stimulate the parathyroids as it does in normal people. Instead, it would have the beneficial effect of moving excess calcium out of the blood, thus reducing serum calcium from too high to normal. The parathyroids would "sleep" through this procedure. They're triggered into action only by a drop in serum calcium below normal levels. In the absence of increased parathyroid activity, bone resorption wouldn't occur. And neither would extra-skeletal calcification, because there would be nothing to prevent the displaced blood calcium from returning to the bones.

In humans, the absence of calcium deposits is determined merely by visual examination, either by the naked eye or by X-rays.[19] In animals, unlike man, it's possible to measure the amount of calcium in the soft tissues at concentrations below those at which X-ray evidence of calcification occurs.

When laboratory animals have been fed diets containing calcium and phosphorus in the ratio found in the average American diet, evidence of soft tissue calcification has similarly been absent. But chemical analysis has shown that the calcium contents of the internal organs have increased.[20]

Whether osteoporosis, in which calcium is lost from bone, is the flipside of the pathological buildup of calcium that clogs and hardens the soft tissues in old age remains to be established, but circumstantial evidence points to this result.

We drink milk by the quart and top it off with calcium supplements. In addition, calcium is now added to everything from cereals to soft drinks. Yet the incidence of osteoporosis in this country remains among the highest in the world, and so does the incidence of atherosclerosis.

Could it be that all of this calcium is precipitating out in our arteries instead of sticking to our ribs? If it's not sticking to our ribs because it's being pulled from them by excess phosphorus, the cure isn't more calcium. It's less phosphorus; particularly, less inorganic phosphorus. And that means less meat.

Section IV

CARDIOVASCULAR DISEASE: THE BLACK PLAGUE OF AFFLUENCE

Chapter 16

Cardiovascular Disease: The Way to a Man's Heart is Through His Stomach

"[P]resent day dietary patterns in the United States and other industrialized countries are very recent sweeping innovations in nutrition. Appreciation of this cardinal fact is fundamental to an understanding of the relationship of diet to the modern epidemic of premature coronary heart disease (CHD) in these nations. Contemporary 'rich' diets [are] markedly different . . . from any ever consumed by wild animals, primates and hominids, most preliterate peoples, most of our ancestors in preindustrial or early industrial Europe (or Africa or Asia), or the majority of mankind today in the developing countries of Africa, Asia, and Latin America."

—J. Stamler, M.D., Northwestern
University Medical School[1]

The World Health Organization describes cardiovascular disease as potentially the greatest epidemic mankind has ever faced. The cardiovascular diseases together are responsible for more than one-half of all American deaths, totaling nearly a million annually. That's more than twice as many as are claimed by cancer, the number two killer. The national annual dollar cost is over $60 billion.

Heart attacks top the list of cardiovascular disease deaths. If you are a man, your chances are 1 in 5 of having a heart attack *before* the age of 60. Heart attacks strike over a million Americans each year and kill over half of them. Nearly half of these deaths are immediate and unexpected. For at least a quarter of them, *sudden death is the first sign of trouble.*[2]

Underlying the cardiovascular diseases are two closely-related conditions, hypertension and atherosclerosis. These conditions are so common in the elderly that they are con-

sidered "normal." But they aren't inevitable. Entire populations manage to escape them. Atherosclerosis and hypertension
are rare among the people of China, Africa, India, and
Latin America, whose diets are predominantly plant foods.[3]

Cardiovascular disease was also rare in this country as
late as the turn of the century. Angina pectoris, the chest
pain foreshadowing a heart attack, was described in a popular medical text published in the early 1900s as "a rare
disease in the public wards of hospitals," of which a "con-
sultant in active practice may see a dozen cases or more a
year." Cardiovascular disease did not start its alarming rise
until about 1920.[4]

How has our diet changed in this century?

From 1900 to 1960, carbohydrate intake dropped by 20
percent and fiber intake dropped by 30 percent. Cholesterol
intake didn't change much, but animal *protein* intake did. In
1900, about half our protein came from plants. In 1960, we
ate more than twice as much animal as vegetable protein.[5]

Actually, 1900 may not be the right date to study, since
cardiovascular disease takes about fifty years to develop.
You can eat a grease-laden, fiber-free diet for that long and
be symptom free.[6] That puts the critical date at about 1870.

What did Americans eat in 1870?

Exhaustive diet surveys weren't done then like they are
today. But if the consumption of animal protein was lower
and the consumption of carbohydrate and fiber was higher,
people must have eaten less meat and more grain. It's been
estimated that Americans ate *five times* as much fiber in the
nineteenth century as they do now.

Henry Ford was so impressed with the changes during his
lifetime that he built Greenfield Village in Dearborn, Michigan, to preserve part of the past. On a visit, your guide will
tell you that in 1947, when Henry Ford died, 4 out of 5
Americans lived in the city. But in 1879, when Henry was
sixteen, four out of five people lived on the farm. Most
farmers were poor.[7] They had a few animals, but they couldn't

afford to butcher them for meat. They needed their cows and chickens for milk, butter, and eggs. Any leftover milk and eggs were sold for money for commodities the farmer couldn't make himself.

There was no refrigeration. Meat was preserved with salt, and salt was expensive. Mincemeat was a popular way to dispose of meat that had started to go bad. The meat's off flavor and odor were disguised by the variety of spices that went into the concoction.

In the summer, there were fresh fruits and vegetables. In the winter, the staple foods were made from stone-ground corn and wheat.

The big change came with powered machinery. Factories took the men from the farm. In the city, you could get ice for your ice box. Later you could get electric refrigerators. Mechanical refrigeration came into general use in the cities in about 1890.

Farm machinery dramatically increased production. There were more animals for slaughter and the means to preserve them. Suddenly meat was available three times a day.

That's when the modern epidemic of cardiovascular disease and its forerunners, hypertension and atherosclerosis, began.

What is atherosclerosis?

Atherosclerosis is a hardening of the blood vessels and a reduction in their diameter caused by the buildup of calcium and fatty material, particularly cholesterol. The calcium is what causes the hardening (or sclerosis) of the arteries. The cholesterol builds up in the arteries when the blood contains so much of it that the artery walls can't absorb it all. Cholesterol may also be manufactured by the body as a sort of patch to cover up damage to the artery walls caused by free radicals and other irritants.

Fats carried in the bloodstream gradually pile up on the walls of the arteries like rust in a pipe. The first sign of atherosclerosis is the appearance of fatty streaks on the inside of the arteries. These fatty streaks later become patches of cholesterol called plaques. Atherosclerotic plaques in the smaller arteries can reduce the size of the opening through which blood is carried by 60–70 percent or more.[8]

Raised coronary lesions (areas in which function has been impaired by atherosclerotic growths) develop in the average man in industrialized countries at about the age of twenty. These lesions spread so that they cover about 2 percent more of the surface of the coronary arteries each year. By the time 60 percent of this surface has been covered with raised lesions, the opening through which blood passes is narrowed enough to set the stage for angina or a heart attack. Until they reach this critical threshold of surface coverage, coronary lesions cause no symptoms. Then they take only minutes—with increased blood vessel spasm or hemorrhage, blockage or clotting—to become clinically evident as chest pain or a heart attack. Atherosclerosis is active in all of us for decades, but the process is a silent one. Its first sign may be its last.[9]

How are atherosclerosis and hypertension related?

When the arteries are narrowed, greater pressure is required to force the blood through, and blood pressure goes up. High blood pressure, in turn, hardens the arteries, because the heart's high-pressure pounding gradually causes the walls to lose their elasticity. As they harden and thicken, the channel for blood is narrowed even further and offers greater resistance to the blood flow. The heart is forced to work more, causing it to enlarge and eventually to fail.

How do the cardiovascular diseases differ?

When the arteries are blocked by atherosclerotic plaques, the organs serviced by those arteries are starved for blood. The type of cardiovascular disease that develops depends simply on the location of the blockage.

When the blockage is in the coronary arteries that carry oxygen to the heart, the result is coronary artery disease. Angina pectoris, or chest pain, is the first sign of this condition. If the blockage causes a starved muscle segment to die, the workings of the whole heart may be disrupted. The condition then is called a myocardial infarction, or heart attack.

A heart attack may be from coronary occlusion—when the coronary artery is entirely blocked—usually a result of deposits of calcium and fatty material piled up high enough to dam the flow channel. It may also be caused by coronary thrombosis—the formation of a blood clot (or thrombus) which has suddenly caught on the roughened, fat-clogged area of the coronary artery and plugged up the vessel.

If the blockage is in arteries leading to the arms or legs, cell death in those extremities is likely. This condition is called necrosis, and it can result in gangrene. Unless proper circulation is restored, the arm or leg tissues may die. Bacterial invasion may follow. The area may swell and blacken, and amputation may be required.

If the blockage is in vessels supplying the brain, a thrombus fixed within a blood vessel may cause some of the brain cells to be starved for blood. This condition, which usually occurs without warning, is called a cerebrovascular accident, or stroke. It may be characterized by coma, weakness or paralysis of the muscles of the extremities on one side, a weakness of facial muscles on one side, slurring of speech or total inability to speak. The neurological damage may range from slight muscle weakness to almost complete paralysis on one side of the body.[10]

Atherosclerosis and hypertension can also cause other problems common to old age. Blockage of the arteries that run to the brain can produce senility.[11] Blockage of other vital arteries can result in impotence.[12] Pressure on the eye from hypertension can cause blindness. Damage to the kidneys from high blood pressure can cause kidney function to stop altogether. In the United States, hypertension is responsible for the kidney failure of at least one of every six patients requiring kidney dialysis or renal transplantation.[13] Atherosclerosis can also cause the hearing loss that is the bane of old age.

Artherosclerosis, hypertension, and the conditions they spawn are all linked to a diet high in animal foods.

What evidence links animal foods to hearing loss?

In populations with heavy animal food intakes, not only is the incidence of heart disease high, but hearing levels tend to be low. Russians living in Moscow, for example, have substantially lower hearing levels than those living in the Georgian Soviet Republic. The diet of Moscovites is rich in animal foods, while the Georgian diet is rich in plant foods. Moreover, diet appears to be the critical variable, because these hearing differences remain when other variables are controlled.

> In a study comparing over 300 Moscovites with the same number of Georgians, hearing was significantly better in the Georgians after the age of forty. Hearing was excellent for their ages even in Georgians over 100 years old—who were also remarkable for their ability to work in the fields. The sharp ears of the Georgian elderly weren't something they were born with, since no significant differences in hearing were found in the nearly 200 children in the two groups. Noise trauma associated with urban living also couldn't explain the differences. The hearing levels of the Georgian factory workers were better than those of the Moscow factory and clerical workers together, although the Moscow clerical workers were exposed to lower levels of noise and should have had better hearing.[14]

Isn't the superior health and longevity of Georgians more likely to be due to a lifetime of physical labor than to their diets?

Exercise is undoubtedly a factor in the general health of these Russians, but it alone doesn't guarantee protection from cardiovascular disease. (See Chapter 17.) And the better hearing of people whose diets are low in animal food has been confirmed in studies in which physical activity wasn't a variable.

> One study compared the hearing of Finnish patients aged 40–59 years who had been confined for at least five years

to the hospital. In one hospital, the diet was the ordinary Finnish one high in saturated fat and cholesterol. In the other, the diet was low in these components and high in unsaturated fat. The patients on the diet low in saturated fat and cholesterol had significantly less coronary heart disease and better hearing at all frequencies than those eating the ordinary Finnish fare. And in this study, diet was the only variable that could explain the differences.[15]

Aren't the culprits saturated fat and cholesterol rather than meat?

All three of these dietary components have been implicated. Again, cholesterol is found only in animal foods. Nearly half the fat in the American diet comes from meat—ten times as much as from eggs, and three times as much as from milk.[16]

Saturated fat and cholesterol are the focus of the prevailing dietary theory of cardiovascular disease, but there is also evidence implicating animal protein. Either way, that implicates meat, which is about half animal fat and half animal protein.[17] Over the last few decades, ten studies have been published comparing data for up to forty countries from the Food and Agriculture Organization (FAO) and the World Health Organization (WHO). All of these studies correlate coronary heart disease with the consumption of animal protein, as well as with saturated fat and cholesterol.[18]

Couldn't the higher incidence of heart disease in industrialized countries be due to other variables, like stress, lack of exercise or heredity?

Possibly. But Japan is a modern industrialized country. Yet the rate of fatal heart attacks among the Japanese is only one-fourth the American incidence. Why? The traditional Japanese diet is low in animal foods. When the Japanese emigrate to the United States and adopt a Western diet, their incidence of heart disease rises to *ten times* that of their countrymen remaining in Japan.[19]

An association with meat rather than level of industrialization is also seen in studies comparing vegetarians and meat-eaters in industrialized countries. They show that the risk factors for cardiovascular disease are greatly reduced in Western vegetarians, although their genes, lifestyles, and exercise and stress levels are similar to Western meat-eaters'.

Aren't butter, cheese, and eggs as bad as meat?

No. A recent large-scale study linking heart disease to meat consumption found no significant association with either butter or cheese, and only a weak association with eggs. This difference is hard to explain, since milk contains as much saturated fat, ounce-for-ounce, as most meats; and cheese contains several times as much. Moreover, one egg contains *twice* as much cholesterol as *five ounces* of meat.[20]

The study followed 25,153 California Seventh Day Adventists (SDAs) for a 20–year period. Some ate meat; some did not. In men aged 45–84 (the group at greatest risk), the relative risk of fatal ischemic heart disease was 70 percent greater for those who ate meat daily than for those who ate none. But the relative risk for men who ate *cheese* daily was 5 percent *lower* than for those who ate none. And for men who drank 2 glasses of milk daily, it was 6 *percent* lower than for those who drank none. Even for men who ate eggs daily, the relative risk was only 4 percent greater than for those who ate none.[21]

Arguably, milk contains some factor that is protective against heart disease. Or was it that the milk-drinking, cheese-eating SDAs were eating milk products instead of meat—the real villain?

How much could I lower my risk of a heart attack by cutting out meat?

By somewhere between a third and two-thirds. This is the cumulative result of studies comparing death rates from heart disease in vegetarians and meat-eaters.

Early studies of this type compared the mortality rates of SDAs and the general population. Among SDA men, the death rate from all causes was only half that predicted for the population as a whole,[22] and the incidence of coronary heart disease was 40 percent lower than predicted.[23]

Studies comparing unique vegetarian groups include other variables and provide only slim evidence that meat is the critical one. This problem, however, was overcome in several recent studies.

One study followed 10,943 people for seven years. Nearly half were vegetarians. Deaths from all causes were 51 percent lower for the vegetarians than predicted from mortality figures for the general population; and the incidence of heart disease was lower by 64 percent. This means that heart disease occurred among the vegetarians only a third as often as in the general population. To eliminate the possibility that the health-conscious orientation of the vegetarians accounted for these differences, the researchers compared them to an equally health-conscious control group recruited from customers of health food shops, subscribers to health magazines, and members of health-related societies. No significant differences were found in the diets and lifestyles of these two groups except meat consumption. Total deaths in both groups were much lower than expected. But the incidence of heart disease in the vegetarians was still nearly a third lower than among the equally health-conscious meat-eaters.[24]

On the basis of these figures, you could lower your actual risk of heart disease by two-thirds if you abstained from meat *and* pursued a generally healthy lifestyle. If the only change you made was to eliminate meat from your meals, you could still reduce that risk by nearly a third.

On the basis of the figures in a second study, *just eliminating meat would reduce your risk by two-thirds*. This study was the California SDA project just discussed. It tracked deaths from heart disease over a 6-year period in 24,044 California SDAs. Both the meat-eaters and the vegetarians were health-conscious SDAs who neither smoked nor drank. Meat was the only variable. Deaths from heart disease were unusually low in both SDA groups. In the 35–64 age group, they were only 28 percent as frequent as in the general California population; and among older SDAs, they were only half as frequent. Yet the death rate from heart disease for SDA vegetarians was still only one-third that for SDA meat-eaters.[25]

A third study, reported in 1988, involved 1,904 German vegetarians. They were followed for 5 years. When deaths among the vegetarians were compared with those expected from standardized mortality ratios, only *one-fifth* as many deaths had occurred as expected from heart disease; only one-half as many had occurred from cancer; and only two-fifths as many had occurred *from any cause*. That means that in any given period, these German vegetarians were only 40 percent as likely to die from *anything* as their sausage-loving fellow countrymen. They weren't merely trading heart disease for something else.[26]

The same was true for the SDA vegetarians. In a 1984 review, the researchers conducting the SDA studies showed that SDAs who ate meat or poultry less than once a week were significantly less likely than those who ate these foods five times a week or more to die from any cause.[27] Meat was positively associated with death, and salads were negatively associated with it. SDAs who ate green salads every day were significantly less likely to die from any cause than those who ate salads less than once a week. A 1988 report by one of these researchers confirmed that meat not only *is* positively correlated with death, but isn't negatively correlated with any investigated cause of death. That means meat, unlike salads, won't protect you from any potentially fatal disease.[28]

If they don't succumb to heart disease, what do vegetarian SDAs die of? It seems an unusually large number die in auto accidents, the fourth leading cause of death in this country. The proposed explanation is that elderly vegetarians are still driving around at an age when other senior citizens are not.[29]

The lower incidence of heart disease in the vegetarians in these studies confirms theoretical predictions based on the risk factors for cardiovascular disease, which are also markedly reduced in vegetarians.

What are the risk factors for cardiovascular disease?

The three traditional ones are high blood pressure, elevated serum cholesterol levels, and smoking. Cardiovascular disease is more likely to occur in the presence of these factors, and less likely to occur in their absence.[30] *All* of them vary directly with the consumption of animal foods.

A fourth predisposing factor has also been suggested by recent studies. Men with elevated serum levels of estradiol have a substantially greater risk of suffering a heart attack than those with low levels of this hormone. In a study conducted by the Pritikin Research Foundation in Santa Monica, California, people eating a high-complex-carbohydrate, low-fat, low-cholesterol diet showed significant reductions not only in serum cholesterol (which dropped 21 percent) and triglycerides (which dropped 50 percent), but in serum estradiol (which dropped 50 percent).[31]

Incidentally, the "Pritikin Lifetime Eating Plan" used to include maintenance intakes of meat, fish, or fowl of up to 3½ ounces per day. This recommendation was reduced in 1988 to 3½ ounces *per week*, an essentially-vegan prescription.[32]

Does even the cardiovascular risk posed by smoking vary with the consumption of animal foods?

Yes, surprisingly. Epidemiological studies link smoking to cardiovascular disease only when the diet is also high in saturated fat and cholesterol—which means animal foods. In populations of heavy smokers with low intakes of saturated fat and cholesterol, like the Japanese, a serious problem with atherosclerosis and coronary disease hasn't been found.[33]

The macrobiotic explanation is that smoking causes problems when tar and nicotine adhere to uric acid deposits in the lungs. These deposits result from the consumption of animal protein.[34]

Of course, smoking still can't be recommended—even for vegetarians. Tar and nicotine aren't the only harmful substances in cigarette smoke. Carbon monoxide also damages the artery walls. By replacing oxygen carried on the blood's hemoglobin, carbon monoxide reduces blood oxygen levels and suffocates the cells the blood feeds.[35]

Moreover, cardiovascular disease isn't the only condition for which smoking is a major risk factor. Others include chronic bronchitis and emphysema, peptic ulcer, and cancer—particularly lung cancer. Lung cancer is the leading cause of cancer deaths among men in this country, and smoking is its major risk factor. Heart disease incidence may be low in Japan, but lung cancer isn't. This cancer is increasing in direct correlation with an increase in cigarette sales in that country.[36]

On the other hand, there is evidence that lung cancer incidence goes down as cholesterol intake goes down, all other factors—including smoking—being equal.[37] Besides being less likely to get heart disease, smokers are less likely to get lung cancer if their diets are low in cholesterol-containing animal foods.

Studies linking animal foods to the other two major risk factors for cardiovascular disease—elevated serum cholesterol levels and high blood pressure—are investigated in the next two chapters.

Chapter 17

The Cholesterol Menace

"Recent data have suggested that a 10 percent reduction in cholesterol concentration might be associated with a 30 percent reduction in the incidence of coronary heart disease. Our data suggest that in Britain the incidence of coronary heart disease may be 24 percent lower in lifelong vegetarians and 57 percent lower in lifelong vegans than in meat eaters."
—*British Medical Journal* (1987)[1]

Epidemiological studies demonstrate direct correlations between meat intake, serum cholesterol, and heart disease. Where meat is scarce, serum cholesterol is low and cardiovascular disease is virtually unknown. In Western meat-eating countries, in contrast, serum cholesterol levels are high, and heart disease has increased over the decades in direct correlation with the increased intake of animal foods.[2]

Americans eat five times as much beef, pork, and poultry as the world average, and fifteen times as much as people in East Asia.[3] Serum cholesterol levels that we consider normal are regarded by the Chinese with alarm. Their average level is 170 mg/dl, below the 220-mg/dl American average by 50 mg/dl or 23 percent.[4]

The cholesterol levels of Western milk-drinking vegetarians are also lower than matched omnivores', by an average of 20 percent; and vegans' are lower by about 30 percent.[5]

Serum cholesterol is lowest in essentially-vegan populations. The Tarahumara Indians described in Chapter 6 are a good example. Their average serum cholesterol is only a little over *half* that in this country. Deaths from cardiac and circulatory diseases are unknown.[6]

In a study of 523 healthy Tarahumara Indians whose ages ranged from 5 to 70 years, the average cholesterol level was 125 mg/dl. This figure included both children and old people. In fact little increase occurred with age. In children, the average level was 116 mg/dl, compared to levels ranging from 153 to 182 mg/dl for typical Midwestern American children. In adult Tarahumara men, the average level was still only 136 mg/dl, compared to 221 mg/dl for adult male Midwesterners.[7]

Couldn't the low cholesterol·levels of the Tarahumara be due to strenuous exercise rather than diet?

Exercise is undoubtedly a factor, but it won't alone explain the absence of cardiovascular disease. Athletic Westerners frequently succumb to heart disease. In many studies, exercise has had only a modest effect on serum cholesterol.[8]

In middle-aged men who ran more than 15 miles a week, serum cholesterol was lower than in age-matched controls by only 5 percent.[9]

For women who exercised three times a week, similar results were seen.[10]

In angina patients who were put on an exercise program, angina incidence was reduced only when this treatment was accompanied by dietary modification. In 32 patients who followed the exercise program combined with a low-fat, high-carbohydrate diet, the number of angina attacks was reduced by 22 percent. But in 40 patients who followed the exercise program alone, it was unaffected.[11]

The level of exercise in these studies was lower than that of the Tarahumara. However, doctors writing in the August 1982 *Journal of the American Medical Association* concluded that even conditioned long-distance marathon runners aren't protected from coronary atherosclerosis. They reported the case of a marathon runner who had been active in competitive athletics since childhood, and had run an average of 50–70 miles a week at an 8-minute-per-mile pace all during his forties. This athletic conditioning didn't save him from progressive angina pectoris, which he developed at the age of 48. His case was only one of a number of recent reports of atheromatous coronary artery disease in runners.[12]

The same is true of Finnish men. Although their lifestyle is physically strenuous, their heart disease incidence is higher than in any other country in the world.[13] Men engaged in farming and lumbering, the predominant occupations in Finland, are frequent victims of coronary disease.[14]

In a study of men in Western Finland aged 50–59 who were engaged in "hard to very hard physical work" (farmers, blacksmiths, loggers, etc.), the average serum cholesterol level was 248 mg/dl—higher than that of sedentary workers in the same area, which averaged 241 mg/dl. In Eastern Finland, the average for men engaged in "hard to very hard physical work" was an even higher 252 mg/dl, compared to 258 mg/dl for the sedentary workers.[15]

Could the low serum cholesterol of the Tarahumara be hereditary?

Not likely. Their Indian relatives in the United States, who eat a more Westernized diet, have cholesterol levels nearly as high as the usual American averages.[16] When the Tarahumara are subjected to heavy doses of dietary cholesterol, their serum cholesterol responds like ours.[17]

But heredity and exercise are potential variables in epidemiological studies. To eliminate them, other studies have compared the cholesterol levels of Western vegetarian and non-vegetarian groups with different diets, but similar lifestyles and genes. These studies confirm the lower cholesterol levels of vegetarians in general, and of vegans in particular. They show that for lacto-ovo-vegetarians the difference is about 20 percent, and for vegans it's about 30 percent. These differences remain when other variables besides animal foods are controlled.

What do these percentages mean in terms of heart disease risk?

The relationship between elevated serum cholesterol and the risk of heart disease has long been debated, but it was essentially resolved in January of 1984. The National Heart, Lung and Blood Institute (NHLBI) released the findings of a $150 million study tracking the incidence of heart disease in 3,806 men over a 7–10 year period. The study established a definite correlation between high amounts of cholesterol in the blood and an increased likelihood of coronary heart disease. It showed that for every 1 percent reduction in serum cholesterol, the risk of heart disease drops by about 2 percent.[18] British researchers reporting in *The Lancet* in 1986 put the figure even higher. They suggested that a 10 percent drop in serum cholesterol translates into a *30 percent* reduction in risk.[19]

Applying even the more conservative formula, eliminating meat from the diet reduces the risk of heart disease by about 40 percent. Eliminating all animal products reduces it by about 60 percent, or nearly two-thirds. A two-thirds reduction in risk means the incidence of heart disease should be only one-third that of the general population. This is the actual observed incidence in vegetarians.[20]

What studies show serum cholesterol is lower even in lacto-ovo-vegetarians, who eat milk products and eggs that are high in saturated fat and cholesterol?

Some of the first studies involved Seventh Day Adventists, who refrain from eating meat, but freely indulge in other animal foods. Yet SDAs have substantially lower cholesterol levels than non-SDAs.[21] These disparities exist although SDAs eat eggs, which contain many times as much cholesterol as lean beef; and cheese, which contains as much cholesterol as most meats, and several times as much saturated fat.

That doesn't necessarily mean milk products and eggs are easier on the arteries than meat. An alternative explanation is simply that SDAs have a lower *total* intake of saturated fat and cholesterol. Meat-eaters eat meat along with milk products and eggs. Vegetarians tend to replace meat with a grain- or bean-based main dish rather than with more milk and eggs.

In an early study comparing the food intakes of lacto-ovo-vegetarians and meat-eaters, the average intake of dietary cholesterol was only 333 mg/day for the vegetarians, compared to 914 mg/day for the non-vegetarians. The difference was nearly 300 percent. The percentage of calories from animal fat in the vegetarian diet was also only about half that in the non-vegetarian diet.[22]

Couldn't the fact that Seventh Day Adventists abstain from alcohol, coffee and cigarettes explain their lower cholesterol levels?

No, because these differences remain when other variables are eliminated.

Strictly vegetarian SDAs were compared with SDAs who ate meat, but whose other habits were the same. The meat-eating SDAs had cholesterol levels that were very close to non-SDA meat-eaters. The average for the meat-eating SDAs was 223 mg/dl—only 6 mg/dl lower than the non-SDA meat-eaters', and 44 mg/dl (or 20 percent) higher than the vegetarian SDAs.'[23]

The same result is reached when the groups compared are chosen for their health orientation rather than their religious affiliation.

Eighty-five vegetarians and 215 non-vegetarians were selected from among the health-conscious patrons of health food stores and subscribers to health food journals. Their diets and habits were comparable except for meat consumption. Few in either group smoked cigarettes, and alcohol consumption was roughly equivalent. Yet serum cholesterol in the vegetarian men was an average of 45 mg/dl lower than in the non-vegetarian men. The percentage difference was again 20 percent, representing a 40 percent reduction in heart disease risk.[24]

At what age are these differences in serum cholesterol apparent?

Studies vary, but at least one reported significant differences as early as adolescence. An Australian study found that partially vegetarian SDA youths were already 18 percent more likely to be victims of heart disease than their strict SDA friends, although they differed from them only in that they ate modest amounts of meat.[25]

What about vegetarians who eat no animal products of any sort?

Their serum cholesterol reaches lows usually seen only in primitive cultures. The percentage reduction from normal American levels is about 30 percent, representing a 60 percent reduction in heart disease risk.

In a study comparing vegans to healthy non-vegetarians matched for age, sex, height, ethnic origin and socioeconomic background, the vegan serum cholesterol level averaged 158 mg/dl—77 mg/dl lower than the 235-mg/dl average of the non-vegetarians. The difference was 30 percent.[26]

A second study compared serum cholesterol in 86 lacto-ovo-vegetarians, 26 vegans, and 88 meat-eaters. The cholesterol levels of vegan men were 82 mg/dl lower than for non-vegetarian men—a reduction of 28 percent. For vegan women, the difference was 89 mg/ dl—or 30 percent. For lacto-ovo-vegetarians, the respective reductions were 16 percent and 9 percent.[27]

A third study involved members of "The Farm," a commune in Tennessee where the daily menu includes no animal products of any sort. Serum cholesterol for the men averaged 125 mg/dl—even lower than in the Tarahumara Indians. Serum cholesterol in a group of healthy non-vegetarian men matched for age and sex averaged 184 mg/dl—again, a difference of 30 percent. For the women, the respective figures were 133 and 174 mg/dl, a difference of 24 percent.[28]

A fourth study involved 116 macrobiotic vegetarians whose dietary staples were whole grains, beans, fresh vegetables, seaweed, and fermented products. Meat and poultry were entirely avoided, and milk, eggs, and fish were eaten rarely. The mean cholesterol level was a low 126 mg/dl, as compared to 184 mg/dl for a matched omnivore control group. The reduction was 32 percent.[29]

Nearly the same percentage reduction resulted in the already low cholesterol levels of lacto-ovo-vegetarian men when virtually all animal foods were eliminated from their diets.[30]

Could these differences be due to differences in weight?

Vegetarians do tend to weigh less than meat-eaters, and people who are heavier tend to have higher serum cholesterol levels. But the differences in cholesterol levels in these studies could still be shown in pairs of subjects matched according to weight.[31]

If serum cholesterol is a function of diet, why is it that some people on low-cholesterol diets have high cholesterol levels, while other people on high-cholesterol diets have low levels?

To some extent, the ability to handle cholesterol is hereditary. Some people are born with a higher proportion than others of high-density lipoprotein cholesterol (the good kind) to low-density lipoprotein cholesterol (the bad kind).[32] But in studies of entire populations, low-density lipoprotein and total cholesterol levels still show a definite correlation with dietary cholesterol, despite individual variations in the ability to handle cholesterol.[33]

What are high-density and low-density lipoproteins?

Lipoproteins are cholesterol-protein packages by which cholesterol and other fatty substances are transported through the blood. Low-density lipoprotein (LDL) carries cholesterol toward the tissues, where it collects and causes the fatty buildup responsible for cardiovascular disease. High-density lipoprotein (HDL) carries cholesterol away from the tissues to the liver, where it is broken down and reused or excreted. Since HDL helps to clean up excess cholesterol by taking it out of circulation, a high proportion of HDL to LDL protects the body from heart disease. A high level of HDL and a low level of LDL is therefore associated with a reduced risk of heart disease.[34]

If some cholesterol actually protects against heart disease, is the total cholesterol level still a valid predictor of heart disease risk?

Yes, because LDL is the *major* cholesterol carrier in human blood, and total plasma cholesterol levels generally reflect LDL cholesterol levels. High levels of either LDL or total cholesterol indicate an increased risk of heart disease.[35]

What low levels of *HDL* indicate, on the other hand, isn't clear. In some populations, HDL levels are low, yet coronary disease is rare.[36] HDL levels can be increased by feeding cholesterol, but there is no suggestion that this improves your chances against coronary disease.[37] Measurement of HDL alone doesn't necessarily predict the risk of vascular disease, and raising HDL levels doesn't necessarily reduce that risk. Lowering LDL levels, on the other hand, clearly does.[38]

A more comprehensive indicator is the ratio of HDL to LDL (or of HDL to total cholesterol).[39]

How do the HDL and LDL cholesterol levels of vegetarians and meat-eaters compare?

LDL ("bad") cholesterol levels are always higher in meat-eaters. Whether HDL ("good") cholesterol levels are also higher varies with the study. But even when they have been, the *ratio* of HDL to LDL (and to total cholesterol) has remained higher in the vegetarians.[40] This factor tends to reduce the risk of heart disease regardless of the absolute HDL level.[41] The idea is basically to have enough HDL to clean up the LDL.

Many studies have shown that LDL cholesterol is substantially lower in vegetarians than meat-eaters, and the ratio of HDL to LDL and to total cholesterol is higher.

A 1985 study compared the plasma lipoprotein levels of lacto-vegetarians and vegans with those found for meat-eaters in the National Institutes of Health Lipid Research Clinics population studies. The respective figures for LDL and HDL were 78 and 43 for vegans, 97 and 46 for lacto-vegetarians and 116 and 51 for meat-eaters. The HDL/LDL ratio was 55 percent in vegans, 46 percent in lacto-vegetarians, and 44 percent in meat-eaters. LDL cholesterol was about 50 percent higher in meat-eaters than in vegans, and about 20 percent higher than in lacto-vegetarians.[42]

In the study cited earlier comparing vegans on The Farm with matched non-vegetarians, the respective mean levels for vegans and controls were 79 versus 118 for LDL, and 37 versus 48 for HDL. The HDL/LDL ratio was 47 percent for the vegans and 41 percent for the meat eaters; and LDL cholesterol was again about 50 percent higher in meat-eaters.[43]

In the macrobiotic vegetarian study also reported previously, the respective mean levels for the macrobiotic group and the controls were 73 versus 118 for LDL, and 42 versus 49 for HDL. The HDL/LDL ratio was 58 percent for the macrobiotics and 42 percent for the meat-eaters. LDL cholesterol was again more than 50 percent higher in the meat-eaters.[44]

Comparable results were obtained in a clinical study in which vegans were given about 8 ounces of beef daily for four weeks. This modest dietary change caused their average total cholesterol level to rise from 140 to 168 mg/dl, an increase of 19 percent. But the average HDL level did not change. The result was a significant increase in the ratio of total to HDL cholesterol on the meat diet. On the vegan diet, it was about 4.5, a ratio characteristic of people with a low risk for heart attacks. On the meat diet, it rose to more than 5, a ratio characteristic of people with a high risk for heart attacks.[45]

Total LDL remains the most important indicator because it makes up about 80 percent of the cholesterol of an adult. Even if you're heavy on the HDL side, you may be at risk if your LDL is also high.[46] Conversely, if your HDL level is low, you may not be at risk if your LDL level is also low. The average HDL level of the Tarahumara Indians is a low 26 mg/dl, but it's balanced by an equally low total cholesterol level of 134 mg/dl. The ratio is 5.2, which for Americans would be considered dangerously high. Yet atherosclerosis among the Tarahumara is virtually non-existent.[47]

Can arterial plaque actually be reduced by reducing serum cholesterol, or is the middle-aged meat-eater already too late?

It's not too late. It's been known for some time that atherosclerotic lesions induced in monkeys by a diet high in saturated fat and cholesterol can be reversed by a diet low in these components. This has now been shown in humans.

Rhesus monkeys were fed a diet high in saturated fat and cholesterol for 17 months. The result was atherosclerosis so severe that the animals' arteries were more than half closed by fatty plaques. At the same time, serum cholesterol increased fivefold. After two months on a diet without saturated fat and cholesterol, serum cholesterol returned to normal; and after 40 months, the atherosclerotic growths had shrunk to less than ⅓ their original size.[48]

In 1987, doctors at the University of Southern California School of Medicine completed a two-year study showing similar results in humans. Coronary plaque was monitored with X-rays in two groups of men who had undergone coronary bypass surgery. Serum cholesterol was lowered in one group by diet and drugs. At the end of the study, 16 percent of this group showed visible arterial improvement, as compared to only 2 percent in the control group.[49]

A study reported in 1988 got these effects solely by changes in lifestyle, without drugs. The patients all had blocked arteries, many severe enough to warrant bypass surgery. One group ate a standard low-fat diet (30 percent fat), exercised and quit smoking. Another group exercised, quit smoking, practiced yoga and meditation, and switched to a vegetarian diet that was only 10 percent fat. Artery blockage dropped significantly in the vegetarian group, while no significant change was seen in the standard low-fat group.[50]

Researchers conclude that advanced atherosclerotic lesions are much more likely to respond favorably to treatment if serum cholesterol is reduced to the minimum found in animals and people eating a diet low in saturated fat and cholesterol. In humans and rhesus monkeys, this value appears to be about 150 mg/dl. Under these conditions, much of the fat in the plaques disappears, and the remaining tissue and cells remodel themselves as they do in the healing of wounds and fractures.[51] Serum cholesterol this low is typically found only in essentially-vegan populations. The 220-mg/dl American average is nearly 50 percent above this optimum level.[52]

How effective is dietary modification as compared to drugs or surgery?

Bypass surgery won't reduce the development of atherosclerotic lesions. In fact, it often has the opposite effect.[53] It's also subject to other serious drawbacks. It's painful and risky, resulting in brain damage in 15 percent of patients.[54]

It's expensive, adding up to a collective national bill of about $5 billion annually—more than we spend in total on medical research on heart disease and its prevention.[55] Worse, in most cases, bypass surgery hasn't been shown to prolong the life of the patient.[56]

Cholesterol-lowering drugs are also subject to drawbacks. Mevacor, the hottest drug now on the prescription market, can reduce serum cholesterol by as much as 30 percent. Unfortunately, it can also cause cataracts and liver dysfunction.[57] A vegan diet is equally effective without these risks. The vitamin niacin also lowers serum cholesterol, but it has to be taken in huge doses that can cause serious skin flushing, itching, and upset stomachs. Bile-acid resins, like Questran and Colestid, can lower serum cholesterol by 15–20 percent. But that's less than the reductions seen on a vegan diet, and they also have to be taken in large amounts to be effective, producing unpleasant side effects.[58]

Bile-acid resins work by forcing the liver to produce more bile acid, the digestive juice that breaks down dietary fats. Cholesterol is thus used up in the blood. You don't, however, have to take a drug to get this effect. Pectin, a common plant fiber, works the same way. Pectin in combination with calcium binds readily to bile acids, rendering them useless as digestive enzymes. The liver senses that there is a shortage of bile acid and compensates by extracting cholesterol molecules from the blood, which are then modified into bile molecules. As a result, the serum cholesterol drops.[59]

A completely vegan diet works better yet. It treats the cause as well as the effect, preventing cholesterol from getting into the arteries in the first place.

A vegan diet not only lowers serum cholesterol and blood pressure but is an effective treatment for angina, the chest pain foreshadowing a heart attack. In a study reported in the *American Heart Journal*, this diet cured severe angina in four out of four patients—a small study sample, but a 100 percent success rate.

One patient was a 44-year-old man who experienced severe attacks of angina on exertion. After eighteen months on a vegan diet, the pain disappeared. After nearly three more years, he could climb 2,000 feet up a steep mountain and walk seven or eight miles without pain. He was followed for four more years, during which he remained pain-free on the diet.

Another patient was a 46-year-old man with severe chest pains when he tried to walk. After three months without animal products, the angina was gone, and he could garden and do heavy work without pain. He was followed for six more years, during which he remained pain free on the diet.

The third patient was a 65-year-old man with chest pains so severe he couldn't walk without stopping every few paces. After five months on the diet, he experienced no chest pains on making fairly strenuous efforts. The sixth month he climbed mountains without pain. He was followed for ten years, during which the pain did not return. He later died of a pulmonary embolism.

The fourth patient was a 48-year-old man with very severe chest pain despite over five years of medication. After six months without animal foods, he could walk much further and the pain was much less. In nine months, the pain had disappeared. In eleven months, he was able to do gardening and fairly heavy work without pain. Then he abandoned the diet. Several years later, he was again having frequent attacks of angina.[60]

For treating chest pain, a vegan diet can be more effective than drugs.

When six angina patients were given an anticoagulating drug, no significant change resulted in their conditions. But when they were put on a vegan diet consisting of rice, fruits, vegetables, and a protein hydrolysate mixture (a specially prepared mixture of amino acids), their angina pain decreased and their ability to exercise increased. In only three weeks their average serum cholesterol dropped by 184 mg/dl, or nearly 40 percent—enough to reduce their risk of a heart attack by 80 percent.[61]

A vegan diet can also be more effective than drugs in reducing the third major risk factor for cardiovascular disease—hypertension.

Chapter 18

High Blood Pressure: Too Much Salt or Too Much Meat?

"Mild hypertension . . . has become a therapeutic dilemma: The steadily rising pressure to treat all such patients is bringing millions of asymptomatic people into lifetime drug therapy; at the same time the results of clinical trials indicate that, for some, the risks of the drugs . . . may outweigh the benefits gained from lowering the blood pressure. Although the levels of hypertension considered to be in need of reduction have progressively come down, the treatment of hypertension has become the leading indication for the use of licit drugs."

—Norman Kaplan, M.D.
Annals of Internal Medicine[1]

High blood pressure has been cited as the leading cause of death in industrialized countries. It's the most common factor in the origins of cardiovascular disease.[2] The American Heart Association estimates that nearly 35 million Americans have it. That's 1 out of every 6.[3] An estimated 850,000 Americans die each year from cardiovascular diseases related to it.

The usual treatment is antihypertensive medication. Once hypertension has been diagnosed, doctors typically prescribe these drugs for the rest of the patient's life.[4] But the unpleasant side effects of the treatment—drowsiness, dizziness, dry mouth, depression, nausea, headache, heart palpitations, and impotence—often prevent patients from following their doctor's advice.

Drugs, however, aren't the only alternative. The dangerously high blood pressures of hypertensive patients can be reduced to safe levels and kept there without pills by switching to a vegan diet. The reported side effects of this treat-

ment are all good ones, including a gener
being, lower serum cholesterol, and impro

Isn't it salt rather than animal prod
blood pressure?

That's the most popular theory, but researchers still de-
bate the extent to which salt is responsible. It seems to raise
blood pressure in susceptible people, but many studies have
found no correlation between salt intake and blood pressure.[6]

Most studies have found the blood pressure of vegetarians
to be significantly lower than meat-eaters', even when their
salt intakes are higher.[7] And in clinical trials, blood pressure
has dropped far more with the avoidance of *both* animal
products and salt than with salt alone.[8]

Even if these suspects are equally guilty, many people
find it easier to go without meat than to go without salt.
Studies we'll look at show a meatless diet is an effective
means of keeping your blood pressure at safe levels, even
when the flavor of your grains and greens is enhanced by
salt.

Why do doctors worry so much about high blood pressure?

Because more than half of all heart attacks and two-thirds
of all strokes occur in people with this symptom.[9]

The association between high blood pressure and cardiovascular disease was demonstrated in the Framingham Heart
Study, which involved 5,209 men and women aged 30 to 62
years living in Framingham, Massachusetts. Beginning in
1949, their blood pressures were taken twice a year for 18
years. Blood pressures were then plotted against clinical
signs of heart disease.

The study showed that people with high blood pressure
(hypertensives) were twice as likely to be victims of either
angina pectoris or heart attacks as those with normal blood
pressure (normotensives). Hypertensives were also three
times as likely to experience heart attacks resulting in sudden death.[10] Interestingly, no association was found between
salt intake and high blood pressure.[11]

The 5-year findings of the more recent Hypertension and Detection Follow-up Program were reported in the *Journal of the American Medical Association* in 1979. The study established that lowering blood pressure markedly reduced the death rate from all causes.[12] A 1988 report in the *American Journal of Clinical Nutrition* observed that the number of major coronary events could be substantially reduced by a modest blood pressure reduction of only 6 mm Hg systolic—and that *this difference was the same as that typically seen between vegetarians and meat-eaters.*[13]

How is hypertension diagnosed?

The blood pulses with each beat of the heart from a high pressure to a low pressure. Blood pressure is measured at these two levels in millimeters of mercury (mm/Hg). The higher level is the systolic pressure; the lower level is the diastolic pressure. Hypertension is usually diagnosed on the basis of the diastolic reading (the lower figure.) But in the Framingham study, a stronger association with coronary heart disease was actually found for the systolic reading (the higher figure).[14]

Participants in the Framingham study with blood pressures of 160/95 were classified as hypertensive, while those having blood pressures of 140/90 were classified as normotensive. The difference between normotensives and hypertensives was only 20 mm systolic and 5 mm diastolic.

Insurance company statistics verify the significance of this modest difference in blood pressure levels. They show that a 45-year-old man with a blood pressure of 120/80 can expect to live to seventy, while a man of the same age with a blood pressure of 140/95 can expect to live six years less.[15]

What evidence links meat to high blood pressure?

Epidemiological surveys link diets low in meat and fish to low blood pressures, and diets high in meat and fish to high blood pressures. These surveys cover the United States, Europe, Japan, China, India, Malaysia, Australia, and the South Pacific Islands.[16] When salt intake has been reported in these studies, the association between meat and high blood pressure has been independent of it. Much has been made of the fact that populations who eat little salt have low blood pressures. With the exception of the Eskimos (discussed in Chapter 20), these populations generally also eat few animal products. Many vegetarian populations eat moderate to high amounts of salt, yet their blood pressures remain low.[17]

A study already discussed compared railway clerks in North and South India. Significantly higher blood pressures were found in the South Indians, who ate six times as much meat. Salt intake, on the other hand, was *inversely* correlated with blood pressure. The North Indians, who had the lowest blood pressures, used between 50 percent and 90 percent more salt than the South Indians, who had the highest blood pressures. Heredity couldn't explain these differences, because when the South Indian clerks transferred to the North and ate the North Indian diet, their blood pressures dropped to levels like the North Indian natives'. Other variables eliminated were age, occupation, body weight, psychological factors and smoking. In fact, the vegetarian North Indians (with the lower blood pressures) smoked 3 times as much as the meat-eating South Indians (with the higher blood pressures).[18]

Another study compared blood pressures in two rural villages in Japan. The people in one village ate 50 percent more animal protein and 100 percent more animal fat—mainly from fish. These people had significantly higher blood pressures and a higher mortality from heart disease, although their salt intakes were again lower than in the other village.[19]

In a New Guinea study, village men receiving extra rations of food that included meat had higher blood pressures than other tribal groups eating a vegetable diet.[20]

In another New Guinea study, the average blood pressure of 200 adults whose diets consisted mainly of vegetables and fruit was only 92/64—25 percent below the 120/80 considered normal in this country.[21]

Among Australian aborigines, a trend toward higher blood pressures is seen in meat-eating groups, whether primitive or "semi-urbanized."[22]

Polynesian studies demonstrate the same trend.[23]

In Germany, lacto-vegetarian monks have lower blood pressures at all ages than meat-eating monks.[24]

In Czechoslovakia, blood pressures go up with meat intake.[25]

In Tokyo, hypertensives eat more animal products than the normal urban Japanese population.[26]

In China, the blood pressures of vegan aborigines whose diets consist mainly of corn range from a low of 99/66 at ages 16–20 to a high of 118/72 at age 64.[27]

In the United States, by contrast, blood pressures are as high as in these elderly aborigines in youth, and they increase with age. In a study of the members of a rural Kentucky community, blood pressure averaged 122/74 at ages 16–19 and had risen to 160/85 by the age of 70.[28]

Couldn't the higher blood pressures of Americans be due simply to the stresses of urban living?

This theory won't explain the statistics. The prevalence of hypertension is considerably higher, for example, among American blacks living in the rural South than among those in large cities, although the city dwellers are subject to urban stress.[29] Meat-eating German monks also have higher blood pressures than vegetarian monks, and neither group is subject to urban stress.[30] Urban vegetarians in industrialized countries have significantly lower blood pressures than their meat-eating counterparts, although they are no less stress ridden.

How much lower are the blood pressures of vegetarians in Western countries?

Studies have found differences of between 5 and 13 mm systolic for milk-drinking vegetarians, and as much as 200 mm systolic for vegans.

A California study comparing lacto-ovo-vegetarian and non-vegetarian male college students demonstrated a 13 mm difference in systolic pressures and a 10 mm difference in diastolic pressures. The mean blood pressure for the vegetarians was 113/65, while for the non-vegetarians it was 126/75.[31]

An Australian study comparing older SDA lacto-ovo-vegetarians and meat-eaters (age range 30–79 years) found a similar spread. The mean average for the vegetarians was 128.7/76.2, while for the non-vegetarians it was 139.3/84.5. Blood pressure also rose less with age in the vegetarians.[32]

In a study of 210 Boston macrobiotic vegetarians aged 16–29, the average blood pressure was 106/60—20 mm systolic and 15 mm diastolic below meat-eaters' in the same age range.[33]

Other variables besides meat consumption have been proposed to explain these differences. SDA vegetarians avoid not only meat but also alcohol, caffeine, and nicotine. But in the Australian study, when the intakes of these substances by non-SDAs were plotted separately against their blood pressure levels, no significant correlations were found.[34]

Other variables have also been eliminated in studies comparing meat-eating Mormons and vegetarian Seventh Day Adventists, two religious groups whose lifestyles otherwise closely resemble each other. The blood pressures of Mormons are higher than SDAs by an average of 5–6 mm systolic and 4–5 mm diastolic.[35]

A recent study compared 113 Mormon omnivores with 93 SDA vegetarians. The two groups were similar in strength of religious affiliation, consumption of alcohol, tea and coffee, and use of tobacco. Yet the SDAs had significantly lower blood pressures, lower cholesterol levels and less obesity. For the men, blood pressure averaged 115.6/68.7 in the SDAs versus 121.1/72.2 in the Mormons; and for the women, it averaged 109.1/66.7 in the SDAs versus 114.9/72.6 in the Mormons. A full 10 percent of the Mormons had mild hypertension (defined as blood pressures over 140/90), as compared to only 1–2 percent of the SDAs. Serum cholesterol was also 8 percent higher for the Mormon men and 21 percent higher for the women.[36]

The reason for these differences between vegetarians and meat-eaters, however, remains a mystery. Reviewing 60 years of studies, researchers writing in the *American Journal of Clinical Nutrition* in 1988 concluded that the factors responsible for lowering the blood pressures of vegetarians are still uncertain.[37]

Could their lower blood pressures be due to a lower salt intake?

No, because *vegetarians don't have lower salt intakes.*[38] A recent study found that the excretion of sodium by vegetarians was greater than for non-vegetarians, reflecting a *higher* salt intake.[39]

In macrobiotic dietary theory, sea salt is actually recommended with vegetables and grains to bring out their "yang" qualities. It isn't recommended, however, with meat, which is already too "yang."[40]

The Boston macrobiotic vegetarians just cited used sea salt regularly in cooking, and nearly half of them also added salty condiments at the table. When dietary variables were plotted against their blood pressures, neither salt nor sugar consumption showed any association with blood pressure. The *only* variable that related significantly to both systolic and diastolic pressure was "percentage of animal food in a meal."[41]

Can the lower blood pressures of vegetarians be explained by their lower consumption of saturated fat?

This theory has been proposed, based on a Finnish study in which thirty couples with normal blood pressures were placed on a diet low in saturated fat. In six weeks, their average blood pressure level dropped 7.5 mm systolic and 2.8 mm diastolic.[42]

These results, however, were confounded by other variables. Not only was the ratio of polyunsaturated to saturated fat increased, but *total* fat was reduced from 36 percent to 24 percent of caloric intake. Fiber, vitamin C, magnesium, and potassium were also modified so they were more like the intakes of vegetarians. In a later Australian study in which other variables were held constant, the substitution of polyunsaturated for saturated fat was not significantly related to changes in blood pressure.[43]

What about fiber?

This theory has also been suggested, but in a 1988 study in which fiber was increased without other dietary changes, no effect on blood pressure was found.[44]

How can the lower blood pressures of vegetarians be explained?

Good question. An Australian review of studies in which possible factors were isolated concluded that neither polyunsaturated fat, saturated fat, cholesterol, potassium, magnesium, sodium, nor total protein intake was independently responsible for the lower blood pressures of vegetarians.[45]

Some vegetarians propose a "karmic factor." When an animal is about to be killed, it experiences fear. This fear generates an adrenalin rush. When a human eats the animal, he also eats this adrenalin, which raises his blood pressure. There is no scientific evidence for this theory, but it's provocative.

How fast can I expect my blood pressure to drop if I change my diet?

A reduction equal to the difference between the blood pressures of SDAs and Mormons can be brought about in a few weeks. In one controlled study, an average drop in blood pressure of 6.8 mm systolic and 2.7 mm diastolic resulted in only three weeks when normally omnivorous men and women switched to a vegetarian diet.[46]

When meat has been fed to vegetarians, their blood pressures have shot up just as fast—and have dropped back down as soon as they returned to meatless fare.

In an early study, meat was fed to people who normally avoided it but were not strict vegetarians. (This condition eliminated the "anxiety factor" that has been hypothesized to raise blood pressure in strict vegetarians with a moral aversion to eating meat.) Their blood pressures rose an average of 14 mm systolic, from 106/62 to 120/66, after only 16 days of meat-eating.[47]

In a later study, 21 macrobiotic vegetarians whose normal diets included almost no animal products ate 8 ounces of beef daily. After 4 weeks, their blood pressures had risen by 3 percent. More alarming were the reported rises in serum cholesterol levels, which went up by 19 percent, and in their pulse rates, which went up by 63 percent. After 2 more weeks without beef, all of these indices had returned to their starting levels.[48]

How much can a vegan diet lower blood pressure in hypertensive patients?

In some studies, their blood pressures have dropped by as much as 30–60 mm systolic.[49] More important, the diet has allowed most of the patients to maintain safe blood pressures without hypertensive medication and its side effects.

A recent Swedish study producing these impressive results involved 26 patients with long-established, hospital-verified hypertension. Treatment with medication reduced the blood pressures of most of them to within the normal range, but they continued to experience disturbing side effects and were concerned about the prospect of lifelong medication. They were sufficiently dissatisfied to be willing to change completely to a vegan regimen—without meat, milk, eggs, or salt—for an entire year.

On this diet, 20 of the 26 patients abandoned their pills, while maintaining blood pressures that were even lower than with medication. The other six achieved lower blood pressures while reducing their daily prescriptions by about half. With drugs alone, the average drop from pre-treatment levels was 47 mm systolic; with diet alone, it was 56 mm systolic.

Other benefits of the vegan diet included an 11 percent drop in serum cholesterol, a 50 percent drop in serum urea, and improvement in eyesight. To the patients, however, the most important benefit was the cessation of drug side effects.[50]

Couldn't the avoidance of salt alone have produced these results?

This isn't likely. In other studies, rigorous sodium deprivation has lowered blood pressure in only 30–50 percent of hypertensive patients. Not only has it been ineffective in the rest, but in some cases it has raised blood pressure and caused adverse clinical effects.[51] Even in patients in whom salt restriction is effective in lowering blood pressure, it doesn't work as well as a vegan diet.

> Ninety patients who were on medication for mild hypertension were divided into two groups. Both were advised to eat less fat and sugar, more cereals and breads (preferably wholemeal), and more fruits and vegetables. One group was also asked to avoid salt. The blood pressures of the salt-restricted group dropped only 5 mm systolic and 3 mm diastolic more than in the controls, and two-thirds of the group remained dependent on their medications.[52]

Comparing the results of this and the Swedish study, a salt-free vegan diet is ten times as effective in lowering blood pressure as salt restriction alone.

Chapter 19

Jack Sprat and the Lean Meat Myth

"Jack Sprat could eat no fat,
His wife could eat no lean;
And so between them both, you see,
They licked the platter clean."

The popular solution to the cholesterol problem is to trim the fat from steaks and chops, or concentrate on leaner meats (chicken and fish). There is, however, evidence that meat protein also raises serum cholesterol, independent of its fat. If that's true, both Mr. and Mrs. Sprat may be at risk.

In a study reported in the June 1982 *Journal of the American Medical Association*, 20 percent reductions in serum cholesterol resulted in healthy young men when the only change made in their diets was to replace animal protein with vegetable protein. Saturated fat and cholesterol were unchanged.

Twenty-four young men whose cholesterol levels were between 140 and 220 mg/dl were divided into three groups. For four weeks, each group received the same diet except for its protein component, which consisted entirely either of (1) soy flour and textured soy protein, (2) egg white, or (3) nonfat dairy products. All three diets contained 35 percent fat, more than half of which was saturated; and all participants ate two egg yolks a day to make sure that any reductions in serum cholesterol weren't due to a corresponding reduction in dietary cholesterol and saturated fat. The total cholesterol levels of the men eating dairy products and egg whites showed no change. The total levels of the men on the soy diet, however, dropped from a mean of 179 to 144 mg/dl—a reduction of 35 mg/dl, or about 20 percent. These men also showed consistent decreases in LDL ("bad") cholesterol, and consistent increases in HDL ("good") cholesterol.[1]

In comparable studies involving healthy young women, the results have been smaller in magnitude but similar in direction.[2] Since the type of protein—animal versus vegetable—was the only variable in these studies, the researchers concluded animal protein independently raises serum cholesterol.

Arguably, plant protein sources merely contain some component that lowers serum cholesterol, which is lacking in animal protein sources.[3] The most likely cholesterol-lowering plant component is fiber. The problem with this theory is that some plant foods lower cholesterol even when their fiber, taken alone, does not. Soybeans and wheat are two examples.[4]

Whatever the reason, it seems that animal protein foods raise serum cholesterol more than plant protein foods, independent of their fat content. That means even lean meat will raise your serum cholesterol as compared to beans.

The protein theory

While the prevailing dietary theory of atherosclerosis focuses on saturated fat and cholesterol, the protein theory actually has a longer history. As early as 1909, the Russian physician A. Ignatowski proposed that the clearest explanation for the high incidence of heart disease among the Russian aristocracy was their increased intake of both animal and total protein.

Only in the 1950s was the protein theory preempted by the fat theory, based on several epidemiological studies showing increased coronary heart disease in populations with high intakes of saturated fat and cholesterol. It's hard to tell from epidemiological studies, though, whether this increased incidence is due to animal fat or animal protein, because the two are inextricably joined in animal foods. Differences in animal protein consumption could as easily explain the statistics. In Africa and Asia, where cholesterol levels and heart disease incidence are low, the daily intake of protein is only about 50 grams—and 90 percent of it comes from plants. In the United States, the per capita protein intake is over 100 grams—and 70 percent of it comes from animals.[5]

Vegans, who eat no animal products, also eat no animal fat or cholesterol. But the differences in the cholesterol intakes of vegans and meat-eaters are alone insufficient to explain the differences in their serum cholesterol levels, which are several times those brought about experimentally by manipulating dietary fat alone.[6] In the NHLBI study discussed in Chapter 17, limiting animal fat intake over a period of years lowered serum cholesterol by only 4 percent.[7] This is a fraction of the reduction seen in vegans, whose serum cholesterol levels are lower than comparable meat-eaters' by a full 30 percent.

In other studies, a rigorous low-fat diet has reduced serum cholesterol by about 10 percent, but this is still only one-third the reduction seen in vegans.[8] And in intractable cases, a strict low-fat diet has had *no* effect on elevated cholesterol levels—while eliminating all animal foods has reduced them an average of 20 percent.[9] This is twice the reduction normally achieved by limiting fat intake alone, even in patients for whom that treatment works.

Wouldn't lean meat still be better than fatty meat?

Fish and light-meat poultry do contain less saturated fat than beef or pork, but in studies in which poultry and fish have replaced red meat in the diet, no significant lowering of serum cholesterol has resulted.[10]

> In a 10½ month study, the participants ate beef as the only meat for three months, poultry and fish for another 3 months, and pork for another three months, in different sequences. Serum cholesterol did not change significantly during any of the dietary periods.[11]

Contrary to popular belief, beef, pork, poultry, and fish contain about the same amount of cholesterol. Moreover, there is no supporting evidence to demonstrate that dietary cholesterol can be avoided by selecting unmarbled meat, or trimming away fat.[12]

There is also no statistically significant difference in the cholesterol content of different *grades* of meat. After cooking, a well-marbled steak contains no more than less-marbled cuts; and muscle meat actually contains about 50 percent *more* cholesterol than meat fat. This anomalous result is explained by the higher water content of muscle meat. Raw, it's about 70 percent water, as compared to 15 percent to 22.5 percent for meat fat. This water is lost in cooking, leaving a more concentrated meat with a higher cholesterol content.[13]

In studies we'll look at in the next chapter, the consumption of fish has produced modest reductions in serum cholesterol. But these reductions are less than you can get by eliminating animal products altogether, and they aren't due to the protein or the cholesterol content of fish. They're due to its unique content of polyunsaturated fatty acids. Fish actually has a high cholesterol content; fish *protein* significantly *raises* the serum cholesterol levels of rabbits, even when isolated from fish fat.

> Groups of rabbits were fed diets in which the fat contents were equivalent, but the protein was varied so that a third of it came either from soy, milk or fish meal. The milk diet resulted in serum cholesterol levels that were half again as high as on the soy diet. The fish meal diet resulted in cholesterol levels that were *nine times* as high as on the soy diet (and six times as high as on the milk diet). When the fish meal was fed with either saturated or unsaturated fat, the same excessive elevation resulted; demonstrating that its protein rather than its saturated fat was responsible for the enormous increase in serum cholesterol.[14]

How do other animal proteins affect serum cholesterol?

In rabbits, all animal proteins raise it and plant proteins lower it. In one study, animal proteins increased rabbit serum cholesterol as much as 200 percent, while plant proteins decreased it as much as 70 percent.[15] Animal protein also induces atherosclerotic lesions in rabbits, while vegetable protein actually inhibits them.[16] In fact, vegetable protein inhibits lesion development in rabbits even when cholesterol is fed along with it.

> Atherosclerosis was induced in rabbits by feeding large amounts of cholesterol. One group was fed cholesterol in combination with a soy protein diet, while another group was fed the same amount of cholesterol without the soy protein. The soy protein actually inhibited the development of the disease. The aortas of the rabbits fed cholesterol plus soy protein showed fewer signs of atherosclerosis than those of the rabbits fed the same diet without soy protein.[17]

There's an obvious problem, of course, with rabbit studies. Rabbits are vegetarian by nature, unaccustomed to handling animal food. Ideally, these tests would be done on people; but it's hard to get people to volunteer—while they're still alive. For evidence in humans, we have to look at autopsy studies of the deceased.

One such study involved 253 men who had died from various causes. Their bodies were autopsied as part of the New Orleans sample of the International Atherosclerosis Project. Dietary histories were obtained by interviewing women who had shared their households. When atherosclerotic lesion involvement was plotted against nutrient intake as a percentage of total calorie intake, only two dietary components were significantly related to the degree of atherosclerosis: animal protein and total fat. Diets high in total fat were associated with 40 percent more raised coronary lesions than diets low in total fat. Diets high in animal *protein* were associated with *50 percent* more raised lesions—more even than diets high in fat. Conversely, diets high in vegetable protein were associated with 36 percent fewer coronary lesions than diets low in vegetable protein. The study suggested that in people, as in rabbits, the degree of atherosclerosis goes up with the consumption not only of fat but of animal protein, and that it goes down with the consumption of vegetable protein.[18] As we saw in Chapter 16, studies comparing food intake data from some forty countries all confirm this correlation.

How does vegetable protein affect human serum cholesterol levels?

In humans, as in rabbits, serum cholesterol drops when animal protein is replaced with vegetable protein in the diet. This dietary maneuver can reduce serum cholesterol by 20 percent to 40 percent—percentage differences like those seen in vegetarians as compared to meat-eaters.[19] When only dietary protein has been changed from meat to vegetable, up to 20 percent reductions have been reported.[20] And when *both* fat and protein have been changed, up to 40 percent reductions have been reported.

In one study, forty-percent reductions in serum cholesterol were reported when textured soy proteins replaced animal proteins in a weight-reducing diet.[21]

In another study, an Oriental-style vegetarian diet based on soybean protein was fed for six months to six middle-aged prison inmates. It contained no animal protein and virtually no animal fat or cholesterol. All the volunteers seemed healthy, but their blood cholesterol levels were elevated (a frequent finding among middle-aged inmates of that prison). In four weeks, the diet produced an average drop in serum cholesterol from about 295 mg/dl to 172 mg/dl—a difference of 123 mg/dl, or 42 percent. In later experiments, other alterations were made in the diet but it continued to include no animal products. When fat was raised from 15 percent to 45 percent of total calories, and when complex starches were replaced with simple sugars, serum cholesterol increased somewhat. But it still averaged about 193 mg/dl—*more than 100 mg/dl below the men's initial levels.*[22]

A recent series of Italian studies involved nearly 200 patients with elevated serum cholesterol levels. All the patients had followed a low-fat, low-cholesterol diet for at least the previous three months without any appreciable effect on serum cholesterol. Then they were put on a diet in which textured soybean protein replaced all animal protein. The result was an average drop in serum cholesterol of 20 percent. Since changing fats hadn't had this effect, the reduction was attributed to the change in proteins.

The first study involved twenty patients. After only three weeks on the soy protein diet, total serum cholesterol dropped an average of 21 percent. LDL cholesterol also dropped significantly.[23]

The second study involved 41 patients. Again their serum cholesterol dropped an average of 20 percent after only three weeks on the soybean protein diet.[24]

The study was then tried on a larger scale, using 127 outpatients. Their average initial serum cholesterol level was 351 mg/dl. After eight weeks on the soy protein diet, this average dropped by 92.5 mg/dl, or 25.3 percent, in the women and by 78.15 mg/dl, or 23.1 percent, in the men. *Every* patient responded by a drop in serum cholesterol of at least 10 percent, although they hadn't responded to the usual low-fat dietary treatment.[25]

The researchers tested whether these results were due simply to a reduction in dietary cholesterol by adding cholesterol to the soy diet. Cholesterol was added at the rate of 500 mg per day, the average amount in the American diet. No measurable effect was seen, either on the reduction in serum cholesterol during the first three weeks on the soy diet, or the stability of the low levels during the next three weeks.[26]

The researchers also tested the soy diet with and without saturated fat. Adding substantial saturated fat reduced its effectiveness, but only by about half. At least half the diet's cholesterol-lowering effect was due to something else. The researchers attributed it to differences in protein. Other studies have confirmed this possibility.

In a European study, the cholesterol levels of patients with very high initial levels were first lowered by the standard low-fat dietary treatment. Textured soy proteins were then added to this diet. The addition of the soy protein reduced plasma cholesterol 12 percent *below* the level achieved by limiting fats alone.[27]

In a University of Kentucky study, twenty patients with initially high serum cholesterol levels were given a seven-day control diet, followed by a twenty-one-day test diet that was the same in saturated and unsaturated fat, cholesterol, total calories, total protein, and simple and complex carbohydrates, but that included either 115 grams of beans or 100 grams of oat bran. On both test diets, total serum cholesterol dropped 19 percent and LDL cholesterol dropped 24 percent—although dietary cholesterol and saturated fat were unchanged.[28]

Couldn't the cholesterol-lowering effects of these plant foods have been due to their high fiber content?

That could explain the oats, but not the beans. Some types of fiber, including oat bran, lower serum cholesterol, but bean fiber doesn't seem to be one of them.[29]

Researchers at the University Hospital of Geneva, Switzerland, tested the effects of two different soybean seed fiber preparations, without the soybeans. Adding twenty-one grams of these preparations to the diet had no effect on fecal neutral steroids (a form in which cholesterol is excreted); and one of the preparations actually caused a 19 percent *increase* in LDL ("bad") cholesterol. The researchers concluded that the cholesterol-lowering effect of soybeans can't be attributed to their fiber content.[30]

One theory proposed to explain the cholesterol lowering of plant fibers is that they bind with dietary fats and speed their transit time through the intestines. The fats thus escape absorption.[31] But for beans, the theory hasn't been borne out by laboratory studies. To test for the effect, the stools are examined for increased amounts of fecal bile acids and neutral steroids (by which cholesterol is excreted). When either soybean fiber or whole beans have been added to the diet, these fecal components haven't changed.[32]

In the Italian studies, a textured soy product was used that simulated whole soybeans. It was only 52 percent protein and contained added minerals, simple and complex sugars, fiber, and saponins (soap-like plant compounds). Arguably, it was these non-protein components that lowered cholesterol, rather than the soy protein itself. But the Italian researchers observed that in animal and human experiments, when the compounds added to their soy protein product were isolated and fed in equivalent amounts, no significant effects on serum cholesterol resulted.[33]

In most studies, wheat fiber, like soy fiber, has appreciably lowered serum cholesterol when eaten alone.[34] But the entire wheat product, including its protein component, hasn't had this effect.

> The cholesterol-lowering effects of wheat were shown in a study in which twelve healthy omnivorous male students were fed a diet that derived its protein principally from bread. The diet was fed for sixty days and contained 46 grams of protein per day (thirty-five grams from wheat bread and the rest from other plant foods). Mean serum cholesterol fell from 155 to 122 mg/dl, a drop of 21 percent.[35]

> In another study, the experimental diet simulated that of the Yemenite Jews of Israel. They have very low serum cholesterol levels, and their staple food is bread. About half the animal protein in a typical Western-type diet was replaced with vegetable protein in the form of bread. The result was a drop in serum cholesterol of 63 mg/dl, or 25 percent. Adding saturated fat and cholesterol in the form of butter didn't significantly change the results. The drop in serum cholesterol from pre-test levels was still 50 mg/dl, or 22 percent.[36]

> In a third study, bread made from rolled oats replaced bread made from wheat. A reduction in serum cholesterol resulted that was 11 percent greater than with the wheat bread. This effect was attributed to oat fiber, which has a known cholesterol lowering effect.[37]

The fiber in vegetarian diets is also insufficient to explain the lower heart disease incidence of vegetarians. In a study discussed in chapter 16, when deaths from heart diseases were plotted over a 7-year period for over 10,000 people, meat intake showed a definite correlation with heart disease. No correlation was found, however, with fiber intake.[38]

What other plant proteins lower serum cholesterol?

Besides wheat and soy, other plant foods known to lower serum cholesterol include garbanzo beans (chickpeas), and green and yellow vegetables. Like soybeans, other beans and grains reduce serum cholesterol by about 20 percent. The cholesterol-lowering capabilities of green and yellow vegetables are less, but they still reach statistical significance.

In a garbanzo bean study, serum cholesterol was intentionally raised by a diet in which half the calories came from butterfat. Adding garbanzo beans caused a 22 percent drop in serum cholesterol over a 20-week period. This result wasn't due to a corresponding reduction in animal fat or protein, since the beans replaced cereal rather than animal food.[39]

When sucrose was replaced with leafy vegetables in experimental diets, serum cholesterol dropped an average of 10 mg/dl.[40] When sucrose was replaced with a supplement composed of seventeen different vegetables, including leaves, fleshy parts and roots, serum cholesterol dropped more than twice this much.[41] The researchers observed that the effect of the vegetables was synergistic (they worked better together than alone), and that an entire vegetarian diet could have an even greater effect.

Could it be the sterols in plant foods that lower serum cholesterol?

These candidates have also been suggested. Plant sterols (or phytosterols) are what vegetables contain instead of cholesterol, and they're structurally similar to it. They are poorly absorbed, and they interfere with the absorption of cholesterol. The result is a reduction in the amount of cholesterol in the blood.[42]

This reduction has been seen, however, only when plant sterols were fed in amounts greater than the usual dietary intake. Cholesterol absorption has been inhibited by plant sterol intake in the range of 1–15 grams per day, while the usual intake is in the range of only 200–300 mg per day.[43]

Yet plant sterols do lower cholesterol; and it's been suggested that you can have your meat and your arteries, too, by taking plant sterols along with your meat.[44] But if the only way to avoid meat's cholesterol raising effects is to strip it of its own fats, and add to it the fiber and sterols that are natural to plant foods, clearly plant protein—not meat—is what the human digestive system is best adapted to handle. Why not get your protein in its natural packaging—in the form of whole plant foods?

Chapter 20

The Diets of Dogs and Eskimos

"Their diet is saturated with fat, cholesterol and protein. They eat little fiber, few carbohydrates and almost no vitamin C or E. According to nutritional dogma, they should be dropping like flies. But the Eskimos of Western Greenland may be among the healthiest people on earth. They have far less cholesterol in their blood than we do, and suffer one-tenth the heart disease."

—August 1985 *Reader's Digest*[1]

Not all accounts paint such an idyllic picture of the predominantly meat-eating Eskimos. While Eskimos are at low risk for heart attack, they're at high risk for strokes.[2] In Alaskan (as opposed to Greenland) Eskimos, atherosclerotic heart disease is rare mainly because few of them reach middle age. Among those who pass the age of 40, the disease is common.[3] Alaskan Eskimos also have an earlier and greater bone loss than any other people in the world—a problem traced directly to their high meat intake.[4] Their serum cholesterol levels also aren't particularly low.[5]

The more primitive Eskimos of Western Greenland do, however, have low serum cholesterol levels and heart disease rates; and this phenomenon is attributed to the large amounts of fish in their diet. Recent studies show that fish consumption lowers serum cholesterol and is linked to a lower heart disease incidence. The effect isn't as great as you can get from eliminating animal foods altogether, and it involves other risks that are avoided by a vegan diet; but as flesh foods go, fish clearly has the most to recommend it.

Greenland Eskimos are at low risk not only for atherosclerosis but for cancer. Fish may also be responsible for this result. While atherosclerosis and breast cancer are linked epidemiologically to diets high in meat, animal fat and fat

191

in general, the exception seems to be fish fat. Both diseases are *negatively* associated with fish consumption, although fish is high in fat.[6] There is also laboratory evidence that fish may be protective against colorectal cancer. In a study reported in 1988, rats fed fish oil and then injected with a cancer-causing agent developed fewer colorectal tumors than rats fed corn oil.[7]

Unfortunately, this protective effect isn't reflected in epidemiological studies. They show the incidence of stomach and bowel cancer goes *up*, rather than down, with fish consumption.[8] The distinction may be that the fish eaten in industrialized countries, unlike the fish eaten by Greenland Eskimos or the fish oil fed to laboratory rats, contains high levels of. pesticide and toxic chemical residues that are potential carcinogens.[9] Broiling and salting may also be responsible. These methods of preparing fish have been blamed for the particularly high stomach cancer rates of Japanese men.[10]

The arterial health of primitive Eskimos has been attributed not only to what they eat, but to how they eat it. Like carnivorous animals, they consume the entire animal in its fresh, raw, salt-free natural state.[11] Eskimos in more civilized areas, who normally cook and salt their food, have blood pressures and an incidence of coronary heart disease like those seen in Western countries. Only Eskimos in the far North, who eat their meat raw and unsalted, have low blood pressures and relatively few signs of atherosclerosis.[12]

The habit of eating animal foods raw may explain the healthy arteries of another primitive people, the African Masai. These nomadic tribesmen live almost exclusively on raw fermented milk, supplemented occasionally with blood and meat. Yet their serum cholesterol averages only about 135 mg/dl, and autopsy examinations show atherosclerosis and coronary heart disease are rare.[13]

Both pasteurization (which involves cooking) and homogenization have been implicated in the modern epidemic of arteriosclerotic heart disease.[14] This may be why milk is associated with low cholesterol levels in these raw-milk-drinking African natives, while American vegetarians who drink pasteurized, homogenized milk have higher serum cholesterol levels than vegetarians who avoid it.

Could the ability of these primitive people to handle cholesterol be hereditary?

There is some evidence for this theory. In studies in which Eskimos have eaten American-style diets that were lower in saturated fat and cholesterol than their normal fare, serum cholesterol levels have dropped to below the usual American averages.[15] And when young Masai men have been given heavy doses of cholesterol, their serum cholesterol has not changed dramatically.[16] But not all studies have confirmed this theory.[17]

Another possibility is that the active lifestyles of these primitive people keep their arteries healthy, Yet remember, Finnish men, whose lifestyles are also very active, have a higher heart disease incidence than men anywhere else in the world.

A third possibility is that the Eskimos and the Masai are protected by what they eat: raw fish for the Eskimos, raw milk for the Masai. The hard-working Finns, who have a very high incidence of heart disease also consume amounts of milk and other animal foods; but their animal foods are heat-treated.[18]

What studies suggest fish is protective against heart disease?

The landmark study was a Dutch one published in the *New England Journal of Medicine* in May of 1985. It reported that deaths from coronary heart disease over a 20-year period were more than 50 percent less among men who ate at least seven ounces of fish a week than among those who ate none.[19]

Later studies have linked fish consumption to lower serum cholesterol levels, but the results of these studies have been inconsistent. At best, the cholesterol-lowering effect has been less than that achieved by abandoning animal foods altogether.

In a study in which 200 grams (about seven ounces) of mackerel replaced 150 grams of full-fat cheese in the daily diet, serum cholesterol dropped only 7.5 percent—not much compared to the 20–40 percent reductions when animal foods

ıminated.[20] Further, the participants had to eat
ent of a large can of mackerel daily to get those
s hardly surprising that fish had a more favorable
.n cheese. Full-fat cheese contains 15 times as much
sᴀ   :d fat as oily fish like mackerel (and 60 times as
much as lean fish).[21] What is surprising is that serum cholesterol was lowered by only 7.5 percent.

Smaller amounts of fish, on the other hand, seem to have
no effect on serum cholesterol. In a Welsh study in which
the participants ate 100 grams (about 4 ounces) or more of
fatty fish twice a week for three months, no significant
changes in total HDL or LDL cholesterol were observed.
The only significant change in blood lipids was a modest 6.7
percent reduction in triglycerides on the fish diet.[22]

In studies using fish oil supplements, the results have
been somewhat better. In one of these studies, fish oil supplements reduced serum cholesterol by 27 percent in 20
patients with very high initial levels. But to achieve that
result, fish oil had to comprise 20–30 percent of the patients'
total calories.[23] In another study, daily doses of fish oil concentrate reduced triglycerides by 37 percent, but serum
cholesterol dropped only 5 percent and that result took two
years to produce.[24]

The inconclusive results of these studies haven't deterred
advertisers from capitalizing on them to boost sales of fish
oil capsules, which grossed about $50 million in 1987. At a
conference at the Massachusetts Institute of Technology the
same year, however, researchers warned that the barrage
of advertising for fish oil capsules is essentially without scientific evidence. Unless consumption of other fatty foods is
curbed, no significant benefits should be expected.[25] If fish
oil is good for the heart, it isn't because it lowers serum
cholesterol.

*What risks are associated with fish consumption that
are eliminated by a vegan diet?*

One is the risk of bone loss, which we looked at in Chapter 11. Another is the risk of cancer from the pesticide and
toxic chemical residues that are particularly high in fish.
Cataracts have also been linked to high seafood intakes.

The culprit seems to be methylmercury, an industrial contaminant found in high levels in seafood.[26]

An additional problem is the flipside of the cholesterol-lowering effect fish is touted for. Fish has a high content of a highly polyunsaturated omega-3 fatty acid called eicosapentaenoic acid. It lowers serum cholesterol by thinning the blood—reducing the tendency of blood platelets to aggregate, or clump together.[27] The factor is adaptive for fish because it keeps their blood from thickening in cold water. But thinner blood means longer bleeding times. Eskimos, who consume large amounts of fish, tend to bleed excessively from wounds and have frequent nosebleeds.[28]

In one study, the bleeding times of Eskimos were nearly twice as long as those of Danes matched for age and sex.[29]

In another study, the only change made in the diets of 107 people with elevated serum cholesterol levels was to give them fish oil supplements. Their bleeding times approximately doubled.[30]

In a third study, called "heroic and foolhardy" by the reporters, a 70-year-old Oxford professor experimented on himself by eating an Eskimo-like diet consisting only of marine animals (seal, fish, crustaceans, and mollusks) for 100 days. His bleeding time rose from 3–4 minutes at the beginning of the study to 50 minutes at the end of it. Nosebleeds and spontaneous bleeding were frequent, and he became quite anemic. These symptoms disappeared after a normal diet was resumed.[31]

The thinner blood of Eskimos may also be responsible for their greater risk of stroke. Because their blood clots less, they bleed more; and cerebral hemorrhage, or bleeding, is the cause of some strokes. The anti-clotting factor in fish oil can also be dangerous for people who are losing blood from accidents or surgery.

In addition, some fish oil capsules can cause vitamin E deficiency, and can produce vitamin A and vitamin D toxicity at high doses.[32]

For people whose cholesterol levels are dangerously high from a lifetime of meat consumption, these risks may be worth taking. The best alternative for normal people, however, is a diet that prevents the problem, rather than treats the symptom.

How can you prevent the problem?

Blood platelet stickiness and clumping come from eating animal fat and animal protein. When these components have been eliminated from the diets of patients with elevated serum cholesterol levels, not only has platelet stickiness been reduced, but serum cholesterol has dropped a full 25 percent.[33]

A 1986 report in the *British Journal of Nutrition* noted that lack of blood fluidity ("sticky blood") characterizes all the known cardiovascular risk factors—high blood pressure, high serum cholesterol, smoking, obesity, lack of exercise, and stress. Conversely, blood fluidity is better than normal in people with reduced risk. These people include young females, sportsmen, and slightly anemic people. (The inference arises that the low iron levels reported in some vegetarians are actually protective against heart disease.) The researchers tested 48 vegetarians and found that they also had better than normal blood viscosity, putting them in the low-risk category for heart disease.[34]

If fish protects the arteries of Eskimos, what protects those of the Masai?

Possibly some factor in raw milk. The most likely milk factor is calcium. Studies show calcium not only lowers serum cholesterol and blood pressure levels, but inhibits the development of plaque in the arteries.[35]

A word of caution, however, if you drink vitamin-D-fortified milk *and* take vitamin supplements. When animals are given a calcium-rich diet that includes a substantial excess of vitamin D, they're *more* likely to develop atherosclerosis. Because of the unusual toxicity of vitamin D, the Food and Nutrition Board has advised against its intake in excess of the recommended daily allowance of 400 international units. This is *both* the normal dosage in vitamin capsules, and the amount added to each quart of vitamin-D-fortified milk. That means people who use both are getting excess vitamin D.[36]

Aside from its calcium content, whether milk itself lowers or raises serum cholesterol remains unsettled. The studies go both ways. (See chapter 21.) The form of the milk may be the critical variable. The milk in the Masai diet is not pasteurized or homogenized. It's also usually fermented. This process improves its digestibility and may discourage the growth of harmful bacteria.[37]

What evidence links resistance to heart disease to the habit of eating animal foods raw?

An association between cooked animal foods and chronic disease was demonstrated in a classic experiment involving 900 cats. The experiment grew out of the observation that laboratory cats who were fed cooked-meat leftovers from an institutional kitchen were poor operative risks, while those fed raw-meat scraps were not.

The study lasted ten years. One group of cats was fed a diet of two-thirds raw meat, one-third raw milk, and cod-liver oil. The second group was fed the same diet, except the meat was cooked.

The cats eating the raw meat reproduced normally and had good resistance to infections and parasites. Their organic development was complete and they functioned normally.

The cats eating cooked meat, on the other hand, developed a number of diseases familiar in human medicine—including cardiac lesions (damaged heart tissue), arthritis, loss of teeth and bones, nephritis (kidney disease), cirrhosis of the liver, and degeneration of the brain and spinal cord. Spontaneous abortion was common, running as high as 70 percent in the second generation. Deliveries were difficult, and many cats died in labor. Mortality rates of the kittens were high. This was frequently due to the failure of the mother to produce milk. Intestinal parasites abounded. Skin lesions and allergies were frequent and became progressively worse from one generation to the next. Pneumonia and empyema (pus in the lung cavity) were among the principal causes of death among the adult cats. By the third generation, the entire strain had died out.

In a follow-up experiment, the meat was raw but the *milk* was cooked or otherwise treated. Again, the cats fed raw milk grew and reproduced normally, but those fed pasteur-

ized or metabolized vitamin D milk developed bone disturbances. The mothers showed lessened reproductive efficiency,
and the kittens showed developmental deficiencies. Cats fed
evaporated milk showed even more damage. The most
marked deficiencies occurred in the cats fed sweetened
condensed milk.[38]

These detrimental effects have been attributed to the de-
naturing of animal proteins by cooking, which impairs their
digestibility; and to the destruction of necessary enzymes,
vitamins, and minerals.[39]

Domestic cats do not become diseased as readily as in this
experiment, probably because the vitamins and minerals
lost in cooking are added back into commercial cat food.
But pet cats, like people, are subject to chronic disease. A
common one among cats is leukemia, or cancer of the blood.
It occurs in domestic animals and birds, but is virtually
non-existent in wild animals. It can be viral, but susceptibility to infection itself appears to be diet related. Animals
eating their natural diets in their native habitats are highly
resistant to infection.[40]

What if I limit my meat intake to sushi and beef tartare?

That alternative might preserve your arteries, but there
would still be the problems of bone loss, and an increased
exposure to toxic chemical residues and bacteria.

You run the risk of ingesting beef tapeworms with your
beef tartare, or of contracting toxoplasmosis, a disease causing birth defects and blindness in newborns. You may in-
gest fish tapeworms with your sushi, or contract infectious
hepatitis or paralytic shellfish poisoning.[41] As noted in Chapter 7, dogs and other carnivores are less susceptible than we
are to infection from raw meat because their intestinal tracts
are shorter and their enzymes are stronger bactericidals.
Raw milk is so likely to contain harmful bacteria that in
most states its sale is illegal, so you couldn't get it if you
wanted to.[42]

Obviously, these risks go up as your fish intake goes up. If
you're eating fish to lower serum cholesterol, you don't
need to make a steady diet of it. Studies show 2 to 3 serv-
ings a week are enough. Generally, the darker the flesh,

the more oil. The oiliest fish are salmon, mackerel, herring, sardines, sablefish, lake trout, fresh tuna, whitefish, and anchovies. Moderately oily fish include halibut, bluefish, rockfish, rainbow and sea trout, ocean perch, bass, hake, pollock, smelt, and mullet. You're better off with these than with fish oil capsules. The capsules are so concentrated that they can produce side effects, and they lack the protein and minerals found in whole fish.[43]

Section V

MEETING YOUR RDAS WITH THE FRUITS OF THE EARTH

Chapter 21

Milk: Studies Find Flaws
in the Perfect Food

"Cow's milk is for the calf."
—Gandhi

If we cut out meat, what are we going to replace it with? Many vegetarians turn to milk, which is not only a good source of protein, but is also the easiest way to get calcium. This is especially true for children, who aren't keen on greens and will eat tofu only if it's well disguised.

Yet whether or not milk is "nature's most perfect food"—particularly in the quantities recommended in this country—is hotly debated. Heavy milk consumption has been linked to breast cancer, heart disease, allergies, arthritis, and multiple sclerosis. In children, it's linked to sudden infant death syndrome, kidney disease, hyperparathyroidism, and insomnia, along with other complaints we'll look at in chapter 24. It's also the leading cause of allergies among children.[1] In fact, milk may be *perfect* only for calves.

If milk is our first food, why would it be the leading cause of allergies?

Cow's milk is much different from human milk. Its use as a substitute for breast milk is a recent social innovation that apparently dates back only several hundred years. Cow's milk contains more than twenty proteins, and some of them are not found in human milk; so our bodies may treat them as foreign. The result is allergy, an immunological reaction in which antibodies are formed to dispose of foreign substances (called antigens).

Milk antibodies can be detected in most healthy babies

and in many apparently healthy adults. Overt evidence of milk allergy is seen in 5–10 percent of white adults, about 70 percent of black adults, about 90 percent of full-blooded American Indians, and a large number of Oriental adults.

For some people, milk intolerance is due to a congenital shortage of lactase, the enzyme that digests milk sugar (lactose). But for most people who can't tolerate milk, the symptoms are caused by its proteins.[2]

In one study, 27 normal babies were fed cow's milk in various forms. Detectable antibodies to cow's milk protein were demonstrated in all of them, although none had previously been suspected of having cow's milk protein allergy.[3]

When beta-lactoglobulin—the protein most frequently responsible for milk sensitivity—is denatured by pasteurization or cooking, it becomes 100 times more allergenic than in its original state. Apparently it reacts with lactose to produce a molecule that can't be broken down further into its amino-acid building blocks. This large molecule is treated by the body as foreign and is attacked.[4]

The signs of milk allergy are indigestion and diarrhea, but you may be allergic to milk without knowing it. Amorphous symptoms like headaches, gas, and depression have also been pinned on this culprit; and even heart disease has been linked to it.[5]

How strong is the correlation between milk consumption and heart disease?

Some studies suggest it's stronger than that with saturated fat and cholesterol.[6]

In a study of 43 countries, a direct link was established between the quantity of milk consumed and the incidence of arteriosclerotic heart disease, while correlations with other dietary components were less consistent. The highest heart disease incidence was found in Finland, which also had the highest per capita consumption of milk products.[7]

A 24-country study produced similar results.[8]

In Switzerland between 1951 and 1976, heart disease mysteriously declined, although animal fat consumption rose by 20 percent. The only direct correlation established for the decline was a 46 percent drop in milk consumption.[9]

Polynesian societies exhibit little evidence of arteriosclerosis, although they have high intakes of saturated fat. The distinction may be that most of their saturated fat comes from plants, mainly coconuts and coconut oil. They do not consume dairy products.[10]

The real villain may not be milk in its fresh, raw state, but the heat treatments we subject it to. Certain primitive peoples consume great quantities of milk and remain free of arteriosclerotic heart disease. These peoples include the African Masai, the rural Zulu, the Samburu, the nomads of Nigeria and Somaliland, the West Africans of Gabon, and the Congolese Pygmies.[11] The milk they drink differs from ours in that it's preserved by fermentation. It's not treated by pasteurization or by homogenization (the even dispersement of fat through the milk).

What evidence links heart disease to pasteurization?

Heat treatment of milk has been implicated in certain epidemiological studies of heart disease.

In the United Kingdom and in Oslo, Norway, at different times in different regions, a sudden steep rise in coronary heart disease was seen within two years of the introduction of Holder pasteurized milk. Holder pasteurization involves heating for a period of thirty minutes at not less than 145 degrees Fahrenheit.

In the United States, the consumption of milk products that were extensively heated—such as evaporated milk and ice cream—doubled from 1931 to 1945; and the consumption of cheese that was pasteurized, processed, or cooked came close to doubling. Heart disease deaths increased twelvefold during the same period.

Meanwhile, populations that consumed either no milk protein (including the Yemenites, the South Vietnamese, the Atiu Mitiaro, and the Hunja) or only fresh, unheated milk (including the Masai and other primitive African tribes) were all free of arteriosclerotic heart disease. But East Indians and Trappist monks, two vegetarian groups who took their milk pasteurized or boiled, were only partly protected by their diets.[12]

Isn't raw milk unsafe?

The FDA thinks so, because it recently banned its interstate sale of raw milk.[13] Certain outbreaks of food poisoning have been traced to it, but certified raw milk producers contend that more can be traced to pasteurized milk.[14]

There is some evidence that infections from raw milk are limited to people who aren't used to it. Dairy farmers frequently drink raw milk without becoming ill. It seems habitual raw-milk drinkers build up an immunity to its microbes and are less susceptible to milk-borne infection.

Among 48 people who had drunk raw milk from an Oregon farm, 76 percent of first time raw-milk drinkers developed an acute gastrointestinal illness. Among 10 others who habitually drank raw milk, none developed the illness; and elevated levels of antibodies to the infecting organisms were found in their blood.[15]

One researcher suggests heart disease is linked to a blue-green bacteria carried in milk. (The bacteria hasn't actually been detected there, but circumstantial evidence suggests the possibility.) These bacteria thrive in hot temperatures and can survive a certain amount of pasteurization. They can't, however, survive in an acid medium. This may explain the absence of heart disease in cultures consuming their milk in fermented forms such as yogurt, buttermilk, and certain cheeses.[16] If this theory proves correct, more stringent pasteurization is warranted.

Even if raw milk were the answer, for many people it's not a practical one because the sale of raw milk is banned in more than half the states.[17]

How does milk affect serum cholesterol?

That question has been extensively researched, but it hasn't been definitively answered. In animals, milk seems to lower serum cholesterol. But human infants fed cow's milk have higher cholesterol levels than those receiving formulas made up of polyunsaturated fats. And in adult humans, the studies go both ways.[18]

If milk doesn't significantly affect serum cholesterol, why would it be linked to heart disease?

There are several alternative hypotheses. Besides the infection theory we just looked at, there are the allergy theory and the homogenization theory.

The allergy theory is based on well-documented evidence that antigen-antibody complexes can promote the deposit of platelets that cause thrombosis. Thrombosis is the obstruction of blood vessels and arteries. It seems that unusually high numbers of milk antibodies are found in the blood of heart disease patients. Milk antibodies are also commonly seen in people with different digestive disorders, including ulcerative colitis, Crohn's disease, and celiac disease. In heart attack cases, these milk antibodies don't result from the heart attack itself because they've been detected before it happens. Researchers postulate that circulating antibodies are built up over many years to counteract circulating milk protein antigens, and that vascular damage results from antigen-antibody complexes that contribute to the deposit of fatty substances in the arteries. The evidence in support of the theory, however, is inconclusive.[19]

The homogenization theory has been proposed by researchers at Fairfield University in Connecticut, who found that homogenization causes an enzyme to enter the bloodstream and damage the arteries. This enzyme—xanthine oxidase—is present in all milk. When milk is drunk raw, the enzyme is digested and passes through the system without harm. But when milk is homogenized, the enzyme is protected from digestion by tiny droplets of fat that surround it,

and it gets carried into the bloodstream. Here, the fat droplets are broken down and the enzyme is freed, producing a
chemical that damages the arteries. Plaque then builds up
where the arteries have been injured, contributing to
atherosclerosis.[20]

*If these theories are correct, why are milk-drinking
vegetarians less susceptible to heart disease than meat-
eaters are?*

Good question. No one theory seems to cover all the
evidence. Arguably, vascular damage has many causes, including xanthine oxidase, milk proteins, meat proteins, fats,
and wandering calcium salts. Meat-eaters are exposed to
more of these suspect substances. Meat-eaters eat meat *and*
drink milk. They also have substantially higher intakes of
saturated fat and cholesterol than milk-drinking vegetarians. The lowest serum cholesterol and blood pressure levels
are seen in vegans, who avoid *both* milk and meat.[21]

How is milk associated with arthritis?

Arthritis is a painful inflammation of the joints that comes
with bone degeneration. Normally, smooth movement of the
joints is aided by a lubricating fluid called synovial fluid, as
well as by cartilage which faces the bone surfaces and
makes the points of contact more pliable. In arthritis, the
synovial fluid is altered, the cartilage deteriorates, and bone
is deposited where the surfaces make contact.[22]

The most common form of arthritis is osteoarthritis. It hits
after about age 45 and is associated with normal wear and
tear on the joints. It may, however, also have a dietary
element. It occurs less frequently in developing than developed populations.[23] It involves an accumulation of extra-
skeletal calcium deposits.

Gout, or gouty arthritis, is a form of arthritis having a
definite dietary component. It's linked to the high purine
content of a high-meat diet.[24]

But the form of arthritis associated in some patients specifically with milk consumption is rheumatoid arthritis. Osteoarthritis and gout develop with age and are "use-and-abuse" diseases. Rheumatoid arthritis strikes earlier and has different origins. It's also the most intractable and crippling form of the disease.

Rheumatoid arthritis involves an immune response that turns against the body. Damaging effects in the joints are apparently caused by a powerful chemical released by the white cells when they attack the invaders.[25] Susceptibility to the disease seems to be genetic, but diet can trigger the condition in the predisposed. A recent study by British arthritis specialists linked it to the common food allergens, and milk topped the list.[26] In case studies, milk challenges have significantly exacerbated the symptoms of rheumatoid arthritis, and the exclusion of milk products has produced significant improvement.[27] Dietary fat has also been implicated. In one study, complete remission was produced in six rheumatoid arthritis patients by removing fats of every sort from their diets.[28]

Epidemiological studies also suggest a dietary element. In non-dairy cultures, the incidence of rheumatoid arthritis is unusually low. In China, its prevalence is less than one-third that in the United States.[29] In a study of 1,183 essentially-vegan South African Bantu, not a single active case was found. Again, heredity won't explain this, because among South African blacks eating Westernized diets, the disease is as common as in whites.[30]

Collin Dong is a physician of Chinese extraction who developed rheumatoid arthritis soon after graduating from Stanford Medical School, where he ate the standard American diet. He cured himself by returning to the Oriental diet of his childhood, which contained no milk products, fruit, or meat except fish. He reports that thousands of patients have also gained relief by this means.[31]

Other forms of rheumatoid arthritis seem to be infectious. One suspect is a milk-borne bacteria, which was found to be four times as prevalent in rheumatoid arthritis victims as in controls. These bacteria could survive pasteurization, but not acidity—another argument in favor of yogurt.[32]

Milk has also been incriminated in laboratory studies with animals. Rheumatoid-like synovial lesions have developed in rabbits when they were fed cow's milk.[33]

How is milk linked to multiple sclerosis?

Multiple sclerosis is a chronic, slowly progressive disease of the central nervous system. It affects the myelin sheath, which serves as an electrical insulator for the nerves of the brain and spinal cord. Its symptoms include palsy, numbness of the face and limbs, weakness, and visual disturbances.

Epidemiologically, multiple sclerosis is correlated with milk consumption. In non-dairy populations, the disease is rare. It is more common in women, and its onset is after adolescence. This is the time when the heavy milk intake of childhood is normally curtailed, especially among silhouette-conscious teenage girls.

One specialist proposes that the disease results from a dependency developed in childhood on the high calcium content of milk. When this calcium intake dwindles in adolescence, serum calcium drops, and the myelin sheath is unable to form properly around the nerves.[34]

Cow's milk contains four times as much calcium as human milk, and the proportion of calcium in the bodies of infants fed cow's milk can be 50 percent higher than in those nursed on human milk.[35] If calcium intake suddenly drops, calcium balance must be restored by the parathyroids. In non-dairy societies, the parathyroids step in to perform this task immediately after weaning. But in dairy societies, calcium intake remains high until adolescence.

Body growth and milk consumption are at their highest levels in infancy, and so is myelinization (the process by which myelin is laid down around the nerves). During adolescence, growth shoots up again, and myelinization shoots up with it—but milk consumption falls off. The high cow's milk intake of childhood may cause a dependency in some children, which leaves their parathyroids underdeveloped. When this calcium intake is curtailed, serum calcium fails to reach adequate levels, adversely affecting myelinization.[36]

The calcium-dependency theory could also explain why Americans, whose calcium intakes are among the highest in the world, also seem to have the highest calcium requirements. Why can't we get by on 300 mg a day like the Bantu? Could it be that our heavy milk consumption from infancy has made us dependent on a high calcium intake? To quote Dr. D. M. Hegsted of Harvard's Department of Nutrition:

"[P]erhaps when high levels of calcium are fed over long periods the 'calcium retaining mechanisms,' whatever these may be, might have little work to do and become atrophied. . . . It is well substantiated that negative calcium balances are common in old age. The traditional view is that we should load up so that we will be well prepared when this time comes. It is possible that this logic is completely false."[37]

Other studies show people who were not breastfed have a higher risk of developing multiple sclerosis later in life. Breast milk contains 5 times as much linoleic acid as cow's milk. Linoleic acid is the building block for nervous tissue. It's an essential fatty acid that must be obtained from food. Apparently babies deficient in linoleic acid develop a weaker nervous system—one that is more likely to break down later.[38]

Other studies associate multiple sclerosis with a diet high in animal fats. A doctor at the University of Oregon found that patients with multiple sclerosis who were given a diet low in animal and total fat early in their disease had a 95 percent chance of getting better or at least getting no worse over the next 20 years.[39]

If I give up milk, where will I get enough calcium?

We'll look at alternative sources of calcium and other minerals in the next chapter. You don't, however, need to give up milk. Moderation is the key.

A single cup of milk supplies about 300 mg of calcium. As we'll see shortly, that's more than half your daily requirement—*if* you're on a low-protein diet. A little on your cereal in the morning, an occasional yogurt, a bit of cheese to flavor your vegetarian casserole is fine. Any remaining calcium requirement is met easily with plant foods. If you're allergic to milk, plant sources can meet the whole requirement—as they do in many cultures without apparent detriment to the bones.

Chapter 22

Minerals: You Don't Have to Choose Between Anemia and Cardiac Arrest

"One may reach the conclusion upon theoretical grounds that the amount of a nutrient required to maintain balance in a 'normal adult' is that amount which his traditional diet supplies. . . . Our estimated requirement of calcium of around 0.7 gm per day simply reflects the dietary habit of the population upon which the studies were done. Had we worked in areas where milk and other calcium containing foods were less common, we would have arrived at estimates of perhaps half as high."

—D. M. Hegsted, M.D.
Harvard University[1]

We've seen that you can get enough protein without animal products, but can you get enough iron without meat, or enough calcium without milk?

You can. In fact, analyses of the diets of modern-day vegans show that they get between 50 percent and 100 percent *more* iron than the average person who eats meat and eggs. The calcium intakes of vegans, if no better than your average milk-drinkers', are also no worse. Various studies report vegan iron intakes ranging from 16 to 27 mg a day, and calcium intakes ranging from about 500 to 1,000 mg a day.[2] The average American iron intake, by contrast, is only 11 mg for women and 17 mg for men. The average calcium intake is only about 500 mg for women and 850 mg for men.[3]

Despite these statistics, nutritional authorities still wag a warning finger at vegans. They point out that it's not the amount of minerals taken in, but the amount absorbed that counts—and mineral absorption is better from animal foods. The minerals in vegetables and grains come packaged along

with fiber and phytate (or phytic acid, an organic phosphorus compound found in all cereals, many legumes and nuts,
and a few fruits, tubers and roots). Fiber and phytate bind
with minerals, so they're less readily absorbed in the
intestines.[4]

*But fiber is essential to the diet. How can something so
good be so bad?*

Good question. The problem may be in the design of the
studies, which have either been short-term, or involved
more fiber and phytate than is normally found in the diet.[5]
When reasonable amounts of fiber have been tested, trace
element balance has not been affected.[6] In studies of long-
term vegetarians accustomed to high-fiber diets, the proph-
esied mineral deficiencies haven't been found.[7]

The problem is illustrated in certain studies of oatmeal,
is high in fiber and phytate. Studies showed a diet composed primarily of it leads to serious calcium loss in man.
Based on these studies, English researchers declared oatmeal unfit for human consumption. These findings nearly
precipitated a civil war among the Scots, for whom oatmeal is a staple food. The hearty physiques of the Scots
attest that oats are a healthful grain for people accustomed
to it.[8]

The diets of rural South African blacks are similarly unhealthy in theory, because they're also very high in fiber
and phytic acid. Yet studies comparing South Africans on
very high and very low intakes of these components reveal
no differences in mean hematological (blood) values, serum
calcium levels, bone thicknesses, or growth rates.[9]

A USDA study reported in 1988 compared the mineral intakes and balances of Asian Indian and American vegetarians and non-vegetarians in the Washington D.C. area. The
fiber intake of the vegetarians was 50–100 percent greater
than for the non-vegetarians. However, it was within the
range shown not to affect mineral balance in other studies
(under 25 grams of neutral detergent fiber per day). And in

fact it didn't affect mineral balances in this study, since calcium, iron, zinc, and copper balances weren't significantly different among the groups.[10]

Note that animal foods, too, contain components that can inhibit mineral absorption. These are their large animal proteins. Meat proteins reduce the absorption of copper, and cow's milk protein reduces the absorption of zinc.[11]

A critical variable in mineral-absorption studies seems to be adaptation. The mineral balance of vegetarians depends on the capacity of their intestinal microflora to digest the substantial amounts of phytate and fiber in their diets. This capacity improves over time. Phytate is destroyed in the gut by an enzyme called phytase, and gut enzymes change only gradually in response to changes in diet.[12]

That adaptation is a slow process was shown in calcium balance studies using Norwegian prisoners. In most of these men, a positive calcium balance was eventually achieved on a low-calcium diet. But in some of them, it took as long as nine months—longer than most balance studies.[13]

The adaptation factor is a good argument for starting children young on a plant-based diet. A 1987 study found that while long-term vegetarians have normal iron levels, "new" vegetarians can be low in this mineral.[14]

On the other hand, low iron levels may not be all bad. A 1986 study found that slightly anemic people are at *lower* than average risk for heart disease.[15] And a study reported in the *New England Journal of Medicine* in 1988 showed that people with unusually high iron levels are at higher than average risk for cancer.[16]

Once adapted to a higher-fiber diet, vegetarians seem to absorb minerals better than meat-eaters when both are fed the same foods. This was demonstrated in a University of Nebraska study that tested the bioavailability of zinc. When the same diet was fed to vegetarians and to meat-eaters, zinc balances were notably better for the vegetarians.[17]

The protein factor

We've already seen that vegetarians retain calcium better than meat-eaters. Adaptation may be a factor; but a more important one seems to be the low protein intakes of vegetarians.

Protein has also been shown to affect the requirements for other minerals. As protein intake goes up, so do mineral requirements. This phenomenon was demonstrated in a 1981 study funded by the USDA. Men were fed diets for 28–30 day intervals providing protein at two levels of daily intake— 40 grams and 100 grams. The lower intake approximated the RDA for women, while the higher intake approximated the American national average for protein intake.[18] Mineral requirements at these two protein levels were:

	100-gm/protein	_40-gm/protein_
Calcium	940 mg	560 mg
Zinc	12.2 mg	5.2 mg
Iron	16 mg	13.5 mg
Copper	1.2 mg	1.0 mg
Magnesium	330 mg	210 mg

The study showed that reducing protein intake by 60 percent reduces calcium requirements by more than a third. It also reduces zinc requirements by more than half, and reduces iron requirements by a sixth.[19]

This variable helps explain the low incidence of osteoporosis among vegans, despite calcium intakes that are inadequate as measured by the RDA. It also throws light on the variability in mineral requirements found by different authorities.

The United States RDA for calcium is 800 mg for adults. Some authorities contend that even this figure is too low. The FAO/WHO Committee on Calcium Requirements, on the other hand, suggests 400–500 mg per day is the actual requirement. Who is right? The diets of meat-eating, milk-drinking women in this country just barely meet the lower FAO/WHO recommendation, and their bone loss rate is high. So for them, the FAO/WHO guidelines are probably too low. Yet women in less developed countries, who have *lower* calcium intakes, also have lower rates of bone loss; so for them, the United States RDA is too high.[20]

Something besides calcium intake obviously enters into the equation. This elusive variable seems to be protein intake. In the USDA study, when protein intake dropped from 100 grams to 40 grams, the calcium requirement also dropped by 40 percent (from 940 mg to 560 mg). On the average American 100-gram/protein diet, the 800 mg U.S. RDA *is* too low. But on a 40-gram/protein diet, even the lower 500-mg FAO/WHO recommendation is sufficient. This was recognized by the Committee that set the United States RDAs:

> "[P]ersons consuming less than the customary United States intake of protein and phosphorus will remain in calcium balance with intakes considerably below the allowance recommended."[21]

How can you get enough calcium without milk?

While milk is considered the ideal calcium source in this country, it's actually an insignificant part of the diet of most of the human race. Readily available fresh milk is a product of technological civilization, and of refrigeration. For people who are either less technologically advanced or less affluent than we are, calcium is provided by vegetables (including roots, tubers, seeds, and the greens of root vegetables such as turnips, beets, and carrots); and by soymilk and its solid counterpart, tofu.

Calcium is absorbed as efficiently from green leaves, soymilk, and tofu as it is from cow's milk. Calcium from these sources is adequate for proper skeletal development. This is true not only for Third World, essentially-vegan populations, but for vegans in industrialized countries. There is no evidence of impaired bone growth or tooth development from lack of calcium, in vegans of either type.[22]

Don't you need meat for iron and zinc?

These are the two minerals for which meat is considered essential, but significant amounts of iron are also found in legumes, green leafy vegetables, whole grains, some nuts and dried fruits; and significant amounts of zinc are found in legumes, nuts, miso, and tofu.[23] Hematological studies demonstrate normal hemoglobin values and serum zinc levels in vegetarians, so their intakes of both minerals are sufficient. This is true although they not only don't eat meat, but do eat large amounts of mineral-binding phytate and fiber.[24]

A 1986 study of vegetarians in Israel found their blood levels of iron and zinc were normal, although their diets included twice as much fiber as a matched meat-eating control group. This was also true for the other minerals studied, calcium, phosphorus, and magnesium.[25]

A 1981 study of 56 middle-aged vegetarian women in Canada reported their blood levels of iron and zinc were actually *higher* than those of meat-eating women.[26] Their serum iron and zinc levels were also higher than in comparably-aged meat-eating women in this country.[27] Interestingly, the use of mineral supplements had no effect on the vegetarians' blood mineral levels. Few of them even took supplements, and those who did had no higher blood mineral levels than those who didn't.

An American study reported in 1988 compared the iron status of women who ate (1) red meat, (2) poultry and fish but no red meat, and (3) milk and eggs, but no flesh foods. The red-meat-eaters had better iron status than the vegetarians, but all groups were within normal limits. And *the vegetarians had better iron status than the women who ate chicken and fish.* The researchers weren't sure why, but they suggested the fish oils eaten by the latter group increased their bleeding tendency and thus their iron loss.[28]

Other studies show hemoglobin levels are normal not only in lacto-ovo-vegetarians but in vegans, whose iron comes entirely from plant foods.[29]

Wouldn't I get more minerals from a vegetarian diet that included milk and eggs than from one that didn't?

It depends on the mineral. Milk-drinking vegetarians get more calcium than both vegans and meat-eaters, but vegans don't need as much calcium because their protein intakes are lower. Vegans get more iron than both milk-drinking vegetarians and meat-eaters.[30] Milk is a very poor source of iron, and eggs provide it in a form that is not only poorly absorbed, but that impairs iron absorption from other foods.[31]

The calcium intakes of milk-drinking vegetarians average about 1,500 mg/day. Vegans average only 600–700 mg.[32] But their intake is still normal—even for this country, where calcium intakes are higher than elsewhere. According to the United States Department of Health and Human Services, the American calcium intake averages only 495 mg for women and 846 mg for men.[33]

If calcium is the long suit of lacto-ovo-vegetarians, it's iron for vegans. Various studies report vegan iron intakes ranging from 19 to 27 mg/day.[34] The average intake of lacto-ovo-vegetarians, by contrast, is only about 15 mg/day.[35] The average for meat-eaters is only about 11 mg/day for women and 17 mg for men.[36]

Considering their high fiber intakes and the absence of meat from their diets, the iron status of long-term vegetarians is much better than expected. Several factors are credited for this phenomenon, including their adaptation to a high-fiber diet, their relatively low protein intakes, and their relatively high vitamin C intakes.[37]

What does vitamin C have to do with iron status?

Vitamin C enhances iron absorption. It does this by forming a chelate, or chemically-bonded compound, that helps carry the iron across the lining of the intestines. Unchelated iron tends either to react with other substances in the intestinal tract forming an insoluble compound that can't be used, or to attach itself to the intestinal lining.[38]

The RDA for iron for premenopausal women is 18 mg. But the amount they need to *absorb* is only 1.5 mg/day. The

18-mg RDA is based on an average absorption rate of only 10 percent, with an additional 3 mg thrown in for good measure. For men, who don't have the problem of monthly iron loss, the respective figures are 10 mg and 1.0 mg.[39]

The most readily-available iron source is "heme" iron—that derived from animal blood. Heme iron is 23 percent absorbed. But it constitutes only about 40 percent of the total iron even in meat, fowl and fish—and only about 10–15 percent of the total iron intake even of meat-eaters.[40] Most dietary iron, for vegetarians and non-vegetarians alike, comes from less readily-available "nonheme" sources. If vegetarians absorb this non-heme iron better than meat-eaters, the balance can be tipped in their favor.

The percentage absorption of nonheme iron from a single food can vary by a factor of *twenty*, depending on the presence of certain other components in the meal. Its absorption is enhanced by meat, citric acid, and ascorbic acid (vitamin C); and inhibited by phosphorus compounds (phytic acid and phosphate additives), caffeine, tannic acid, and oxalic acid (found in chocolate, rhubarb and spinach).[41]

In one study, a high fiber intake from fruits and vegetables had no inhibitory effect on iron absorption. Researchers postulated the high dietary content of ascorbic and citric acid offset any inhibitory effect of fiber.[42]

In another study, a maximal fiber intake resulted in a two-fold difference in iron absorption; but this difference was modest compared to the three- to five-fold changes produced by ascorbic acid, meat and tea consumed in normal amounts.[43]

In the past, nutritionists emphasized the importance of meat to enhance nonheme iron absorption, but recent studies show iron absorption can be equally good from a vegetarian meal, in which vitamin C substitutes for meat as an iron enhancer. When a vegetarian meal is supplemented with a fresh vegetable salad containing vitamin C, the nonheme iron absorption rate doubles. When the meal includes cauliflower (which is particularly high in vitamin C), it triples. Adding cauliflower actually increases iron absorption more than adding meat. Sauerkraut and borscht soup are other good iron enhancers.[44] Soybeans contain a substance that inhibits iron absorption, but in a study in which vitamin C was added to a soy-based meal, its nonheme iron absorption rate was 21 percent—equivalent to the heme iron in meat.[45]

That means it's best to eat a salad or vegetable containing vitamin C along with your beans, grains, and greens, and to refrain from chasing them down with coffee or tea. (Coffee lovers, take heart: Coffee drunk an hour before the meal won't affect iron absorption.[46])

Megadoses of vitamin C, however, aren't necessary. The amount in ordinary vegetables and fruits will do. In fact, taking heavy doses of vitamin C with your iron foods can be harmful, since they can lead to iron overload.[47]

What about zinc?

Deficiencies in zinc intake have been reported for vegetarians at lower caloric intakes,[48] yet their *serum* zinc levels remain normal.[49] This may be because the theoretical deficiencies are based on the 15-mg American RDA, which many authorities consider too high. The Canadian recommendation is only 9 mg/day; and this is easily met by the diets of vegetarians and vegans, even at lower caloric levels.[50] The lower recommendation should be sufficient particularly where protein intake is low, as it is among essential-vegans. In the USDA study discussed earlier, a mere 5.2 mg satisfied zinc requirements on a low-protein diet.[51]

A recent study found no evidence of zinc deficiency in Bengalese men although their daily zinc intake was less than 6 mg, far below the 15-mg U.S. RDA. The Indian researchers noted the diets of many populations are low in this mineral, yet the *symptoms* of zinc deficiency are absent.[52] The explanation may again be that their protein intakes are equally low, reducing mineral requirements proportionately.

Even during pregnancy, when zinc requirements are particularly high, a vegetarian diet seems to provide enough zinc without either meat or supplements.

In a study of the bioavailability of zinc in the diets of pregnant and non-pregnant women, the substitution of plant foods for meat failed to affect zinc bioavailability or zinc utilization in either group.[53]

A study comparing pregnant vegetarians and pregnant meat-eaters found no significant differences in zinc levels in the blood, hair or urine of the women. This was true whether or not they took zinc supplements.[54]

In a 1985 commentary, the editor of the *British Journal of Obstetrics and Gynaecology* maintained that the National Research Council's RDA for zinc is grossly overestimated. He concluded that there is no solid evidence that zinc requirements during pregnancy can't be met by ordinary diets, either omnivorous or vegetarian; and that much better evidence was necessary before British doctors should be persuaded to provide zinc supplements for pregnant women, since artificial supplements are never free of side effects.[55]

Chapter 23

Vitamins and Minerals Without Pills

"If we lived entirely on raw, fresh plant foods, as our ancestors did millions of years ago, there would be no need for concern about getting adequate amounts of the essential foods such as vitamins."

—Linus Pauling[1]

Vitamin pills and nutritional supplements have grown into a two-billion-dollar industry in this country. Half the population relies on them. Yet this may not be healthy, because our bodies can use only so much of even essential nutrients without getting into trouble. Artificial vitamins and minerals can interfere with the operation of other nutrients and with each other. Overdoses can have dangerous side effects.[2]

Vegetarians are particularly prone to vitamin-pill popping, although studies show that they can get everything they need from their food.[3] Even vegans have maintained good health without supplements, and their food comes entirely from plants.[4]

Don't vegans at least need a supplemental source of B12?

Vitamin B12 is the sticking point. It's the only vitamin that isn't normally available in plant foods. Yet vegans have gone for many years without B12 supplements, with no visible ill effects.[5] One reason is that B12 stores are depleted very slowly. Normal stores in omnivores are sufficient to maintain adequate serum levels for up to five years, and it may take 10–20 years for symptoms of deficiency to appear.[6] Another reason was suggested recently by Indian researchers, who showed that B12 is manufactured by bacteria in the small intestines.[7]

Unfortunately, you can't count on your own intestinal microflora for B12. The requisite bacteria, while prevalent in the small intestines of vegetarians in India, tend to be scarce in the upper small bowels of people in industrialized countries. And even Indians are susceptible to B12 deficiency when they emigrate westward, although their diets remain unchanged. It appears that their intestinal microflora become similar to those of people living in the new country.[8]

One difference is the widespread use in Western countries of pesticides, which exterminate soil bacteria that can be a source of B12 in ordinary plant foods. Another is the use of antibiotics, which wipe out friendly intestinal bacteria along with unfriendly ones.[9]

Despite the scarcity of microorganisms in the Western gut, clinical signs of B12 deficiency are absent from most vegans even in industrialized countries.[10] Cases of pernicious anemia have been reported among them, particularly before the problem was recognized.[11] Yet the condition is no more common among vegans than among meat-eaters.[12]

Arguably, this is because most vegans now know about vitamin B12 and take supplements. But Dr. Victor Herbert, writing in the September 1988 *American Journal of Clinical Nutrition*, concluded that most B12 sources relied on by vegans contain almost none of the true B12 molecule (called cobalamin). What they contain instead are B12 analogues. These cobalamin look-alikes react like cobalamin in the standard assay used to determine B12 content, but they don't react like it in the human body. B12 analogues can actually lead to B12 deficiency, because they take the place of true cobalamin. They are like keys that fit into a lock but don't turn it. They end up keeping the true key out.[13]

If traditional vegan B12 sources aren't effective, why isn't pernicious anemia more common among them?

Good question. The problem may be in the RDA, which many authorities now feel is grossly overstated. The present RDA for anyone over six years of age is 3 micrograms (mcg). But Dr. Herbert shows that no one needs more than 1 mcg a

day, and the actual minimum requirement is probably around
.1 mcg.[14] That's only ⅟₃₀th the present RDA—so little that you
could get it from plant foods alone.

What plant foods contain vitamin B12?

The only ones common to the Western diet are legumes
(including peas, beans, peanuts, and alfalfa), and they contain only marginal amounts. They get their cobalamin from
bacteria that grow in their nodules and on their roots. These
marginal amounts can be doubled or tripled by sprouting,
which also increases the synthesis of other vitamins.[15]

How many sprouts would I have to eat to satisfy the RDA for vitamin B12?

To meet the 3-mcg requirement would take from ⅜ to a
whole pound of legumes, even when sprouted.[16] Few people eat this many sprouts in a day, although the sproutarian
school of vegetarianism recommends they be the mainstay
of the meal. The little square cartons you get at the supermarket weigh only a quarter of a pound.

If eating that many sprouts daily seems difficult, consider
that it would take 11½ pounds daily of chicken meat to
meet the same requirements.[17] At the .1-mcg level, a tenth
of these amounts would meet the requirement. That's about
2½ ounces of chicken meat, or one ounce of sprouts. At
this level, raw sprouts are a practical B12 source for people
who like them.

What about other vegan B12 sources?

Sources traditionally relied on by macrobiotic vegetarians
include tempeh and miso, which are soybean products fermented by bacteria; certain seaweeds and sea vegetables,
including kombu and wakame; and the single-celled algae,
spirulina, and chlorella. Unfortunately, according to Dr. Herbert, these products don't contain cobalamin in appreciable

amounts. Their B12 seems to be in the unusable analogue form.

Other popular B12 sources are fortified brewer's yeast and nutritional yeast, but yeast itself doesn't contain vitamin B12. The medium it's grown on has to be enriched with it. These yeasts can't be recommended for other reasons. They generally have a very low calcium/phosphorus ratio, and they may contribute to yeast infections in the susceptible.[18]

For the hard-core vegan, Dr. Herbert recommends true cobalamin purchased in tablet form.[19]

What about for the not-so-hardcore: How much animal food would I have to eat to satisfy B12 requirements?

Not much. Vitamin B12 is stored in the body and doesn't need to be eaten daily. Even at the outdated 3-mcg level, four ounces of beef liver will meet the requirement *for an entire month*. And 4 ounces of oysters, or 8 ounces of mackerel or herring, will do it for a week. To meet the more modest 1-mcg requirement, 8 ounces of salmon or trout once a week are sufficient.[20]

Of course, you don't need flesh foods at all to meet B12 requirements. At the 1-mcg level, a quarter of a cup of milk or yogurt, or 3.5 ounces of cheese, or half an egg will do it for the day.[21] If the true minimum requirement is only .1 mcg, these modest amounts of milk, cheese, or eggs will hold you for more than a week.

What about other vitamins and minerals?

Other nutrients are easily supplied by a diet of plant foods. In fact, vegetarians get *more* of most vitamins and minerals than meat-eaters.[22] This include vegans, although they avoid animal products altogether.

A 1984 study demonstrating this point came from Sweden, where veganism is popular enough to have been studied by researchers. The study compared the mineral intakes of middle-aged vegans, lacto-vegetarians, and meat-eaters. It found that for lacto-vegetarians, intakes of selenium, potassium, and magnesium were nearly double omnivores';

intakes of calcium, zinc, and copper exceeded omnivores'; and iron intakes equalled omnivores'. For vegans, intakes of magnesium, copper, and folate tripled omnivores'; intakes of iron and zinc were 50 percent greater than omnivores'; and calcium intakes equalled omnivores'. The vegan diet was significantly below the omnivore diet only in the trace elements iodine and selenium.[23]

Aren't iodine and selenium problems for vegans?

The iodine intakes of the Swedish vegans, while below those of omnivores, were sufficient to prevent symptoms of iodine deficiency.[24] Meat isn't actually a good source of iodine. Seafood is, but so are sea vegetables like kelp and dulse, and vegetables grown in iodine-rich soil. In Sweden, in areas where the soil is iodine-poor, iodine requirements are generally satisfied with iodized salt.

As for the trace mineral selenium, the daily requirement hasn't been established. Selenium is found in seafood and unprocessed meats, but it's also contained in whole grains. Although its content in grains varies in different areas, no deficiency has been reported among vegetarians even in low-selenium areas. In fact, their blood selenium levels are no different from meat-eaters' in the same area.[25] A 1989 study comparing the breast milks of vegetarian and omnivorous women found that the selenium content of the vegetarians' milk was one-third greater than the omnivores', *although selenium intakes were the same*. The researchers could not explain this difference, but noted that bioavailability of selenium is greater from some vegetables than from animal sources.[26]

It has been theorized that selenium is a cancer-protecting agent. Yet New Zealand, with one of the lowest selenium intake levels, has no more breast cancer than the United States, where selenium intake is more than twice as great.[27] At least one study reported that blood selenium levels in cancer patients were actually higher than for people who didn't have cancer. What distinguished the cancer patients wasn't their selenium intake but their meat intake, which was also significantly higher than for people without cancer.[28]

What about vitamins?

Vitamins, like minerals, are abundantly supplied by the plant kingdom. This was shown in a 1984 study from Great Britain, another country where veganism is popular. The researchers found that the standard vegan diet provided twice as much vitamin C and 50 percent more vitamin A than the ordinary mixed diet.[29]

The vegans were low in vitamin B12, riboflavin, and vitamin D, but they showed no signs of clinical deficiency. Riboflavin (vitamin B2), like vitamin B12, can be synthesized by intestinal organisms.[30] In other studies, the vegan intake of riboflavin has exceeded the RDA. No symptoms of deficiency have been reported among vegans, whether or not they ate milk products and eggs.[31] Besides organ meats, brewer's yeast, milk, and eggs, other good sources of riboflavin include whole grains, beans, peas, seeds and leafy green vegetables.

As for vitamin D, *no* natural foods supply enough of it to satisfy the daily requirement. You can meet the requirement with fortified milk—but only because the vitamin was added by the processors.[32]

Where did we get our vitamin D before modern science came up with this alternative?

The main source of vitamin D is the sun. Studies show that blood levels of the vitamin are only weakly correlated with dietary intake. A much stronger correlation has been shown with exposure to sunlight. The evidence for this association is particularly compelling because it comes from England, where the sun rarely shines. British studies show that the sun is the principal source of vitamin D, even when it isn't shining. A summer holiday at the beach affords better protection against vitamin D deficiency in the winter than vitamin D supplements.[33]

Another advantage of getting your vitamin D from the sun is that you can't overdose on it. A Cambridge University researcher warns that taking vitamin D orally is potentially dangerous, as well as being ineffective and unnatural.[34]

You could, of course, contract skin cancer from regular overdoses of sunshine, but only modest exposure is necessary to avoid vitamin D deficiency. Researchers at Tufts University recently determined that in the summer, adequate vitamin D nutrition is supplied by exposure of just the hands, face, and arms for 10–15 minutes a day, three times a week.[35]

Aren't vitamin D supplements at least necessary for the elderly and young children?

These are the two groups most likely to need vitamin D supplements: children because their bones are rapidly developing, and old people because their ability to transform ultraviolet light is limited.

The minimal exposure to sunlight recommended by the Tufts researchers, however, was made specifically for the elderly. British researchers have also found that blood levels of the vitamin are raised more by gardening than by cod liver oil, even in senior citizens. They showed that residents of an old people's home who could spend some time in the garden had normal vitamin D levels, while those confined indoors did not.[36]

Children living in the country or in the Southwest also get enough vitamin D from the sun; but vitamin D supplements may be advisable for children under six living in generally cloudy, northern industrial areas.

Rickets, caused by vitamin D deficiency, was a common problem at the turn of the century in these areas, in part because air pollution from burning coal filtered out the already scarce ultraviolet rays. In the 1930s, the problem was virtually eliminated by fortifying milk with vitamin D and by giving children supplements of cod liver oil.

Several cases of rickets were reported in a 1979 study of vegan children living in Boston. The problem, however, wasn't their diet. It was their failure to use the artificially fortified foods that correct the deficiency. All were children under three who had never received vitamin D supplements or vitamin D-fortified milk. They were completely cured by supplements of the vitamin.[37] In other studies, exposure to sunlight alone has proved an effective treatment for rickets.[38]

If these children lived in the United Kingdom, they could obtain vitamin D without going off their vegan diets. The food the British supplement with vitamin D is margarine rather than milk.[39] The solution isn't animal products, because before vitamin D-fortification, rickets was rife even among meat-eating, milk-drinking children in northern industrial areas. The solution is vitamin D supplements, an unnatural remedy to an unnatural environmental condition brought about by the Industrial Revolution.

Aren't supplements necessary to compensate for the poor mineral quality of our exhausted soil?

This is probably the strongest argument in favor of supplements. Even if plant foods are our natural diet, they may no longer be well-balanced storehouses of vitamins and minerals. Chemical fertilizers upset the balance of minerals and micoorganisms in the soil. They bombard the plant's roots with certain nutrients to the exclusion of others that are equally important, and render the soil's natural minerals less available to the plant. Pesticides wreak even more havoc.

One way around this problem is to eat only organically grown vegetables and fruits, but you may not be able to find them or afford them.

The easier alternative is to supplement, but that doesn't necessarily mean popping pills. Certain natural supplementary foods can help cover any deficiencies in your diet without exposing you to toxic overdose and vitamin/mineral imbalance. Seaweeds and sea vegetables, single-celled green algae, sprouts, blackstrap molasses, wheatgrass juice, and tofu are storehouses of nutrients.

Sea plants and algae may not be the reliable sources of B12 they were once thought to be, but they're still rich mines of minerals. Sea plants include kelp, dulse, kombu, arame, wakame, hiziki, nori, agar, and algae. They are 10–30 percent protein, and contain all eight essential amino acids. Vitamins, too, are supplied by these plants much more liberally than by other foods.[40] Orientals use them to enhance the flavor and nutrient value of their staple rice and vegetables.

Spirulina has gotten mixed reviews. Analysts at the University of California, Berkeley, think it doesn't offer anything that can't be had in a cheaper form.[41] But it's producers argue that spirulina's rich stores of organic vitamins, minerals, proteins, and nucleic acids are more easily absorbed than synthetic supplements, which may actually be toxic to the body. Spirulina's cell walls are naturally soft proteins, because it evolved before cellulose walls. In fact, it's been around more than three billion years. It came from the original single-celled photosynthetic life form that produced the earth's atmospheric oxygen and allowed life to evolve.[42]

One authority has written a book promoting spirulina as a revolutionary aid in weight loss. She contends that its nutrients are assimilated more quickly than other foods, so it enters the blood stream and travels to the hypothalamus more quickly. The hypothalamus is the part of the brain responsible for sending out hunger signals. When it's satisfied, so is your urge for more food. That means you're satisfied with less.[43]

Another natural supplementary food is blackstrap molasses, which is a rich source of calcium and iron. A mere tablespoon contains 137 mg of calcium (a quarter of the FAO/ WHO requirement) and 3.2 mg of iron (a third of the RDA for a man).[44] Its taste is a little too strong to use as a sweetener, except in moderation in recipes. As a supplement, however, it can be taken by the spoonful. Unlike iron pills, which can bring bowel function to a grinding halt, blackstrap molasses has the advantage of being mildly laxative.

Sprouts are another wonder food. Seeds and beans are rich sources of many nutrients, and sprouting increases their content. In fact, their nutrient content increases by more than can be explained by the loss of dry matter in the conversion from seed to sprout. The seed's carbohydrate content goes down and its protein content goes up. How remains a mystery, unless the sprouting seed pulls nitrogen (the missing element in carbohydrate) from the air. Sprouts also have a higher vitamin content than the seeds from which they sprang.[45] And they're tasty.

Wheatgrass juice is a cult health food made in a special juicer from the green grass of the sprouted wheat plant. It does *not* have the advantage of being tasty. But it's reputed to be another very rich source of nutrients[46]—although you can't prove it by the USDA, which does not recognize it as food.

Wheat germ, the embryo of the wheat kernel, is another popular supplementary food. Like brewer's yeast, it can be recommended only with qualification. It's a good source of B vitamins, iron, vitamin E, and protein; and a cup contains a full 18.8 mg of zinc. Unfortunately, its high fat content makes wheat germ go rancid quickly. The reason it's usually separated out in milling is that it contains fat that limits the keeping quality of the flour.[47] You're probably better off getting the germ along with the flour, in the form of stone-ground whole-wheat flour that has been only lightly milled.

Then there is tofu, which can be one of your best nutritional allies. Tofu is the curd that results when soy milk is separated into curds and whey. Soymilk is made by blending soaked whole soybeans with water, straining out the pulp, then cooking, cooling, and flavoring. Tofu can be digested by people who have trouble with either cow's milk or the whole soybeans from which this smooth bean cheese is made.

Tofu is as high as milk in calcium and protein. It's also as high in fat, but it contains no cholesterol and has a better balance of minerals—including *forty-three times* as much iron.[48] In fact, milk is such a poor source of iron that chronic dieters who rely heavily on yogurt, cottage cheese, and skim milk can end up anemic.

Admittedly, milk rates higher in taste, but tofu is so mild-flavored and versatile, it can be slipped into hundreds of recipes without impairing their flavor. (See Recipes.)

Chapter 24

Raising a Healthy Child on Grains and Greens

"Little Tommy Tucker
Sang for his supper;
What shall we give him?
White bread and butter."

As a mother who once called bread and butter junk food, I was shocked to read that a diet that is 75 percent bread—whole wheat *or* white—can support children in good health.

This was the result of a landmark study that monitored the growth of 310 undernourished German school children after World War II. The study was particularly important because it took place at a time when children grow rapidly. Any dietary deficiency—especially in iron, calcium, and protein—would be easily detected. The children ate only one ounce of meat and 1–2 cups of milk *per week*. By accepted standards, their diet was hopelessly deficient. Yet they did remarkably well on it. They gained 50 percent more weight in a year than was predicted on the basis of normal growth rates; and they showed no signs of any deficiencies.[1]

The bread was fortified with calcium, so it's not clear from this study whether the diet alone would have provided enough of this mineral. But the majority of the world's children get their calcium from vegetarian sources.[2] The researchers established that the bread diet provided enough protein and iron.[3] The children's hemoglobin concentrations remained normal, despite their high requirements for iron during a year of rapid growth.

Contrary to the expectations of the researchers, the high fiber content of the bread didn't seem to affect mineral absorption. Any fiber-induced impairment in mineral absorption should have been reflected in the children's growth rates and general health. But when the children were divided into groups and given bread of different refinements (from whole wheat to white), no differences could be detected among the groups.

In another variation on the experiment, the children's milk intakes were increased from ¼ cup to 2 cups a day over a six-month period. Again, no change was seen in their growth rates or general health. This finding upset the prevailing theories that plant proteins could be effectively used only in combination with animal proteins, and that calcium could be effectively absorbed only from milk.

There were other unexpected findings. The enrichment of white flour with iron and B-vitamins had no apparent effect on its nutritive value. Wholemeal flour and white flour proved to be equally nutritious. Why? Probably because white flour has nearly as much protein as whole wheat flour and, although it has fewer vitamins and minerals, it also has less of the fiber and phytate that inhibit vitamin and mineral absorption.[4]

It must be noted, however, that the white bread in this study wasn't the over-processed, spongy version popular today. Modern commercial white bread is produced in high-volume, high-speed mills that virtually wipe out the nutritive value of the grain. What's left is a pasty-white flour consisting of nothing but empty calories. Some ninety nutrients are removed in this process. A few are added back artificially, but the law requires only four, and even these few chemical additions may do more harm than good. The elemental iron commonly used for the fortification of flour can be toxic in excess doses. And it doesn't do much good, because its bioavailability is extremely low.[5]

In determining the nutritive value of bread, the degree of refinement may be less important than the way it's milled. The ideal method is traditional stone grinding, in which wheat berries are crushed slowly between two stones without tearing the germ. The nutrients and oils of the grain are thus substantially preserved.

Can a vegan diet support the nutrient needs of children?

This isn't clear from the study with German schoolchildren because the diet wasn't totally vegan, and the bread was fortified with calcium. But healthy babies are easily reared without meat, as generations of Seventh Day Adventists can attest. They're also easily reared without cow's milk. Infants allergic to milk are simply switched to commercial soy-based formulas.[6] If you can raise healthy children without one of these animal foods, you should be able to raise them without either. Neither is necessary for protein, and they aren't interchangeable as mineral sources. Milk is an excellent source of calcium, but a very poor source of iron. Meat is an excellent source of iron, but a very poor source of calcium.[7] You can't satisfy the mineral requirements of a child who is allergic to milk by giving him meat, or those of a child who eats no meat by giving him milk. Tofu, grains, and greens are more appropriate substitutes in either case. In addition, they'll satisfy the child's protein needs.

The only nutrient in meat and milk that children can't get from these substitutes is vitamin B12. Vegan mothers, however, can supplement their children's diets like their own. Even without supplementation, uncomplicated vitamin B12 deficiency is extremely rare, among children as well as adults, vegan or otherwise.[8]

As we saw in the last chapter, vitamin D can be a problem for children in cloudy, northern areas, whether or not they eat animal products. The problem was solved for milk-drinking children by adding the vitamin to milk. For non-milk-drinking children, you can add the same supplements to the diet in concentrated form. If cod liver oil is unacceptable, there are synthetic vitamin D drops you can use. Ten micrograms daily are recommended for children in the winter months.[9]

So you *can* raise your child without animal products. Whether you should is another question, which we'll look at later.

Is it possible to sustain a healthy pregnancy without animal products?

It is. This was the finding of a study of mothers on "The Farm," a vegan community in Tennessee. The first subjects were 143 mothers who had given birth on The Farm. They had been vegans an average of six years before giving birth. Vitamin B12 was supplied in their diets by B12-fortified soymilk, and they took prenatal vitamins, calcium, and iron. They also received regular prenatal medical care. Their pregnancies were normal and they gained sufficient weight. This was true although the mean weight of adult vegans was found to be twenty pounds less than that of either non-vegetarians or milk-drinking vegetarians with similar caloric intakes and physical activities.

The birth weights of the vegan infants also failed to differ significantly from those of infants in the general population. The weight and height of vegan children on The Farm were found to meet or exceed the growth curves of the National Center for Health Statistics' Health and Nutrition Examination Survey and the Centers for Disease Control.

A 1987 followup of 775 vegan mothers on The Farm showed that the incidence of preeclampsia, a toxemic condition that strikes in late pregnancy and can be very dangerous, was extremely low. Preeclampsia is marked by high blood pressure, swollen ankles, and protein in the urine. It is often associated with the consumption of fast foods—hamburgers, fried chicken, and french fries cooked in beef tallow—and with a rapid weight gain. The very low incidence of preeclampsia among vegan mothers suggests that a vegan diet can actually insure a healthier and safer pregnancy than the usual American diet.[10]

Can healthy children be reared without animal products?

Again, the answer is yes. This was shown not only in the studies of American vegans on The Farm just cited, but in a series of studies involving vegan children in England.

A British study reported in 1978 included three children, as well as six adults, who had been vegans from birth. All of the participants were pronounced healthy. Their blood counts were normal, and none had a serum B12 level indicating deficiency. The researchers concluded from this and other studies that vegan pregnancies, and the health of vegan children, "appear to be essentially normal."[11]

In another report, the same researchers observed that the average vegan serum cholesterol level was remarkably low; and that the breast milk of vegan mothers had a low proportion of palmitic acid and a high proportion of linoleic acid. This finding suggested that vegan breast milk has a marked cholesterol-lowering effect. The researchers concluded that a vegan diet may be the best diet to prevent cardiovascular disease.[12]

A 1988 update reported thirty years of follow-up on these same British vegans. Some had been tracked since before birth because their mothers were studied while pregnant. The researchers concluded that the children developed quite normally, although they tended to be shorter and leaner than meat-eating children.[13]

Vegan children on The Farm, on the other hand, were as tall and weighed as much as meat-eating children. Moreover, it hasn't been established that short stature is a detrimental trait. When shorter Third World people emigrate to the United States, their children tend to grow taller than their parents. But tall American women also tend to have hips that are too narrow for their babies during birth. Also, their jaws are sometimes too narrow for their teeth. Latin American women are short, but their hips are wide enough for easy deliveries, and their jaws display wide sets of teeth.

The British researchers found no evidence that the stamina of vegan children was impaired by their diet. Their mental development was also quite normal. The researchers concluded that children can be satisfactorily reared on an appropriately selected vegan diet. To meet energy needs, they recommended that cereals, legumes, and nuts be stressed over watery fruit and vegetables. For vitamins B-12 and D, they recommended supplements.[13]

Another study that included vegan children was reported in 1982. It investigated the nutritional status of children raised on lacto-ovo-vegetarian, macrobiotic, and vegan diets living in Boston. Again, the examining physician pronounced these vegetarian children in good health. Their hematological and biochemical indices failed to differ significantly either from each other or from normal values. The researchers noted that "certain hematological parameters . . . suggested that further investigation of iron deficiency anemia was called for in approximately a quarter" of the vegetarian children. They observed, however, that iron deficiency anemia is common even among meat-eating children.[14] In fact, the average serum iron level for the vegetarians in this study was slightly *higher* than that reported for meat-eating children of the same age in the general population.[15]

On the plus side, the vegan children's vitamin A and complex carbohydrate intakes were high, their fat and salt intakes were low, and their serum cholesterol levels were far below either meat-eating children's or the other vegetarians'. By these parameters, the vegan children were healthier than normal.

Children who eat no meat may also be brighter than normal. This was the finding of a study designed to test the contrary hypothesis: that the absence of meat in the diet impairs mental development. The average mental age of the vegetarian children tested turned out to be more than a year beyond their chronological age.[16]

What about reports of nutritional deficiency among children on subsistence-level plant diets in other countries?

Mineral deficiencies have been reported in certain vegan infants in the Middle East, but their principal food was a thin homemade soymilk. It failed to satisfy not only their mineral requirements but their basic energy and protein requirements.[17]

Rickets and other signs of calcium deficiency have also been seen in vegetarian Asian children living in the United Kingdom. Oddly, vegetarian Caucasian children living in the same country don't have this problem, and neither do Asian vegetarian children living in their native countries.[18]

This anomaly has been explained by two variables: sunshine and yeast. Chapatis made from whole wheat flour are a staple of Asian vegetarians. These chapatis are unleavened. That is, they haven't been fermented with yeast to make the bread rise. Yeasts and other sourdough organisms increase the availability of minerals, apparently by producing enzymes that destroy some of the phytic acid in the bran of the wheat.[19] When the unleavened chapatis in the diets of Asian children living in Great Britain have been replaced with leavened bread, their serum calcium concentrations have increased dramatically.[20]

Asian children living in Asia don't have the same problems because the sun shines there more often. Vitamin D is necessary for the absorption of calcium, and the sun is its principal source. Asians eating chapati flour fortified with vitamin D have normal blood levels of the vitamin even in Britain.[21]

Among children in India, iron deficiency anemia is commonly reported, despite the apparently adequate iron content of their vegetarian diets. This condition is attributed in part to infestations of parasites, which cause anemia due to blood loss. Another factor is the absence of iron-absorption enhancing substances in the diet. Meat and vitamin C intakes are very low. Even children often take their meals with tea, which contains tannin, an iron absorption inhibitor.[22] Further, the Indian diet is based on rice, which is very low in iron. Western vegetarian diets are generally based on wheat, which contains sixteen times as much iron as rice.[23]

Despite these defects in the Indian diet, a recent study reported that vegetarian Indian children were actually taller, heavier, and more likely to survive childhood than meat-eating Indian children. The author's explanation was that the vegetarian children got more food, due to the high cost of meat; and that the meat-eating children were more susceptible to infection, due to sanitation problems in the meat market.[24]

In this country, a 1978 report of megaloblastic anemia and neurological abnormalities in a breast-fed infant of a vegan mother led to an editorial in *Nutrition Reviews* warning that "strict vegetarianism in Western countries is a form of food faddism which can have serious consequences."[25] Another reviewer, however, reached a different conclusion. He pointed out that the vegan mother's serum B12 was normal. That meant that she should have been able to transfer sufficient B12 to her infant, if he had been normal. In fact, the investigators suspected an inborn error of metabolism in the infant. Therefore he wasn't representative of normal infancy.[26]

The same reviewer showed that most studies finding inadequate B12 status in vegans are unconvincing. In the absence of complicating factors like malabsorption of B12 (either inborn, or caused by disease or drugs), clinical problems are unlikely to develop in vegans even without B12 supplementation.[27]

In any case, most vegans are now apprised of the problems and use some supplementary source of B12.[28]

If children aren't allergic to milk, aren't they better off with it than without it?

Milk is definitely the easiest way to get calcium into children. Most authorities stress its importance in their diets.[29] But children who don't eat meat don't need as much calcium.[30] Dr. Frank Oski, a pediatrician at the State University of New York, has argued that unmodified cow's milk shouldn't be a part of the diet at any age. He notes that in the first year of life, cow's milk is linked to iron deficiency anemia, gastrointestinal bleeding, and food allergy. After infancy, it's linked to lactose intolerance, atherosclerosis, and possibly other diseases—including cataracts, milk-borne infections, lymphatic leukemia, and schizophrenia.[31]

Among infants fed whole milk from early infancy, more than half are reported to be anemic. This is true even of those receiving iron-fortified cereals and pediatric care.[32] Milk is too low in iron to meet iron requirements. And for infants, it's typically the main source of nutrition. Not only is milk itself low in iron, but it appears to decrease iron absorption from other foods.[33] It can also cause gastrointestinal bleeding, further contributing to iron loss. In children with this problem, the bleeding can be slowed or stopped by substituting soy formula for cow's milk.[34]

Among children with recurrent abdominal pain, studies show about a third are lactose intolerant. Lactose, or milk sugar, is digested in the infant by an intestinal enzyme called lactase. Europeans typically retain this enzyme into adulthood, but other races don't. Lactase and lactose-digesting ability decline in the majority of the world's population after age five. When the lactose intolerant drink milk, they experience cramping, bloating, gas, and diarrhea.[35]

Even in children without these problems, the saturated fat and cholesterol in milk are linked to the development of arterial plaque, foreshadowing cardiovascular disease.[36] The *symptoms* of this modern scourge don't show up until later in life, but the atherosclerotic process itself begins soon after birth. Fatty streaks composed primarily of cholesterol can be found in the blood vessels during the first year of life. At that age, the condition has been attributed to cow's milk.[37] And atherosclerotic plaques may appear in the arteries as early as three to four years of age.[38]

> In a hospital in Philadelphia, 44 percent of the children autopsied had definite evidence of atherosclerosis, as indicated by the development of fatty plaques on the inner walls of their arteries.[39]

Nonfat milk isn't an ideal solution either, because some butterfat seems to be necessary to aid in the absorption of calcium from the milk.[40]

So should I rear my child without animal foods?

Despite what's been said so far, unless your child is allergic to milk, or you're a vegan for ethical reasons, the answer is probably no. It will stand your child's heart and arteries in good stead for adulthood, but it's not a practical alternative for most people.

Raising vegan children takes more careful planning than for adults. Children's protein needs are proportionately higher, and their stomach capacity is limited. They're also much more finicky eaters. Spinach is a major battle. Collard greens are out of the question. The high-fiber diet recommended for adults with high serum cholesterol levels and sluggish bowels isn't necessarily good for children. It can impair the absorption of mineral and protein intakes that are already limited. And to get sufficient energy can require digesting more bulk than tiny stomachs can accommodate.

On top of that is the psychological barrier. The radical approach is liable to upset your in-laws and your pediatrician. Your child may suffer greater psychological damage from being denied hot dogs and ice cream at birthday parties than physical damage from indulging in them.

The point here is simply that children, like adults, *can* live healthily on essentially-vegan fare. You needn't worry that you're jeopardizing their health by cutting down on these high-fat, high-protein heart attack precursors. Children don't need meat at all. They also don't need the daily quart of milk that used to be recommended. For children 1–3 years old, half that amount will provide 90 percent of their B12 requirement, 75 percent of their calcium requirement, and 50 percent of their vitamin D requirement.[41]

Even if your children aren't yet in the high-risk category for a heart attack, it's better not to teach them to expect high-fat animal foods with every meal. Food habits are developed in childhood; and so are the number of fat cells they will carry through life. Americans suffer more from obesity (overnutrition) than undernutrition, and obesity begins in childhood. Children who are taught early in life to love the foods of the earth are likely to have good eating habits later.

The American Academy of Pediatrics, the National Heart, Lung and Blood Institute, and the American Heart Association have all recently revised their dietary guidelines for children. The new guidelines are lower in cholesterol and fat (especially saturated fat), and higher in polyunsaturated fat. Vegetarian diets meet these recommendations much better than the usual American diet.[42]

How do I teach my children to love the foods of the earth?

This admittedly takes imagination and persistence, but it's worth the effort.

Babies are less opinionated about their food than five-year-olds. The earlier you introduce your children to a variety of natural foods, the better.

Sometimes renaming helps. When my kids were small, they turned a cold shoulder to sliced zucchini, but "garden cookies" appealed to them. They didn't care for celery but would eat "ants on a log" (celery lined with peanut butter and raisins). They thought "Pac Pellet Cereal" was puffed millet. And it took them a long time to figure out that their "milkshakes" contained tofu instead of milk.

How you serve their food can also affect its appeal. Cute children's dishes with small, non-forbidding portions help. Or you can cut and shape the food to look friendly and winsome.

The hardest problem to fight is the sugar habit. Start by avoiding hidden sugars. Buy plain canned fruits and applesauce instead of sweetened fruits, and all-natural peanut butter instead of the sugared variety. Make your own popsicles by freezing fruit juice. For other ideas, see Recipes.

Chapter 25

Vegan Solutions to the Food Crisis

"I have no doubt that it is part of the destiny of the human race, in its gradual improvement, to leave off eating animals, as surely as the savage have left off eating each other when they came in contact with the more civilized."
—Henry David Thoreau

So far, I've avoided ethical issues and focused on the medical evidence. But having concluded that we'd be better off if we slashed our intake of animal products, it's now appropriate to look at the ethical implications. Not only are there the lives of millions of cows and chickens at stake, but a mass conversion to an essentially-vegan diet would go a long way toward feeding the starving Third World.

The case for change is supported not only by medical but by economic, sociological, and agricultural considerations. On nutritional grounds, few experts dispute that industrialized populations eat too much meat and animal fat, too many milk products, and too little dietary fiber. On economic grounds, the case for a switch from meat to grains is even more compelling.[1]

Animal husbandry for meat production is a notoriously inefficient use of our increasingly limited resources. For every pound of protein we obtain from the cow, we must feed it about sixteen pounds of protein from sources that could be used directly as food for humans.[2] To put beef on the table also requires about 4 times as much water as will furnish the same number of calories from wheat. Altogether, a 1-pound steak costs about 5 pounds of grain, 1,500 gallons of water, and 35 pounds of eroded topsoil.[3]

This inefficient use of land has contributed to the world protein crisis. Since 16 pounds of fodder protein are needed to produce one pound of protein from beef, a small increase in demand for meat leads to enormous increases in the indirect consumption of soy and grain proteins. This means a sharp decrease in the amount of these foods available for human consumption, especially in poorer countries. Rising demand for soybean and grain fodders pushes up their prices, further aggravating the shortages in these poorer countries.[4]

To look at this crisis in terms of protein is actually misleading, because virtually all plant foods provide sufficient protein to meet human needs. The world protein shortage is really a world calorie shortage. If the land required to make a pound of meat protein could yield sixteen times as much soy protein, it could yield *fifty* times as many calories—if it were planted with potatoes and greens.[5]

Further, we *need* only half as much protein as we now eat. By FAO/WHO standards, we need only a quarter as much. We also need substantially fewer calories. If we filled up on high-fiber plant foods, we'd be satisfied by fewer calories. The essentially-vegetarian Hunzas face Himalayan winters as severe as those endured by the meat-eating Eskimos. Yet the Hunzas eat only half as many calories as the Eskimos.[6]

A low caloric intake is more than just adequate for good health. It can extend life. The diets of long-lived peoples have two chief traits in common: a low intake of calories and a low intake of meat. They also typically have a carbohydrate content of 70–80 percent (mostly complex), compared to our 35–45 percent; a fat content of 10–15 percent, compared to our 40–45 percent; and a protein content of 10–15 percent, compared to our 15–20 percent.[7]

It's been estimated that an adult's yearly food needs could be met with 1½ bushels of corn, one bushel of soybeans, 1,100 pounds of potatoes and 550 pounds of green vegetables. Using organic farming methods only, this yield would require a third of an acre of arable land. In this country, 2.5 acres per person are devoted to cropland. The amount of arable land actually available per person is 3.5 to 4 acres. Only half of this land is now producing crops. Grazing animals occupy the other half. And only 20 percent of our crops are feeding humans. The United States, which currently feeds less than 7 percent of the world's population, could actually feed 60 percent.[8]

Even India could feed its own people, if its arable crop land weren't limited primarily to rice, and were diversified with corn, soybeans, potatoes, and greens. In India, there are only two acres of land per person, and only half an acre each is available for cultivation. But that's still ⅙ of an acre more than is necessary to sustain a person on these calorie-dense crops.

Using the same figures, the Soviet Union produces enough grain to feed not only its own people, but all of Africa and Europe. Yet it has had to resort to importing American wheat to meet a growing demand for meat. The grain is now feeding livestock.[9]

According to one British economist, Britain too could feed itself, if it stopped trying to support 150 million hens, 30 million sheep and 15 million cattle in addition to its 60 million humans. Britain is heavily dependent on imports, but two-thirds of its home-grown grain goes to feed livestock. Thirty pounds of cattle feed are needed to produce one pound of beef. Even the hen, the most efficient converter of fodder to protein, requires a food intake that's over three times its output. If the British lived on a vegetarian diet, four times its population could be supported without resorting to food imports.[10]

According to another British analyst, one out of eight people in the world is undernourished or starving. Yet farm animals consume enough food to feed four times the human population. That means that the world's agricultural output is actually enough to support five times its present population.[11]

What about vitamin and mineral deficiencies in impoverished countries?

These deficiencies are reported to be widespread, but the real problem isn't lack of animal food. It's lack of food in general, and ignorance of efficient land use and nutritional needs. In India, most of Latin America and Asia, and much of Africa, diets tend to center around a single grain. If part of the available crop land were devoted to leafy greens, intakes of vitamins and minerals would be boosted, and so would the number of available calories. Protein, vitamins, and minerals in grains and beans could be increased by sprouting; and by stone grinding rather than refining.[12]

According to some authorities, nutritional deficiencies in Third World countries are more apparent than real. They're determined by reference to the Recommended Daily Allowances, which include margins of safety that can make them double actual physiological needs. For women in pregnancy and lactation, for example, recommended intakes include nearly 100 grams of protein and 1,200 mg of calcium. Among developing populations, reaching these levels is generally out of the question. Yet nearly all Third World women successfully nurse their babies, usually for long periods, without apparent detriment to the babies or themselves.[13]

In British surveys, many people have had intakes below official recommendations without signs of malnutrition.[14] Researchers writing in the *American Journal of Clinical Nutrition* concluded:

> "Because of increases in population, and because obviously there are limits to increases in food production, the huge bulk of the world's inhabitants will ultimately be *compelled* to consume a largely vegetarian diet. Rather than aiming to produce faster growing or taller children, or seeking to learn what *more* can be added, with advantage, to the already ample diets of most Western populations, we should be concentrating on studying the converse. Knowledge must be acquired of the relatively low levels of nutrients intakes, for young and old, which are compatible with good health and well being. . . ."[15]

Isn't cattle grazing the only productive use possible for large portions of our non-arable public lands?

The vast majority of our federal public lands are grazed by livestock. Contrary to popular belief, however, this use is only marginally productive in terms of food. And it's highly destructive of the land.

Most of our beef comes from private lands in the East which are fertile enough to support crops. Less than ⅓ of

the total amount of red meat in the United States is produced in the Western states. This includes that produced on
both public and private land. Most of this production comes
from artificially irrigated pastures and feedlots on private
lands, rather than from natural desert terrain.

Over 48 percent of the land area of the eleven Western
states is federal public land. This area, which includes over
90 percent of all federal lands in the United States outside
Alaska, is our collective heritage. Nearly all of it is being
grazed by the livestock industry—323 million acres in all.
Yet it produces only 2 percent of the total amount of beef in
the United States.[16] Moreover, the public lands grazing industry is heavily subsidized. This tiny percent costs us nearly
as much in taxes as the value of the beef itself, which we
pay for again at the market.

But the greatest cost is to the land itself, which has seriously
deteriorated in the hands of the cattle industry. According to a
1981 report by the U.S. Council on Environmental Quality,
overgrazing is the leading cause of desertification, the process
by which our Western lands are losing their productivity.[17]

In fact, grazing has been blamed for more environmental
destruction throughout the world than any other single cause.
In Africa, overgrazing has stripped the land of ground cover,
and left the trampled and caked earth unable to absorb
rain. This causes famine.[18]

In this country, livestock grazing became a huge business
in the 1870s and 1880s. Gold fever was also "grass fever."
Cattlemen rushed to extract every possible dollar from our
Western grasslands, by overpopulating them with cattle and
sheep. As a result, over 700 million acres of grassland were
degraded and destroyed. The National Park Service says
that the vast flatlands and broad desert valleys that are now
wastelands of sagebrush, tumbleweed, and cheatgrass were
once rich with perennial grasses and flowering plants. By
1936, a Department of Agriculture report concluded that
rangeland productivity had deteriorated by more than 50
percent from it's original level.

The livestock industry argues that the animals help spread
seeds and trample them into the ground. This would be true
if the plants were lightly grazed. Domestic, stationary livestock ambush each blade of grass as it emerges. The plants
are so ravaged that they have trouble making it to seeding

time. Livestock strip off most of the grass and green plants on the ground, as well as leaves from shrubs and trees. This not only kills desirable plants and prevents their seeding, but allows undesirable ones to expand their territories. In little more than a century, many millions of acres of rich grasslands have become deserts.

When vegetation cover is stripped off, soil erosion increases. Topsoil that has been pulverized by trampling cattle is easily blown or washed away. The hard, sun-baked land loses its ability to hold water, and desertification sets in. According to the U.S.D.A., only agriculture itself outranks grazing as a cause of soil damage and loss.

Cattle tend to congregate around water, where they trample the streamsides and collapse their banks. The streams become wider and shallower, and their unprotected banks become susceptible to flooding. Water temperatures go up, algae that reduce the water's oxygen content increase, and fish die.

Cattle are also a major source of pollution of these public waters, which cover half the land in the eleven Western states. Tons of cattle manure and urine are discharged into them daily. Livestock are more susceptible to disease and parasites than are wild animals, and many people have become sick from this water. Cattle and sheep diseases and parasites also spread to wild animals. The screwworm fly, propagated by cattle, killed three-fourths of the fawns in the Southern United States. Hoof and mouth disease killed many more thousands of deer in the West.

Cattle fences restrict the free movement and prevent the migration of wild animals, thus limiting their access to food. Fences also keep out people, giving the illusion that our collective public lands are privately owned. Campers who dare to cross the fences share their campgrounds with cattle.

To protect the sacred cow, cattle predators and competitors have been systematically eliminated. These two categories include most other animals. The government spends millions each year to slaughter predators for the public lands livestock grazing industry. Millions more (nearly $17 million in 1986) are spent to domesticate or slaughter competitor wild horses and burros on public lands. To this end, most of the large mammals of the West have been brutally exterminated—including the buffalo, grizzly bear, black bear, fox, coyote, grey wolf, jaguar, lynx, bobcat, mountain lion, moose, elk, pronghorn, bighorn sheep, mule, and white-tail deer.

These predators used to exterminate the pests that were their natural enemies. Without them, the government must undertake this task. Rabbits, rats, mice, squirrels, and gophers are poisoned with airdrops of poison grain, spreading poison throughout the environment and killing many other animals.

Insect pests thrive on both cattle and overgrazing. These pests, too, are killed in poisoning campaigns with dangerous insecticides. In 1979, the government spent nearly $10 million for this purpose. On top of this, the livestock themselves are treated with insecticides, fungicides, fumigants, antibiotics, tranquilizers, hormones, and steroids, which find their way into the bodies of humans.

Vegetation that won't support cattle is removed by spraying with dangerous herbicides, burning, or bulldozing. The area may then be seeded by the government with an imported wheatgrass that transforms thousands of acres of diverse plant life into a single form good only for grazing livestock. While seeding allegedly aids in soil erosion control, wheatgrass is no better than natural revegetation for this purpose, and it may actually be worse. What wheatgrass is good for is cattle fodder.

Who profits from all this? A handful of ranchers. Forty percent of public grazing is controlled by only 3 percent of the nation's stockmen. Only 30,000 permittees control 273 million acres of public land—an average of 9,100 acres each.

The government charges these cattlemen only 20 percent as much to lease its rangelands as private range owners charge for the same amount of forage. Half of this money goes back to the grazing districts for range improvements (including barbed wire fences, livestock industry access roads, grass seedings, and waterholes). That means the effective lease rate is only 10 percent of the market value. In 1978, Congress passed the Rangelands Improvement Act, authorizing more than $2 billion for range management programs over the next twenty years. That's $100 million a year, or more than ten times the $9.2 million the United States Treasury netted from grazing fees in 1985.[19]

The public lands grazing industry is one of the most heavily subsidized businesses in the country. Yet the amount of our annual beef intake that actually comes from public lands is only enough to make about six hamburgers for each of us.[20] The sacrifice of only one hamburger every two months could save our public lands.

What will happen to currently existing herds, if no lands are devoted to feeding them?

The easy answer is that we'll eat them—although I won't, and you won't if you've been persuaded by the medical evidence.

As more people turn to plant foods, out of choice or necessity, meat demand must drop. Prudent cattlemen will sell off their herds and turn to more productive endeavors. Children, having watched their fathers succumb to heart disease and cancer, will start to eat grains and greens. The remaining cattle will roam free on our non-arable land or, like the buffalo, be destined for zoos and reservations.

Americans have always been big beef eaters. The quest for new grazing lands helped to push the frontier westward. But there are no more frontiers, and there is insufficient land left on this planet to feed both the human population and the domesticated animals that increase our agricultural needs by a factor of four. It may someday be said of cattle as of the buffalo:

> "[T])he existence of 60 million bison in the heart of the United States and the existence of Kansas City were incompatible. . . . Kansas City, like it or not, was bound to come, and the bison was bound to go."[21]

Recipes

ADVENTURES IN COOKING WITH GRAINS, GREENS, AND BEANS

Essentially Vegan Recipes

Here are some sample high-complex-carbohydrate recipes that can satisfy your protein and mineral needs without
recourse to meat and with only marginal recourse to other
animal foods. If you're going hardcore with veganism, you
can eliminate animal foods altogether by making the following substitutions:

For milk, use commercial soymilk. (Experiment; some
brands are better than others.)

For butter, use margarine or cold-pressed vegetable oil.
Seven tablespoons of oil replace eight of butter or margarine.

For yogurt and cheese, substitute commercial soy yogurt
or soy cheese. In the following recipes, yogurt and cheese
are optional and can be satisfactorily omitted without replacement. Buttered whole wheat breadcrumbs are a tasty
alternative to grated cheese toppings.

The vegan alternative to sour cream is tofu blended with
lemon juice until smooth and creamy. For a sour cream
substitute that's still milk-based but lower in calories, blend
a cup of low-fat cottage cheese with 2 tablespoons of skim
milk and 1 tablespoon of lemon juice. Non-fat yogurt also
works. For a whipped cream substitute, blend low-fat, part-
skim Ricotta cheese until smooth. It's still dairy, but it contains five times as much protein, four times as much calcium
and only half as many calories as even "light" whipping
cream.

To avoid the high cholesterol content of egg yolk, substitute 2 egg whites for 1 whole egg. Often eggs can be omitted
altogether, simply by increasing the liquid in the recipe or
adding tofu in egg-sized portions. If that doesn't work, you
can use commercial egg replacer or, better yet, make your
own. Substitute one of the following mixtures for each
egg:

(1) 1 tablespoon arrowroot (a healthful cornstarch alternative), 1 tablespoon soy flour (which binds better than regular flour), and 2 tablespoons water (more or less); or

(2) 2 tablespoons flour, ½ tablespoon shortening, ½ teaspoon baking powder, and 2 tablespoons water.

Many of the following recipes contain tofu, which is high in calcium, iron and protein. These nutrients make it a great vegan maintenance food. Unfortunately, tofu is also high in fat, so it's *not* a great diet food. Although its fat has the advantage of being unsaturated and cholesterol-free, tofu contains *as much* of it as milk. Even worse, of course, are nuts, cheese and eggs. Until you've dropped down to your desired weight, it's best to cut these ingredients down or out and concentrate on plain grains and greens.

BREAKFAST

Spiced Oat Bran

Oat bran has several advantages over wheat bran. For one, oat bran lowers serum cholesterol. Wheat bran doesn't. In a study at the University of California at Irvine, serum cholesterol was lowered 5 percent merely by eating 2 oat bran muffins a day. (For oat bran muffins, see "Breads.") Oat bran is less woody than wheat bran and therefore easier on your delicate intestinal membranes. And it can be cooked alone as a cereal, while wheat bran has to be added to something else. Here's one cereal possibility:

1 cup oat bran
2 cups water
¼ cup chopped dates or raisins
½ tsp cinnamon
¼ tsp nutmeg
⅓ tsp sun-dried sea salt

Boil water. Add ingredients very slowly, stirring constantly to prevent lumps. Cook over low heat 1 minute, stirring constantly.

Spiced Oatmeal

If you can't get into oat bran in the morning, the same seasonings make a great bowl of oatmeal. Two bowls of oatmeal give you as much fiber as one of oat bran. Oats are also higher in protein and quicker to cook than any other grain. The healthiest are old-fashioned rolled oats. The "quick" and "instant" kinds have been heat treated for fast cooking, which causes nutritive losses. And old-fashioned rolled oats cook in just 5 minutes, so there's no need to resort to the heat processed variety.

Grandpa Brown's Oatmeal Waffles

When you get bored with oatmeal as a hot cereal, you can turn it into waffles.

1½ cups instant oatmeal
1¼ cups milk or soymilk
1 egg (preferably free range)
2 tsp baking powder (Royal and Rumford brands are free of aluminum preservatives)
¼ tsp sea salt
3 tbsp butter or margarine

Combine all ingredients in blender and blend on medium speed for 5 minutes. Let set until thick (about 30 minutes). Preheat waffle iron (about 5 minutes). Fill iron and cook waffle until steam stops coming from it (about 7–10 minutes). Makes three 7½" round waffles.

Tofu Blueberry Waffles

These tasty oatmeal waffles are totally vegan. Two waffles give you 16 grams of protein and 5 mg of iron—at least ⅓ of your daily requirement for each.

8 oz. tofu
3 cups water
¼ cups stone ground corn meal
¼ cup oil
3 tbsp honey
1 tbsp lemon juice
½ tsp vanilla
1 tsp sea salt
4 cups quick oats
1 cup blueberries (fresh or frozen)

Blend all ingredients except blueberries and oatmeal in blender. Add oatmeal and blend again (or mix with oatmeal in bowl). Fold in blueberries. Let stand until thick (about 2 hours). Heat waffle iron. Brush hot iron with butter or oil, pour batter and close. Bake waffles until steam quits rising from iron (about 10 minutes).

Hot Wheat Bran Cereal

Wheat bran, on the other hand, has the advantage over oat bran of promoting regularity. If that's your objective in the morning, try this proven natural remedy (to be prepared the night before).

½ cup whole grain cereal (cracked wheat, millet, bulgur wheat, seven-grain, etc.)
½ cup wheat bran
3 cups water
dried fruit and salt to taste

Combine ingredients and bring to a boil. Turn off heat and let soak overnight. Reheat in the morning. Serves 2.

Millet with Dates and Nuts

Millet is generally considered bird food in this country, but it's a staple grain in many parts of the world. This recipe turns it into a tasty breakfast cereal. The coconut in the recipe is optional, since coconut is one of the few plant foods that are high in saturated fat. Note, however, that in essentially-vegan natives whose diets are high in coconut oil, heart disease incidence remains low.

1 cup millet
¾ tsp sea salt
4 cups water
¾ cup chopped dates
½ cup slivered almonds
½ cup unsweetened grated coconut

Add salt to water and bring to a boil. Add millet and simmer for 15 minutes. Add remaining ingredients and simmer 5 minutes more. Serve as is, or with milk or soymilk, and pure maple syrup or honey.

Grandma Brown's Sugarless Granola

Here's a natural alternative to commercial granola, which is heavily laced with refined sugar.

3 tbsp peanut butter
2 tbsp butter or margarine
⅓ cup pure maple syrup
½ cup water
1 tsp vanilla
½ tsp almond flavoring

Combine ingredients in saucepan. Heat to melt, mixing thoroughly. In a large bowl, mix:

6 cups oatmeal
1½ cups wheat bran
½ cup coconut
½ cup sunflower seeds
¼ cup chopped nuts (walnuts or pecans)
½ cup bulgur wheat (cooked)

Pour saucepan mixture over grains, seeds and nuts, mixing thoroughly. Pour into a large pan and bake at 300 degrees for 20 minutes. Stir. Lower heat to 275 degrees and bake 40 minutes more.

Tofu Pancakes

Beans are the major protein source of the predominantly vegetarian Third World, but my children won't touch them. The solution? Tofu, a yogurt-like soybean derivative that can be used in treats that children love, such as pancakes and French toast. This recipe is modified from *Cook with Tofu* by Christina Clarke (New York: Avon Books 1981). If you get 6 pancakes from it, each contains 9 grams of protein, 70 mg of calcium and 2 mg of iron. My kids easily eat two each at a sitting. That's 18 grams of protein, 140 mg of calcium and 4 mg of iron; or, for a 10-year-old, over half the U.S. RDA for protein, nearly half the RDA for iron, and a sixth the RDA for calcium. By FAO/WHO criteria, it's an even greater percentage of these requirements.

   2 cups whole wheat pastry flour (or unbleached white)
   1¾ tsp baking soda
   ½ tsp salt
   1 cup water
   ¼ cup oil or clarified butter
   1 tbsp honey
   1 tbsp lemon juice
   8 oz. tofu, mashed with a fork
   2 eggs

Combine dry ingredients in a mixing bowl. Combine wet ingredients in a blender, adding tofu gradually until smooth. Combine the 2 mixtures, stirring quickly. Heat on lightly oiled griddle. (If first pancake is too thick, add a bit of water; if too thin, add flour.)

Tofu Buckwheat Pancakes

Tofu can actually improve the taste of buckwheat pancakes by diluting the strong buckwheat flavor. The batter is best if prepared the night before.

   1 tsp active dry yeast
   ½ cup lukewarm water
   1 tbsp pure maple syrup

Dissolve yeast in water. Add syrup and let sit about 5 minutes (until bubbly). Meanwhile, blend:

8 oz. tofu
1 tbsp butter
½ tsp sea salt
1½ cups water

Add:

1½ cups whole grain buckwheat flour
½ cup stone ground whole wheat flour

Combine all ingredients. Beat or blend until smooth. Cover and let rise overnight. Spoon batter onto griddle and fry in a small amount of butter.

Tofu French Toast

My kids can each eat 3 slices of this French toast at a meal. This gives them 22 grams of protein, 230 mg of calcium and 5 mg of iron. For a 10-year-old, that's two-thirds of the U.S. RDA for protein, half the requirement for iron, and nearly a third of the requirement for calcium.

1 tsp lemon juice
6 oz. very fresh, soft tofu (if it's sour, children will notice)
3 eggs
2 tbsp pure maple syrup
⅜ tsp sea salt
6 slices whole grain bread

Blend all ingredients except bread. Pour into shallow dish. Dip bread into mixture, coating both sides. Lay dipped bread on well-oiled baking sheet and bake at 500 degrees about 5 minutes on each side, or until lightly browned. For children and those who can afford the calories, serve with butter and pure maple syrup. For adults on a diet, serve with warm, unsweetened applesauce.

Tofu Corn Cakes

Corn is the staple grain of the Indians of Mexico and Central America, including the extremely athletic Tarahumara. (See Chapter 6.) Corn is low in protein, but these tofu corn cakes aren't. One of them gives you 11 grams of protein, as well as 184 mg of calcium and 2 mg of iron.

    12 oz. tofu
    1 egg
    ½ cup soymilk or milk
    4 tbsp butter or margarine
    1 tbsp baking powder
    1 tsp sea salt
    1 cup stone ground corn meal
    1 cup stone ground whole wheat flour

Blend all ingredients except corn meal and flour in blender. Add corn meal and flour. Blend again. Pour batter onto hot, lightly greased griddle and brown on both sides. Makes 6 cakes about 6″ in diameter.

Corn Cakes Colonial-Style

Corn was also a staple for the British colonists, who had trouble growing their imported grains on American soil. The Indians' maize became the colonists' corn, the medieval English word for grain. Colonial-style corn cakes used the whole corn kernel.

    10-oz. package frozen corn kernels, thawed
    ¼ cup stone ground whole wheat flour
    1 egg, beaten
    ⅓ cup milk or soymilk
    ½ tbsp raw sugar
    ⅛ tsp sea salt
    ½ tsp baking soda
    ⅛ tsp nutmeg

Combine all ingredients. Cook on griddle like pancakes. Makes eight 4″ cakes.

LUNCH

Salad

Salad is the dieter's basic lunch, but it doesn't have to be the boring iceberg-lettuce-with-a-cherry-tomato version often served in restaurants. Anything green, yellow, red, or brown in the vegetable section of the produce department can go into it. Looseleaf green and romaine are the most nutritious types of lettuce. Spinach, mustard greens, and celantro are also rich in nutrients. Grated beets and carrots add not only vitamins but flavor, texture, and color. Seeds and nuts add protein. Sunflower seeds add iron. Sprouts are nutrient-rich. And bread makes your salad a satisfying meal. Your salad's only liability may be the dressing, but you can remedy that by making your own.

Vinegar and Oil Dressing

To avoid the detrimental effects of heat-processed oil, as well as the sugar and other additives commonly found in vinegar-and-oil dressings, try making your dressing from scratch. Combine 2 parts of a good polyunsaturated cold-pressed oil (like safflower oil), with 1 part vinegar or lemon juice. Add fresh or dried herbs or mustard (dried or prepared) to taste.

Lemon and Honey Dressing

   ½ cup cold-pressed vegetable oil
   ½ cup fresh lemon juice
   1½ tsp honey

Blend in blender, or shake in a jar with the lid on.

Vinegar, Oil and Honey Dressing

⅓ cup honey
¾ cup cold-pressed vegetable oil
3 tbsp red wine vinegar
1½ tsp onion juice
¾ tsp sea salt
¼ tsp natural stone ground mustard

Blend in blender.

Tofu Avocado Dressing

The same seasonings can be used to make a dressing based on tofu. It has the advantage of being free of processed oils, which are susceptible to free radical formation. (See Chapter 4.) Combine all of the ingredients in the previous recipe except oil with 8 ounces of tofu and a quarter of an avocado. Blend in blender until smooth.

SANDWICHES, SPREADS, AND DIPS

Contrary to what your local sandwich bar may have led you to believe, avocado-cheese-and-sprouts is *not* the only palatable alternative to meat. Here are some other sandwich and spread possibilities that are lower in cholesterol and higher in protein.

Wanja's Coriander Paste

The staple foods of the Bantu tribes of Kenya are ugali, a sort of dry porridge made from white corn meal; and sukuma wiki, a dark, tough green that is very high in nutrients and is prepared by stir-frying. Coriander is another nutritious leafy green that is a Kenyan favorite. This tasty paste can be used as a spread or dip, or can be mixed with plain yogurt and used as a dressing or dip. It's also good as a side dish with Indian curries for dipping chapatis.

6 bunches fresh coriander
½ cup cashew nuts
2 tbsp lemon juice
1 medium green chili pepper
½ tsp black pepper
½ tsp salt
¼ cup water

Mix ingredients in a blender or food processor.

Hummus

Hummus is a Middle Eastern bread spread made with tahini, the sesame equivalent of peanut butter. Hummus is both lower in fat and higher in protein than butter or margarine. Its major constituent is garbanzo beans (chickpeas). Unlike butter, which raises serum cholesterol, garbanzo beans lower it. Hummus is best made from dry beans, but canned will do. If you start with the dry beans, wash them thoroughly and let them soak overnight. Discard soaking water and simmer in an equal amount of new water for 2 hours, or until tender.

4 cups cooked garbanzo beans
¼ cup lemon juice
¼ cup tahini
⅔ tsp garlic salt
2 cloves garlic
½ small onion

Combine all ingredients in food processor until smooth. Serve in pita bread as a sandwich or with pita strips as a dip.

Tofu/Tomato Sandwich Spread

Two tablespoons of this tasty spread—enough for one sandwich—contain only 45 calories.

  7 oz. tofu
  3 tomatoes
  ½ cup water
  2 tbsp butter
  ¾ tsp sea salt
  ½ tsp onion powder
  ½ tsp garlic powder
  ¼ tsp basil
  ⅔ cup soy flour

Blend everything except soy flour. Add soy flour and blend again. Pour into 1½ quart casserole. Bake at 400 degrees for 10 minutes, then at 325 degrees for 50 minutes. Makes 3 cups.

Carrot Sandwiches

  ½ cup peanut butter
  1 cup grated carrots
  4 tsp cold-pressed mayonnaise

Mix ingredients. Spread on whole grain bread. Top with alfalfa sprouts or lettuce if desired.

Nut-Meat-Loaf Sandwiches

Any of the vegetarian nut or bean loaves can be sliced cold for a delicious sandwich. (See Dinner.)

Bean Dip

This high-protein dip is good with baked tortilla chips or in bean tostadas.

1 cup black beans, dry
5 cups water
1 tbsp sea salt
½ onion, chopped fine
2 large cloves garlic
1 tbsp chili powder or to taste
2 bay laurel leaves
1½ tbsp oil
corn tortillas

Cook beans in salted water until soft (about 1 hour). Drain and blend in blender to a paste. Saute onions and garlic in oil. Add seasonings, bay leaves and beans. Cook covered over low heat for 10 minutes. Add water as necessary for desired consistency.

Tortilla Chips

Cut corn tortillas into strips. Toast in 300-degree oven for about 5 minutes.

Bean Tostada

Spread bean dip on corn tortillas that have been toasted for about 5 minutes in a 300-degree oven. Top with shredded cabbage or lettuce, then with salsa. For non-dieters, mashed avocado or sour cream (imitation, for vegans) is also delicious.

Mexican Salsa

1 tomato
2 jalapeno chili peppers
¼–½ onion
1 small clove garlic
¼ tsp sea salt

Boil tomato, chili peppers, onion, and garlic until soft. Combine all ingredients in blender. If you're in a hurry, all you really need are the tomato and chili peppers.

Guacamole

Although avocados are high in fat, half an avocado still contains only 153 calories. Its fat is mainly monounsaturated, which means it lowers cholesterol without risking cancer. (See Chapter 4.) Avocados are also good sources of vitamins A and B6, folic acid, niacin, potassium, and magnesium. Guacamole is good as a dip or on tostadas and other Mexican creations.

    2 ripe avocados
    1 ripe tomato
    ½ onion, finely minced
    jalapeno chili peppers, chopped
    lemon juice
    salt
    pepper
    garlic

Peel tomato, first dropping it in boiling water if necessary to loosen skin. Mash tomato and avocado. Mix with onion, chili peppers and seasonings to taste.

Kachumbari (Kenyan Hot Sauce)

This sauce will liven up even the most boring vegetable casserole.

    6 red onions, very thinly sliced
    6 tomatoes, chopped
    ¼ cup vinegar or lime juice
    ¼ tsp salt
    1 long green chili pepper, chopped

Wash onions in salted water. Soak for about five minutes, then squeeze water out, crushing onions slightly to soften. Combine onions and tomatoes with vinegar or lime juice. Add chili pepper. For a version that's more like salad, add 2 chopped medium-sized cucumbers, 2 chopped medium-sized carrots, and 4 chopped lettuce leaves.

SOUP

Soups are another way to get your luncheon vegetables in a low-calorie but highly palatable form. Any combination of fresh vegetables will make a soup, but here are some ideas for starters.

Zucchini Soup

This delicious soup is additive-free and vitamin-rich. The same basic recipe works for carrot soup, spinach soup, etc. Just cook up your choice of vegetable, blend, and add sauteed onions and seasonings.

    6 medium-sized zucchini
    1 tbsp butter or margarine
    ½ onion, chopped fine
    2½ tbsp seasoned stock base
    ½ tsp sea salt (or to taste)

Cover zucchini with water. Bring to a boil, reduce heat and simmer until soft. Blend with enough cooking water to make about 3½ cups of puree. Saute onion in butter or margarine until transparent. Add puree and bring to a boil. Add additional cooking water as needed for desired consistency. Add seasonings.

Kale, Collards, and Other Woody Greens

You can use the same method and ingredients to prepare kale, collard greens, mustard greens, and other nutrient-dense, dark leafy vegetables. They're too woody to blend to a soup, but they make a tasty mash that is good over rice and other grains.

Garbanzo Bean Soup

The cholesterol-lowering garbanzo bean makes a great soup. Good with corn tortillas heated directly over a gas flame.

1 cup dry garbanzo beans, soaked overnight (or 2 cups canned)
2 cloves garlic, minced
1 small onion, chopped
1 tbsp butter or margarine
4 fresh tomatoes, chopped (or 1 large can)
1 tbsp parsley (chopped fresh or dried)
1 tsp sea salt
3 cups water
½ cabbage, shredded
½ cube bouillon
caynenne pepper to taste, if desired

Discard soaking water. Add 4 cups new water and simmer for one hour. (Mexican cooks slip the skins off the beans after soaking, but it takes time and isn't essential.) In a large pot, saute garlic and onion in butter until onion is transparent. Add tomatoes and parsley. Bring to a boil and simmer for 5 minutes. Drain beans and add to mixture along with cabbage and 2 cups of water. Cover and simmer 20 minutes. Makes about 2 quarts.

Cauliflower Soup

½ white onion
3 cloves garlic
3 potatoes
3 carrots
½ cauliflower, chopped
salt
thyme
3 cups water
2 cups tomato sauce (16-oz. can)
2 bay leaves

Chop vegetables into bite-sized pieces. Boil cauliflower separately for 2 minutes; throw out water. Bring 3 new cups of water to a boil. Add all ingredients. Simmer for 5 minutes.

Benita's Lentil Soup

Lentils are a popular Third World source of protein, providing 15.6 grams of it per cup.

    5–6 cups water
    1¼ cups lentils
    ½ cup rice
    1 onion, chopped
    2 stalks celery, finely diced
    1 6-oz. can tomato paste
    1 tbsp bouillon
    ½ tsp oregano
    1 clove garlic, crushed

Combine ingredients. Cook in pressure cooker 20 minutes, or simmer in covered pan about 45 minutes.

DINNER

Tofu Millet Casserole

Millet is the staple grain in many areas of Africa, China, and India. A sixth of this tasty millet casserole supplies 20 grams of protein, 350 mg of calcium, and 7 mg of iron for only 400 calories (including the optional grated cheese topping). That's ⅖ of the daily protein requirement and ⅔ of the calcium and iron requirements of an adult man. And it's supplied by only ⅐ of his daily allotment in calories.

1½ cups dry millet
3 cups water, seasoned with 1 tsp sea salt
1½ lb fresh broccoli, chopped (or 10 oz. frozen, thawed, chopped)
3 carrots, chopped
2 tbsp butter or margarine
1 medium onion, chopped
8 oz. mushrooms, sliced
1 clove garlic, minced
2 sprigs celantro, chopped
1 tsp marjoram
½ tsp basil
¼ tsp thyme
1–2 tsp sea salt
1 tsp flavored bouillon
chopped jalapeno chili pepper to taste (optional)
pepper to taste
8 oz. tofu, mashed with fork
¾ cup (3 oz.) shredded cheddar cheese (optional)

Bring water to a boil. Add millet, reduce heat, and simmer for 20 minutes or until water is absorbed. Steam broccoli and carrots until just soft. Meanwhile, melt butter in large frying pan over medium heat. Saute onion, garlic, mushrooms, and chili pepper about 5 minutes. Add broccoli, carrots, and seasonings to frying pan mixture and cook 2 minutes more, stirring constantly. Turn off heat. Stir in tofu and millet. Top with cheese if desired; or top with buttered whole wheat bread crumbs. Can also be served with plain yogurt to cool down the chili pepper. Pour into 2-quart casserole and bake for 15 minutes at 350 degrees.

Black Beans

Black beans are a favorite protein booster in Latin America, where heart disease is low.

1 lb. black beans, dry
3 tbsp oil
1 medium-sized onion, chopped
½–¾ jalapeno chili pepper, chopped
2 tomatoes, chopped

Cook beans in salted water 1½ hours or until soft. Saute onion and chili pepper in oil until onion is transparent. Add tomatoes and cook for 1 minute. Mash beans lightly and add to frying pan mixture. Heat 5 minutes more.

Marina's Vegetable Burritos

These vegetable burritos are healthier than the beef version, and your guests will probably say they taste better.

1½ tbsp butter or oil
2½ carrots
½ green pepper
3 zucchini
1 cup chopped mushrooms
1 small onion
2 tomatoes
1 tbsp tomato sauce
¼ tsp dill
sea salt to taste
black beans, cooked and mashed (optional)
tortillas (for homemade, see following recipe)

Chop carrots into tiny pieces and sauté in butter or oil. While carrots are cooking, chop other vegetables except tomatoes. (If you don't have this particular combination of vegetables on hand, use whatever you have—celery, broccoli, etc.) Add chopped vegetables to carrots and continue sautéing. Blend tomatoes in blender. Add blended tomatoes and remaining ingredients to frying pan mixture and heat through. Heat tortillas, either by wrapping in aluminum foil and warming in 500-degree oven for 10 minutes, or by warming in frying pan or directly over gas flame, without oil. Spread a line of black beans down each (if you've got them handy, or you can just use the mixed vegetables for filling). Top with vegetable mixture and roll up burrito-fashion. Serve with Mexican salsa. (See Lunch.) If you can afford the calories, add mashed avocado or sour cream (imitation, for vegans).

Home-Made Tortillas

You can buy tortillas ready made, but they won't compare to homemade ones. The only essential ingredients are water and corn tortilla mix (Masa Harina, which is available at major grocery stores). Oil is not used, and salt is optional. Moisten flour with just enough water to shape. Form into 1″ balls. Flatten in a wax-paper-lined tortilla press or with a rolling pin. Heat but don't grease non-stick frying pan. Reduce heat to low and cook each 30 seconds on a side.

White Beans

1 lb. white beans (dry)
2 tbsp olive oil
1 small onion, chopped
½ green bell pepper, chopped
1 clove garlic
½ tsp thyme
3 bay leaves
8 oz. can tomatoes
⅔ tsp sea salt or to taste
1 tsp hot sauce or to taste
1 tsp red wine vinegar

Soak beans overnight. Discard soaking water, add 2 quarts fresh water and cover. Simmer 30–40 minutes or until tender. Sauté onion and pepper in oil with garlic and thyme until onions are transparent. Drain beans and add 2 cups of water. Combine frying pan mixture with beans, tomatoes, and bay leaves, and simmer for 15 minutes. Add salt, hot sauce, and red wine vinegar to taste.

Lentils

1½ cups lentils
4 cups water
½ onion, chopped
2 cloves garlic, chopped
2½ tomatoes, chopped
1 tsp sea salt
½ tsp dried parsley
⅛ tsp thyme
2 tsp butter or oil

Wash lentils. Cover with 4 cups water and bring to a boil. Simmer until soft (about 30 minutes). Saute onion and garlic in butter or oil for 2 minutes. Add tomatoes and cook on low heat for 7 minutes more. Add lentils with water and seasonings. Bring to a boil. Reduce heat and simmer about 20 minutes, or until done.

Coco's Sweet Lentils

This tasty Mexican lentil dish is sweetened with fruit.

1½ cups dry lentils
3 cups water
1 onion, chopped
1 tsp butter or oil
4 tomatoes, diced
3 cloves garlic, chopped (or ¼ tsp garlic powder)
¼ tsp cumin powder
1 apple, diced
1 banana, diced

Bring water to a boil. Add lentils; reduce heat and simmer, covered, for 40 minutes. In the meantime, sauté onion and garlic in butter or oil until onions are transparent. Add diced tomatoes and cook until soft. Add lentils and fruit. Cook covered for 20 minutes more over low heat.

Doug's 20-Minute Beans and Rice

For the man who can't wait.

> 1 small onion, chopped
> 1 tsp butter or margarine
> 1 16-oz. can black or pinto beans
> 1 10-oz. can stewed tomatoes
> 1 green pepper, chopped
> ½ tsp oregano
> ¼ tsp black pepper
> rice

Cook rice according to package directions. Microwave onion with butter or margarine for 3 minutes. Add green pepper and microwave 3 minutes more. Add remaining ingredients and microwave 10 minutes more. Serve over rice.

Tofu Burgers

Tofu can replace meat in that all-American favorite, the hamburger. These patties contain no saturated fat and no cholesterol.

> 1 lb. tofu, extra firm
> ¾ cup shredded carrots
> ½ cup finely-chopped onion
> 1 tbsp chopped or dried parsley
> 1 tbsp soy sauce
> ½ tsp garlic powder
> ½ tsp sea salt, or to taste
> ¼ tsp pepper
> 1 cup whole wheat bread crumbs (made by putting 1 slice dry or toasted bread through blender)

Drain and rinse tofu, place in a dish towel and close up ends. Squeeze out excess water by kneading for several minutes, until tofu has the texture of dry cottage cheese. Mix with remaining ingredients, except save ½ the breadcrumbs for later. Form into patties and coat with the following mixture:

½ cup whole wheat bread crumbs
½ tsp sea salt
½ tsp garlic powder
½ tsp powdered ginger

Bake on non-stick or lightly oiled baking sheet at 350 degrees for 15 minutes on each side, or until done. Serve like hamburger with lettuce, tomato, and mayonnaise on whole wheat buns or English muffins.

Sweet Dal

In India, digestive problems associated with beans and peas are eliminated by preparing them in the form of dal (sautéed legumes), which contains traditional Indian seasonings known for their gas-relieving properties. Dal is the basic protein dish in northern India, where heart disease and cancer are both rare. Half a cup at a meal is enough to satisfy protein requirements. Indians generally fry their seasonings separately before adding the vegetables, but you can substitute an equal amount of curry powder. Indians fry in ghee, or clarified butter from which the water and milk solids have been removed. Ghee won't scorch or turn black when heated and needn't be refrigerated. These characteristics suggest it is both less carcinogenic (cancer-producing) and less atherogenic (heart-disease-producing) than butter. You can buy it at Indian grocery stores or make your own.

This dal recipe is good made with red lentils or with Masoor Dal, a split yellow mung bean available at Indian grocery stores.

¼ cup raisins
1 cup red lentils
2 tbsp ghee or butter
1 onion, chopped
2 carrots, diced
2 medium-sized apples, chopped
3 tbsp whole wheat flour
½ cup soymilk or milk
½ cup water
1 tbsp curry powder
1 tsp sea salt
⅛ tsp pepper
hot chopped chili peppers to taste (optional)

Soak raisins in water until soft (about 1 hour). Simmer beans in lightly salted water in covered pan until soft (about 15 minutes). Chop onion and carrots and saute in butter or ghee until onions are transparent. Chop apples. Mix flour, salt, pepper and curry powder with onions and carrots. Add drained beans and 1 cup of the bean cooking water; then add remaining ingredients. Simmer for 30 minutes, stirring as needed to prevent sticking. Serve with whole wheat chapatis, or over brown or Basmati rice. May be topped with plain nonfat yogurt, coconut, or chopped peanuts.

David's Eggplant Curry

This curry is filling and satisfying, yet low in calories.

1 large eggplant
1 onion
2 tomatoes
1 cup water
1 tbsp olive oil
1 tbsp or 1 cube bouillon
1 tsp curry powder
1 tsp ground coriander
½ tsp cumin
salt and white pepper to taste

Cut 8 lengthwise slits in eggplant. Bake 1 hour, or until soft. Peel and chop. Drop tomatoes in boiling water for a minute to loosen skins. Peel and chop. Chop onion and saute in olive oil until transparent. Add tomatoes, eggplant, water, and seasonings. Simmer 10 minutes. Add more water if necessary for proper consistency. Serve over rice pilaf:

> 1 cup brown or long-grain white rice
> 1 tbsp olive oil
> 1¾ cups water
> 2 tsp bouillon

Sauté rice in oil until lightly browned. Add water and bouillon. Bring to a boil, reduce heat, and simmer 2 minutes. Serve curry over rice. Top with chopped peanuts, plain yogurt, or raisins.

Stir-Fried Vegetables

Conventional wisdom favors boiling over frying because it requires less fat. But to make your boiled vegetables palatable, you're probably going to butter them anyway. Boiling means valuable vitamins will be lost in the water. Sautéing vegetables in a small amount of oil seals in their vitamins and enhances their flavor at the same time. This stir-fry recipe works for any vegetable, but some particularly healthy ones to try are collards, mustard greens, and turnip greens. All provide generous amounts of calcium.

> vegetables, thinly sliced
> 2 tsp vegetable oil
> 2 tbsp lemon juice
> 1 tbsp water

Heat non-stick frying pan. Add oil, then vegetables. Stir with wooden or plastic spoon or spatula 1–2 minutes, or until vegetables are translucent. Add remaining ingredients, cover and cook 2–3 minutes more. Add soy sauce at the table.

Vegan Chow Mein

This Seventh Day Adventist version of the Chinese stir-fry
favorite is high in calcium, low in calories, and delicious. It
comes from *Ten Talents* by Frank and Rosalie Hurd (College-
dale, Tenn.: College Press, 1985), a source highly recommended for other vegan recipe ideas.

3 tbsp oil
¼ cup water
½ tsp sea salt
½ tsp onion powder
chicken-flavored seasoning (optional)
3 cups celery, sliced in thin diagonal pieces
2 cups onion, sliced thin or in rings
2 cups bean sprouts (soy or mung)
1 cup mushrooms, sliced
1 cup tofu, cubed
¼ cup green peas or parsley (optional)

Heat oil, water, and seasonings in large skillet. Add vegetables and cook covered until just tender (about 15 minutes).
Frozen peas or chopped parsley may be added at the end
for color, cooking with the lid off. Cover vegetables with
sauce:

1¼ cups water or liquid drained from vegetables
¼ tsp sea salt or kelp
1¼ tbsp arrowroot starch

Stir until thick. Serve with soy sauce over brown rice.

Bulgur Pilaf

Bulgur wheat is a basic grain of the Middle East, where
cholesterol levels are low. This tasty recipe is straight off the
Old World Bulgur Wheat Box, only slightly modified.

1 cup uncooked bulgur wheat
1 cup water
1 cup tomato juice
1 medium-sized tomato, finely chopped
2 tbsp butter or margarine
¼ cup raisins
¼ cup nuts (almonds or walnuts)
¼ tsp cinnamon
⅛ tsp cloves
⅛ tsp allspice
¼ tsp salt or to taste

Melt butter or margarine in wok or large skillet. Add bulgur; stir fry until it begins to crackle and turn color. Boil water and tomato juice together, then let cool. Add to the bulgur, cover, and simmer about 45 minutes, or until the water has evaporated. Add remaining ingredients and cook over low heat to desired dryness.

Vegetarian Cottage Pie

This creation is modeled on the British beef-and-potato cottage pie. It's not any lower in calories than the beef version, but it's a lot lower in cholesterol and saturated fat. It tastes great, and your guests may not believe it's meatless.

7 medium-sized potatoes
½ cup milk or soymilk
3 tbsp butter or margarine
1 medium-sized onion
1½ cups walnuts or almonds
2 cups breadcrumbs (made by blending whole grain bread
    in blender or nut grinder, 1 slice at a time)
1½ cups water
2 tbsp Worcestershire sauce
1 tsp basil
½ tsp marjoram
2 tsp sea salt
⅛ tsp pepper
1 medium tomato, sliced

Peel and quarter potatoes. Steam in steamer until soft (about 20 minutes). While they're cooking, chop onion and saute in 1 tablespoon butter. Grind nuts and bread in nut grinder or blender, a little at a time. Combine with onions. Add 1–½ cups boiling water (or enough to give the consistency of uncooked meatloaf). Add Worcestershire sauce, 1 teaspoon salt and other seasonings, and mix well. Spread mixture in greased baking dish. Mash potatoes with milk or soymilk, 3 tablespoons butter, and 1 teaspoon each salt and pepper. Spread potatoes on top of nut mixture. Garnish with tomato slices and chopped almonds. Bake at 400 degrees for 30 minutes, or until potatoes are golden brown on top.

Tofu/Carrot/Nut Loaf

Vegetarian bean and nut loaves are not only good for dinner. Cold and sliced, with mayonnaise on a whole wheat English muffin, they can surpass hamburger for lunch the next day.

    8 oz. tofu
    1 clove garlic
    1½ tsbp butter
    2 eggs
    ¾ tsp sea salt
    pepper to taste
    2 carrots, grated
    2 tomatoes, chopped
    ½ onion, chopped
    1 cup walnuts, chopped
    1 cup whole grain breadcrumbs (made by putting bread
        through a blender, 1 slice at a time)
    1½ tbsp Worcestershire sauce
    4 bay laurel leaves

In blender, combine tofu, garlic, butter, eggs, salt, and pepper. Stir in remaining ingredients and pour into oiled casserole. Bake for 45 minutes at 350 degrees. Serves 6.

Celery Nut Loaf

1 cup soymilk or milk
1 egg
1 cup chopped walnuts
1½ cups chopped onion
½ cup chopped celery
1 cup whole wheat bread crumbs (made by putting bread
  through blender)
1 clove garlic
2 tbsp Worcesterhire sauce
sea salt to taste

Beat egg, combine with soymilk or milk. Pour mixture over
remaining ingredients and mix well. Bake in oiled 1-quart
casserole 1½ hours at 325 degrees.

Tofu Zucchini Pudding

5 large zucchini squash, sliced but not peeled
1 small onion, diced
2 tbsp butter or margarine
8 oz. tofu, mashed with fork
2 eggs, beaten slightly
1½ cups whole wheat bread, crumbled and soaked in ½
  cup milk or soymilk
¾ tsp sea salt
2 tbsp Worcestershire sauce
¼ tsp pepper
½ cup grated cheddar cheese

Steam zucchini until soft. Sauté onion in butter until transparent. Combine all ingredients except cheese. Pour into
lightly greased 8″ × 8″ × 2″-casserole. Top with grated cheese.
Bake at 350 degrees for 45 minutes. Serves 6–8.

Green Casserole

A sixth of this tasty casserole gives you 11.5 grams of protein,
211 mg of calcium, and 3 mg of iron for only 200 calories.

⅔ cup chopped onion
1 clove garlic
3 tbsp butter or margarine
1½ cups chopped fresh tomatoes (about 3 tomatoes)
½ lb. green beans, stemmed and snapped (or 10-oz. package frozen)
¾ lb. fresh broccoli, chopped (or 10-oz. package frozen, chopped)
1 lb. tofu, mashed with a fork
1½ cups whole wheat breadcrumbs (made by putting whole wheat bread through blender, 1 slice at a time)
¼ cup Parmesan cheese (optional)
½ tsp salt

Steam broccoli and green beans until just soft. Sauté onion and garlic in 2 tablespoons butter until onion is transparent. Add tomatoes and heat to boiling. Add tofu, broccoli and beans; heat through. Pour into 1½-quart casserole. Saute breadcrumbs and Parmesan cheese in 1 tablespoon butter. Sprinkle evenly over casserole. Cook at 350 degrees for 20 minutes.

Quick Tofu/Corn/Tomato Casserole

Here's another version of the same basic tofu/vegetable/breadcrumb recipe which takes only 15 minutes to prepare. A sixth of it gives you 10 grams of protein, nearly 100 mg of calcium, and 3 mg of iron for 211 calories.

14 oz. tofu
2 cups tomatoes (1 1-lb. can, drained)
2 cups frozen corn, thawed
1 green pepper, chopped
1 tsp sea salt
1 tsp maple syrup
2 tbsp butter or margarine, softened
1 cup Italian seasoned breadcrumbs

Mash tomatoes and tofu in bowl with fork. Add remaining ingredients except ⅔ cup breadcrumbs. Pour into baking dish. Sprinkle remaining breadcrumbs over top. Bake uncovered at 375 degrees for 30 minutes.

Tofu Creamed Corn

    ¼ cup chopped green pepper
    ¼ cup chopped onion
    1 tbsp butter or margarine
    ½ tsp sea salt
    ⅛ tsp pepper
    3 tbsp stone ground whole wheat flour
    1½ cups milk or soymilk
    8 oz. tofu, cut into ½" cubes
    10-oz. package frozen corn, thawed

Sauté onion and pepper in butter. Stir in salt and pepper. Gradually add flour, then milk or soymilk. Add tofu and corn. Heat through. Serves 4.

Tofu Pasta

Pasta goes back to the ancient Etruscans, but in this country its popularity dates from the Italian immigrations of 1880–1920. Two ounces of dry pasta (or 5 ounces cooked) contain about 7 grams of protein and 210 calories, only 2% of which come from fat. Pasta contains thiamine, niacin and riboflavin; and the whole wheat version is a good source of fiber. With bottled, packaged or frozen sauces, you can make a pasta meal in a flash. But they probably contain objectionable ingredients, so you're better off starting from scratch. One-sixth of this homemade pasta sauce gives you 10 grams of protein, 150 mg of calcium, and 3 mg of iron for only 130 calories.

1 onion, chopped
3 cloves garlic, minced
1 tbsp butter or oil
4 tomatoes, chopped
½ green bell pepper, chopped
1 jalapeno chili pepper, chopped
1 bay leaf
½ tsp basil
½ tsp oregano
¾ tsp sea salt
¼ tsp pepper
16–20 oz. tofu
1 cup mushrooms, sliced lengthwise
1 lb. pasta noodles

Saute onions and garlic in butter or oil until onions are transparent. Add tomatoes and pepper. Heat to boiling. Add seasonings. Blend tofu in blender to consistency of Ricotta cheese. Add tofu and mushrooms to tomato mixture. Cover and simmer 15 minutes. Serve over pasta prepared according to package directions. Also good over rice.

Helen's Tofu Spaghetti Sauce

1 tbsp olive oil
½ cup chopped onions
1 28-oz. can tomato sauce
1 6-oz. can tomato paste
2 cups carrots, very finely grated (or peeled, steamed, and blended in a blender)
16 oz. tofu, diced
½ cup Parmesan cheese
2 cups chopped mushrooms
1 medium zucchini, chopped
1 tsp oregano
¼ tsp garlic salt

Simmer about 20 minutes. Best prepared several hours before the meal or the night before, and left in the refrigerator so flavors can mix.

Working Mothers' Easy Pasta

Boil whole grain pasta or spaghetti according to package directions. Add a package of frozen Chinese-style mixed vegetables to the boiling water. When heated through, drain and rinse. Sprinkle with Parmesan cheese, butter, and salt to taste. Serve as is, or pour into casserole, top with grated cheese, and bake in oven at 350 degrees until cheese melts.

BREAD

Nothing does more for your image as a homemaker than homebaked bread. But who has time to make it? You do, with your food processor, your blender, and these easy recipes.

Tofu Corn Bread

This corn bread takes only 10 to 15 minutes to prepare. The tofu increases its protein, calcium, and iron contents by about 50 percent.

    1 cup stone ground corn meal
    1 cup whole wheat flour
    1 tbsp baking powder
    8 oz. tofu
    ¼ cup maple syrup
    4 tbsp butter or margarine
    1 tsp sea salt
    1 egg
    ½ cup milk or soymilk

Mix dry ingredients. Blend remaining ingredients in blender. Then combine the two mixtures. Pour into oiled glass loaf pan and bake at 400 degrees for 45–50 minutes, or until toothpick comes out clean.

Food-Processor-Quick Homebaked Whole Grain Bread

Even yeast breads can now fit into the busy working womans' schedule. The secret is the handy food processor, which has revolutionzed breadmaking. This basic bread takes only about 30 minutes of actual preparation time. Rising and baking, of course, take several hours more.

    1 pkg active dry yeast
    1½ tbsp brown sugar
    1¼ cups warm water
    3 cups stone ground whole wheat flour
    1½ tsp sea salt

Combine sugar and yeast with warm water in a small bowl and set aside. Prepare food processor for processing with steel blade. Place flour and salt in food processor bowl, and add yeast mixture through chute. Process at high speed until dough forms into a ball. Break dough in half, then break each half into 3 or 4 pieces. Press pieces against steel blade and process at high speed until dough again forms a ball. Break the ball into several more pieces and repeat the process. Then repeat with the other half. Combine the kneaded halves into a ball and place in a buttered bowl, turning to butter all sides. Cover and let rise about 1 hour, until doubled in size. Punch down, shape into a loaf, and place in oiled glass loaf pan. Cover and let rise about 45 minutes, until doubled again. Bake at 425 degrees until golden brown (20–30 minutes).

Oat Bran Muffins

Oat bran muffins are a popular way to lower serum cholesterol.

    1¾ cups skim milk or soymilk
    1½ cups oat bran
    1 egg, beaten (or ¼ cup egg substitute)
    ¼ cup brown sugar, packed firm
    1 tsp cinnamon
    4 tsp cold-pressed vegetable oil
    1 cup stone ground whole wheat flour
    2 tsp baking powder

Combine milk and oat bran in bowl. Add egg, brown sugar, cinnamon, and oil. Mix well. Combine flour and baking powder and add to oat bran mixture, mixing sufficiently to moisten dry ingredients. Line muffin tin with paper baking cups. Fill each cup ⅔ full. Bake until light golden brown (about 20 minutes). Makes 1 dozen.

Apple-Cinnamon Oat Bran Muffins

2½ cups oat bran
1¼ tsp ground cinnamon
1 tbsp baking powder
½ cup evaporated skim milk
¾ cup frozen apple juice concentrate
2 egg whites or 1 large whole egg
3 tbsp honey
1 medium apple, cored and chopped but not peeled
¼ cup chopped walnuts
1 tsp baking soda
pinch salt

Preheat oven to 425 degrees. Mix dry ingredients in a bowl. In another bowl, mix evaporated milk, juice concentrate, egg, and honey. Blend in dry ingredients, then add chopped apple and walnuts. Line a muffin tin with 12 paper muffin cups and fill with batter. You can fill the cups more than if using wheat flour, because oat bran doesn't rise much. Bake for 17 minutes.

Oat Bran Banana Bread

Here's another painless way to eat oat bran. This and the next two breads are sweetened with fructose, which has the advantage over sucrose that it causes less of a rise in blood sugar levels. (See Chapter 3.) It's also a bit sweeter than sugar, teaspoon-for-teaspoon, so you need less.

½ tbsp lemon juice
½ cup milk or soymilk
1 cup oat bran
1 small banana, mashed
1 egg
⅓ cup fructose
1 cup stone ground whole wheat flour
1 tsp baking powder
1 tsp sea salt
½ tsp baking soda
4 tbsp butter or margarine

Mix milk and lemon juice. Let sit for a few minutes to sour.
Mix oat bran, banana, and milk together. Add beaten egg,
then fructose. Sift flour, baking powder, salt, and baking
soda together. Add to mixture. Heat butter to soften and stir
into batter. Pour into oiled glass loaf pan. Bake at 350
degrees for 45 minutes.

Tofu Banana Bread

You can also use banana bread to slip tofu into your family
menu.

¾ cup fructose
¼ cup butter or margarine
2 cups ripe bananas
8 oz. tofu
⅔ cup milk or soymilk
2 eggs
1 tsp vanilla
2 cups stone ground whole wheat pastry flour
1 tsp baking soda
½ tsp sea salt
1 cup chopped walnuts

Combine all ingredients except flour and nuts in blender.
Mix with flour in bowl. Add nuts, mixing just enough to
blend. Turn into oiled glass loaf pan. Bake at 350 degrees
for 40 minutes, or until toothpick comes out clean.

GUILT-REDUCED DESSERTS

CAKES

Tofu Date Cake

For 180 calories, this oil-free cake gives you 4 mg of iron, 136 mg of calcium, and 8 grams of protein. Calorie-for-calorie, that's 38 times as much iron, 4 times as much calcium, and 3½ times as much protein as in ordinary white cake. You also get more cake. And it takes only 15 minutes to prepare.

    16 oz. tofu
    ½ cup honey or maple syrup
    1 cup soymilk or milk
    2 eggs
    1 tsp sea salt
    1 tsp baking soda
    1 tsp cinnamon
    1 tsp nutmeg
    1 cup stone ground corn meal
    1 cup chopped dates

Combine all ingredients except dates in blender, adding corn meal last. Pour into oiled 8″ × 8″ pan. Sprinkle dates evenly over top. Bake at 350 degrees for 35–40 minutes, or until toothpick comes out clean.

Vegan Applesauce Cake

This cake is both sugarless and eggless.

> 2 cups whole wheat pastry flour (or 1 cup whole wheat and 1 cup unbleached white flour)
> 1 tsp baking soda
> ½ tsp cinnamon
> ¼ tsp cloves
> ⅛ tsp ginger
> ½ tsp sea salt
> 1¼ cups applesauce
> ¼ cup oil
> ½ cup honey
> ½ cup walnuts, chopped
> ½ cup raisins

Sift together dry ingredients. In another bowl, combine applesauce with oil and honey. Stir dry ingredients gradually into wet ingredients. Fold in nuts and raisins. Pour into oiled and lightly floured baking pan (9″ × 9″). Bake at 350 degrees, or until toothpick comes out clean (about 40 minutes). Cool in pan before slicing.

Tofu Rice Cake

The healthiest sweeteners are fruits and their juices. This moist cake is sweetened mainly with apple juice.

> 3 cups unsweetened apple juice
> 2 cups stone ground corn meal
> 8 oz. tofu
> 1 egg
> ⅓ cup whole wheat pastry flour
> 2 tbsp butter or margarine
> 1 tsp cinnamon
> 2 tbsp sesame seeds
> ⅔ tsp sea salt
> ¼ cup fructose
> 1 tbsp vanilla
> 2 cups cooked brown rice

Boil apple juice and pour slowly over corn meal in large bowl, mixing thoroughly to prevent lumps. Let sit for 10 minutes. Blend remaining ingredients except rice in a blender until smooth. Combine all ingredients. Pour into oiled and lightly floured 9″ × 9″ glass cake pan. Bake at 400 degrees for 15 minutes. Reduce heat to 350 degrees and bake 60 minutes more, or until toothpick comes out clean.

Pineapple Nut Cake

4/22/92

This cake is sweetened mainly with pineapple.

4 tbsp butter or margarine
½ cup fructose
1 egg
¼ cup soymilk or milk
⅔ cup frozen pineapple juice, thawed but undiluted
2 cups stone ground whole wheat pastry flour (or 1 cup whole wheat and 1 cup unbleached white flour)
1 tsp baking soda
½ tsp sea salt
½ cup walnuts, chopped
1 8-oz. can crushed pineapple, drained

Cream together butter and fructose. Add egg and beat with a spoon. Add soymilk or milk, and juice concentrate. Mix well. Sift flour, soda, and salt together. Add gradually to juice mixture, mixing well. Mix in walnuts and undrained crushed pineapple. Pour into oiled cake pan and bake at 350 degrees for 50 minutes. Allow to cool before cutting. May be topped with lemon icing (below).

ICINGS AND TOPPINGS

Lemon Icing

2 tbsp butter or margarine
¼ cup honey
1½ tsp grated lemon rind

Melt butter over low heat. Remove from heat and mix in honey and lemon rind. When somewhat cooled, dribble uniformly over cake.

Peanut Butter Topping

¾ cup peanut butter (made from peanuts and salt only)
½ cup honey or maple syrup
6 tbsp milk or soymilk
½ tsp vanilla

Mix with electric mixer. Good as an icing on cake or a topping for waffles and pancakes.

PUDDINGS

Oat-Bran Apple Pudding

This recipe replaces fiberless white flour with cholesterol-lowering oat bran, and it's sweetened mainly with fruit.

1 cup oat bran
2 tbsp safflower or corn oil
⅛ tsp sea salt
3 medium-sized apples
⅛ cup raisins
⅛ cup slivered almonds
½ tsp cinnamon
3 tbsp maple syrup
½ cup apple juice

Combine oat bran, oil, and salt. Mix into a crumbly dough. Peel, core, and chop apples. Place in 1-quart oiled baking dish. Stir in raisins, almonds, and cinnamon. Cover with oat bran mixture. Combine apple juice and maple syrup, and pour over top. Cover with aluminum foil and bake at 350 degrees about 45 minutes, or until apples are soft when stuck with a fork. Good with vanilla tofu ice cream, yogurt, or milk.

Whole-Grain Bread Pudding

Bread pudding is a handy way to use up old bread.

- 3 cups whole grain breadcrumbs (made in blender, blending one slice at a time) or whole grain bread cubes (made from dry bread)
- 2 cups milk or soymilk
- 2 tbsp butter or margarine
- 2 eggs, slightly beaten
- ½ cup raw turbinado sugar
- 1 tsp cinnamon
- ¼ tsp sea salt
- ½ cup seedless raisins

Scald milk with butter, heating almost to boiling. Combine ingredients, pour into baking dish, and place in pan containing 1″ of hot water. Bake at 350 degrees for 45 minutes, or until inserted knife comes out clean. Serves 6.

Vegan Bread Pudding

Same as above, but omit eggs, use soymilk for the milk, substitute ⅓ cup honey for raw sugar, and add a tsp of soy flour.

Brown Rice Pudding

Kids who aren't crazy about brown rice will still go for brown rice pudding.

1½ cups cooked brown rice
2 cups milk or soymilk
¼ cup fructose
¼ tsp sea salt
1 egg
⅔ cup raisins
1 tbsp butter or margarine
½ tsp vanilla
cinnamon or nutmeg to taste

Cook rice, 1½ cups milk or soymilk, fructose, and salt over medium heat, stirring as needed until thick (15–20 minutes). Beat egg and blend with remaining milk. Combine with rice mixture and raisins. Cook 2 minutes more, stirring constantly. Add vanilla and butter or margarine. Sprinkle with cinnamon or nutmeg.

GRANDMA'S PIES

You may not lose weight eating these pies, but they're healthier than the ordinary variety. They're made with whole wheat flour instead of white flour, and they're sweetened with fructose instead of white sugar. Fructose actually gives the fillings a better flavor than white sugar, and you need less of it for the same sweetening power.

Whole Wheat Crust

Whole wheat flour is harder to manipulate than white flour, but its deficiencies can be overcome by using whole wheat pastry flour, which is finer and lighter in texture; and by covering the dough with plastic wrap while you work with it.

2¼ cups whole wheat pastry flour (or 1 cup whole wheat and 1¼ cup unbleached white)
½ cup vegetable oil
¼ cup cold milk or soymilk

Sift dry ingredients together and stir. Form a well in the center. Put vegetable oil in a 1-cup measuring cup, add milk and mix. Pour into the well in the flour, then stir until thoroughly mixed. Wrap mixture in plastic wrap, form into a ball, and cut ball in half. Dampen counter and lay a sheet of plastic wrap on it. Place half the dough on the plastic wrap and cover with another sheet. Roll dough flat with a rolling pin, still covered with plastic wrap. Remove top sheet of plastic wrap. Slide hand under bottom crust and sheet, lift, and invert on pie tin. Peel off bottom sheet. Repeat with second ball for second crust.

Pumpkin Pie

A whole cup of pumpkin contains only 81 calories and less than a gram of fat. You can make pie with canned pumpkin, but it won't compare to starting from scratch. If using fresh pumpkin, choose small or medium-sized pie pumpkins (not the Halloween variety). Cut into strips, and peel off skin and seeds. Cut into 1″ cubes. Simmer covered in about ½″ of water until soft (45 minutes to an hour). Drain thoroughly. Blend in blender until smooth. This recipe makes 2 pies.

    3 cups cooked pumpkin
    3–4 eggs, slightly beaten
    1½ cups nonfat milk or soymilk
    1⅓ cups fructose
    2 tsp cinnamon
    ½ tsp ground cloves
    ⅜ tsp ginger
    ⅛ tsp sea salt

Mix wet ingredients and dry ingredients separately, then combine. Pour into two single crusts. Bake at 425 degrees until crust begins to brown (about 35 minutes). Reduce heat to 400 degrees and bake 20–25 minutes more. Pie is done when pumpkin is no longer runny when shaken, or inserted knife comes out clean.

Apple Pie

⅔ cup fructose
2 tbsp whole wheat pastry flour
2–3 tsp lemon juice
¾ tsp cinnamon
⅛ tsp sea salt
5–6 apples, peeled and sliced
1 tbsp butter or margarine

Mix dry ingredients together. Mix apples with lemon juice, then with dry ingredients. Arrange in bottom crust. Dot with butter or margarine. Make small slits in top crust with knife, 1½″ apart. Dampen rim of lower crust and lay top crust over top, sealing edges together with a fork. Trim edges and flute with fingers. Bake at 400 degrees for 45 minutes, or until edges are golden brown. Reduce heat to 375 degrees for 15 minutes more, or until apples feel soft when poked with a toothpick.

Blueberry Pie

4 cups fresh blueberries (2 small cartons), washed, stemmed
    and drained
¾ cup fructose
½ tsp cinnamon
3 tbsp tapioca
⅛ tsp sea salt
1 tbsp lemon juice
1 tbsp butter or margarine

Mix dry ingredients together. Add lemon juice and mix with berries. Fill bottom pie crust and dot with butter. Cover and bake as for apple pie on upper rack of oven. When blueberries are about to bubble over, protect oven with a sheet of aluminum foil on rack below pie (but not before, since foil blocks heat).

SHAKES AND SMOOTHIES

Papaya/Banana Smoothie

Besides apple juice concentrate, another useful fruit sweetener is papaya juice concentrate. To make a good smoothie, blend with bananas and any other appropriate fruit you have on hand (berries, pears, pineapple). Dilute with water to taste.

Tofu/Banana Smoothie

I'm throwing in this disguised tofu recipe because my kids used to like it. Now that they've tasted real milkshakes, they're no longer interested. You have to catch them young.

2 ripe bananas
7 oz. very fresh tofu
1 cup papaya juice concentrate
2 cups water
honey and vanilla to taste

Blend until smooth.

Strawberry Tofu Shake

This one, however, they're still crazy about; and it's very easy to make. The only problem is the sugar in the frozen strawberries. If you're hardcore, you can buy fresh strawberries and add honey.

5–10 oz. tofu
5 oz. frozen sweetened sliced strawberries
blend until smooth

FOOTNOTES

Footnotes

Chapter 1
VEGANISM: AN OLD DIET WITH A NEW NAME

1. T. Taylor, *Life of Pythagoras* (London: Watkins, 1965).
2. R. Rizek, E. Jackson, "Current Food Consumption Practices and Nutrient Sources in the American Diet," in *Animal Products in Human Nutrition* (New York: Academic Press, 1982), pages 150–51, citing *Nationwide Food Consumption Survey 1977–78*, Prelim. Rep. No. 1, Sci. Educ. Admin., U.S. Dept. of Agriculture.
3. "Diets of Early Miocene African Hominoids," *Nature* 268:628–30 (1977).
4. See R. Olson, et al., "The Effect of Low-Protein Diets Upon Serum Cholesterol in Man," *American Journal of Clinical Nutrition* 6(3):310–321 (1958).
5. *Ibid*; S. Eaton, M. Konner, "Paleolithic Nutrition: A Consideration of Its Nature and Current Implications," *New England Journal of Medicine* 312(5):283–89 (1985).
6. "Seventh Day Adventist Studies," *Vegetarian Times* (April 1986), page 12; see also M. Batten, "Life Spans," *Science Digest* 92(2):46 (February 1984); D. Georgakas, *The Methuselah Factors* (New York: Simon and Schuster, 1980), page 200.
7. R. Frentzel-Beyme, et al., "Mortality Among German Vegetarians: First Results After Five Years of Follow-Up," *Nutrition and Cancer* 11:117–26 (1988).
8. H. Kahn, et al., "Association Between Reported Diet and All-Cause Mortality," *American Journal of Epidemiology* 119:775–87 (1984).
9. T. Van Itallie, " 'Morbid Obesity': A Hazardous Disorder That Resists Conservative Treatment," *American Journal of Clinical Nutrition* 33:358–63 (1980).
10. F. Ellis, V. Montegriffo, "The Health of Vegans," *Plant Foods for Human Nutrition* 2:93–103 (1971); M. Abdulla, et al., "Nutrient Intake and Health Status of Vegans," *American Journal of Clinical Nutrition* 34:2464–77 (1981); M. Burr, et al., "Plasma Cholesterol and Blood Pressure in Vegetarians," *Journal of Human Nutrition* 35:437–41 (1981).

11. F. Ellis, et al., note 10.
12. C. Adams, *Nutritive Value of American Foods in Common Units* (Washington D.C.: Agricultural Research Service, USDA 1975). A gram of protein contains only 4 calories, while a gram of fat contains 9. A 2.9-ounce patty of cooked lean ground beef (21% fat) contains 19.8 grams of protein and 16.6 grams of fat, for a total of 79.2 calories from protein and 149.4 calories from fat.
13. R. Rizek, et al., note 2.
14. U.S. Dept. of Agriculture, *Agriculture Statistics 1985* (Washington D.C.: U.S. Government Printing Office 1985), page 497.
15. Calculated from figures given in F. Ashbrook, *Butchering, Processing and Preservation of Meat* (New York: Van Nostrand Reinhold Co., 1955), assuming an average lifespan of 74 years.
16. J. Anderson, "Health Implications of Wheat Fiber," *American Journal of Clinical Nutrition* 41:1103–12 (1985). See H. Trowell, D. Burkitt, eds., *Western Diseases: Their Emergence and Prevention* (London: Edward Arnold, 1981).
17. See Chapters 9, 15, and 16.
18. A. Rydning, et al., "Prophylactic Effect of Dietary Fiber in Duodenal Ulcer Disease," *The Lancet* (October 2, 1982) pages 736–39 (1982); see Chapter 3.
19. B. Ershoff, "Antitoxic Effects of Plant Fiber," *American Journal of Clinical Nutrition* 27:1395–98 (1974).
20. *Ibid.*
21. See Chapter 19.
22. R. Ballentine, *Diet & Nutrition* (Honesdale, Pa.: Himalayan International Institute, 1982), pages 71–72; see Chapter 22.
23. See R. Good, et al., "Nutritional Modulation of Immune Responses," *Federation Proceedings* 39:3098–3104 (1980); H. Trowell, "Hypertension, Obesity, Diabetes Mellitus and Coronary Heart Disease," in H. Trowell, D. Burkitt, eds., *Western Diseases: Their Emergence and Prevention* (London: Edward Arnold, 1981), pages 3–32; H. Valkenburg, "Osteoarthritis in Some Developing Countries," *Journal of Rheumatology* (suppl. 10) 10:20–22 (1983).
24. R. Rizek, et al., note 2; J. Anderson, "Health Implications of Wheat Fiber," *American Journal of Clinical Nutrition* 41:1103–12 (1985); C. Adams, note 12.
25. W. Brown, W. Karmally, "Coronary Heart Disease and the Consumption of Diets High in Wheat and Other Grains," *American Journal of Clinical Nutrition* 41:1163–71 (1985); C. Edwards, et al., "Utilization of Wheat by Adult Man," *Ibid.* 24:169–71 (1971); R. Rizek, et al., note 2, page 138; R. Ols0n, et al., note 4; J. Nelson, "Wheat: Its Processing and Utilization," *American Journal of Clinical Nutrition* 41:1070–76 (1985); B. Ershoff, note 19.
26. *Dorland's Illustrated Medical Dictionary*, 26th ed. (Philadelphia: W.B. Saunders Co. 1974), page 261.

27. See Chapter 5.
28. See Chapter 11.

Chapter 2
ALL CALORIES ARE NOT EQUAL

1. L. Cornaro, *Discourses on the Sober Life: How to Live 100 Years* (Mokelumne Hill, Cal.: Health Research), page 53.
2. N. Gustafson, "Losing Weight While Eating Well," *Vegetarian Times* (February 1984), pages 16–18; O. Mickelsen, et al., "Effects of a High Fiber Bread Diet on Weight Loss In College-age Males," *American Journal of Clinical Nutrition* 32:1703–09 (1979). Interestingly, *only* the overweight lose weight on a high-fiber diet. Thin rats and thin people seem to instinctively eat more food to make up for the difference in calories. See A. Sullivan, et al., "Caloric Compensatory Responses to Diets Containing Either Non-Absorbable Carbohydrate or Lipid by Obese and Lean Zucker Rats," *American Journal of Clinical Nutrition* 31:S261–66 (1978); and J. Hunt, et al., note 8.
3. I. Romieu, et al., "Energy Intake and Other Determinants of Relative Weight," *American Journal of Clinical Nutrition* 47:406–12 (1988). A similar study involving middle-aged men was reported in the same volume. It found that obese men, like obese women, ate more fat and less carbohydrate and fiber than non-obese men (although they did not eat more protein); and their caloric intake bore no significant relation to their weight. See D. Dreon, et al., "Dietary Fat: Carbohydrate Ratio and Obesity in Middle-Aged Men," *American Journal of Clinical Nutrition* 47:995–1000 (1988).
4. K. Duncan, et al., "The Effects of High and Low Energy Density Diets on Satiety, Energy Intake and Eating Time of Obese and Non-Obese Subjects," *American Journal of Clinical Nutrition* 37:763–67 (1983).
5. R. Barnett, "Why Fat Makes You Fatter," *American Health* (May 1986), pages 38–41; D. Porte Jr., S. Woods, "Regulation of Food Intake and Body Weight by Insulin," *Diabetologia* 20:274–80 (1981).
6. J. Wurtman, "Neurotransmitter Control of Carbohydrate Consumption," *Annals of the New York Academy of Sciences* 443:145–51 (1985); N. Gustafson, note 2.
7. G. Bray, "Obesity—A Disease of Nutrient or Energy Balance?", *Nutrition Reviews* 45(2):33–43 (1987).
8. J. Hunt, et al., "Energy Density of Food, Gastric Emptying, and Obesity," *American Journal of Clinical Nutrition* 31:S259–60 (1978).
9. T. Van Itallie, "Dietary Fiber and Obesity," *American Journal of Clinical Nutrition* 31:S43–52 (1978).
10. T. Van Itallie, "Fiber and Obesity: Summary and Recommendations," *American Journal of Clinical Nutrition* 31:S252 (1978).

11. J. Cummings, "Nutritional Implications of Dietary Fiber," *American Journal of Clinical Nutrition* 31:S21–29 (1978).
12. G. Haber, et al., "Depletion and Disruption of Dietary Fiber: Effects on Satiety, Plasma-Glucose, and Serum-Insulin," *The Lancet* (October 1, 1977), page 679.
13. J. Cummings, note 11; J. Kelsay, "A Review of Research on Effects of Fiber Intake on Man," *American Journal of Clinical Nutrition* 31:S142–59 (1978).
14. R. Barnett, note 5, quoting Jean-Pierre Flatt, professor of biochemistry, University of Massachusetts Medical Center, Worcester.
15. O. Mickelsen, et al., "Experimental Obesity: I. Production of Obesity in Rats by Feeding High-Fat Diets," *Journal of Nutrition* 57:541–54 (1955); R. Schemmel, et al., "Conversion of Dietary to Body Energy in Rats as Affected by Strain, Sex and Ration," *Journal of Nutrition* 102:1187 (1972).
16. P. Donald, et al., "Body Weight and Composition in Laboratory Rats: Effects of Diets with High or Low Protein Concentrations," *Science* 211:185–86 (1981); see "Dietary Protein and Body Fat Distribution," *Nutrition Reviews* 40(3):89–90 (1982).
17. See R. Passmore, Y. Swindells, "Observations on the Respiratory Quotients and Weight Gain of Man after Eating Large Quantities of Carbohydrate," *British Journal of Nutrition* 17:331–39 (1963); P. Bjorntorp, L. Sjostrom, "Carbohydrate Storage in Man: Speculations and Some Quantitative Considerations," *Metabolism* 27:1853–65 (1978); K. Acheson, et al., "Nutritional Influences on Lipogenesis and Thermogenesis after a Carbohydrate Meal," *American Journal of Physiology* 246:E62–70 (1984).
18. See E. Danforth, "Diet and Obesity," *American Journal of Clinical Nutrition* 41:1132–45 (1985).
19. V. Dole, et al., "Treatment of Obesity with a Low Protein Calorically Unrestricted Diet," *American Journal of Clinical Nutrition* 2:381–91 (1954); L. Allen, et al., "Protein-Induced Hypercalciuria: a Longer Term Study," *American Journal of Clinical Nutrition* 32:741–49 (1979).
20. K. Acheson, et al., "Glycogen Synthesis Versus Lipogenesis after a 500 Gram Carbohydrate Meal in Man," *Metabolism* 31(12):1234–40 (1982). One man even put butter on his bread (totaling five pats); he too lost body fat.
21. *Ibid.*; see note 17.
22. E. Danforth, note 18.
23. R. Barnett, note 5.
24. *Ibid.*; N. Gustafson, note 2.
25. H. Trowell, "Hypertension, Obesity, Diabetes Mellitus and Coronary Heart Disease," in H. Trowell, D. Burkitt, eds., *Western Diseases: Their Emergence and Prevention* (London: Edward Arnold 1981), pages 3–32.
26. See R. Peat, *Nutrition for Women* (Eugene, Ore.: Kenogen 1981), page 82.

27. D. Grimes, C. Gordon, "Satiety Value of Wholemeal and White Bread," *The Lancet* 2:106 (1978); see Chapter 24.
28. O. Mickelsen, et al., note 2.
29. *Ibid*; P. Burkholder, "Vitamins in Dehydrated Seeds and Sprouts," *Science* 97:562–64 (1943); R. Peat, note 26.
30. S. Kazimierz Kon, A. Klein, "The Value of Whole Potato in Human Nutrition," *Biochemical Journal* 22(1):258–60 (1928); see Chapter 5.
31. E. Whitney, E. Hamilton, *Understanding Nutrition* (New York: West Publishing Co., 1984), pages 208–09.
32. E. Whitney, et al., note 31, page 210; B. Singh, et al., "Liquid Protein Diets and *Torsade de Pointes*," *JAMA* 240 (2):115–19 (1978).
33. See "Lipogenic Adaptations Related to Pattern of Food Intake," *Nutrition Reviews* 30(7):151–57 (1972).
34. *Ibid*; see S. Reiser, et al., "Isocaloric Exchange of Dietary Starch and Sucrose in Humans," *American Journal of Clinical Nutrition* 32:1659–69 and 32:2206–16 (1979).

Chapter 3
BREAD VS. SUGAR:
ALL CARBOHYDRATES ARE NOT EQUAL

1. *King Richard II*, Act I.
2. R. Ballentine, M.D., *Diet and Nutrition* (Honesdale, Pa.: Himalayan International Institute, 1982), pages 59–60.
3. D. Jenkins, et al., "The Diabetic Diet, Carbohydrate and Differences in Digestibility," *Diabetologia* 23:477–84 (1982); G. Haber, et al., "Depletion and Disruption of Dietary Fibre: Effects on Satiety, Plasma-glucose, and Serum-insulin," *The Lancet* (October 1, 1977) page 679.
4. D. Jenkins, et al., note 3.
5. H. Himsworth, "The Physiological Activation of Insulin," *Clinical Science* 1:1 (1933).
6. J. Anderson, K. Ward, "High-Carbohydrate, High-Fiber Diets for Insulin-treated Men with Diabetes Mellitus," *American Journal of Clinical Nutrition* 32:2312–21 (1979); E. Bierman, "Diet and diabetes," *American Journal of Clinical Nutrition* 41:1113–16 (1985). See J. McDougall, M.D., *McDougall's Medicine* (Piscataway, N.J.: New Century Publishers, Inc., 1985), page 203.
7. D. Jenkins, et al., note 3.
8. J. Anderson, et al., note 6.
9. *Ibid.*; D. Jenkins, et al., note 3.
10. S. Reiser, et al., "Isocaloric Exchange of Dietary Starch and Sucrose in Humans I. Effects on Levels of Fasting Blood Lipids," *American Journal of Clinical Nutrition* 32:1659–69 (1979). In another study, when bread was substituted for fat in

a Western-style high-fat diet, serum cholesterol dropped by 29 mg/dl; but when sugar was substituted for the bread, it rose by 15 mg/dl. A. Cohen, et al., "Effect of Interchanging Bread and Sucrose as Main Source of Carbohydrate in a Low Fat Diet on the Serum Cholesterol Levels of Healthy Volunteer Subjects," *American Journal of Clinical Nutrition* 19:46 (1966).

11. See R. Ahrens, "Sucrose, Hypertension and Heart Disease: An Historical Perspective," *American Journal of Clinical Nutrition* 27:403–22 (1974); S. Reiser, et al., note 10; E. Cheraskin, et al., *Diet and Disease* (New Canaan, Conn.: Keats Publishing, Inc., 1977), page 308.

12. H. Trowell, D. Burkitt, *Western Diseases: Their Emergence and Prevention* (London: Edward Arnold, 1981).

13. A. Cohen, et al., note 10; S. Reiser, et al., note 10; M. Albrink, "Dietary Fiber, Plasma Insulin, and Obesity," *American Journal of Clinical Nutrition* 31:S277–S279 (1978).

14. M. Albrink, note 13.

15. S. Reiser, et al., note 10.

16. M. Albrink, note 13; E. Cheraskin, et al., note 11, page 308. Elevated insulin levels in response to a sugar load are also symptomatic of cardiovascular disease, to which diabetics are particularly prone. D. Jenkins, et al., note 3.

17. D. Snowdon, R. Phillips, "Does a Vegetarian Diet Reduce the Occurrence of Diabetes?" *American Journal of Public Health* 75:507–12 (1985).

18. *Ibid.* See also D. Snowdon, "Animal Product Consumption and Mortality Because of All Causes Combined, Coronary Heart Disease, Stroke, Diabetes, and Cancer in Seventh-Day Adventists," *American Journal of Clinical Nutrition* 48:739–48 (1988).

19. S. Reiser, et al., note 10; R. Ahrens, note 11.

20. "How Safe Is Aspartame?", *University of California, Berkeley Wellness Letter* 3(5):1–2 (1987).

21. K. Porikos, et al., "Effect of Covert Nutritive Dilution on the Spontaneous Food Intake of Obese Individuals: A Pilot Study," *American Journal of Clinical Nutrition* 30:1638–44 (1977).

22. See D. Palm, *Diet Away Your Stress, Tension & Anxiety* (New York: Pocket Books, 1977), pages 81–82.

23. See Chapter 13.

24. See R. Peat, *Nutrition for Women* (Eugene, Ore.: Kenogen, 1981), pages 76, 89; "Coffee–Not Guilty," *University of California, Berkeley Wellness Letter* 3(6):2 (March 1987).

Chapter 4
SALVAGING THE JOYS OF BUTTER FOR YOUR BREAD

1. See E. Shell, "The Sweet Taste of . . . Fat," *American Health* (May 1986), page 94.
2. R. Rizek, E. Jackson, "Current Food Consumptin Practices and Nutrient Sources in the American Diet," in D. Beitz, R. Hansen, eds., *Animal Products in Human Nutrition* (New York: Academic Press, 1982), page 150.
3. Assuming a pat to a slice. See C. Adams, *Nutritive Value of American Foods in Common Units* (Washington D.C.: Agricultural Research Service, USDA 1975), page 39.
4. See J. Kinsella, et al., "Metabolism of *Trans* Fatty Acids with Emphasis on the Effects of *Trans, Trans*-Octadecadienoate on Lipid Composition, Essential Fatty Acid, and Prostaglandins: An Overview," *American Journal of Clinical Nutrition* 34: 2307–18 (1981).
5. See M. Enig, et al., "Dietary Fat and Cancer Trends—A Critique," *Federation Proceedings* 37(9):2215–20 (1978); L. Thomas, "Mortality from Arteriosclerotic Heart Disease and Consumption of Hydrogenated Oils and Fats," *British Journal of Preventive and Social Medicine* 29:82–90 (1975); W. Martin, "The Combined Role of Atheroma, Cholesterol, Platelets, the Endothelium and Fibrin in Heart Attacks and Strokes," *Medical Hypotheses* 15:305–22 (1984).
6. J. Booyens, "Polyunsaturated Fatty Acids and Margarines: Reply," *South African Medical Journal* 66:793–94 (1984); J. Kinsella, et al., note 4.
7. L. Thomas, et al., "Concentrations of *Trans* Unsaturated Fatty Acids in the Adipose Body Tissue of Decedents Dying of Ischaemic Heart Disease Compared with Controls," *J. Epidemiol. Comm. Health* 37:22–24 (1983).
8. J. Booyens, et al., "The Role of Unnatural Dietary *Trans* and *Cis* Unsaturated Fatty Acids in the Epidemiology of Coronary Artery Disease," *Medical Hypotheses* 25:175–82 (1988).
9. F. Kummerow, et al., "The Influence of Three Sources of Dietary Fats and Cholesterol on Lipid Composition of Swine Serum Lipids and Aorta Tissue," *Artery* 4(4):360–84 (1978); T. Toda, et al., "Comparative Study of the Atherogenicity of Dietary Trans, Saturated and Unsaturated Fatty Acids on Swine Coronary Arteries," *J. Nutr. Sci. Vitaminol.* 31:233–41 (1985); J. Kinsella, et al., note 4.
10. See D. Kramsch, et al., "Atherosclerosis: Prevention by Agents Not Affecting Abnormal Levels of Blood Lipids," *Science* 213:1511 (1981); S. Broitman, et al., "Polyunsaturated Fat, Cholesterol and Large Bowel Tumorigenesis," *Cancer* 40:2455–63 (1977); M. Pearce, "Incidence of Cancer in Men on a Diet High in Polyunsaturated Fat," *Lancet* 1:464 (1971). In other studies, however, suggestions of a possible increase in colon cancer in populations taking a diet high in polyunsaturated

oils have not been substantiated. See K. Liu, et al., "Dietary Cholesterol, Fat and Fibre and Colon Cancer Mortality," *Lancet* 2:782–85 (1979); S. Goodnight, et al., "Polyunsaturated Fatty Acids, Hyperlipidaemia and Thrombosis," *Arteriosclerosis* 2:87–113 (1982). See also M. Jain, et al., "A Case-Control Study of Diet and Colo-Rectal Cancer," *International Journal of Cancer* 26:757–68 (1980), associating colo-rectal cancer with saturated fat and animal fat, but not with polyunsaturated fat.

11. See M. Kushi, *The Cancer Prevention Diet* (New York: St. Martin's Press, 1983), pages 100–01.

12. B. Ames, "Dietary Carcinogens and Anticarcinogens: Oxygen Radicals and Degenerative Diseases," *Science* 221:1256–64 (1983); D. Pearson, S. Shaw, *Life Extension* (New York: Warner Books, 1982), pages 100–19, 363–69.

13. B. Ames, note 12; R. Williams, *Nutrition Against Disease* (New York: Pitman Publishing Corp., 1971), pages 269–70.

14. A. Bonanome, S. Grundy, "Monounsaturated Fatty Acids for Plasma Cholesterol-Lowering Diets," *Nutrition & the M.D.* 15(1):1–3 (1989); R. Mensink, et al., "Effect on Blood Pressure of Two Diets Differing in Total Fat But Not in Saturated and Polyunsaturated Fatty Acids in Healthy Volunteers," *American Journal of Clinical Nutrition* 47:976–80 (1988).

15. D. Vesselinovitch, et al., "Atherosclerosis in the Rhesus Monkey Fed Three Food Fats," *Atherosclerosis* 20:303–21 (1974); D. Vesselinovitch, et al., "The Effect of Various Diets on Atherogenesis in Rhesus Monkeys," *Atherosclerosis* 35:189–207 (1980); R. Wissler, "Principles of the Pathogenesis of Atherosclerosis," in E. Braunwald, ed., *Heart Disease: A Textbook of Cardiovascular Medicine* (W. B. Saunders Co., 1984), page 1196.

16. D. Pearson, et al., note 12, pages 368–69.

17. L. Lawson, et al., "Suppression of Arachidonic Acid in Lipids of Rat Tissues by Dietary Mixed Isomeric *Cis* and *Trans* Octadecenoates," *Journal of Nutrition* 113:1927–1835 (1983); D. Ponder, N. Green, "Effects of Dietary Fats and Butylated Hydroxytoluene on Mutagen Activation in Rats," *Cancer Research* 45:558–60 (1985). See G. Null, S. Null, *How to Get Rid of the Poisons in Your Body* (New York: Arco Publishing Co., Inc., 1978), pages 202–05; "BHT: Weighing the Benefits and Risks," *Nutrition Action* (September 1977), pages 6–7.

18. See D. Pearson, et al., note 12, pages 110, 371. The authors also recommend certain supplements as antioxidants: vitamins E, C, B1, B5, B6 and A, cysteine, selenium, and zinc.

19. See H. Adlercreutz, et al., "Diet and Plasma Androgens in Postmenopausal Vegetarian and Omnivorous Women and Postmenopausal Women with Breast Cancer," *American Journal of Clinical Nutrition* 49:433–42 (1989).

20. B. Ames, note 12.

21. See R. Williams, note 13, pages 271–73, noting that calcium absorption requires the presence of sufficient fat, and fat ab-

sorption requires the presence of sufficient calcium. But if either of these components is excessive, absorption of the other is depressed.

22. Against margarine: see studies cited in note 6. In favor of margarine: see J. Rossouw, A. Benade, "Polyunsaturated Fatty Acids and Margarines," *South African Medical Journal* 66:793 (1984); J. Hunter, "Consumption of Trans Acids in Relation to Heart Disease," *Journal of Epidemiology and Community Health* 38:346–47 (1984). Against butter: see M. Jain, et al., note 10; J. Lubin, et al., "Dietary Factors and Breast Cancer Risk," *International Journal of Cancer* 28:685–89 (1981). In favor of butter: see studies cited in notes 25–26.

23. J. Kirschmann, *Nutrition Almanac* (New York: McGraw-Hill Book Co., 1984), pages 257, 263.

24. J. Groen, et al., "Influence of the Nature of the Fat in Diets High in Carbohydrate (Mainly Derived from Bread) on the Serum Cholesterol," *American Journal of Clinical Nutrition* 17:296–304 (1965).

25. K. Ho, "The Masai of East Africa—Some Unique Biological Characteristics," *Archives of Pathology* 91:387 (1971).

26. S. Malhotra, "Dietary Factors Causing Hypertension in India," *American Journal of Clinical Nutrition* 23:1353–63 (1970); S. Malhotra, "Epidemiology of Ischaemic Heart Disease in India with Special Reference to Causation," *British Heart Journal* 29:895–905 (1967); S. Malhotra, "Serum Lipids, Dietary Factors and Ischemic Heart Disease," *American Journal of Clinical Nutrition* 20(5):462–74 (1967).

27. R. Ballentine, *Diet and Nutrition* (Honesdale, Pa.: Himalayan International Institute, 1978), pages 92, 106.

28. "Stearic Acid and Blood Lipids," *Nutrition & the M.D.* 15(1):3–4 (1989).

29. B. Rolls, et al., "Food Intake in Dieters and Nondieters after a Liquid Meal Containing Medium-Chain Triglycerides," *American Journal of Clinical Nutrition* 48:66–71 (1988). The effect was only good for non-dieters. Dieters ate as much lunch after the medium- as after the long-chain triglycerides.

30. "Calcium, Vitamin D and Heart Disease," *Science News* 127(9):141 (1985); R. Williams, note 13, pages 268–73; S. Dreizen, et al., "Influence of Milk and Selected Milk Products on the Development of Medial Arteriosclerosis in the Rat," *Journal of Atherosclerosis Research* 6:537–47 (1966).

31. See Chapters 19 and 21.

32. H. Rowsell, et al., "Comparison of Effects of Butter and Egg Yolk on Development of Atherosclerosis in Swine," *Circulation* 20:970–71 (1959).

Chapter 5
PROTEIN: ENOUGH BEATS A FEAST

1. D. Hegsted, et al., "Lysine and Methionine Supplementation of All-Vegetable Diets for Human Adults," *Journal of Nutrition* 56:555–75 (1955).
2. National Research Council Committee on Dietary Allowances, *Recommended Dietary Allowances* (Washington, D.C.: National Academy of Sciences, 1980), page 46; see note 5.
3. See D. Miller, P. Mumford, "The Nutritive Value of Western Vegan and Vegetarian Diets," *Plant Foods for Human Nutrition* 2:201–13 (1972) (summarizing many studies); M. Hardinge, F. Stare, "Nutritional Studies of Vegetarians. 1. Nutritional, Physical, and Laboratory Findings," *American Journal of Clinical Nutrition* 2:73 (1954); M. Abdullah, et al., "Nutrient Intake and Health Status of Vegans. Chemical Analyses of Diets Using the Duplicate Portion Sampling Technique," *American Journal of Clinical Nutrition* 34:2464–77 (1981).
4. H. Linkswiler, "Importance of Animal Protein in Human Nutrition," in D. Beitz, R. Hansen, eds., *Animal Products in Human Nutrition* (New York: Academic Press, 1982), page 272.
5. See, e.g., J. Howe, et al., "Nitrogen Retention of Adults Fed Six Grams of Nitrogen from Combinations of Rice, Milk and Wheat," *American Journal of Clinical Nutrition* 559–63 (1972); D. Agarwal, et al., "Determination of Protein Requirements on Vegetarian Diet in Healthy Female Volunteers," *Indian Journal of Medical Research* 79:60–67 (1984); B. Bhatia, et al., "Determination of Protein Requirements in Healthy Male Volunteers on Vegetarian Diet," *Indian Journal of Medical Research* 77:658–67 (1983); E. Veiga, et al., "The Nutritive Value of a Rice and Soybean Diet for Adults," *Nutrition Research* 5:577–83 (1985).
6. D. Hegsted, et al., note 1.
7. See P. Lemon, et al., "The Importance of Protein for Athletes," *Sports Medicine* 1:474–84 (1984); B. Brenner, et al., "Dietary Protein Intake and the Progressive Nature of Kidney Disease," *New England Journal of Medicine* 307(11):652–59 (1982).
8. See Chapter 12.
9. See F. Coe, et al., "The Contribution of Dietary Purine Over-Consumption to Hyperuricosuria in Calcium Oxalate Stone Formers," *Journal of Chronic Diseases* 29:793–800 (1976); A. Lehninger, *Biochemistry* (New York: Worth Publishers, Inc., 1977), pages 741–42; A. Reunanen, et al., "Hyperuricemia as a Risk Factor for Cardiovascular Mortality," *Acta Med. Scand.* (Suppl.) 668:49–59 (1982); W. Robertson, et al., "The Effect of High Animal Protein Intake on the Risk of Calcium Stone-Formation in the Urinary Tract," *Clinical Science* 57:285–88 (1979); W. Robertson, et al., "Dietary Changes and the Incidence of Urinary Calculi in the U.K. Between 1958 and 1976," *Journal of Chronic Diseases* 32:469–76 (1979).

10. PAG Bulletin, 5(3) (September 1975).
11. P. Donald, et al., "Body Weight and Composition in Laboratory Rats: Effects of Diets with High or Low Protein Concentrations," Science 211:185–86 (1981); Joint FAO/WHO Ad Hoc Expert Committee, Energy and Protein Requirements, Techn. Report No. 522 (Geneva: World Health Organization 1973).
12. P. Payne, "Safe Protein-Calorie Ratios in Diets," American Journal of Clinical Nutrition 28:281–86 (1975); D. Calloway, H. Spector, "Nitrogen Utilization During Caloric Restriction," Journal of Nutrition 56:533–53 (1956).
13. Calculated from tables in J. Kirschmann, Nutrition Almanac (New York: McGraw Hill Book Co., 1984).
14. Ibid.
15. H. Oomen, "Interrelationship of the Human Intestinal Flora and Protein Utilization," Proceedings of the Nutrition Society 29:197–206 (1970).
16. See H. Trowell, "The Development of the Concept of Dietary Fiber in Human Nutrition," American Journal of Clinical Nutrition 31:S3–S11 (1978).
17. D. Miller, et al., note 3; S. Miller, Food for Thought (Englewood Cliffs, N.J.: Prentice-Hall, Inc., 1979), pages xii, 47–48; E. Cheraskin, et al., Diet and Disease (New Canaan, Conn.: Keats Publishing, Inc., 1977), pages 7–28.
18. V. Young, N. Scrimshaw, "Relation of Animal to Human Assays of Protein Quality," in American Medical Association, Nutrients in Processed Foods: Proteins (Acton, Mass.: Publishing Sciences Group, Inc., 1974), pages 85–98; S. Vaghefi, et al., "Lysine Supplementation of Wheat Proteins: A Review," American Journal of Clinical Nutrition 27:1231–46 (1974).
19. D. Hegsted, "Nitrogen Requirements and Utilization," in American Medical Association, Nutrients in Processed Foods: Proteins (Acton, Mass.: Publishing Sciences Group, Inc., 1974), pages 5–9; C. Edwards, et al., "Utilization of Wheat by Adult Man: Nitrogen Metabolism, Plasma Amino Acids and Lipids," American Journal of Clinical Nutrition 24:169–71 (1971); D. Hegsted, et al., note 1; S. Bolourchi, et al., "Wheat Flour as a Source of Protein for Adult Human Subjects," American Journal of Clinical Nutrition 21:827–35 (1968).
20. M. Hardinge, et al., "Nutritional Studies of Vegetarians. V. Proteins and Essential Amino Acids," Journal of the American Dietetic Association 48:25–28 (1966).
21. S. Laidlaw, et al., "Plasma and Urine Taurine Levels in Vegans," American Journal of Clinical Nutrition 47:660–63 (1988).
22. S. Rana, T. Sanders, "Taurine Concentrations in the Diet, Plasma, Urine and Breast Milk of Vegans Compared with Omnivores," British Journal of Nutrition 56:17–27 (1986).
23. M. Hardinge, et al., note 20.
24. C. Edwards, et al., note 19.
25. S. Bolourchi, et al., note 19.

26. S. Vaghefi, et al., "Lysine Supplementation of Wheat Proteins: A Review," *American Journal of Clinical Nutrition* 27:1231–46 (1974) (noting that studies to the contrary allowed insufficient time for adaptation to the wheat protein diet).
27. C. Edwards, et al., note 19.
28. J. Howe, et al., "Nitrogen Retention of Adults Fed Six Grams of Nitrogen from Combinations of Rice, Milk, and Wheat," *American Journal of Clinical Nutrition* 25:559–63 (1972). See R. Ballentine, *Transition to Vegetarianism* (Honesdale, Pa.: Himalayan International Institute, 1987), page 96.
29. S. Kazimierz Kon, A. Klein, "The Value of Whole Potato in Human Nutrition," *Biochemical Journal* 22(1):258–60 (1928).
30. R. Ballentine, note 28, page 95.
31. *Ibid*; C. Jacobs, J. Dwyer, "Vegetarian Children: Appropriate and Inappropriate Diets," *American Journal of Clinical Nutrition* 48:811–18 (1988).
32. See S. Bolourchi, et al., note 19; H. Oomen, note 15; W. Connor, et al., "The Plasma Lipids, Lipoproteins, and Diet of the Tarahumara Indians of Mexico," *American Journal of Clinical Nutrition* 31:1131–41 (1978).
33. *Ibid.*; W. Connor, et al., note 32.

Chapter 6
MEAT OR WHEAT: WHICH IS THE
BREAKFAST OF CHAMPIONS?

1. B. Balke, C. Snow, "Anthropological and Physiological Observations on Tarahumara Endurance Runners," *American Journal of Physical Anthropology* 23:293–302 (1965).
2. W. Connor, et al., "The Plasma Lipids, Lipoproteins, and Diet of the Tarahumara Indians of Mexico," *American Journal of Clinical Nutrition* 31:1131–42 (1978).
3. C. Lumholtz, "Tarahumara Life and Customs," *Scribner's Magazine* 16:296–311 (1894); W. Bennett, R. Zingg, *The Tarahumara, an Indian Tribe of Northern Mexico* (Chicago: University of Chicago Press, 1935).
4. B. Balke, et al., note 1; see also D. Groom, "Cardiovascular Observations on Tarahumara Indian Runners—the Modern Spartans," *American Heart Journal* 81(3):304–14 (1971).
5. R. Chittenden, *The Nutrition of Man* (London: Heinemann, 1909).
6. See H. Munro, J. Allison, eds., *Mammalian Protein Metabolism*, vol. II (New York: Academic Press, 1964), pages 24–27; G. Pitts, et al., "Dietary Protein and Physical Fitness in Temperate and Hot Environments," *Journal of Nutrition* 27:497 (1944); R. Darling, et al., "Effects of Variations in Dietary Protein on the Physical Well Being of Men Doing Manual Work," *Journal of Nutrition* 28:273 (1944); L.Holt, et al., "The Concept of Protein Stores and Its Implications in Diet," *Journal of the American Medical Association* 181:699–705 (1962).

7. See J. Brooke, "Carbohydrate Nutrition and Human Performance," in J. Parizkova, V. Rogozkin, eds., *Nutrition, Physical Fitness, and Health* (Baltimore: University Press, 1978), pages 43–44; F. Ellis, V. Montegriffo, "The Health of Vegans," *Plant Foods for Human Nutrition* 2:93–103 (1971), page 101; *Vegetarian Times*, February 1984, page 58; July 1984, page 6; September 1984, pages 20–21; November 1984, page 8; December 1984, page 43; January 1985, page 25; April 1985, page 46; September 1985, page 8; August 1987, page 17.

8. N. Hanne, et al., "Physical Fitness, Anthropometric and Metabolic Parameters in Vegetarian Athletes," *Journal of Sports Medicine* 26:180–85 (1986).

9. H. Bieler, M.D., *Food Is Your Best Medicine* (New York: Ballantine Books, 1982), pages 43–44, 188, 193, 222–5. See also E. Abravanel, note 10, whose popular dietary theories are based on Dr. Bieler's.

10. E. Abravanel, M.D., *Dr. Abravanel's Body Type Diet and Lifetime Nutrition Plan* (New York: Bantam Books, 1983), pages 4–5, 15, 17–18, 25.

11. S. Vaghefi, et al., "Lysine Supplementation of Wheat Proteins: A Review," *American Journal of Clinical Nutrition* 27:1231–46 (1974); S. Bolourchi, et al., "Wheat Flour as a Source of Protein for Adult Human Subjects," *American Journal of Clinical Nutrition* 21:827–35 (1968).

12. J. Watts, et al., "Nitrogen Balance for Young Adult Males Fed Two Sources of Non-Essential Nitrogen at Two Levels of Total Nitrogen Intake," *Metabolism* 13:172 (1964).

13. W. Evans, V. Hughes, "Dietary Carbohydrates and Endurance Exercise," *American Journal of Clinical Nutrition* 41:1146–54 (1985); J. Brooke, note 7. The contention that protein is burned only if the diet is low in carbohydrate is based on nitrogen balance studies, in which no increase in urinary nitrogen excretion has been seen with physical activity. It is contested by Lemon, et al. (note 18), but only at levels of heavy exercise exceeding four hours at a time.

14. See W. Evans, et al., note 13.

15. *Ibid.*

16. *Ibid.*

17. *PAG Bulletin*, 5(3) (September 1975).

18. P. Lemon, et al., "The Importance of Protein for Athletes," *Sports Medicine* 1:474–84 (1984).

19. J. Durnin, "Protein Requirements and Physical Activity," in J. Parizkova, et al., note 7, pages 53–59.

20. A. Robeznieks, "Andreas Cahling: Mind Over Muscle," *Vegetarian Times* (April 1985), page 46.

Chapter 7
THE GORILLA IN YOUR BUSINESS SUIT

1. *The Descent of Man*, Chapter 6.
2. E. Danforth, "Diet and Obesity," *American Journal of Clinical Nutrition* 41:1132–45 (1985).
3. J. Stamler, "Population Studies," in R. Levy, et al., *Nutrition, Lipids, and Coronary Heart Disease* (New York: Raven Press, 1979), vol. 1, pages 30–31, 41.
4. S. Washburn, R. Moore, *Ape Into Man* (Boston: Little Brown & Co., 1974), page 21; A. Dixson, *The Natural History of the Gorilla* (New York: Columbia Press, 1981), pages 52, 54, 60–66. It's been said that man's digestive system closely resembles the omnivorous pig's. But the resemblance is not so close as with the great apes; and while the domesticated pig is an omnivore, most native hog species are herbivores. See K. Schmidt-Nielsen, et al., *Comparative Physiology: Primitive Mammals* (Cambridge: Cambridge University Press, 1978), page 57.
5. D. Fossey, *Gorillas in the Mist* (Boston: Houghton Mifflin Co., 1983), page 51; A. Dixson, note 4, pages 111, 115.
6. G. Schaller, *The Year of the Gorilla* (Chicago: University of Chicago Press, 1964), page 198; D. Fossey, note 5, page 51.
7. A. Dixson, note 4, page 115; R. Rizek, E. Jackson, "Current Food Consumption Practices and Nutrient Sources in the American Diet," in D. Beitz, R. Hansen, eds., *Animal Products in Human Nutrition* (New York: Academic Press 1982), pages 156–57.
8. J. Goodall, *In the Shadow of Man* (Boston: Houghton Mifflin, 1971), page 199.
9. R. Ewer, *The Carnivores* (Ithaca, N.Y.: Cornell University Press, 1973), pages 24, 35–41; G. Montgomery, ed., *The Ecology of Arboreal Folivores* (Washington D.C.: Smithsonian Institution Press, 1978), pages 136, 138, 154, 178.
10. A. Dixson, note 4, page 39.
11. See note 9.
12. L. Goldstein, ed., *Introduction to Comparative Physiology* (New York: Holt, Rinehart & Winston, 1977), page 391; A. Dixson, note 4, pages 45, 48; W. Clark, *The Antecedents of Man: An Introduction to the Evolution of the Primates* (Edinburgh: At the University Press, 1962), pages 74–82.
13. L. Goldstein, note 12, page 391; P. Rodman, J. Cant, *Adaptations for Foraging in Nonhuman Primates: Contributions to an Organismal Biology of Prosimians, Monkeys, and Apes* (New York: Columbia Press, 1984), page 252.
14. "Diets of Early Miocene African Hominoids," *Nature* 268: 628–30 (1977).
15. See Chapters 3, 8–20 (meat and chronic disease); B. Hunter, *Additives Book* (New Canaan, Conn.: Keats Publishing, Inc., 1980) (additives and chronic disease); R. Ahrens, "Sucrose,

Hypertension, and Heart Disease: An Historical Perspective,"
American Journal of Clinical Nutrition 27:403–22 (1974) (sugar
and cardiovascular disease); G. Campbell, "Diabetes in Asians
and Africans in and Around Durban," *South African Medical
Journal* 50:760 (1976) (sugar and diabetes); E. Freis, "Salt,
Volume and the Prevention of Hypertension," *Circulation*
53(4):589–94 (1976) (salt and hypertension).

16. W. Voegtlin, *The Stone Age Diet* (New York: Vantage Press,
1975), pages 132–33.

17. S. Eaton, M. Konner, "Paleolithic Nutrition: A Consideration
of Its Nature and Current Implications," *New England Journal of
Medicine* 312(5):283–89 (1985); R. Jackson, et al., "Influence
of Polyunsaturated and Saturated Fats on Plasma Lipids and
Lipoproteins in Man," *American Journal of Clinical Nutrition*
39:589–97 (1984); B. Phillipson, et al., "Reduction of Plasma
Lipids, Lipoproteins, and Apoproteins by Dietary Fish Oils in
Patients with Hypertriglyceridemia," *New England Journal of
Medicine* 312:1210–16 (1985).

18. S. Eaton, et al., note 17; B. Brenner, et al., "Dietary Protein
Intake and the Progressive Nature of Kidney Disease," *New
England Journal of Medicine* 307(11):652–59 (1982).

19. B. Brenner, et al., note 18. One of the few exceptions is the
genetic retention into adulthood of lactase, the intestinal enzyme that digests lactose, or milk sugar. But this genetic
change occurred mainly in North Americans and Europeans.
Many African and Asian adults are still unable to digest milk
products. S. Eaton, et al., note 17; M. Gordon, *Animal Physiology: Principles and Adaptations* (New York: Macmillan Publishing Co., Inc., 1977), page 40.

20. C. Lockhead, "Carving Out a Precut Meat Market," *Washington Times Insight* (August 17, 1987), pages 44–45.

21. However, a degree of ruminant function is now being as-
cribed to the human colon. See D. Jenkins, et al., "The diabetic Diet, Dietary Carbohydrate and Differences in Digestibility," *Diabetologia* 23:477–84 (1982).

22. A. Dixson, note 4, page 54.

23. The omnivorous rat manages to digest both plant and animal
matter efficiently, but it possesses certain regulatory mechanisms that we lack (discussed in Chapter 8).

24. P. Rodman, et al., note 13, page 252; H. Vonk, J. Western,
*Comparative Biochemistry and Physiology of Enzymatic Diges-
tion* (London: Academic Press, 1984), pages 470–72; G. Montgomery, note 9, page 209; C. Prosser, F. Brown, *Comparative
Animal Physiology* (Philadelphia: W. B. Saunders Co., 1961),
pages 116, 138, 148.

25. D. Georgakas, *The Methuselah Factors* (New York: Simon &
Schuster 1980), page 199; C. Prosser, et al., note 24, pages 112,
138; H. Vonk, et al., note 24, pages 107, 461–64; B. Drasar, M.
Hill, *Human Intestinal Flora* (New York: Academic Press,
1974), page 76.

Chapter 8
DEAD MEAT: YOU ARE WHAT YOU EAT

1. See S. Eaton, M. Konner, "Paleolithic Nutrition: a Consideration of Its Nature and Current Implications," *New England Journal of Medicine* 312(5):283–89 (1985); P. Henrikson, "Periodical Disease and Calcium Deficiency," *Acta Odontologica Scandinavica*, vol. 26, suppl. 50 (1968), pages 121–22; F. Pottenger, "The Effect of Heat-Processed Foods and Metabolized Vitamin D Milk on the Dentofacial Structures of Experimental Animals," *American Journal of Orthodontics and Oral Surgery* 32(7):467–85 (July 1946); R. Wissler, D. Vesselinovitch, "Experimental Models of Human Atherosclerosis," *Annals New York Academy of Sciences* 149:907–23 (1968). See also M. Gerson, *A Cancer Therapy: Results of Fifty Cases* (Del Mar, Ca.: Totality Books, 1977), page 146, and D. Howell, *Food Enzymes for Health and Longevity* (Woodstock Valley, Conn.: Omangod Press, 1980), page 79, both discussing studies in which groups of rats fed ordinary human food developed all the degenerative diseases and pathology known in human beings within one generation, while rats feeding from the soil maintained perfectly healthy organs through many generations; and R. Wissler, "Development of Atherosclerotic Plaque," in E. Braunwald, ed., *The Myocardium: Failure and Infarction* (New York: HP Publishing Co. 1974), page 155, discussing the induction of atherosclerosis in rhesus monkeys by feeding an American-type diet made up of mixed ordinary human foods.

2. M. Krause, L. Mahan, *Food, Nutrition, and Diet Therapy* (Philadelphia: W. B. Saunders, Co., 1984), pages 563–64, 602–03, 674; A. Reunanen, et al., "Hyperuricemia as a Risk Factor for Cardiovascular Mortality," *Acta Medica Scandinavica* (Suppl.) 668:49–59 (1982); H. Selye, *Calciphylaxis* (Chicago: University of Chicago Press, 1962), pages 406–31.

3. See, e.g., M. Burr, et al., "Plasma Cholesterol and Blood Pressure in Vegetarians," *Journal of Human Nutrition* 35:437–41 (1981); W. Robertson, et al., "The Effect of High Animal Protein Intake on the Risk of Calcium Stone-Formation in the Urinary Tract," *Clinical Science* 57:285–88 (1979); R. Mazess, W. Mather, "Bone Mineral Content of North Alaskan Eskimos," *American Journal of Clinical Nutrition* 27:916–25 (1974).

4. L. Abell, et al., "Cholesterol Metabolism in the Dog," *J. Biol. Chem.* 220:527–35 (1955); P. Henrikson, note 1; D. Howell, note 1, pages 77–80; B. Lapin, L. Yakovleva, *Comparative Pathology in Monkeys* (Springfield, Ill.: Charles C. Thomas, Publisher, 1960), pages 147, 254; R. Wissler, D. Vesselinovitch, note 1.

5. E. Quintao, et al., "Effects of Dietary Cholesterol on the Regulation of Total Body Cholesterol in Man," *Journal of Lipid Research* 12:233–46 (1971); J. Stamler, "Population Studies,"

in R. Levy, et al., eds., *Nutrition, Lipids, and Coronary Heart Disease* (New York: Raven Press, 1979), pages 25–88; R. Wissler, "Principles of the Pathogenesis of Atherosclerosis," in E. Braunwald, ed., *Heart Disease: A Textbook of Cardiovascular Medicine* (W. B. Saunders Co., 1984), page 1183.

6. K. Carroll, H. Hamilton, "Effects of Dietary Protein and Carbohydrate on Plasma Cholesterol Levels in Relation to Atherosclerosis," *Journal of Food Science* 40:18–23 (1975); R. Wissler, et al., note 4; L. Abell, et al., note 4.

7. D. Pertsemlidis, et al., "Regulation of Cholesterol Metabolism in the Dog. I. Effects of Complete Bile Diversion and of Cholesterol Feeding on Absorption, Synthesis, Accumulation, and Excretion Rates Measured During Life," *Journal of Clinical Investigation* 52:2353–66 (1973); A. Bhattacharyya, D. Eggen, "Mechanism of the Variability in Plasma Cholesterol Response to Cholesterol Feeding in Rhesus Monkeys," *Artery* 11(4):306–26 (1983); A. Lehninger, *Biochemistry* (New York: Worth Publishers, Inc., 1977), page 835; E. Quintao, et al., note 5; P. Nestel, A. Poyser, "Changes in Cholesterol Synthesis and Excretion When Cholesterol Intake Is Increased," *Metabolism* 25(12): 1591–99 (1976).

8. J. Emes, T. Nowak, *Introduction to Pathophysiology* (Baltimore: University Park Press, 1983), pages 264–265; Royal College of Physicians of London, *Medical Aspects of Dietary Fibre* (Pitman Medical, 1980), pages 95, 98.

9. Royal College of Physicians, note 8, pages 95–96; F. Pixley, et al., "Effect of Vegetarianism on Development of Gall Stones in Women," *British Medical Journal* 291:11–12 (1985); D. Kritchevsky, D. Klurfeld, "Influence of Vegetable Protein on Gallstone Formation in Hamsters," *American Journal of Clinical Nutrition* 32:2174–76 (1979).

10. See, e.g., D. Kritchevsky, et al., "Experimental Atherosclerosis in Rabbits Fed Cholesterol-Free Diets. Part 9. Beef Protein and Textured Vegetable Protein," *Atherosclerosis* 39:169–75 (1981); G. Descovich, et al., "Multicentre Study of Soybean Protein Diet for Outpatient Hypercholesterolaemic Patients," *Lancet* 8197:709–12 (1980); and other studies discussed in Chapter 19.

11. D. Kromhout, et al., "The Inverse Relation Between Fish Consumption and 20-Year Mortality from Coronary Heart Disease," *New England Journal of Medicine* 312:1205–9 (1985).

12. M. Weiner, "Cholesterol of Foods Rich in Omega-3 Fatty Acids," *New England Journal of Medicine* 315(13):833 (1986); T. A. Simopoulos, N. Salem Jr., "Purslane: A Terrestrial Source of Omega-3 Fatty Acids," *Ibid.*

13. I. Munro, S. Charbonneau, "Environmental Contaminants," in H. Roberts, ed., *Food Safety* (New York: John Wiley & Sons, 1981), page 155; R. Ballentine, *Diet and Nutrition* (Honesdale, Pa.: Himalayan International Institute, 1982), page 119; B. Ershoff, "Antitoxic Effects of Plant Fiber," *American Journal of Clinical Nutrition* 27:1395–98 (1974).

14. J. Ayres, et al., *Chemical and Biological Hazards in Food* (New York: Hafner Publ., 1969), page 144; T. Corbett, *Cancer and Chemicals* (Chicago: Nelson-Hall, 1977), page 81; I. Munro, et al., note 13, pages 141–80.
15. J. Hergenrather, et al., "Pollutants in Breast Milk of Vegetarians," *New England Journal of Medicine* (March 26, 1981), page 792.
16. R. Mazess, W. Mather, "Bone Mineral Content of North Alaskan Eskimos," *American Journal of Clinical Nutrition* 27:916–25 (1974).
17. See Chapter 11.
18. See Chapter 12.
19. See Chapter 13.
20. See, e.g., G. Laflamme, J. Jowsey, "Bone and Soft Tissue Changes with Oral Phosphate Supplements," *Journal of Clinical Investigation* 51:2834–40 (1972), and other studies discussed in Chapter 15.
21. P. Henrikson, note 1 pages 121–22.
22. P. Upton, J. L'Estrange, "Effects of Chronic Hydrochloric and Lactic Acid Administrations on Food Intake, Blood Acid-Base Balance and Bone Composition of the Rat," *Q. J. Exp. Physiol.* 62:223–35 (1977); R. Bell, et al., "Effect of a High Protein Intake on Calcium Metabolism in the Rat," *Journal of Nutrition* 105:475–83 (1975); Y. Kim, H. Linkswiler, "Effect of Level of Protein Intake on Calcium Metabolism and on Parathyroid and Renal Function in the Adult Human Male," *Journal of Nutrition* 109:1399–1404 (1979); M. Miettinen, et al., "Effect of Cholesterol Lowering Diet on Mortality from Coronary Heart Disease and Other Causes: a Twelve-Year Clinical Trial in Men and Women," *Lancet* 2:835–38 (1972).
23. See Chapter 13.
24. M. Krause, et al., note 2, pages 149, 153.

Chapter 9
THE CANCER CONNECTION

1. *Washington Post* (May 12, 1977), page A17.
2. R. Hur, *Food Reform* (Austin, Tex.: Heidelberg Publishers, 1975), page 1; J. Berg, "Can Nutrition Explain the Pattern of International Epidemiology of Hormone-Dependent Cancers?" *Cancer Research* 35:3345–50 (1975); P. Hill, et al., "Diet and Endocrine-Related Cancer," *Cancer* 39:1820–26 (1977); A. Walker, B. Walker, "Recommended Dietary Allowances and Third World Populations," *American Journal of Clinical Nutrition* 34:2319–21 (1981).
3. L. Cohen, "Diet and Cancer," *Scientific American* 257(5):42–48 (1987).

4. See, e.g., R. Phillips, "Role of Life-Style and Dietary Habits in Risk of Cancer Among Seventh-Day Adventists," *Cancer Research* 35:3513–22 (1975); T. Hirayama, "Epidemiology of Breast Cancer with Special References to the Role of Diet," *Preventive Medicine* 7:173–95 (1978); P. Nair, "Correlates of Diet, Nutrient Intake, and Metabolism in Relation to Colon Cancer," *American Journal of Clinical Nutrition* 40:880–86 (1984); B. Drasar, M. Hill, *Human Intestinal Flora* (New York: Academic Press, 1974), pages 212–14, 222–24. An exception among meat-eaters are the low-risk Mormons, discussed at note 11.

5. B. Reddy, "Influence of Dietary Fat, Protein, and Fiber on Colon Cancer Development," in D. Beitz, R. Hansen, eds., *Animal Products in Human Nutrition* (New York: Academic Press, 1982), page 441; B. MacMahon, et al., "Etiology of Human Breast Cancer: A Review," *Journal of the National Cancer Institute* 50:21–42 (1973); C. Huang, et al., "Fiber, Intestinal Sterols, and Colon Cancer," *American Journal of Clinical Nutrition* 31:516–26 (1978).

6. H. Adlercreutz, et al., "Diet and Plasma Androgens in Post-menopausal Vegetarian and Omnivorous Women and Postmenopausal Women with Breast Cancer," *American Journal of Clinical Nutrition* 49:433–42 (1989).

7. E. Farber, "Chemical Carcinogenesis," *New England Journal of Medicine* 305(23):1379–89 (1981); P. Nair, note 4; J. Berg, note 3.

8. L. Cohen, note 3; National Research Council, *Diet, Nutrition and Cancer* (Washington D.C.: National Academy Press, 1982), Chapter 5; W. Willett, B. MacMahon, "Diet and Cancer—An Overview (Part II)," *New England Journal of Medicine* 310(11): 697–703 (1984).

9. "Japanese Study Confirms Anti-Cancer Properties of Vegetables," *Vegetarian Times* (March 1985), pages 15–16.

10. M. Kushi, *The Cancer Prevention Diet* (New York: St. Martin's Press, 1983), page 101.

11. J. Enstrom, "Cancer Mortality Among Mormons in California During 1968–75," *Journal of the National Cancer Institute* 65:1073–82 (1980); D. Burkitt, "Colonic-Rectal Cancer: Fiber and Other Dietary Factors," *American Journal of Clinical Nutrition* 31:S58–S64 (1978). Cancer mortality among California Mormon adults is 50–75 percent that of the general California population for most cancer sites, while lifetime SDAs have mortality rates which are about 40 percent of the general California rates. See J. Enstrom, "Cancer Mortality Among Mormons," *Cancer* 36:825–41 (1975). Concerning the higher serum cholesterol and blood pressure levels of Mormons, see Chapter 18.

12. L. Cohen, note 4.

13. See M. Howell, "Diet as an Etiological Factor in the Development of Cancers of the Colon and Rectum," *Journal of Chronic*

Diseases 28:67–80 (1975); O. Manousos, et al., "Diet and Colorectal Cancer: A Case-Control Study in Greece," *International Journal of Cancer* 32:1–5 (1983); W. Haenszel, et al., "Large-Bowel Cancer in Hawaiian Japanese," *Journal of the National Cancer Institute* 51(6):1765–79 (1973); M. Jain, et al., "A Case-Control Study of Diet and Colo-Rectal Cancer," *International Journal of Cancer* 26:757–68 (1980); W. Willett, et al., note 8.

14. International Agency for Research on Cancer Intestinal Microecology Group, "Dietary Fibre, Transit-Time, Faecal Bacteria, Steroids, and Colon Cancer in Two Scandinavian Populations," *Lancet* (July 30, 1977), pages 207–11.

15. S. Malhotra, "Gastrointestinal Cancer," *Gut* 8:361 (1967). See discussion in Chapter 18.

16. R. Clarke, T. Bauchop, *Microbial Ecology of the Gut* (London: Academic Press, 1977), pages 301–05; B. Drasar, M. Hill, *Human Intestinal Flora* (New York: Academic Press, 1974), pages 193–225.

17. B. Drasar, et al., note 16, pages 197–204; W. Visek, et al., "Nutrition and Experimental Carcinogenesis," *Cornell Veterinarian* 68:3 (1978); J. Cummings, et al., "The Effect of Meat Protein and Dietary Fiber on Colonic Function and Metabolism. II. Bacterial Metabolites in Feces and Urine," *American Journal of Clinical Nutrition* 32:2094–2101 (1979).

18. J. Cummings, et al., "The Effect of Meat Protein and Dietary Fiber on Colonic Function and Metabolism. I. Changes in Bowel Habit, Bile Acid Excretion, and Calcium Absorption," *American Journal of Clinical Nutrition* 32:2086–93 (1979); W. Willett, et al., note 8; P. Nair, N. Turjman, "Role of Bile Acids and Neutral Sterols in Familial Cancer Syndromes of the Colon," *Diseases of the Colon and Rectum* (September 1983), pages 629–32. An association between a high-cholesterol intake and cancer incidence seems to be contradicted by studies demonstrating low serum cholesterol levels in cancer patients but these low levels have been shown to result not from the diet but from the preclinical cancer itself. See R. Sherwin, et al., "Serum Cholesterol Levels and Cancer Mortality in 361,662 Men Screened for the Multiple Risk Factor Intervention Trial," *JAMA* 257(7):943–48 (1987).

19. N. Turjman, et al., "Diet, Nutrition Intake, and Metabolism in Populations at High and Low Risk for Colon Cancer: Metabolism of Bile Acids," *American Journal of Clinical Nutrition* 40:937–41 (1984); P. Nair, et al., note 18.

20. N. Turjman, et al., note 19.

21. W. Willett, et al., note 8.

22. *Ibid.*; L. Cohen, note 3; D. Burkitt, note 11.

23. P. Rodman, J. Cant, *Adaptations for Foraging in Nonhuman Primates* (New York: Columbia University Press, 1984), page 252; I. McDonald, A. Warner, *Digestion and Metabolism in the Ruminant* (Armidale, Australia: University of New England

Publishing Unit, 1975), pages 165–69.

24. H. Trowell, D. Burkitt, eds., *Western Diseases: Their Emergence and Prevention* (London: Edward Arnold Ltd., 1981); D. Burkitt, "Epidemiology of Cancer of the Colon and Rectum," *Cancer* 28:3 (1971).

25. S. Ettinger, *Textbook of Veterinary Internal Medicine: Diseases of the Dog and Cat*, vol. 2 (Philadelphia: W. B. Saunders Co., 1983), pages 1366–71.

26. R. Lechowich, "Controlling Microbial Contamination of Animal Products," in D. Beitz, R. Hansen, eds., *Animal Products in Human Nutrition* (New York: Academic Press, 1982), page 386.

27. T. Sugimura, "Tumor Initiators and Promoters Associated with Ordinary Foods," in M. Arnott, et al., eds., *Molecular Interrelations of Nutrition and Cancer* (New York: Raven Press, 1982), page 3; B. Commoner, et al., "Mutagenic Analysis as a Means of Detecting Carcinogens in Foods," *Journal of Food Protection* 41(12):996–1003 (1978); H. Hayatsu, et al., "Fecal Mutagenicity Arising from Ingestion of Fried Ground Beef in the Human," *Mutation Research* 143:207–11 (1985); U. Kuhnlein, et al., "Mutagens in Feces from Vegetarians and Non-Vegetarians," *Mutation Research* 85:1–12 (1981); R. Hur, note 2, page 12.

28. L. Bjeldanes, et al., "Mutagens from the Cooking of Food. II. Survey by Ames Salmonella Test of Mutagen Formation in the Major Protein-Rich Foods of the American Diet," *Fd. Chem. Toxic.* 20:357–63 (1982); J. Felton, et al., "Mutagens from the Cooking of Food. III. Survey by Ames Salmonella Test of Mutagen Formation in Secondary Sources of Cooked Dietary Protein," *ibid.* 20:365–69; N. Spingarn, et al., "Formation of Mutagens in Cooked Foods. II. Foods with High Starch Content," *Cancer Letters* 9:7–12(1980).

29. L. Bjeldanes, et al., note 28; J. Felton, et al., note 28.

30. M. Ikeda, et al., "A Cohort Study on the Possible Association Between Broiled Fish Intake and Cancer," *Gann* 74:640–48 (1983).

31. See M. Pariza, et al., "Mutagens in Heat-Processed Meat, Bakery and Cereal Products," *Fd. Cosmet. Toxicol.* 17:429–30 (1979); and notes 23–27.

32. R. Phillips, note 4; D. Snowdon, "Diet and Ovarian Cancer," *JAMA* 254(3):356 (1985).

33. S. Malhotra, note 15; C. Huang, et al., note 5; T. Hirayama, "Changing Patterns of Cancer in Japan with Special Reference to the Decrease in Stomach Cancer Mortality," in H. Hiatt, et al., eds., *Origins of Human Cancer, Book A: Incidence of Cancer in Humans* (Cold Spring Harbor Laboratory, 1977), page 57.

34. W. Willett, et al., note 8; A. Gregor, et al., "Comparison of Dietary Histories in Lung Cancer Cases and Controls with Special Reference to Vitamin A," *Nutrition and Cancer* 2:93–97 (1980).

35. S. Tannenbaum, "Industrial Processing," in American Medical Association, *Nutrients in Processed Foods: Proteins* (Acton, Mass.: Publishing Sciences Group, Inc., 1974), pages 131–38; S. Davidson, et al., *Human Nutrition and Dietetics* (London: Churchill Livingstone, 1979), pages 211–12; D. Vaughan, "Processing Effects," in C. Bodwell, ed., *Evaluation of Proteins for Humans* (Westport, Conn.: Avi Publishing Co., Inc., 1977), page 255. Intense or prolonged heating, on the other hand, impairs the digestibility of any food.

36. L. Goldstein, ed., *Introduction to Comparative Physiology* (New York: Holt, Rinehart & Winston, 1977), page 400; I. Liener, "Protease Inhibitors and Hemagglutinins of Legumes," in C. Bodwell, ed., *Evaluation of Proteins for Humans* (Westport, Conn.: Avi Publishing Co., Inc., 1977), pages 284–317.

37. S. Davidson, et al., note 35.

38. E. Siguel, "Cancerostatic Effect of Vegetarian Diets," *Nutrition and Cancer* 4(4):285–90 (1983).

39. See B. Reddy, et al., "Metabolic Epidemiology of Large Bowel Cancer. Fecal Bulk and Constituents of a High-Risk North American and Low-Risk Finnish Population," *Cancer* 42:2832–38 (1978); O. Jensen, R. MacLennan, "Dietary Factors and Colo-Rectal Cancer in Scandinavia," *Israel Journal of Medical Science* 15:329–34 (1979); L. Teppo, E. Saxen, "Epidemiology of Colon Cancer in Scandinavia," *Israel Journal of Medical Science* 15:322–28 (1979).

40. J. Berg, note 2. The incidence of hormone-dependent cancers is also 5 times as great in the U.S. as among black African women—but not among black African men, who are particularly prone to prostate cancer. Why is unknown.

41. See T. Shultz, J. Leklem, "Nutrient Intake and Hormonal Status of Premenopausal Vegetarian Seventh-Day Adventists and Premenopausal Nonvegetarians," *Nutrition and Cancer* 4(4):247–59 (1983); G. Phillips, "Hyperestrogenemia, Diet, and Disorders of Western Societies," *American Journal of Medicine* 78:363–66 (1985); J. Lubin, et al., "Dietary Factors and Breast Cancer Risk," *International Journal of Cancer* 28:685–89 (1981); B. Howie, T. Shultz, "Dietary and Hormonal Interrelationships Among Vegetarian Seventh-Day Adventists and Non-Vegetarian Men," *American Journal of Clinical Nutrition* 42:127–34 (1985); B. Goldin, et al., "Effect of Diet on Excretion of Estrogens in Pre- and Postmenopausal Women," *Cancer Research* 41:3771–73 (1981); K. Carroll, "Experimental Evidence of Dietary Factors and Hormone-Dependent Cancers," *Cancer Research* 35:3374–83 (1975); P. Hill, et al., "Diet and Endocrine-Related Cancer," *Cancer* 39:1820–26 (1977).

42. See K. Carroll, note 41; P. Hill, note 41; K. Horowitz, W. McGuire, "Estrogen Control of Progesterone Receptor in Human Breast Cancer," *J. Biol. Chem.* 253:2223–28 (1978); R. Good, et al., "Nutritional Modulation of Immune Responses," *Federation Proceedings* 39:3098–3104 (1980); G. Phillips, note

41. While clear correlations between breast cancer incidence and fat intake have been shown in epidemiological studies, no such correlation was observed in a recent study of nearly 90,000 American nurses, in whom reductions in fat intake from 44 percent to 32 percent of total calories did not significantly affect breast cancer risk. See W. Willett, et al., "Dietary Fat and the Risk of Breast Cancer," *New England Journal of Medicine* 316(1):22–28 (1987). One theory is that there is a threshold fat level somewhere below 32 percent that can be tolerated without increased risk, and that anything over that threshold puts women in the high-risk category. Another possibility is that only milk fat, not all fat, is correlated with increased risk. Types of fat were not distinguished in this study. (See text at note 51.) W. Willett, et al., note 8, suggests breast cancer may be related to obesity only in older women.

43. D. Topping, W. Visek, "Nitrogen Intake and Tumorigenesis in Rats Injected with 1,2-Dimethylhydrazine," *Journal of Nutrition* 106:1583–90 (1976); A. Lorincz, R. Kuttner, "Response of Malignancy to Phenylalanine Restriction," *Nebraska State Medical Journal* (December 1965), pages 609–17.

44. J. Berg, note 2.

45. B. Howie, et al., note 41. The plasma levels of these hormones are also inversely correlated with fiber intake, in both vegetarians and meat-eaters. This factor is thought to be protective for the meat-eating Mormons, who also have a low incidence of hormone-dependent cancer. See text at note 11.

46. P. Hill, et al., "Diet and Urinary Steroids in Black and White North American Men and Black South African Men," *Cancer Research* 39:5101–05 (1979).

47. M. Rosenthal, et al., "Effects of a High-Complex-Carbohydrate, Low-Fat, Low-Cholesterol Diet on Levels of Serum, Lipids and Estradiol," *American Journal of Medicine* 78:23–27 (1985).

48. See B. Howie, et al., note 41; T. Shultz, et al., note 41; B. Goldin, et al., note 41. However, W. Willett, et al., note 8, point out that the findings of studies of low-risk Asian women are inconsistent, and the relation between dietary factors and hormonal levels remains inadequately defined.

49. B. Goldin, et al., note 41.

50. P. Hill, et al., "Gonadotrophin Release and Meat Consumption in Vegetarian Women," *American Journal of Clinical Nutrition* 43:37–41 (1986).

51. S. Gaskill, et al., "Breast Cancer Mortality and Diet in the United States," *Cancer Research* 39:3628–37 (1979); P. Stocks, "Breast Cancer Anomalies," *British Journal of Cancer* 24:633–43 (1970).

52. S. Gaskill, et al., note 51; T. Hirayama, "Epidemiology of Breast Cancer with Special Reference to the Role of Diet," *Preventive Medicine* 7:173–95 (1978).

Chapter 10
KIDNEYS ON STRIKE

1. B. Brenner, et al., "Dietary Protein Intake and the Progressive Nature of Kidney Disease: The Role of Hemodynamically Mediated Glomerular Injury in the Pathogenesis of Progressive Glomerular Sclerosis in Aging, Renal Ablation, and Intrinsic Renal Disease," *New England Journal of Medicine* 307(11):652–59 (1982) (emphasis added).
2. "Largely Vegetarian Diet Curbs Kidney Disease, Study Finds," *Los Angeles Times* (September 6, 1984); O. Mickelsen, note 6, pages 109–10.
3. S. Klahr, M. Purkerson, "Effects of Dietary Protein on Renal Function and the Progression of Renal Disease," *American Journal of Clinical Nutrition* 47:146–52 (1988).
4. See A. Reunanen, et al., "Hyperuricemia as a Risk Factor for Cardiovascular Mortality," *Acta Med. Scand.* (Suppl.) 668:49–59 (1982); B. Aschner, note 23.
5. J. Emes, T. Nowak, *Introduction to Pathophysiology* (Baltimore: University Park Press, 1983), page 300.
6. O. Mickelsen, "Michigan Seventh-Day Adventists: What Are the Benefits of a Vegetarian Diet?", in *Nutrition and Vegetarianism* (Chapel Hill, No. Car.: Health Sciences Consortium, 1981), page 108.
7. *Ibid.*, page 111; B. Armstrong, et al., "Urinary Sodium and Blood Pressure in Vegetarians," *American Journal of Clinical Nutrition* 32:2472–76 (1979); W. Mitch, et al., "The Effect of a Keto Acid—Amino Acid Supplement to a Restricted Diet on the Progression of Chronic Renal Failure," *New England Journal of Medicine* 311:623–29 (1984).
8. B. Drasar, M. Hill, *Human Intestinal Flora* (New York: Academic Press, 1974), page 226.
9. *Ibid.*, pages 226–30; G. Phillips, et al., "The Syndrome of Impending Hepatic Coma in Patients with Cirrhosis of the Liver Given Certain Nitrogenous Substances," *New England Journal of Medicine* 247(7):239–46 (1952).
10. J. Fenton, et al., "Milk-and-Cheese Diet in Portal-Systemic Encephalopathy," *Lancet* 1:164–66 (1966). The researchers proposed that milk protein may undergo less degradation by putrefactive bacteria; or that the intestinal bacteria may change, reducing the number of ammonia-producing organisms.
11. M. Uribe, et al., "Treatment of Chronic Portal-Systemic Encephalopathy with Vegetable and Animal Protein Diets," *Digestive Diseases and Sciences* 27(12):1109–16 (1982). This effect may be due to the accompanying increase in dietary fiber. Fiber enhances bacterial metabolism and increases the incorporation of nitrogen into fecal bacteria, so that more nitrogen is excreted with the fecal matter. See F. Weber Jr., et al., "Effects of Vegetable Diets on Nitrogen Metabolism in Cirrhotic Subjects," *Gastroenterology* 89:538–44 (1985).

12. J. Emes, et al., note 5, pages 271–303.

13. B. Brenner, et al., note 1.

14. *Ibid.*; D. Sandberg, et al., "Severe Steroid-Responsive Nephrosis Associated with Hypersensitivity," *Lancet* (February 19, 1977), pages 388–91; J. Sancho, et al., "Immune Complexes in IgA Nephropathy: Presence of Antibodies Against Diet Antigens and Delayed Clearance of Specific Polymeric IgA Immune Complexes," *Clin. Exp. Immunol.* 54:194–202 (1983).

15. M. Blum, et al., "Protein Intake and Kidney Function in Humans: Its Effect on 'Normal Aging,' " *Archives of Internal Medicine* 149:211–212 (1989).

16. M. Wiseman, et al., "Dietary Composition and Renal Function in Healthy Subjects," *Nephron* 46:37–42 (1987).

17. B. Brenner, et al., note 1; S. Ettinger, *Textbook of Veterinary Internal Medicine: Diseases of the Dog and Cat*, 2d ed., vol. 2 (Philadelphia: W.B. Saunders Co., 1983), pages 1757–58; J. Emes, et al., note 5, pages 286–87, 300.

18. See N. Gretz, et al., "Does a Low-Protein Diet Really Slow Down the Rate of Progression of Chronic Kidney Failure?", *Blood Purif.* 7:33–38 (1989); W. Mitch, et al., "The Effect of a Keto Acid—Amino Acid Supplement to a Restricted Diet on the Progression of Chronic Renal Failure," *New England Journal of Medicine* 311:623–29 (1984); G. Maschio, et al., "Effects of Dietary Protein and Phosphorus Restriction on the Progression of Early Renal Failure," *Kidney International* 22:371–76 (1982); N. Gretz, et al., "Low-Protein Diet Supplemented by Keto-Acids in Chronic Renal Failure: A Prospective Controlled Study," *Kidney International* 24 (Suppl. 16):S263–67 (1983); G. Barsotti, et al., "Restricted Phosphorus and Nitrogen Intake to Slow the Progression of Chronic Renal Failure: A Controlled Trial," *ibid.* at S278–84; K. Vetter, et al., "Influence of Keto-Acid-Treatment on Residual Renal Function in Chronic Renal Insufficiency," *ibid.* at S350.

19. W. Mitch, et al., note 18. The diet contained 1,500 mg of calcium and less than 600 mg of phosphorus, a calcium/phosphorus ratio of 2:1. (See Chapter 13.)

20. J. Emes, et al., note 5, pages 271–303; *Los Angeles Times*, note 2.

21. N. Bricker, et al., "Calcium, Phosphorus, and Bone in Renal Disease and Transplantation," *Archives of Internal Medicine* 123:543–53 (1969); L. Ibels, A. Alfrey, "Effects of Thyroparathyroidectomy, Phosphate Depletion and Diphosphonate Therapy on Acute Uraemic Extra-Osseous Calcification in the Rat," *Clinical Science* 61:621–26 (1981); L. Ibels, et al., "Arterial Calcification and Pathology in Uremic Patients Undergoing Dialysis," *American Journal of Medicine* 66:790–96 (1979). Oddly, arterial fat deposits in these patients *aren't* accelerated. It's the unusually rapid calcification of the arteries that worsens their condition. But an increase in dietary fat can accelerate

the loss of renal function—at least in mice. See V. Kelley, S. Izui, "Enriched Lipid Diet Accelerates Lupus Nephritis in NZBxW Mice," *American Journal of Pathology* 111:288–97 (1983).

22. See G. Maschio, et al., note 18.
23. R. Ballentine, M.D., *Diet & Nutrition* (International Himalayan Institute 1978), pages 113–14; B. Aschner, M.D., *Arthritis Can Be Cured* (New York: Arco Publishing, Inc., 1979), page 9.
24. I. Pave, "So You Thought Gout Was a Thing of the Past?", *Business Week* (October 5, 1987), page 129; R. Ballentine, note 31, page 114.
25. B. Nordin, *Metabolic Bone and Stone Disease* (New York: Churchill Livingstone, 1984), pages 271–77; J. Emes, et al., note 5, pages 297–98; O. Zechner, et al., "Nutritional Risk Factors in Urinary Stone Disease," *Journal of Urology* 125:51–54 (1981).
26. W. Robertson, et al., "Should Recurrent Calcium Oxalate Stone Formers Become Vegetarians?", *British Journal of Urology* 51:427–31 (1979).
27. W. Robertson, et al., "Dietary Changes and the Incidence of Urinary Calculi in the U.K. Between 1958 and 1976," *Journal of Chronic Diseases* 32:469–76 (1979).
28. W. Robertson, et al., "Prevalence of Urinary Stone Disease in Vegetarians," *Eur. Urol.* 8:334–39 (1982).
29. W. Robertson, et al., "The Effect of High Animal Protein Intake on the Risk of Calcium Stone-Formation in the Urinary Tract," *Clinical Science* 57:285–88 (1979); B. Nordin, note 25, page 275; A. Licata, "Acute Effects of Increased Meat Protein on Urinary Electrolytes and Cyclic Adenosine Monophosphate and Serum Parathyroid Hormone," *American Journal of Clinical Nutrition* 34:1779–84 (1981).
30. W. Robertson, et al., note 29. Compare J. Brockis, et al., "The Effects of Vegetable and Animal Protein Diets on Calcium, Urate and Oxalate Excretion," *British Journal of Urology* 54:590–93 (1982), in which animal protein intake was associated with urinary calcium but not with urinary oxalate at modest levels of intake. Vegetable protein intake, on the other hand, did have some association with urinary oxalate. The researchers suggested that this was due to the oxalate content of plant foods. They were unable, however, to demonstrate that moderately high dietary oxalate affects urinary oxalate.
31. B. Nordin, note 25, pages 277–98; W. Robertson, et al., note 28.
32. See Chapters 11–12.
33. B. Nordin, note 25, pages 289, 310; F. Coe, et al., "The Contribution of Dietary Purine Over-Consumption to Hyperuricosuria in Calcium Oxalate Stone Formers," *Journal of Chronic Diseases* 29:793–800 (1976).
34. T. Ohkawa, et al., "Rice Bran Treatment for Patients with Hypercalciuric Stones: Experimental and clinical Studies," *Journal of Urology* 132:1140–45 (1984); M. Modlin, "Urinary Phos-

phorylated Inositols and Renal Stones," *Lancet* (November 22, 1980), pages 1113–14.

35. "Urinary Calcium and Dietary Protein," *Nutrition Reviews* 38(1):9–10 (1980); J. Brockis, et al., note 30.
36. J. Brockis, et al., note 30. What calcium intake was correlated with was urinary oxalate, but the correlation was a negative one—the *less* calcium ingested, the *more* oxalate excreted. The finding suggests that a severe reduction in calcium intake not only wouldn't help but could hurt recurrent stone formers, since it would increase urinary oxalate.
37. N. Breslau, et al., "Relationship of Animal Protein-Rich Diet to Kidney Stone Formation and Calcium Metabolism," *Journal of Clinical Endocrinology and Metabolism* 66:140–46 (1988).

Chapter 11
TOO LITTLE CALCIUM OR TOO MUCH MEAT?

1. From the motion picture "Reuben, Reuben."
2. P. Henrikson, "Periodontal Disease and Calcium Deficiency," *Acta Odontologica Scandinavica*, vol. 26, suppl. 50 (1968), pages 118–20.
3. See D. Smith, et al., "Mineral Metabolism in Relation to Ageing," *Proceedings of the Nutrition Society* 27:201 (1968); and notes 12–25 and 35.
4. A. Marsh, et al., "Cortical Bone Density of Adult Lacto-Ovo-Vegetarian and Omnivorous Women," *Journal of the American Dietetic Association* 76:148–51 (1980).
5. N. Breslau, et al., "Relationship of Animal Protein-Rich Diet to Kidney Stone Formation and Calcium Metabolism," *Journal of Clinical Endocrinology and Metabolism* 66:140–46 (1988).
6. G. Lewinnek, et al., "The Significance and a Comparative Epidemiology of Hip Fractures," *Clin. Ortho. Related Res.* 152:35–43 (1980); Consensus Development Conference, "Osteoporosis," *JAMA* 252:799–802 (1984); W. Harris, R. Heaney, "Skeletal Renewal and Metabolic Bone Disease (Concluded)," *New England Journal of Medicine* 280(6):303–11 (1969); J. Jowsey, *Metabolic Diseases of Bone* (Philadelphia: W.B. Saunders Co. 1977), page 286.
7. C. Lee, et al., "Effects of Supplementation of the Diets with Calcium and Calcium-Rich Foods on Bone Density of Elderly Females with Osteoporosis," *American Journal of Clinical Nutrition* 34:819–23 (1981).
8. J. Shapiro, et al., "Osteoporosis," *Archives of Internal Medicine* 135:563 (1975).
9. K. Yano, et al., "The Relationship Between Diet and Bone Mineral Content of Multiple Skeletal Sites in Elderly Japanese-American Men and Women Living in Hawaii," *American Journal of Clinical Nutrition* 42:877–88 (1985); M. Notelovitz, M. Ware, *Stand Tall!* (Gainesville, Fla.: Triad Publishing Co., 1982), page 37.

10. See P. Baker, J. Angel, "Old Age Changes in Bone Density: Sex and Race Factors in the United States," *Human Biology* 37(2):104–19 (1965); J. Chalmers, K. Ho, "Geographical Variations in Senile Osteoporosis," *Journal of Bone and Joint Surgery* 52–B:667–75 (1970); G. Lewinnek, et al., note 6.
11. C. Paterson, "Calcium Requirements in Man: A Critical Review," *Postgraduate Medical Journal* 54:244–48 (1978).
12. A. Walker, "The Human Requirements of Calcium: Should Low Intakes Be Supplemented?", *American Journal of Clinical Nutrition* 25:518–30 (1972); C. Paterson, note 11; G. Kolata, "How Important is Dietary Calcium in Preventing Osteoporosis?", *Science* 233:519–20 (1986).
13. G. Lewinnek, et al., note 6.
14. A. Walker, note 12; O. Mickelsen, "Michigan Seventh-Day Adventists: What Are the Benefits of a Vegetarian Diet?", in J. Anderson, ed., *Nutrition and Vegetarianism: Proceedings of Public Health Nutrition Update* (Health Sciences Consortium: Chapel Hill, 1981), pages 115–17; see Chapter 22.
15. G. Kolata, note 12; R. Smith, B. Frame, "Concurrent Axial and Appendicular Osteoporosis," *New England Journal of Medicine* 273:73–78 (1965); S. Garn, "Calcium Requirements for Bone Building and Skeletal Maintenance," *American Journal of Clinical Nutrition* 23(9):1149–50 (1970).
16. D. Hegsted, et al., "A Study of the Minimum Calcium Requirements of Adult Men," *Journal of Nutrition* 46:181 (1952). This adaptation did not occur in the absence of vitamin D, underlining the importance of sunshine to insure adequate calcium absorption. Note that older Caucasians in Western countries do not readily adapt to reduced calcium intakes, arguably because their diets are high in protein, which pulls calcium from the bones. See R. Marcus, "The Relationship of Dietary Calcium to the Maintenance of Skeletal Integrity in Man— an Interface of Endocrinology and Nutrition," *Metabolism* 31(1):93–102 (1982); A. Walker, note 12.
17. S. Garn, note 15.
18. I. Shenolikar, "Absorption of Dietary Calcium in Pregnancy," *American Journal of Clinical Nutrition* 23:63 (1970).
19. R. Luyken, F. Luykoning, "Studies on Physiology of Nutrition in Surinam. XII. Nutrition and Development of Muscular, Skeletal and Adipose Tissues in Surinam Children," *American Journal of Clinical Nutrition* 22:519 (1969).
20. C. Paterson, note 11; A. Walker, note 12.
21. O. Mickelsen, note 14, page 116.
22. S. Davidson, et al., *Human Nutrition and Dietetics* (Edinburgh: Churchill Livingstone, 1979), page 92.
23. J. Chalmers, et al., note 10.
24. R. Heaney, et al., "Calcium Nutrition and Bone Health in the Elderly," *American Journal of Clinical Nutrition* 36:986–1013 (1982).
25. A. Walker, note 12.

26. See W. Shurtleff, A. Aoyagi, *The Book of Tofu* (Brookline, Mass.: Autumn Press 1975), page 17; O. Mickelsen, note 14.

27. See notes 38–42.

28. B. MacMahon, P. Cole, "Oestrogen Profiles of Asian and North American Women," *Lancet* 2:900–02 (1971); L. Dickinson, et al., "Estrogen Profiles of Oriental and Caucasian Women in Hawaii," *New England Journal of Medicine* 291(23):1211–13 (1974); B. Goldin, et al., "Effect of Diet on Excretion of Estrogens in Pre- and Postmenopausal Women," *Cancer Research* 41:3771–73 (1981). See also "Dietary and Hormonal Interrelationships Among Vegetarian Seventh-Day Adventists and Nonvegetarian Men," *American Journal of Clinical Nutrition* 42:127–34 (1985). The significance of these variations remains to be established. See "Estrogen Excretion Patterns and Plasma Levels in Vegetarian and Omnivorous Women," *Nutrition Reviews* 41(6):180–83 (1983); G. Lewinnek, et al., note 6; P. Baker, et al., note 10.

29. This may be true only for older black males. P. Baker, note 10; see P. Walker, note 12.

30. A. Walker, B. Walker, "Metacarpal Bone Dimensions in Young and Aged South African Bantu Consuming a Diet Low in Calcium," *Postgraduate Medical Journal* 47:320–25 (1971); A. Walker, et al., "Cortical Thickness of Bone in Underprivileged Populations," *American Journal of Clinical Nutrition* 23:244–45 (1970).

31. S. Garn, et al., "Compact Bone in Chinese and Japanese," *Science* 143:1439–40 (1964).

32. O. Mickelsen, note 14, pages 117–19; T. Sanchez, et al., "Bone Mineral in Elderly Vegetarian and Omnivorous Females," in R. Mazess, ed., *Proceedings: Fourth International Conference on Bone Measurement* (U.S. Department of Health and Human Services, National Institutes of Health Publication No. 80–1938, 1980), pages 94–98.

33. R. Mazess, W. Mather, "Bone Mineral Content of North Alaskan Eskimos," *American Journal of Clinical Nutrition* 27:916–25 (1974).

34. *Ibid.*

35. *Ibid.*; C. Heller, "The diet of Some Alaskan Eskimos and Indians," *Journal of the American Dietetic Association* 45:425 (1965); G. Mann, et al., "The Health and Nutritional Status of Alaskan Eskimos," *American Journal of Clinical Nutrition* 11:31 (1962). Compare J. Ellestad-Sayed, et al., "Twenty-Four Hour Urinary Excretion of Vitamins, Minerals, and Nitrogen by Eskimos," *American Journal of Clinical Nutrition* 28:1402–07 (1975), in which low calcium intakes were reported.

36. R. Mazess, et al., note 33; R. Mazess, et al., "Bone Mineral and Vitamin D in Aleutian Islanders," *American Journal of Clinical Nutrition* 42:143–46 (1985).

37. R. Mazess, et al., note 33.

38. F. Ellis, et al., "Incidence of Osteoporosis in Vegetarians and Omnivores," *American Journal of Clinical Nutrition* 25:555

(1972). A later report by the same researchers stated their earlier findings were contradicted "in some cases." See F. Ellis, et al., "Osteoporosis in British Vegetarians and Omnivores," *American Journal of Clinical Nutrition* 27:769–70 (1974).

39. O. Mickelsen, note 14, pages 117–19.
40. A. Marsh, et al., "Cortical Bone Density of Adult Lacto-Ovo-Vegetarian and Omnivorous Women," *Journal of the American Dietetic Association* 76:148–51 (1980).
41. Confirmed in: T. Sanchez, et al., note 32 (mean decrease in bone mineral for vegetarians was lower than for meat-eaters by 40 percent); A. Marsh, et al., "Bone Mineral Mass in Adult Lacto-Ovo-Vegetarian and Omnivorous Males," *American Journal of Clinical Nutrition* 37:453–56 (1983) (bone loss for vegetarian men was less than half that for meat-eating men, though not statistically significant); A. Marsh, et al., note 42. Not confirmed in: I. Hunt, et al., "Food and Nutrient Intake of Seventh-Day Adventist Women," *American Journal of Clinical Nutrition* 48:850–51 (1988).
42. A. Marsh, et al., "Vegetarian Lifestyle and Bone Mineral Density," *American Journal of Clinical Nutrition* 48:837–41 (1988).

Chapter 12
EXCESS PROTEIN: THE CALCIUM DRAIN

1. R. Walker, H. Linkswiler, "Calcium Retention in the Adult Human Male as Affected by Protein Intake," *Journal of Nutrition* 102:1297–1302 (1972).
2. See, e.g., M. Krause, L. Mahan, *Food, Nutrition, and Diet Therapy* (Philadelphia: W.B. Saunders Co., 1984), page 150.
3. See R. Walker, et al., note 1; N. Johnson, et al., "Effect of Level of Protein Intake on Urinary and Fecal Calcium and Calcium Retention of Young Adult Males," *Nutrition* 100:1425–30 (1970).
4. R. Walker, et al., note 1.
5. U.S. Department of Agriculture, *Nutritive Value of American Foods in Common Units*, Agriculture Handbook No. 456 (Washington, D.C.: Agricultural Research Service, 1975); Food and Nutrition Board Committee on Dietary Allowances, *Recommended Dietary Allowances* (Washington, D.C.: National Academy of Sciences, 1980), page 46. See Chapter 5.
6. M. Hegsted, et al., "Urinary Calcium and Calcium Balance in Young Men as Affected by Level of Protein and Phosphorus Intake," *Journal of Nutrition* 111:553–62 (1981). The relationship applies only when dietary phosphorus is held constant. See Chapter 13.
7. See R. Walker, et al., note 1; N. Johnson, et al., note 3; L. Allen, et al., "Protein-Induced Hypercalciuria: A Longer Term Study," *American Journal of Clinical Nutrition* 32:741–49

(1979); C. Anand, H. Linkswiler, "Effect of Protein Intake on Calcium Balance of Young Men Given 500 mg Calcium Daily," *Journal of Nutrition* 104:695–700 (1974); R. Schwartz, et al., "Metabolic Responses of Adolescent Boys to Two Levels of Dietary Magnesium and Protein. II. Effect of Magnesium and Protein Level on Calcium Balance," *American Journal of Clinical Nutrition* 26:519–23 (1973); J. Chu, et al., "Studies in Calcium Metabolism. II. Effects of Low Calcium and Variable Protein Intake on Human Calcium Metabolism," *American Journal of Clinical Nutrition* 28:1028–35 (1975).

8. S. Margen, J. Chu, N. Kaufmann, D. Calloway, "Studies in Calcium Metabolism. I. The Calciuretic Effect of Dietary Protein," *American Journal of Clinical Nutrition* 27:584–89 (1974).

9. D. Beitz, R. Hansen, eds., *Animal Products in Human Nutrition* (New York: Academic Press, 1982), page 272.

10. A. Davis, *Let's Have Healthy Children* (New York: Signet Books, 8th rev. ed., 1981), pages 90, 162.

11. N. Johnson, et al., note 3. The additional 93 grams of protein in the high-protein diet came from milk and wheat. Calcium and phosphorus levels were maintained constant and equal at 1400 mg/day. The diets were each maintained for 45 days, an amount of time generally considered sufficient for adaptation.

12. L. Allen, et al., note 7.

13. *Ibid.*

14. J. Jowsey, "Osteoporosis: Its Nature and the Role of Diet," *Postgraduate Medicine* 60(2):75–79 (1976).

15. B. Krolner, S. Nielsen, "Bone Mineral Content of the Lumbar Spine in Normal and Osteoporotic Women: Cross-Sectional and Longitudinal Studies," *Clinical Science* 62:329–36 (1982).

16. R. Marcus, "The Relationship of Dietary Calcium to the Maintenance of Skeletal Integrity in Man—An Interface of Endocrinology and Nutrition," *Metabolism* 31(1):93–102 (1982).

17. R. Heaney, R. Recker, "Effects of Nitrogen, Phosphorus, and Caffeine on Calcium Balance in Women," *Journal of Laboratory and Clinical Medicine* 99:46–55 (1982).

18. D. Smith, et al., "Age and Activity Effects on Rate of Bone Mineral Loss," *Journal of Clinical Investigation* 58:716–21 (1976).

19. M. Hegsted, H. Linkswiler, "Long-Term Effects of Level of Protein Intake on Calcium Metabolism in Young Adult Women," *Journal of Nutrition* 111:244–51 (1981).

20. As found for the nuns in the previous study whose diets contained 102 grams of protein.

21. B. Nordin, *Metabolic Bone and Stone Disease* (London: Churchill Livingstone, 1973), page 30.

22. R. Walker, et al., note 1.

23. S. Schuette, et al., "Studies on the Mechanism of Protein-Induced Hypercalciuria in Older Men and Women," *Journal of Nutrition* 110:305–15 (1980).

24. See A. Albanese, et al., "Problems of Bone Health in the Elderly," *New York State Journal of Medicine* 75:326–36 (1975);

E. Smith Jr., et al., "Physical Activity and Calcium Modalities for Bone Mineral Increase in Aged Women," *Medicine and Science in Sports and Exercise* 13(1):60–64 (1981); C. Lee, et al., "Effects of Supplementation of the Diets with Calcium and Calcium-Rich Foods on Bone Density of Elderly Females with Osteoporosis," *American Journal of Clinical Nutrition* 34:819–23 (1981).

25. A. Albanese, et al., note 24.
26. See G. Kolata, "How Important Is Dietary Calcium in Preventing Osteoporosis?", *Science* 233:519–20 (1986); B. Riggs, et al., "Effects of Oral Therapy with Calcium and Vitamin D in Primary Osteoporosis," *Journal of Clinical Endocrinology and Metabolism* 42:1139–44 (1976); J. Shapiro, et al., "Osteoporosis: Evaluation of Diagnosis and Therapy," *Archives of Internal Medicine* 135:563–67 (1975).
27. L. Allen, et al., "Reduction of Renal Calcium Reabsorption In Man by Consumption of Dietary Protein," *Journal of Nutrition* 109:1345–50 (1979); S. Schuette, et al., "Renal Acid, Urinary Cyclic AMP, and Hydroxyproline Excretion as Affected by Level of Protein, Sulfur Amino Acid, and Phosphorus Intake," *Journal of Nutrition* 111:2106–16 (1981).
28. M. Reidenberg, et al., "The Response of Bone to Metabolic Acidosis in Man," *Metabolism* 15(3):236–41 (1966); J. Lemann Jr., E. Lennon, "Role of Diet, Gastrointestinal Tract and Bone in Acid-Base Homeostasis," *Kidney International* 1:275–79 (1972); R. Farquharson, et al., "Studies of Calcium and Phosphorus Metabolism. XIII. The Effect of Ingestion of Phosphorus on the Excretion of Calcium," *Journal of Clinical Investigation* 10:251 (1931); A. Wachman, D. Bernstein, "Diet and Osteoporosis," *Lancet* 1: 958–59 (1968).
29. S. Schuette, et al., note 27. While fruit is acidic in the mouth, the end-products of the digestion of fruit and vegetables are alkaline.
30. J. Lemann, A. Relman, "The Relation of Sulfur Metabolism to Acid-Base Balance and Electrolyte Excretion: The Effects of DL-Methionine in Normal Man," *Journal of Clinical Investigation* 38:2215–23 (1959); J. Brockis, et al., "The Effects of Vegetable and Animal Protein Diets on Calcium, Urate and Oxalate Excretion," *British Journal of Urology*, 54:590– 93 (1982).
31. D. Yuen, H. Draper, "Long-Term Effects of Excess Protein and Phosphorus on Bone Homeostasis in Adult Mice," *Journal of Nutrition* 113:1374–80 (1983).
32. S. Schuette, et al., note 27; see Chapter 13.

Chapter 13
PHOSPHORUS: THE CALCIUM ANTAGONIST

1. G. Anderson, H. Draper, "Effect of Dietary Phosphorus on Calcium Metabolism in Intact and Parathyroidectomized Adult Rats," *Journal of Nutrition* 102:1123–32 (1972), citing many studies.

2. See H. Spencer, et al., "Effect of a High Protein (Meat) Intake on Calcium Metabolism in Man," *American Journal of Clinical Nutrition* 31:2167–80 (1978); H. Spencer, "Further Studies on the Effect of a High Protein Diet on Calcium Metabolism in Man," *Federation Proceedings* 40:885 (1981). But see R. Marcus, note 13; C. Annand, et al., "Effect of Protein Intake on Calcium Balance of Young Men given 500 mg Calcium Daily," *Journal of Nutrition* 104:695–700 (1974).

3. See J. Brockis, et al., "The Effects of Vegetable and Animal Protein Diets on Calcium, Urate and Oxalate Excretion," *British Journal of Urology* 54:590–93 (1982).

4. See notes 5, 11, 13, 14.

5. H. Draper, et al., "Osteoporosis in Aging Rats Induced by High Phosphorus Diets," *Journal of Nutrition* 102:1133–42 (1972). In the diet with the highest phosphorus concentration, phosphorus was 3 times the intake of calcium recommended for growing rats. The human phosphorus intake goes up to about 2,500 mg/day, which is also about 3 times the RDA for calcium (800 mg).

6. See, e.g., R. Goldsmith, et al., "Effects of Phosphorus Supplementation on Serum Parathyroid Hormone and Bone Morphology in Osteoporosis," *Journal of Clinical Endocrinology and Metabolism* 43:523–32 (1976), page 529; H. Draper, et al., note 5.

7. H. Draper, et al., note 5.

8. See, e.g., R. Hammond, E. Storey, "Measurement of Growth and Resorption of Bone in Rats Fed Meat Diet," *Calc. Tiss. Res.* 4:291–304 (1970); D. Gaster, et al., "Differential Effects of Low Calcium Diets on the Bones of Mice and Rats," *Nutr. Dicta* 9:200–7 (1967).

9. P. Scott, "Problems Encountered in Studying the Nutrition of the Cat," *Proceedings of the Nutrition Society* 16:77 (1957); P. Scott, "Calcium and Iodine Deficiency in Meat-Fed Cats with Reference to Osteogenesis Imperfecta," *Proc. Cong. Brit. Small Anim. Vet. Assoc.* (New York: Pergamon Press, 1959), page 84; L. Krook, et al., "Nutritional Secondary Hyperparathyroidism in the Cat," *Cornell Veterinarian* 53:224–40 (1962).

10. P. Henrikson, "Periodontal Disease and Calcium Deficiency: An Experimental Study in the Dog," *Acta Odontologica Scandinavica* 36 (Supp. 50) (1968), page 122.

11. J. Jowsey, et al., "Long-Term Effects of High Phosphate Intake on Parathyroid Hormone Levels and Bone Metabolism," *Acta Orthop. Scand.* 45:801–08 (1974). A follow-up study located the displaced bone calcium in the soft tissues. See G. Laflamme, J. Jowsey, "Bone and Soft Tissue Changes with Oral Phosphate Supplements," *Journal of Clinical Investigation* 51:2834–40 (1972).

12. A biopsy involves the removal of a small piece of living tissue for microscopic examination.

13. R. Goldsmith, et al., note 6. The researchers concluded that bone resorption was increased and bone formation was sup-

pressed. This conclusion was questioned in R. Marcus, "The Relationship of Dietary Calcium to the Maintenance of Skeletal Integrity in Man—An Interface of Endocrinology and Nutrition," *Metabolism* 31(1):93–102 (1982), pages 99–100, on the grounds that the method used measured only the total resorption and formation surfaces without measuring the rate of either process. But Goldsmith, et al., labeled this argument spurious because no investigator had demonstrated a divergence between the percentage of resorptive surface and the rate of resorption, and other studies demonstrated their concurrence. (At page 530.)

14. S. Hulley, et al., "The Effect of Supplemental Oral Phosphate on the Bone Mineral Changes During Prolonged Bed Rest," *Journal of Clinical Investigation* 50:2506 (1971).

15. P. Henrikson, "Periodontal Disease and Calcium Deficiency: an Experimental Study in the Dog," *Acta Odontologica Scandinavica* 26 (Supp. 50) (1968), pages 106–08.

16. "Hypocalcemia in Newborn Infants Fed Cow's Milk," *Nutrition Reviews* 26:299–301 (1968).

17. *Ibid.*; J. Jowsey, *Metabolic Diseases of Bone* (Philadelphia: W.B. Saunders Co., 1977), pages 87–89; T. Sie, et al., "Hypocalcemia, Hyperparathyroidism and Bone Resorption in Rats Induced by Dietary Phosphate," *Journal of Nutrition* 104: 1195–201 (1974).

18. See A. Albanese, et al., "Problems of Bone Health in the Elderly," *New York State Journal of Medicine* 75:326–36 (1975).

19. U.S. Department of Agriculture, *Nutritive Value of American Foods*, Agriculture Handbook No. 456 (Washington, D.C.: U.S. Government Printing Office, 1975).

20. The daily intake comes to 817.5 mg., calculating from the USDA figures for annual meat intake given in Chapter 1 and taking the amount of phosphorus in halibut as typical for seafood, in pork roast and cured pan-broiled ham as typical for pork, in broiled chicken as typical for chicken, and in lean round steak as typical for beef.

21. W. Shurtleff, A. Aoyagi, *The Book of Tofu* (Brookline, Mass.: Random House, 1975), page 24.

22. J. Kirschmann, *Nutrition Almanac* (New York: McGraw-Hill Book Co., 1984).

23. *Ibid.* An exception is brewer's yeast. Some varieties have a Ca/P ratio as bad as that in meat. The ratio in rice and many other grains isn't a particularly favorable one, except in relation to meat. Orientals balance their rice with tofu and seaweed.

24. J. Jowsey, note 17, page 89.

25. See L. Kramer, et al., "Mineral and Trace Element Content of Vegetarian Diets," *Journal of the American College of Nutrition* 3:3–11 (1984); M. Read, D. Thomas, "Nutrient and Food Supplement Practices of Lacto-Ovo-Vegetarians," *Journal of the American Dietetic Association* 82(4):401–04 (1983).

26. G. Anderson, et al., note 1.

27. A. Walker, "The Human Requirement of Calcium: Should Low Intakes Be Supplemented?", *American Journal of Clinical Nutrition* 25:518–30 (1972).

28. See Chapter 12.

29. G. Siu, et al., "Self-Regulation of Phosphate Intake by Growing Rats," *Journal of Nutrition* 111:1681–85 (1981). The study showed rats choose a diet containing the appropriate Ca/P ratio *instinctively*. Groups of growing rats were offered a choice of diets. The concentration of calcium was always 0.6 percent, but the concentration of phosphorus varied from 0.1 percent to 1.8 percent. All growing rats given the opportunity chose mixtures containing about twice as much calcium as phosphorus. This ratio approaches that in growing rat bone, which dominates calcium and phosphorus requirements in the growing animal. When the same experiment was tried with adult rats, they chose a diet containing roughly equal amounts of calcium and phosphorus. Their bones had quit growing.

30. J. Jowsey, note 17, pages 288–89; J. Jowsey, "Osteoporosis: Its Nature and the Role of Diet," *Postgraduate Medicine* 60(2):75–79 (1976).

31. J. Jowsey, P. Balasubramaniam, "Effect of Phosphate Supplements on Soft-Tissue Calcification and Bone Turnover," *Clinical Science* 42:289–99 (1972).

32. See M. Anderson, et al., "Long-Term Effect of Low Dietary Calcium: Phosphate Ratio on the Skeleton of *Cebus albifrons* Monkeys," *Journal of Nutrition* 834–39 (1977). The study involved ringtail monkeys caught in the wild. No significant bone loss was seen when the animals were fed a diet containing a Ca/P ratio of 1:4, although the experiment was continued a full 7 years. But in another study, involving baboons, when the Ca/P ratio was dropped to 1:8, the animals developed blood and bone changes indicative of a Ca/P imbalance in 16 months. The biochemical changes that occurred were indicative of secondary nutritional hyperparathyroidism. See J. Pettifor, et al., "The Effect of Differing Dietary Calcium and Phosphorus Contents on Mineral Metabolism and Bone Histomorphometry in Young Vitamin D-Replete Baboons, *Calcified Tissue International* 36:668–76 (1984).

33. J. Pettifor, et al., note 32; D. Cordy, "Osteodystrophia Fibrosa Accompanied by Visceral Accumulation of Lead," *Cornell Veterinarian* 47:480–90 (1957).

34. L. Krook, R. Barrett, "Simian Bone Disease—A Secondary Hyperparathyroidism," *Cornell Veterinarian* 52:459–92 (1962).

35. *Ibid.* Secondary hyperparathyroidism can also result from a Ca/P imbalance in the blood caused by malfunctioning kidneys. But this isn't the problem in monkeys with simian bone disease, since their kidneys are normal.

Chapter 14
HOW MEAT STRESSES YOUR PARATHYROIDS

1. A. Licata, "Acute Effects of Increased Meat Protein on Urinary Electrolytes and Cyclic Adenosine Monophosphate and Serum Parathyroid Hormone," *American Journal of Clinical Nutrition* 34:1779–84 (1981).
2. See R. Goodhart, M. Shils, *Modern Nutrition in Health and Disease*, 6th ed. (Philadelphia: Lea & Febiger, 1980), pages 295, 305; M. Krause, L. Mahan, *Food, Nutrition and Diet Therapy* (Philadelphia: W.B. Saunders Co., 1984), pages 151, 153; J. Jowsey, *Metabolic Diseases of Bone* (Philadelphia: W.B. Saunders Co., 1977), page 282; and Chapter 15.
3. E. Reiss, et al., "The Role of Phosphate in the Secretion of Parathyroid Hormone in Man," *Journal of Clinical Investigation* 49:2146–49 (1970).
4. R. Bell, et al., "Physiological Responses of Human Adults to Foods Containing Phosphate Additives," *Journal of Nutrition* 107:42–50 (1970).
5. See A. Licata, "Acute Effects of Increased Meat Protein on Urinary Electrolytes and Cyclic Adenosine Monophosphate and Serum Parathyroid Hormone," *American Journal of Clinical Nutrition* 34:1779–84 (1981); J. Jowsey, "Editorial: Quantitative Microradiography," *American Journal of Medicine* 40(4):485–91 (1966); P. Henrikson, "Periodontal Disease and Calcium Deficiency: An Experimental Study in the Dog", *Acta Odontologica Scandinavica* 26 (Supp. 50) (1968), pages 112–13, 118–20; L. Krook, et al., "Nutritional Secondary Hyperparathyroidism in the Cat," *Cornell Veterinarian* 53:224–240 (1962), page 234.
6. H. Draper, et al., "Osteoporosis in Aging Rats Induced by High Phosphorus Diets," *Journal of Nutrition* 102:1133–42 (1972).
7. J. Weinmann, H. Sicher, *Bone and Bones: Fundamentals of Bone Biology* (St. Louis: C.V. Mosby Co., 1955), pages 243, 246.
8. J. Jowsey, note 5; J. Jowsey, *Metabolic Diseases of Bone* (Philadelphia: W.B. Saunders Co. 1977), pages 286–88. Some osteoporotic patients, however, actually have reduced PTH levels. The osteoporotic syndrome in these patients apparently results from a different metabolic derangement. See "Osteoporosis and Calcium Balance," *Nutrition Reviews* 41:83–85 (1983).
9. P. Henrikson, note 5, pages 112–13, 118–20; L. Krook, et al., note 5, page 234.
10. L. Krook, et al., note 5; J. Jowsey, *Metabolic Diseases of Bone*, note 8, page 240; N. Bricker, et al., "Calcium, Phosphorus, and Bone in Renal Disease and Transplantation," *Archives of Internal Medicine* 123:543–53 (1969). The bone loss accompanying kidney failure has also been attributed to the almost universal occurrence of metabolic acidosis in the course

of chronic renal disease. Calcium is thought to be released from the skeleton as a buffer, by the mechanism explained in Chapter 12.

11. N. Bricker, et al., note 10; L. Ibels, A. Alfrey, "Effects of Thyroparathyroidectomy, Phosphate Depletion and Diphosphonate Therapy on Acute Uraemic Extraosseous Calcification in the Rat," *Clinical Science* 61:621–26 (1981).

12. A. Arieff, S. Massry, "Calcium Metabolism of Brain in Acute Renal Failure. Effects of Uremia, Hemodialysis and Parathyroid Hormone," *Journal of Clinical Investigation* 58:387–92 (1974).

13. G. Barsotti, et al., "Reversal of Hyperparathyroidism in Severe Uremics Following Very Low-Protein and Low-Phosphorus Diets," *Nephron* 30:310–13 (1982). The diet included only 250–300 mg. of phosphorus and 14 grams of protein a day. The sole animal food permitted was butter.

14. L. Ibels, et al., note 11.

15. G. Alexander, et al., "Pyrophosphate Arthropathy: A Study of Metabolic Associations and Laboratory Data," *Annals of the Rheumatic Diseases* 41:377–81 (1982).

16. P. Henrikson, note 5, page 104; J. Jowsey, L. Raisz, "Experimental Osteoporosis and Parathyroid Activity," *Endocrinology* 82:384–96 (1968); A. Albanese, et al., "Problems of Bone Health in the Elderly," *New York State Journal of Medicine* 75:326–36 (1975); L. Lutwak, et al., "Calcium Deficiency and Human Periodontal Disease," *Israel Journal of Medical Sciences* 7(3):504–05 (1971).

17. P. Henrikson, note 5, pages 106–08.

18. See E. Reiss, et al., note 3, in which one gram of supplemental phosphorus was given orally to five normal adults. Serum calcium decreased only slightly—by 0.3 to 1.1 mg/dl of blood. But this slight decrease was sufficient to cause an increase in serum PTH of between 60 and 125%. See also Chapter 13.

19. T. Sie, et al., "Hypocalcemia, Hyperparathyroidism and Bone Resorption in Rats Induced by Dietary Phosphate," *Journal of Nutrition* 104:1195–1201 (1974).

20. R. Bell, et al., note 4.

21. *Ibid.* L. Hebert, et al., "Studies of the Mechanism by Which Phosphate Infusion Lowers Serum Calcium Concentration," *Journal of Clinical Investigation* 45(12):1866–94 (1966).

Chapter 15
SPECULATING ABOUT PATHOLOGICAL CALCIFICATION

1. J. Emes, T. Nowak, *Introduction to Pathophysiology* (Baltimore: University Park Press, 1983), page 104.

2. H. Selye, *Calciphylaxis* (Chicago: University of Chicago Press, 1962), pages 406–31, 435–7; H. Blumenthal, et al., "The Inter-

relation of Elastic Tissue and Calcium in the Genesis of Atherosclerosis," *American Journal of Pathology* 26:989 (1950); D. Kramsch, et al., "Components of the Protein-Lipid Complex of Arterial Elastin. Their Role in the Retention of Lipid in Atherosclerotic Lesions," *Adv. Exp. Med. Biol.* 43:193 (1974); R. Eisenstein, et al., "Mineral Binding by Human Arterial Elastin Tissue," *Lab. Invest.* 13:1198 (1964); M. Oliver, et al., "Detection of Coronary-Artery Calcification During Life," *Lancet* 1:891 (1964); L. Ibels, et al., "Arterial Calcification and Pathology in Uremic Patients Undergoing Dialysis," *American Journal of Medicine* 66:790–6 (1979); D. Doyle, "Tissue Calcification and Inflammation in Osteoarthritis," *Journal of Pathology* 136:199–216 (1982); J. Gerster, et al., "Olecranon Bursitis Related to Calcium Pyrophosphate Dihydrate Crystal Deposition Disease," *Arthritis and Rheumatism* 25(8):989–96 (1982).

3. L. Ibels, et al., note 2; M. Rawlings, *Beyond Death's Door* (New York: Thomas Nelson Inc., Publishers, 1978), page 41.

4. B. Trump, et al., "The Cellular and Subcellular Characteristics of Acute and Chronic Injury with Emphasis on the Role of Calcium," in R. Cowley, B. Trump, eds., *Pathophysiology of Shock, Anoxia, and Ischemia* (Baltimore: Williams & Wilkins, 1982), page 25.

5. A. Keys, "The Diet and the Development of Coronary Heart Disease," *Journal of Chronic Diseases* 4:364–80 (1956).

6. M. Anderson, et al., "Chemical and Pathological Studies on Aortic Atherosclerosis," *A.M.A. Archives of Pathology* 68:380–91 (1959).

7. S. Davidson, et al., *Human Nutrition and Dietetics* (New York: Churchill Livingstone, 1979), page 334.

8. D. Barr, "Pathological Calcification," *Physiological Reviews* 12:593–624 (1932), pages 596–98, 608–09. Although excess serum calcium is the logical suspect, the association demonstrated experimentally is actually with excess serum phosphorus. Serious calcification has resulted when serum phosphorus was high, even when serum calcium was low; and calcification has not resulted when serum phosphorus was low, even when serum calcium was unusually high.

9. When calcium salts crystallize into bone, they are laid down in the skeleton in a definite pattern governed by the collagen fibers in the bone matrix. A similar matrix has been found in all types of soft-tissue calcium deposits, including calcinosis in the skin, tuberculous, and arteriosclerotic calcifications, and the calcium in dental tartar and kidney stones. This matrix seems to come from the resorption of bone. Microscopic examination reveals that during bone resorption, not only calcium salts but the bone matrix itself disappears. See J. Howard, "Clinical and Laboratory Research Concerning Mechanisms of Formation and Control of Calculous Disease by the Kidney," *Journal of Urology* 72(6):999–1008 (1954).

10. D. Barr, note 8, page 611; J. Ennever, et al., "Calcification by Proteolipid from Atherosclerotic Aorta," *Atherosclerosis* 35:209–13 (1980).

11. M. Modlin, "Urinary Phosphorylated Inositols and Renal Stone," *Lancet* (November 22, 1980), pages 113–14.

12. E. MacKay, J. Oliver, "Renal Damage Following the Ingestion of a Diet Containing an Excess of Inorganic Phosphate," *Journal of Experimental Medicine* 61:319–34 (1935).

13. M. Clapp, "The Effect of Diet on Some Parameters Measured in Toxicological Studies in the Rat," *Laboratory Animals* 14:253–61 (1980); M. Clapp, et al., "Control of Nephrocalcinosis by Manipulating the Calcium:Phosphorus Ratio in Commercial Rodent Diets," *Laboratory Animals* 16:130–32 (1982).

14. See K. Bauer, P. Griminger, "The Effect of Immobilization and Dietary Phosphorus on Bone Density of Mature Female Rats," *Nutrition Research* 5:405–12 (1985), reporting a study in which the Ca/P ratio of the diets of rats was changed from 1.2:1 to 1:2.4. The calcium contents of the rats' kidneys increased to 55 times their original contents, and their phosphorus contents doubled. See also H. Draper, et al., "Osteoporosis in Aging Rats Induced by High Phosphorus Diets," *Journal of Nutrition* 102:1133–42 (1972), a study in which rats were fed diets having the calcium concentration recommended for growing rats and a Ca/P ratio that varied from 2:1 to 1:3. Those on the high-phosphorus diet wound up with 10 times as much calcium in their kidneys as those on the low-phosphorus diet, and one rat had 100 times as much. The human equivalent of the high-phosphorus diet would contain about 800 mg of calcium (the concentration recommended for growing humans) and 2,400 mg of phosphorus (3 times the RDA for calcium) —amounts commonly found in the American diet. (See Chapter 13.) See also K. Bauer, P. Griminger, "Long-Term Effects of Activity and of Calcium and Phosphorus Intake on Bones and Kidneys of Female Rats," *Journal of Nutrition* 113:2111–21 (1983).

15. See J. Jowsey, P. Balasubramaniam, "Effect of Phosphate Supplements on Soft-Tissue Calcification and Bone Turnover," *Clinical Science* 42:289–299 (1972), reporting a 6-month rabbit study in which the experimental diet contained the amount of phosphorus per pound of body weight found in the ordinary human diet. The Ca/P ratio was 1:2. The control animals were fed a diet containing the same amount of calcium but only half as much phosphorus, giving a ratio of 1:1. Calcium loss from the bones of the experimental animals was demonstrated by a five- to twelve-fold increase in the number of holes per X-ray cross-section. No gross evidence of soft tissue calcification was found, but when samples of the soft tissues were separated and weighed, all of those taken from the phosphate-supplemented animals contained more calcium than the controls. In the abdominal aortas, calcium was greater by 37

percent; in the kidneys, by 25 percent; in the hearts, by 15 percent; and in the livers, by 12 percent. The study showed that extra-skeletal calcification can occur although gross evidence of it is lacking, a finding significant for human studies limited to that type of examination. Calcium increased in all areas tested except the blood (from which the calcium deposited elsewhere presumably originated). Bone calcium increased; but bone collagen increased at an even faster rate, resulting in porous, spongy bones. In a companion study reported by the same researchers, the amounts of dietary calcium and phosphorus were increased, but the Ca/P ratio was still 1:2 for the experimental animals, while it was 2:1 for the control animals. After 2 months, calcium deposits were visible on X-ray examination in both the kidneys and the aortas of the experimental animals. In their aortas, total calcium had increased a thousandfold.

16. G. Laflamme, J. Jowsey, "Bone and Soft Tissue Changes with Oral Phosphate Supplements," *The Journal of Clinical Investigation* 51:2834–40 (1972). The study was a follow-up of one discussed in Chapter 14, in which X-ray examination clearly indicated a loss of bone calcium in dogs given phosphate, although urinary calcium was no different than on an unsupplemented control diet. See J. Jowsey, et al., "Long-Term Effects of High Phosphate Intake on Parathyroid Hormone Levels and Bone Metabolism," *Acta Orthop. Scand.* 45:801–08 (1974). The purpose of the follow-up study was to determine what happened to the lost bone calcium, if it wasn't excreted. Whether bone was being added or lost was determined by comparing the amount of osteoblastic activity with the amount of osteoclastic activity on the bone surfaces. This examination revealed bone resorption had doubled, and bone formation had decreased by even more. Bone loss was confirmed by determining the actual mineral content of the bones. After ten months, it had decreased by about 7 percent, and the bones had twice as many holes per X-ray cross-section as before phosphate treatment. Scattered calcium deposits were found in the lenses of eight of the ten phosphate-supplemented dogs, and in five of the eight these deposits were associated with cataracts. (Cataracts form from calcium deposits on the lens of the eye and are evidence of extra-skeletal calcification.) The dogs were then killed and their organs examined microscopically for soft-tissue calcification, which was found in the kidneys, tendons, thoracic aortas, and hearts of the phosphate-supplemented dogs.

17. L. Hebert, et al., "Studies of the Mechanism by Which Phosphate Infusion Lowers Serum Calcium Concentration," *Journal of Clinical Investigation* 45(12):1886–94 (1966), page 1893; R. Breuer, J. LeBauer, "Caution in the Use of Phosphates in the Treatment of Severe Hypercalcemia," *Journal of Clinical Endocrinology* (27:695 (1967); S. Shakney, J. Hasson, "Precip-

itous Fall in Serum Calcium, Hypotension, and Acute Renal Failure After Intravenous Phosphate Therapy for Hypercalcemia," *Annals of Internal Medicine* 66:906–16 (1967); R. Goldsmith, S. Ingbar, "Inorganic Phosphate Treatment of Hypercalcemia of Diverse Etiologies," *New England Journal of Medicine* 274(1):1–7 (1966).

18. See, e.g., R. Goldsmith, et al., "Phosphate Supplementation as an Adjunct in the Therapy of Multiple Myeloma," *Archives of Internal Medicine* 122:128–33 (1968).

19. G. Laflamme, et al., note 16.

20. J. Jowsey, et al., note 15.

Chapter 16
CARDIOVASCULAR DISEASE:
THE WAY TO A MAN'S HEART IS THROUGH HIS STOMACH

1. J. Stamler, "Population Studies," in R. Levy, et al., eds., *Nutrition, Lipids, and Coronary Heart Disease* (New York: Raven Press, 1979), vol. 1, pages 25–88, at page 30 (quoting W. Raab).

2. "The Lipid Research Clinics Coronary Primary Prevention Trial Results," *JAMA* 251(3):351–64 (1984); T. Gordon, W. Kannel, "Premature Mortality from Coronary Heart Disease: The Framingham Study," *Coronary Heart Disease* 215(10):1617–25 (1971); R. Levy, "Current Status of the Cholesterol Controversy," *American Journal of Medicine* 74(5A):1–4 (1983).

3. J. Stamler, note 1, pages 30–31, 41.

4. *Osler's Principles and Practice of Medicine*, quoted in P. Rank, "Milk and Arteriosclerosis," *Medical Hypotheses* 20:317–38 (1986).

5. P. Rank, note 4.

6. R. Levy, note 2.

7. B. Ershoff, "Antitoxic Effects of Plant Fiber," *American Journal of Clinical Nutrition* 27:1395–98 (1974).

8. Whether fatty streaks are precursors of atherosclerotic plaque is still debated. Microscopic examination of the arteries of people from different populations at autopsy has shown that those with higher fat intakes and higher serum cholesterol levels tend to have more coronary fatty streaks in young adulthood and more fat in those fatty streaks. They also have more advanced atherosclerotic lesions in middle age. See R. Wissler, "Principles of the Pathogenesis of Atherosclerosis," in: E. Braunwald, ed., *Heart Disease: A Textbook of Cardiovascular Medicine* (W. B. Saunders Co., 1984), page 1189; J. Stamler, note 1, page 45.

9. D. Blankenhorn, "Will Atheroma Regress with Diet and Exercise?", *American Journal of Surgery* 141:644–45 (1981).

10. J. Leonard, M.D., et al., *Live Longer Now* (New York: Grosset & Dunlap, 1974), pages 360–61; R. Wagman, ed., *The New Family and Medical Guide* (Chicago: J. G. Ferguson Publishing Co., 1974), pages 250–51, 254–57.

11. T. Muckle, J. Roy, "High-Density Lipoprotein Cholesterol in Differential Diagnosis of Senile Dementia," *Lancet* (May 25, 1985), pages 1191–92.

12. R. Virag, et al., "Is Impotence an Arterial Disorder?", *Lancet* 8422:181–87 (1985).

13. N. Kaplan, "Systemic Hypertension: Mechanisms and Diagnosis," in E. Braunwald, note 8, page 875.

14. See S. Rosen, et al., "Epidemiologic Hearing Studies in the USSR," *Archives of Otolaryngology* 91:424–28 (1970).

15. A. Keys, et al., "Serum-Cholesterol Studies in Finland," *Lancet* 2:175 (1958).

16. R. Rizek, E. Jackson, "Current Food Consumption Practices and Nutrient Sources in the American Diet," in D. Beitz, R. Hansen, *Animal Products in Human Nutrition* (New York: Academic Press 1982), pages 150–51. A few vegetable fats are also saturated. They include coconut oil, palm kernel oil, cashew nuts, cocoa butter (a fat in chocolate), and (to a lesser extent) hydrogenated vegetable shortening and margarine.

17. This evidence is presented in detail in Chapter 19. Meat is about half fat and half protein by weight. A pound of regular ground beef contains 81.2 grams of protein and 96.2 grams of fat. A pound of dark-meat chicken contains 26.7 grams of protein and 29.3 grams of fat. A pound of bacon contains 39 grams of protein and 261 grams of fat. See J. Kirschmann, *Nutrition Almanac* (New York: McGraw Hill Book Co., 1984). But counted by the calorie, meat is substantially higher in fat than in protein, since a gram of fat contains more than twice as many calories as a gram of protein.

18. Significant positive correlations were also shown for total protein, total fat, total calories, and sucrose; and significant negative correlations were shown for vegetable fat, vegetable protein, and total carbohydrate (expressed as a percentage of total calories). See J. Stamler, note 1, pages 32–41, citing many studies.

19. J. Stamler, note 1, pages 41, 49–52; S. Yamamoto, "Japan," in H. Trowell, D. Burkitt, eds., *Western Diseases: Their Emergence and Prevention* (London: Edward Arnold, 1981), at page 338; "Hold the Eggs and Butter," *Time* (March 26, 1984), pages 56–63. However, even the Japanese are now eating more animal foods, and heart disease is increasing. See note 36.

20. *Time*, note 19.

21. D. Snowdon, et al., "Meat Consumption and Fatal Ischemic Heart Disease," *Preventive Medicine* 13(5):490–500 (1984). "Ischemic heart disease" is an international disease classification that includes 90 percent of all heart disease deaths.

22. F. Lemon, R. Waldon, "Death from Respiratory System Disease Amongst Seventh-Day Adventist Men," *JAMA* 198:117

(1966). This result is a bit confusing, since death occurs as frequently in vegetarians as in meat-eaters: once for each. But if the people in one group tend to live longer than those in another group, the number of deaths *per thousand, per year,* will be less in the former group.

23. E. Wynder, et al., "Cancer and Coronary Artery Diseases Among Seventh-Day Adventists," *Cancer* 12:1016 (1959). For women, who are less prone to heart disease than men, heart disease incidence was lower than predicted by 15 percent.

24. M. Burr, P. Sweetnam, "Vegetarianism, Dietary Fiber, and Mortality," *American Journal of Clinical Nutrition* 36:873–77 (1982).

25. R. Phillips, et al., "Coronary Heart Disease Mortality Among Seventh-Day Adventists with Differing Dietary Habits: A Preliminary Report," *American Journal of Clinical Nutrition* 31:S191–S198 (1978).

26. R. Frentzel-Beyme, et al., "Mortality Among German Vegetarians: First Results After Five Years of Follow-Up," *Nutrition and Cancer* 11:117–26 (1988).

27. H. Kahn, et al., "Association Between Reported Diet and All-Cause Mortality," *American Journal of Epidemiology* 119:775–87 (1984).

28. D. Snowdon, "Animal Product Consumption and Mortality Because of All Causes Combined, Coronary Heart Disease, Stroke, Diabetes and Cancer in Seventh-Day Adventists," *American Journal of Clinical Nutrition* 48:739–48 (1988).

29. A. Robeznieks, "What Nutritional Research Is Finding Out About Vegetarian Diets," *Vegetarian Times* (April 1986), page 12, quoting Dr. David Snowdon.

30. R. Levy, note 2.

31. M. Rosenthal, et al., "Effects of a High-Complex-Carbohydrate, Low-Fat, Low-Cholesterol Diet on Levels of Serum Lipids and Estradiol," *American Journal of Medicine* 78:23–27 (1985).

32. "Questions and Answers About the Pritikin Lifetime Eating Plan," *Center Post* 9(3):2 (1988).

33. H. Blackburn, "Diet and Mass Hyperlipidemia: A Public Health View," in R. Levy, et al., eds., *Nutrition, Lipids, and Coronary Heart Disease* (New York: Raven Press, 1979), vol. 1, page 315.

34. N. Muramoto, *Healing Ourselves* (New York: Avon Books, 1973), page 47. The correlation between uric acid levels and meat consumption is discussed in Chapter 10.

35. J. Emes, T. Nowak, *Introduction to Pathophysiology* (Baltimore: University Park Press, 1983), pages 112–13.

36. H. Hiatt, et al., eds., *Origins of Human Cancer*, Book A, Cold Spring Harbor Conferences on Cell Proliferation, Vol. 4 (Cold Spring Harbor Laboratory, 1977), pages 25, 61–62, 71–72, 101. However, the consumption of animal protein also more than doubled during the same period, and coronary heart disease also increased. See H. Trowell, D. Burkitt, *Western Diseases:*

Their Emergence and Prevention (London: Edward Arnold, 1981), pages 337–41; J. Stamler, note 1, page 53.

37. M. Hinds, et al., "Dietary Cholesterol and Lung Cancer Risk Among Men in Hawaii," *American Journal of Clinical Nutrition* 37:192–93 (1983).

Chapter 17
THE CHOLESTEROL MENACE

1. M. Thorogood, et al., "Plasma Lipids and Lipoprotein Cholesterol Concentrations in People with Different Diets in Britain," *British Medical Journal* 295:351–53 (1987).

2. See A. Keys, "Diet and Development of Coronary Artery Disease," *Journal of Chronic Diseases* 4:364 (1956); H. Bang, J. Dyerberg, "Plasma Lipids and Lipoproteins in Greenlandic West Coast Eskimos," *Acta Medica Scandinavica* 192:85–94 (1972).

3. W. Shurtleff, A. Aoyagi, *The Book of Tofu* (Brookline, Mass.: Autumn Press, Inc., 1975), page 17.

4. "Cholesterol Goals," *Harvard Medical Newsletter* 9(5):5 (1984).

5. See studies discussed at notes 19–30.

6. D. Groom, "Cardiovascular Observations on Tarahumara Indian Runners—the Modern Spartans," *American Heart Journal* 81:304–14 (1971).

7. W. Connor, et al., "The Plasma Lipids, Lipoproteins, and Diet of the Tarahumara Indians of Mexico," *American Journal of Clinical Nutrition* 31:1131–42 (1978).

8. See G. Mann, et al., "Exercise in the Disposition of Dietary Calories: Regulation of Serum Lipoprotein and Cholesterol Levels in Human Subjects," *New England Journal of Medicine* 253:349 (1955); H. Taylor, et al., "Physical Activity, Serum Cholesterol and Other Lipids in Man," *Proceedings of the Society for Experimental and Biological Medicine* 95:383 (1957); H. Montoye, et al., "The Effects of Exercise on Blood Cholesterol in Middle-Aged Men," *American Journal of Clinical Nutrition* 7:139 (1959); W. Brumbach, "Changes in the Serum Cholesterol Levels of Male College Students Who Participated in a Special Physical Exercise Program," *Research Quarterly* 32:147 (1961); J. Ribeiro, et al., "The Effectiveness of a Low Lipid Diet and Exercise in the Management of Coronary Artery Disease," *American Heart Journal* 108(5):1183–89 (1984); L. Klevay, et al., "Influence of Dietary Lipids on Plasma Cholesterol and Lipoprotein Fractions in Trained Athletes," *Clinical Research* 29(4):754A (1981).

9. P. Wood, et al., "The Distribution of Plasma Lipoproteins in Middle-Aged Male Runners," *Metabolism* 25(11):1249–57 (1976).

10. K. Van der Eems, A. Ismail, "Serum Lipids: Interactions Be-

tween Age and Moderate Intensity Exercise," *British Journal of Sports Medicine* 19(2):112–14 (1985).

11. J. Ribeiro, et al., "The Effectiveness of a Low Lipid Diet and Exercise in the Management of Coronary Artery Disease," *American Heart Journal* 108(5):1183–89 (1984).

12. J. Handler, et al., "Symptomatic Coronary Artery Disease in a Marathon Runner," *JAMA* 248(6):717–19 (1982).

13. J. Stamler, "Population Studies," in R. Levy, et al., eds., *Nutrition, Lipids, and Coronary Heart Disease* (New York: Raven Press, 1979), page 39.

14. A. Keys, et al., "Serum-Cholesterol Studies in Finland," *Lancet* (July 26, 1958) pages 175–78.

15. *Ibid.*

16. P. Savage, et al., "Serum Cholesterol Levels in American (Pima) Indian Children and Adolescents," *Pediatrics* 58:274 (1976).

17. M. McMurry, et al., "Dietary Cholesterol and the Plasma Lipids and Lipoproteins in the Tarahumara Indians: A People Habituated to a Low Cholesterol Diet After Weaning," *American Journal of Clinical Nutrition* 35:741–44 (1982).

18. Lipid Research Clinics Program, "The Lipid Research Clinics Coronary Primary Prevention Trial Results," *JAMA* 251(3):351–74 (1984).

19. M. Martin, et al., "Serum Cholesterol, Blood Pressure and Mortality: Implications from a Cohort of 361,662 Men," *Lancet* ii:933–36 (1986).

20. M. Burr, P. Sweetnam, "Vegetarianism, Dietary Fiber, and Mortality," *American Journal of Clinical Nutrition* 36:873–77 (1982); R. Phillips, et al., "Coronary Heart Disease Mortality Among Seventh-Day Adventists with Differing Dietary Habits: A Preliminary Report," *American Journal of Clinical Nutrition* 31:S191–S198 (1978).

21. See R. Walden, et al., "Effect of Environment on the Serum Cholesterol-Triglyceride Distribution Among Seventh-Day Adventists," *American Journal of Medicine* 36:269–276 (1964), finding the cholesterol levels of SDA women to be 20–30 percent lower than in age-matched New York City women, and those of SDA men to be 5–30 percent lower than in age-matched New York City men. The cholesterol levels of SDA men also reached their peak 10 years later than in New York City men, which topped out at the early age of 44. See also L. Simons, et al., "The Influence of a Wide Range of Absorbed Cholesterol on Plasma Cholesterol Levels in Man," *American Journal of Clinical Nutrition* 31:1334–39 (1978), comparing serum cholesterol in healthy SDA vegetarians and non-vegetarians of all ages. The average level for the SDAs was 179 mg/dl and for the non-SDAs was 229 mg/dl, a difference of 22 percent.

22. M. Hardinge, F. Stare, "Nutritional Studies of Vegetarians: 2. Dietary and Serum Levels of Cholesterol," *Journal of Clinical Nutrition* 2(2):83 (1954).

23. L. Simons, et al., note 21. See also R. West, O. Hayes, "Diet and Serum Cholesterol Levels," *American Journal of Clinical Nutrition* 21:853–62 (1968), in which other variables were eliminated by comparing 233 matched pairs of vegetarian and non-vegetarian SDAs who attended the same church and were of the same sex, marital status, height, weight, occupation, and approximate age. The average cholesterol level of the vegetarians was 185 mg/dl and of the non-vegetarians was 196 mg/dl. The 6 percent difference was smaller than in the study by Simons, et al., probably because the "vegetarians" included semi-vegetarians who ate meat as often as 3 times a week. But the difference was still large enough to be statistically significant. When meat intake and serum cholesterol were plotted against each other, they increased together.

24. M. Burr, et al., "Plasma Cholesterol and Blood Pressure in Vegetarians," *Journal of Human Nutrition* 35:437–41 (1981).

25. "Serum Cholesterol and Triglyceride Levels in Australian Adolescent Vegetarians," *British Medical Journal* 2:87 (1976). Compare R. West, et al., note 23; M. Hardinge, F. Stare, "Nutritional Studies of Vegetarians. II. Dietary and Serum Levels of Cholesterol," *American Journal of Clinical Nutrition* 2:83–88 (1954); M. Hardinge, et al., "Nutritional Studies of Vegetarians. IV. Dietary Fatty Acids and Serum Cholesterol Levels," *American Journal of Clinical Nutrition* 10:516 (1962).

26. A. Sanders, et al., "Studies of Vegans: The Fatty Acid Composition of Plasma Choline Phosphoglycerides, Erythrocytes, Adipose Tissue, and Breast Milk, and Some Indicators of Susceptibility to Ischemic Heart Disease in Vegans and Omnivore Controls," *American Journal of Clinical Nutrition* 31:805–13 (1978). The vegans had avoided all animal products for an average of 8 years.

27. M. Hardinge, et al., note 25. The vegans had maintained the dietary regime for at least 5 years, while the lacto-ovo-vegetarians had maintained it throughout life.

28. J. Burslem, et al., "Plasma Apoprotein and Lipoprotein Lipid Levels in Vegetarians," *Metabolism* 27(6):711–19 (1978).

29. F. Sacks, et al., "Plasma Lipids and Lipoproteins in Vegetarians and Controls," *New England Journal of Medicine* 292:1148–51 (1975).

30. R. Walden, et al., "Effect of Environment on the Serum Cholesterol-Triglyceride Distribution Among Seventh-Day Adventists," *American Journal of Medicine* 36:269–76 (1964).

31. F. Sacks, et al., note 29.

32. D. Small, "Cellular Mechanisms for Lipid Deposition in Atherosclerosis," *New England Journal of Medicine* 297(16):873–77 (1977).

33. J. Stamler, note 13, pages 32–41, 56–57.

34. D. Small, note 32.

35. See Lipid Research Clinics Program, note 18; R. Lees, A. Lees, "High-Density Lipoproteins and the Risk of Atheroscle-

rosis," *New England Journal of Medicine* 306(25):1546–47 (1982).

36. D. Robinson, et al., "High-Density-Lipoprotein Cholesterol in the Masai of East Africa: A Cautionary Note," *British Medical Journal* 1:1249 (1979).

37. J. Masarei, et al., "Vegetarian Diets, Lipids and Cardiovascular Risk," *Aust. N.Z. J. Med.* 14:400–04 (1984).

38. D. Robinson, et al., note 36; M. Green, et al., "The Ratio of Plasma High-Density Lipoprotein Cholesterol: Age-Related Changes and Race and Sex Differences in Selected North American Populations. The Lipid Research Clinics Program Prevalence Study," *Circulation* 72(1):93–104 (1985) (citing the NHLBI Type II Coronary Intervention Study).

39. *Ibid.*

40. See M. Burr, et al., note 24 (HDL levels higher in vegetarians); J. Gear, et al., "Biochemical and Haematological Variables in Vegetarians," *British Medical Journal* 280:1415 (1980) (HDL levels equivalent in vegetarians and meat-eaters); and studies discussed at notes 42–44 (HDL levels higher in meat-eaters).

41. In the NHLBI study (note 18), an increase in HDL cholesterol was only weakly associated with a decreased heart disease risk; but a decrease in LDL cholesterol and an increase in the *ratio* of HDL to total cholesterol were both strongly associated with a decreased risk.

42. F. Sacks, et al., "Plasma Lipoprotein Levels in Vegetarians: The Effect of Ingestion of Fats From Dairy Products," *JAMA* 254(10):1337–41 (1985).

43. J. Burslem, et al., note 28.

44. F. Sacks, et al., note 29.

45. F. Sacks, et al., "Effect of Ingestion of Meat on Plasma Cholesterol of Vegetarians," *JAMA* 246(6):640–44 (1981). See also J. Masarei, et al., "Effects of a Lacto-Ovo-Vegetarian Diet on Serum Concentrations of Cholesterol, Triglyceride, HDL-C, HDL$_2$-C, HDL$_3$-C, Apoprotein-B, and Lp(a)," *American Journal of Clinical Nutrition* 40:468–79 (1984).

46. See S. Siwolop, "Curbing Killer Cholesterol," *Business Week* (October 26, 1987), pages 122–23.

47. M. Rosenthal, et al., "Effects of a High-Complex-Carbohydrate, Low-Fat, Low-Cholesterol Diet on Levels of Serum Lipids and Estradiol," *American Journal of Medicine* 78:23–27 (1985).

48. M. Armstrong, et al., "Regression of Coronary Atheromatosis in Rhesus Monkeys," *Circulation Research* 27:59–67 (1970). The same reversal resulted when the saturated fat and cholesterol were replaced with corn oil (a polyunsaturated vegetable fat), demonstrating that the atherosclerotic growths weren't caused by dietary fat *per se*, but by saturated fat and cholesterol.

49. "Cardiovascular Cleanup," *University of California, Berkeley Wellness Letter* 3(12):1 (1987).

50. Report by Dr. Dean Ornish at the American Heart Associa-

tion's 61st Scientific Session. See "Ohmmm . . . It's About Your Heart," *Body, Mind and Spirit Magazine* (March/April 1989), page 59.

51. R. Wissler, D. Vesselinovitch, "Studies of Regression of Advanced Atherosclerosis in Experimental Animals and Man," *Annals of the New York Academy of Sciences* 275:363–78 (1976).

52. "Cholesterol Goals," *Harvard Medical School Health Letter* 9(5):5 (1984).

53. E. Glassman, et al., "Changes in the Underlying Coronary Circulation Secondary to Bypass Grafting," *Circulation* 49,50 (suppl.2):80–83 (1974).

54. "Brain Damage After Open-Heart Surgery," *Lancet* 1:1161 (1982).

55. T. Preston, "Coronary Bypass Surgery: Remedy or Racket?" *Reader's Digest* (April 1985).

56. The exception is the small group of cases with extensive disease in all three coronary arteries, but with good function in the left ventricle (the chamber of the heart from which blood is pumped to the rest of the body); in other words, those patients likely to die without the operation, yet healthy enough to survive it. See "Coronary Artery Bypass Surgery—Indications and Limitations," *Lancet* 2:511 (1980).

57. S. Siwolop, note 46; J. Byrne, "The Miracle Company," *Business Week* (October 19, 1987), pages 84–90.

58. S. Siwolop, note 46.

59. B. Rensberger, "Mystery of High-Fiber Diet Unraveled," *Washington Post* (October 26, 1987), page A7.

60. F. Ellis, T. Sanders, "Angina and Vegan Diet," *American Heart Journal* 93(6):803–05 (1977).

61. P. Kuo, et al., "The Effect of Lipemia Upon Coronary and Peripheral Arterial Circulation in Patients with Essential Hyperlipemia," *American Journal of Medicine* 26:68–75 (1959).

Chapter 18
HIGH BLOOD PRESSURE:
TOO MUCH SALT OR TOO MUCH MEAT

1. N. Kaplan, "Non-Drug Treatment of Hypertension," *Annals of Internal Medicine* 102:359–73 (1985).

2. N. Kaplan, "Systemic Hypertension: Mechanisms and Diagnosis," in E. Braunwald, ed., *Heart Disease: A Textbook of Cardiovascular Medicine* (Philadelphia: W. B. Saunders Co., 1984), page 849.

3. American Heart Association, *A Guide to Heart Facts* (1981).

4. G. Subak-Sharpe, ed., *The Physicians' Manual for Patients* (New York: Times Books, 1984), page 35.

5. O. Lindahl, et al., "A Vegan Regimen with Reduced Medication in the Treatment of Hypertension," *British Journal of*

Nutrition 52:11–20 (1984), discussed in text at note 50.

6. See C. Farleigh, et al., "Measurement of Sodium Intake and Its Relationship to Blood Pressure and Salivary Sodium Concentration," *Nutrition Research* 5:815–26 (1985); F. Simpson, "Salt and Hypertension: A Skeptical Review of the Evidence," *Clinical Science* 57:463S–48OS (1979); J. Laragh, M. Pecker, "Dietary Sodium and Essential Hypertension: Some Myths, Hopes, and Truths," *Annals of Internal Medicine* 98(Part 2):735–43 (1983).

7. B. Armstrong, et al., "Urinary Sodium and Blood Pressure in Vegetarians," *American Journal of Clinical Nutrition* 32:2472–76 (1979); S. Malhotra, "Dietary Factors Causing Hypertension in India," *American Journal of Clinical Nutrition* 23:1353–63 (1970).

8. See text at notes 50–52.

9. N. Kaplan, note 2.

10. E. Amsterdam, A. Holmes, *Take Care of Your Heart* (New York: Facts on File Publications, 1984), pages 48–52.

11. See J. Laragh, et al., note 6.

12. Hypertension Detection and Follow-up Program Cooperative Group, "Five-Year Findings of the Hypertension Detection and Follow-up Program. I. Reduction in Mortality of Persons with High Blood Pressure, Including Mild Hypertension," *JAMA* 242:2562–71 (1979).

13. B. Margetts, et al., "Vegetarian Diet in Mild Hypertension: Effects of Fat and Fiber," *American Journal of Clinical Nutrition* 48:801–05 (1988).

14. W. Kannel, et al., "Systolic Versus Diastolic Blood Pressure and Risk of Coronary Heart Disease: The Framingham Study," *American Journal of Cardiology* 27(4):335–45 (1971).

15. K. O'Malley, et al., *High Blood Pressure* (New York: Arco Publishing, Inc., 1982), pages 18–19.

16. See F. Sacks, et al., "Blood Pressure in Vegetarians," *American Journal of Epidemiology* 100(5):390–98 (1974). Compare W. Norman-Taylor, W. Rees, "Blood Pressures in Three New Hebrides Communities," *British Journal of Preventive and Social Medicine* 17:141–44 (1963), in which no significant differences in blood pressure were observed between members of vegetarian and non-vegetarian communities in the New Hebrides, and no appreciable rise in blood pressure with age was noted in either group. However, animal fat intake was low in both groups, and yam, taro, and banana constituted the staple foods of both.

17. See F. Sacks, "Vegetarian Diets and Cardiovascular Risk Factors," in *Nutrition and Vegetarianism* (Chapel Hill, No. Car.: Health Sciences Consortium, 1981), pages 135–38.

18. S. Malhotra, "Dietary Factors Causing Hypertension in India," *American Journal of Clinical Nutrition* 23:1353–63 (1970).

19. T. Kimura, M. Ota, "Epidemiologic Study of Hypertension: Comparative Results of Hypertensive Surveys in Two Areas

in Northern Japan," *American Journal of Clinical Nutrition* 17:381–90 (1965).

20. I. Maddocks, "Blood Pressure in Melanesians," *Medical Journal of Australia* 1:1123–26 (1967).
21. R. Barnes, "Incidence of Heart Disease in a Native Hospital in Papua," *Medical Journal of Australia* 2:540–41 (1961).
22. J. Casley-Smith, "Blood Pressure in Australian Aborigines," *Medical Journal of Australia* 1:627–33 (1959).
23. I. Prior, et al., "Sodium Intake and Blood Pressure in Two Polynesian Populations," *New England Journal of Medicine* 279:515–20 (1968); J. Hunter, "Diet, Body Build, Blood Pressure and Serum Cholesterol Levels in Coconut-Eating Polynesians," *Federation Proceedings* 21(4):36–43 (Pt. 2) (1963).
24. F. Saille, "Influence of Vegetarian Food on the Blood Pressure," *Med. Clin.* 26:929–31 (1930).
25. S. Hejda, et al., "Diet and Blood Pressure," *Lancet* 1:1103 (1967).
26. S. Isobe, S. Nagamine, "On the Quantity and Quality of Fat and Oil Ingested by Japanese People (Report 2): Fat Intakes of the Hypertensive Patients," *Ann. Rep. Natl. Inst. Nutr.* (Tokyo 1962), pages 41–42.
27. W. Morse, et al., "Blood Pressure Amongst Aboriginal Ethnic Groups of Szechwan Province, West China," *Lancet* 1:966–67 (1937).
28. J. Kotchen, et al., "Blood Pressure Trends with Aging," *Hypertension* 4(supp.III):128–35 (1982).
29. E. Freis, "Salt, Volume and the Prevention of Hypertension," *Circulation* 53(4):589–94 (1976).
30. See F. Saille, note 24.
31. A. Donaldson, "The Relation of Protein Foods to Hypertension," *Calif. West. Med.* 24:328–30 (1926).
32. B. Armstrong, et al., "Blood Pressure in Seventh-Day Adventist Vegetarians," *American Journal of Epidemiology* 105:444–49 (1977).
33. F. Sacks, et al., "Blood Pressure in Vegetarians," *American Journal of Epidemiology* 100(5):390–98 (1974). (For the blood pressures of meat-eating college students of the same age range, see note 31.) See also E. Ernst, et al., "Blood Rheology in Vegetarians," *British Journal of Nutrition* 56:555–560 (1986), finding that vegans had lower blood pressures than lacto-ovo-vegetarians, who had lower blood pressures than controls. While most studies have found lower blood pressure in vegans, at least one did not. See T. Sanders, T. Key, "Blood Pressure, Plasma Renin Activity and Aldosterone Concentrations in Vegans and Omnivore Controls," *Human Nutrition: Applied Nutrition* 41A:204–11 (1987).
34. See note 32.
35. I. Rouse, et al., "Vegetarian Diet, Lifestyle and Blood Pressure in Two Religious Populations," *Clin. Exp. Pharmacol. Physiol.* 9:327–30 (1982).

36. I. Rouse, et al., "Vegetarian Diet, Blood Pressure and Cardio-vascular Risk," *Aust. N.Z. J. Med.* 14:439–43 (1984).
37. L. Beilin, et al., "Vegetarian Diet and Blood Pressure Levels: Incidental or Causal Association?", *American Journal of Clinical Nutrition* 48:806–10 (1988).
38. See, e.g., M. Abdulla, et al., "Nutrient Intake and Health Status of Lacto-Vegetarians: Chemical Analyses of Diets Using the Duplicate Portion Sampling Technique," *American Journal of Clinical Nutrition* 40:325–38 (1984).
39. B. Armstrong, et al., "Urinary Sodium and Blood Pressure in Vegetarians," *American Journal of Clinical Nutrition* 32:2472–76 (1979).
40. N. Muramoto, *Healing Ourselves* (New York: Avon Books, 1973), pages 8–9, 70.
41. F. Sacks, et al., note 33.
42. J. Iacono, et al., "Effect of Dietary Fat on Blood Pressure in a Rural Finnish Population," *American Journal of Clinical Nutrition* 38:860–69 (1983). See also J. Iacono, et al., "Reduction in Blood Pressure Associated with High Polyunsaturated Fat Diets That Reduce Blood-Cholesterol in Man," *Preventive Medicine* 4:426–43 (1975); J. Judd, et al., "Effects of Diets Varying in Fat and P/S Ratio on Blood Pressure in Man," *Federation Proceedings* 38:387 (1979).
43. B. Margetts, et al., "Dietary Fats and Blood Pressure," *Aust. N.Z. Med. J.* 14:444–47 (1984). See also B. Margetts, et al., note 13.
44. B. Margetts, et al., note 13. See also J. Brussaard, et al., "Blood Pressure and Diet in Normotensive Volunteers: Absence of an Effect of Dietary Fiber, Protein, or Fat," *American Journal of Clinical Nutrition* 34:2023–29 (1981), in which changes in dietary fiber did not produce significant changes in blood pressure. Compare J. Anderson, "Health Implications of Wheat Fiber," *American Journal of Clinical Nutrition* 41:1103–12 (1985) and studies cited therein, in which blood pressure was lowered but dietary fiber may not have been the responsible agent, because the experimental diets were also lower in total fat; and A. Wright, et al., "Dietary Fiber and Blood Pressure," *British Medical Journal* 2:1541–43 (1979), in which fiber seemed to cause small but still significant reductions in blood pressure.
45. L. Beilin, "Vegetarian Approach to Hypertension," *Can. J. Physiol. Pharmacol.* 64:852–55 (1986).
46. I. Rouse, et al., "Blood-Pressure Lowering Effect of a Vegetarian Diet: Controlled Trial in Normotensive Subjects," *Lancet* (January 1, 1983), pages 5–9. Fifty-nine men and women aged 25–63 with normal blood pressures were divided into 3 groups. All ate their meals in the same hospital dining room, and all ate the same omnivorous diet for the first 2 weeks. Two groups then alternately switched to a lacto-ovo-vegetarian diet for another 3 weeks. While on the meatless diet, the partici-

pants were asked to copy the normal diets of vegetarians by choosing vegetable rather than animal fats and eating more fruit and whole grain cereals. Salt was allowed as desired. The blood pressures of the group eating meat throughout the experiment didn't change significantly, while those of the other 2 groups dropped an average of 6.8 mm systolic and 2.7 mm diastolic during the vegetarian period.

47. A. Donaldson, note 31.
48. F. Sacks, et al., "Effect of Ingestion of Meat on Plasma Cholesterol of Vegetarians," *JAMA* 246:640–44 (1981). The 3 percent rise in blood pressure, while modest by comparison, was enough to be statistically significant. It was also greater than in studies in which normal amounts of salt have been added to the diets of people in the same age group. This change has produced no increase in blood pressure. See W. Kirkendall, et al., "The Effect of Dietary Sodium Chloride on Blood Pressure, Body Fluids, Electrolytes, Renal Function, and Serum Lipids of Normotensive Man," *Journal of Laboratory and Clinical Medicine* 87:418–34 (1976); F. Luft, et al., "Cardiovascular and Humoral Responses to Extremes of Sodium Intake in Normal Black and White Men," *Circulation* 60:697–706 (1979).
49. See, e.g., W. Kempner, "Treatment of Hypertensive Vascular Disease with Rice Diet," *American Journal of Medicine* 4:545–77 (1948); E. Huen, ["Vegetarian Fruit Juices in Therapy in Obesity and Hypertension"], *Fortschr. Therap.* 12:403–11 (1936); O. Lindahl, et al., note 5.
50. O. Lindahl, et al., note 5.
51. T. Beard, et al., "Randomised Controlled Trial of a No-Added-Sodium Diet for Mild Hypertension," *Lancet* 8296:455–58 (1982).
52. J. Laragh, et al., note 6.

Chapter 19
JACK SPRAT AND THE LEAN MEAT MYTH

1. "Switch to Soy Protein for Boring but Healthful Diet," *JAMA* 247(22):3045–46 (1982).
2. See G. Walker, et al., "The Effect of Animal Protein and Vegetable Protein Diets Having the Same Fat Content on the Serum Lipid Levels of Young Women," *Journal of Nutrition* 72:317–21 (1960), in which two groups of women were fed diets that were similar in protein (45–50 grams), fat, cholesterol, and the ratio of polyunsaturated to saturated fatty acids; but the protein in one was primarily animal-derived, while in the other it came from plant sources (rice, legumes, gluten flour, cereals), except for ½ cup of milk. After 6 weeks, the average cholesterol level had dropped 7 percent more on the vegetable-

protein than the animal-protein diet—enough to be statistically significant. See also K. Carroll, et al., "Hypocholesterolemic Effect of Substituting Soybean Protein for Animal Protein in the Diet of Healthy Young Women," *American Journal of Clinical Nutrition* 31:1312–21 (1978), in which healthy college women ate a normal mixed diet for 37 days, then ate the same diet except that animal protein was replaced with soy protein for the next 41 days. Animal fat and cholesterol were kept the same by providing the soy protein in the form of specially prepared meat substitutes that contained the animal fats of the corresponding meat (ham, beef, or chicken). The women's cholesterol levels dropped an average of 9 mg/dl, or 5%, on the soy-protein diet. When the experiment was run in the reverse order, the effect was also reversed: serum cholesterol increased an average of 9 mg/dl, or 5 percent.

3. This theory has been proposed to explain studies in which purified plant proteins have failed to lower serum cholesterol as compared to animal proteins. See, e.g., W. Holmes, et al., "Comparison of the Effect of Dietary Meat Versus Dietary Soybean Protein on Plasma Lipids of Hyperlipidemic Individuals," *Atherosclerosis* 36:379–87 (1980); R. Shorey, et al., "Determinants of Hypocholesterolemic Response to Soy and Animal Protein-Based Diets," *American Journal of Clinical Nutrition* 34:1769–78 (1981); A. Campbell, et al., "Serum Lipids of Men Fed Diets Differing in Protein Quality and Linoleic Acid Content," *American Journal of Clinical Nutrition* 17:83–87 (1965). In some studies finding no effect of soy as compared to animal protein, the animal protein used was casein, which seems to be less atherogenic than meat protein. Thus in studies in which soy and casein have been compared, *both* have lowered serum cholesterol as compared to the subjects' usual pre-test meat diets, although dietary cholesterol and saturated fat were unchanged. See J. van Raaij, et al., "Influence of Diets Containing Casein, Soy Isolate, and Soy Concentrate on Serum Cholesterol and Lipoproteins in Middle-aged Volunteers," *American Journal of Clinical Nutrition* 35:925–34 (1982); J. van Raaij, et al., "Effects of Casein Versus Soy Protein Diets on Serum Cholesterol and Lipoproteins in Young Healthy Volunteers," *American Journal of Clinical Nutrition* 34:1261–71 (1981).

4. D. Zilversmit, "Dietary Fiber," in R. Levy, et al., eds., *Nutrition, Lipids and Coronary Heart Disease*, vol. 1 (New York: Raven Press, 1979), pages 162–63.

5. *JAMA*, note 1; "Plant Foods and Atherosclerosis," *Nutrition Reviews* 35:148–50 (1977).

6. T. Sanders, et al., "Studies of Vegans: The Fatty Acid Composition of Plasma Choline Phosphoglycerides, Erythrocytes, Adipose Tissue, and Breast Milk, and Some Indicators of Susceptibility to Ischemic Heart Disease in Vegans and Omnivore Controls," *American Journal of Clinical Nutrition* 31:805–13

(1978); G. Fraser, et al., "The Effect of Various Vegetable Supplements on Serum Cholesterol," American Journal of Clinical Nutrition 34:1272–77 (1981).

7. Lipid Research Clinics Program, "The Lipid Research Clinics Coronary Primary Prevention Trial Results," *JAMA* 251:351–64 (1984). The 30 percent reduction seen in vegans is also the percentage reduction that would have been required to bring the elevated levels of the participants in this study to normal. Their average initial level was 292 mg/dl—33 percent above the 220 mg/dl then considered normal.

8. R. Levy, et al., note 4, page 273.

9. See text at notes 22–28.

10. M. Flynn, et al., "Dietary 'Meats' and Serum Lipids," *American Journal of Clinical Nutrition* 35:935–42 (1982).

11. D. Thomsen, "Steaking Out Cholesterol," *Science News* 124(18): 281 (1983).

12. B. O'Brien, R. Reiser, "Human Plasma Lipid Responses to Red Meat, Poultry, Fish, and Eggs," *American Journal of Clinical Nutrition* 33:2573–80 (1980); M. Flynn, et al., note 10.

13. M. Flynn, et al., note 10.

14. N. Goulding, et al., "Reversible Hypercholesterolaemia Produced by Cholesterol-Free Fish Meal Protein Diets," *Atherosclerosis* 49:127–37 (1983).

15. K. Carroll, H. Hamilton, "Effects of Dietary Protein and Carbohydrate on Plasma Cholesterol Levels in Relation to Atherosclerosis," *Journal of Food Science* 40:18–23 (1975). The tendency of the proteins tested to increase serum cholesterol ranked as follows, from most to least: extracted whole egg, skim milk powder, lactalbumin, casein, fish protein, beef protein, pork protein, raw egg protein, rapeseed flour, wheat gluten, peanut protein, pea protein, soybean protein, and fava bean protein. The cutoff between increasing and decreasing serum cholesterol levels was between the last of the animal proteins and the first of the vegetable proteins. See also D. Kritchevsky, et al., "Experimental Atherosclerosis in Rabbits Fed Cholesterol-Free Diets. Part 9. Beef Protein and Textured Vegetable Protein," *Atherosclerosis* 39:169–75 (1981).

16. D. Meeker, H. Kesten, "Effect of High Protein Diets on Experimental Atherosclerosis of Rabbits," *Archives of Pathology* 31(2):147–62 (1941). One group of rabbits was fed a diet containing defatted, cholesterol-free casein (a protein in milk). A second group was fed the same diet except the casein was replaced with soy protein (which is also cholesterol-free). Cholesterol levels on the casein diet rose an average of 37 percent above the normal level for rabbits and were accompanied by clear evidence of atherosclerosis in the form of atheromatous plaques in the rabbits' aortas. On the soy protein diet, serum cholesterol remained normal, and the aortas contained no atheromatous plaques.

17. *Ibid.*
18. M. Moore, et al., "Dietary-Atherosclerosis Study on Deceased Persons," *Journal of the American Dietetic Association* 38:216–23 (1976).
19. See Chapter 17.
20. See notes 1, 2.
21. R. Hodges, et al., "Dietary Carbohydrates and Low Cholesterol Diets: Effects on Serum Lipids of Man," *American Journal of Clinical Nutrition* 20(2):198–208 (1967).
22. P. Kuo, et al., "The Effect of Lipemia Upon Coronary and Peripheral Arterial Circulation in Patients with Essential Hyperlipemia," *American Journal of Medicine* 26:68–75 (1959). See also H. Liebermeister, H. Toluipur, "Senkung des cholesterinspiegel durch Zusatz von Pektinen and Sojaprotein zur Reduktionsiat," *Dtsch. Med. Wschr.* 10:333 (1980), in which serum cholesterol was reduced by 184 mg/dl—or nearly 40 percent—in 6 patients whose initial cholesterol level averaged 484.5 mg/dl, after only 3 weeks on a vegan diet consisting of rice, fruits, vegetables, and a protein hydrolysate mixture.
23. C. Sirtori, et al., "Soybean-Protein Diet in the Treatment of Type-II Hyperlipoproteinaemia," *Lancet* 1(8006):275–77 (1977).
24. C. Sirtori, et al., "Clinical Experience with the Soybean Protein Diet in the Treatment of Hypercholesterolemia," *American Journal of Clinical Nutrition* 32:1645–58 (1979).
25. G. Descovich, et al., "Multicentre Study of Soybean Protein Diet for Outpatient Hypercholesterolaemic Patients," *Lancet* 8197:709–12 (1980).
26. C. Sirtori, et al., note 23.
27. W. Richter, et al., "The Effect of a Mixture of Soybean Protein and Pectin on Lipoprotein Lipids and Lipoproteins," in *7th International Symposium on Drugs Affecting Lipid Metabolism, Milan*, Abstr. 101 (1980).
28. J. Anderson, et al., "Hypocholesterolemic Effects of Oat-Bran or Bean Intake for Hypercholesterolemic Men," *American Journal of Clinical Nutrition* 40:1146–55 (1984). The beans were either pinto or navy (cooked or as soup). The oat bran was in the form of hot cereal and oat bran muffins.
29. See D. Zilversmit, note 4. Although wheat bran, the most popular of the fiber supplements, also hasn't lowered serum cholesterol in most studies, psyllium has, as have pectin and guar gum (when given in substantial amounts).
30. T. Schweizer, et al., "Metabolic Effects of Dietary Fiber from Dehulled Soybeans in Humans," *American Journal of Clinical Nutrition* 38:1–11 (1983). Although LDL cholesterol increased, the HDL/LDL ratio was not significantly changed.
31. D. Kritchevsky, "Dietary Fiber and Disease," in L. Ellenbogen, ed., *Controversies in Nutrition* (N.Y.: Churchill Livingstone, 1981), page 40.
32. J. Anderson, et al., note 28.

33. G. Descovich, et al., note 25.
34. D. Zilversmit, note 4.
35. C. Edwards, et al., "Utilization of Wheat by Adult Man: Nitrogen Metabolism, Plasma Amino Acids and Lipids," *American Journal of Clinical Nutrition* 24:169–71 (1971).
36. J. Groen, et al., "Influence of the Nature of the Fat in Diets High in Carbohydrate (Mainly Derived from Bread) on the Serum Cholesterol," *American Journal of Clinical Nutrition* 17:296–304 (1965).
37. A. de Groot, et al., "Cholesterol-Lowering Effect of Rolled Oats," *Lancet* 2(7302):303–4 (1963).
38. M. Burr, P. Sweetnam, "Vegetarianism, Dietary Fiber, and Mortality," *American Journal of Clinical Nutrition* 36:873–77 (1982).
39. K. Mathur, et al., "Hypocholesterolaemic Effect of Bengal Gram: A Long-Term Study in Man," *British Medical Journal* 1:30–1 (1968).
40. G. Fraser, et al., "The Effect of Various Vegetable Supplements on Serum Cholesterol," *American Journal of Clinical Nutrition* 34:1272–77 (1981).
41. F. Grande, et al., "Sucrose and Various Carbohydrate-Containing Foods and Serum Lipids in Man," *American Journal of Clinical Nutrition* 27:1043 (1974). See also J. Robertson, et al., "The Effect of Raw Carrot on Serum Lipids and Colon Function," *American Journal of Clinical Nutrition* 32:1889–92 (1979), in which raw carrots reduced serum cholesterol by 11 percent.
42. S. Davidson, et al., *Human Nutrition and Dietetics*, 7th ed. (New York: Churchill Livingstone, 1979), page 50.
43. S. Grundy, "Dietary Fats and Sterols," in R. Levy, et al., note 4, page 91; F. Mattson, et al., "Optimizing the Effect of Plant Sterols on Cholesterol Absorption in Man," *American Journal of Clinical Nutrition* 35:697–700 (1982).
44. F. Mattson, et al., note 43.

Chapter 20
THE DIETS OF DOGS AND ESKIMOS

1. T. Hager, "Take Fish to Heart," *Reader's Digest* (August 1985), pages 127–30.
2. "Fish Oil Pills: Jumping the Gun," *University of California, Berkeley Wellness Letter* 3(5):1 (1987).
3. J. Arthaud, "Cause of Death in 339 Alaskan Natives as Determined by Autopsy," *Archives of Pathology* 90:433 (1970).
4. R. Mazess, W. Mather, "Bone Mineral Content of North Alaskan Eskimos," *American Journal of Clinical Nutrition* 27:916–25 (1974).

5. See H. McGill Jr., "The Relationship of Dietary Cholesterol to Serum Cholesterol Concentration and to Atherosclerosis in Man," *American Journal of Clinical Nutrition* 32:2664–2702 (1979); and studies in note 15.

6. L. Kaizer, et al., "Fish Consumption and Breast Cancer Risk: An Ecological Study," *Nutrition and Cancer* 12:61–68 (1989).

7. R. Nelson, et al., "A Comparison of Dietary Fish Oil and Corn Oil in Experimental Colo-Rectal Carcinogenesis," *Nutrition and Cancer* 11:215–20 (1988).

8. M. Ikeda, et al., "A Cohort Study on the Possible Association Between Broiled Fish Intake and Cancer," *Gann* 74:640–48 (1983); L. Kolonel, et al., "Nutrient Intakes in Relation to Cancer Incidence in Hawaii," *British Journal of Cancer* 44:332–39 (1981).

9. I. Munro, S. Charbonneau, "Environmental Contaminants," in H. Roberts, ed., *Food Safety* (New York: John Wiley & Sons, 1981), page 155.

10. See Chapter 9.

11 H. Bieler, *Food Is Your Best Medicine* (New York: Ballantine Books, 1982), pages 115–16.

12. J. Annand, "The Case Against Heated Animal Protein," *Journal of Atherosclerosis Research* 3:153–56 (1963); O. Schaefer, "Eskimos (Inuit)," in H. Trowell, et al., eds. *Western Diseases* (London: Edward Arnold Ltd., 1981), pages 113–21.

13. K. Ho, "The Masai of East Africa—Some Unique Biological Characteristics," *Archives of Pathology* 91:387 (1971).

14. See Chapter 21.

15. See S. Feldman, et al., "Lipid and Cholesterol Metabolism in Alaskan Arctic Eskimos," *Archives of Pathology* 94:45 (1972); S. Feldman, et al., "Carbohydrate and Lipid Metabolism in the Alaskan Arctic Eskimo," *American Journal of Clinical Nutrition* 28:588 (1975).

16. See K. Ho, et al., note 13.

17. See J. Day, et al., "Anthropometric, Physiological and Biological Differences Between Urban and Rural Masai," *Atherosclerosis* 23:357 (1976), in which the serum cholesterol levels of urban Masai who had adopted a Western diet averaged 203 mg/dl, 25 percent higher than for rural Masai. See also H. Bang, et al., "Plasma Lipid and Lipoprotein Patterns in Greenlandic West Coast Eskimos," *Lancet* 1:1143 (1971), in which serum cholesterol levels in Eskimos living in their native habitat were lower than in either Danes or Eskimos living in Denmark.

18. J. Stamler, "Population Studies," in R. Levy, et al., eds., *Nutrition, Lipids, and Coronary Heart Disease*, vol. 1 (New York: Raven Press, 1979), page 39; J. Annand, "The Case Against Heated Milk Protein," *Atherosclerosis* 13:137–39 (1971).

19. D. Kromhout, et al., "The Inverse Relation Between Fish Consumption and 20-Year Mortality from Coronary Heart Disease," *New England Journal of Medicine* 312(19):1205–09 (1985).

20. T. von Lossonczy, et al., "The Effect of a Fish Diet on Serum Lipids in Healthy Human Subjects," *American Journal of Clinical Nutrition* 31:1340–46 (1978).
21. C. Wallis, "Hold the Eggs and Butter," *Time* (March 26, 1984), pages 56–63.
22. A. Fehily, et al., "The Effect of Fatty Fish on Plasma Lipid and Lipoprotein Concentrations," *American Journal of Clinical Nutrition* 38:349–51 (1983).
23. B. Phillipson, et al., "Reduction of Plasma Lipids, Lipoproteins, and Apoproteins by Dietary Fish Oils in Patients with Hypertriglyceridemia," *New England Journal of Medicine* 312:1210–16 (1985).
24. R. Saynor, et al., "The Long-Term Effect of Dietary Supplementation with Fish Lipid Concentrate on Serum Lipids, Bleeding Time, Platelets, and Angina," *Atherosclerosis* 50:3–10 (1984).
25. See M. Specter, "Fish Oil: No Panacea for Heart Disease," *Washington Post* (October 11, 1987), page A11.
26. "Fish May Not Be See-Food," *Vegetarian Times* (August 1984), page 13.
27. M. Specter, note 25; A. Ahmed, B. Holub, "Alteration and Recovery of Bleeding Times, Platelet Aggregation and Fatty Acid Composition of Individual Phospholipids in Platelets of Human Subjects Receiving a Supplement of Cod-Liver Oil," *Lipids* 19(8):617–24 (1984).
28. "Marine Oils and Platelet Function in Man," *Nutrition Reviews* 42:189–91 (1984).
29. J. Dyerberg, H. Bang, "Hemostatic Function and Platelet Polyunsaturated Fatty Acids in Eskimos," *Lancet* 433–35 (1979).
30. R. Saynor, et al., note 24.
31. See *Nutrition Reviews*, note 28.
32. "Fish Oil Pills: Jumping the Gun," *University of California, Berkeley Wellness Letter* 3(5):1 (1987).
33. L. McDonald, M. Edgill, "Dietary Restriction and Coagulability of the Blood in Ischaemic Heart-Disease," *Lancet* 1:996–98 (1958); C. Mills, et al., "Relation of Clumping and Disintegration of Platelets to Body Metabolism," *Chinese Journal of Physiology* 2(2):219–28 (1928).
34. E. Ernst, et al., "Blood Rheology in Vegetarians," *British Journal of Nutrition* 56:555–60 (1986).
35. See A. Howard, "The Masai, Milk and the Yogurt Factor: An Alternative Explanation," *Atherosclerosis* 27:383–85 (1977); H. Yacowitz, et al., "Effects of Oral Calcium Upon Serum Lipids in Man," *British Medical Journal* 1:1352 (1965); N. Johnson, et al., "Effects on Blood Pressure of Calcium Supplementation of Women," *American Journal of Clinical Nutrition* 42:14–17 (1985); "Calcium, Vitamin D and Heart Disease," *Science News* 127(9):141 (1985).
36. "Calcium, Vitamin D and Heart Disease," note 35 V. Stults, "Nutritional Hazards," in H. Roberts, ed., *Food Safety* (New York: John Wiley & Sons, 1981), page 82; J. Moon, *Pathologi-*

cal Calcification (George Ohsawa Macrobiotic Foundation, 1974), pages 4–26.

37. See P. Rank, "Milk and Arteriosclerosis," *Medical Hypotheses* 20:317–38 (1986), postulating that arteriosclerosis is a chronic infectious disease caused by blue-green bacteria carried in milk; and that the Masai avoid the disease by fermenting their milk, thereby discouraging microbial growth and contamination.

38. F. Pottenger, "The Effect of Heat-Processed Foods and Metabolized Vitamin D Milk on the Dentofacial Structures of Experimental Animals," *American Journal of Orthodontics and Oral Surgery* 32(7):467–85 (1946).

39. See American Medical Association, *Nutrients in Processed Foods: Proteins* (Acton, Mass.: Publishing Sciences Group, Inc., 1974), pages 131–47; J. Love, "Constituents of Animal Proteins That Are Affected by Cooking and Processing," in D. Beitz, R. Hansen, eds., *Animal Products in Human Nutrition* (New York: Academic Press 1982), pages 180–93.

40. S. Ettinger, *Textbook of Veterinary Internal Medicine: Diseases of the Dog and Cat*, vol. 2 (Philadelphia: W. B. Saunders Co., 1983), pages 2,034–35; B. Lapin, L. Yakovleva, *Comparative Pathology in Monkeys* (Springfield, Ill.: Charles C. Thomas, Publisher, 1960), pages 176, 245.

41. H. Roberts, note 36, pages 16, 58, 214–21; "Sushi Lovers: Beware of Parasites," *Science News* 127(9):141 (1985).

42. See C. Sugarman, "The Impact of the Raw Milk Ban," *Washington Post* (August 26, 1987).

43. See *University of California, Berkeley Wellness Letter*, note 32.

Chapter 21
STUDIES FIND FLAWS IN THE PERFECT FOOD

1. J. Boulloche, et al., "The Value of Serum IgE Assay in Milk Aspiration and the Sudden Infant Death Syndrome," *Acta Paediatr. Scand.* 75(4):530–33 (1986); D. Sandberg, et al., "Severe Steroid-Responsive Nephrosis Associated with Hypersensitivity," *Lancet* (February 19, 1977), pages 388–91; "Dietary Phosphorus and Secondary Hyperparathyroidism in Infants Receiving Humanized Cow's Milk Formula," *Nutrition Reviews* 44(3):107–09 (1986); A. Kahn, et al., "Insomnia and Cow's Milk Allergy in Infants," *Pediatrics* 76(6):880–84 (1985); J. McDougall, "Milk in Mother's Diet May Cause Infant Colic," *Vegetarian Times* (February 1985), page 54.

2. S. Freier, B. Kletter, "Milk Allergy in Infants and Young Children," *Clinical Pediatrics* 9(8):449–54 (1970); J. Emes, T. Nowak, *Introduction to Pathophysiology* (Baltimore: Univer-

sity Park Press, 1983), pages 423–32; D. Davies, "Hypothesis: An Immunological View of Atherogenesis," *Journal of Atherosclerosis Research* 10:253–59 (1969); R. Williams, *Nutrition Against Disease* (New York: Pitman Publishing Co. 1971), page 188; J. Johnson, et al., "Lactose Malabsorption Among Adult Indians of the Great Basin and American Southwest," *American Journal of Clinical Nutrition* 31:381–87 (1978).

3. "Antibody Formation to Cow's Milk Protein or Soya Protein," *Nutrition Reviews* 41(3):80–82 (1983).

4. S. Freier, et al., note 2; J. Annand, "Further Evidence in the Case Against Heated Milk Protein," *Atherosclerosis* 15:129–33 (1972). In the study discussed at note 3, the greatest antibody response was seen in the group fed pasteurized milk.

5. T. Randolph, R. Moss, *An Alternative Approach to Allergies* (New York: Lippincott & Crowell, Publishers, 1979), page 16; see discussion at note 19.

6. See P. Rank, "Milk and Arteriosclerosis," *Medical Hypotheses* 20:317–38 (1986).

7. J. Segall, "Is Milk a Coronary Heart Hazard?", *British Journal of Preventive and Social Medicine* 31:81 (1977).

8. S. Seely, "Diet and Coronary Disease. A Survey of Mortality Rates and Consumption Statistics of 24 Countries," *Medical Hypotheses* 7:907 (1981).

9. E. Guberan, "Surprising Decline in Cardiovascular Mortality in Switzerland: 1951–76," *Journal of Epidemiology and Community Health* 33:114 (1979).

10. J. Hunter, "Diet, Body-Build, Blood Pressure, and Serum Cholesterol Levels in Coconut-Eating Polynesians," *Federation Proceedings* 21 (suppl. 11), page 36 (1962); I. Prior, et al., "Cholesterol, Coconuts, and Diet on the Polynesian Atolls: A Natural Experiment," *American Journal of Clinical Nutrition* 34:1552 (1981).

11. J. Annand, "Hypothesis: Heated Milk Protein and Thrombosis," *Journal of Atherosclerosis Research* 7:797–801 (1967).

12. *Ibid*; J. Annand, "The Case Against Heated Animal Protein," *Journal of Atherosclerosis Research* 3:153–56 (1963).

13. C. Sugarman, "The Impact of the Raw Milk Ban," *Washington Post* (August 26, 1987).

14. Literature circulated by Steuve's Natural of California, the only American dairy that produces certified raw milk and raw milk products. Compare P. Rank, note 6.

15. M. Blaser, et al., "The Influence of Immunity on Raw Milk-Associated *Campylobacter* Infection," *JAMA* 257(1):43–46 (1987).

16. P. Rank, note 6.

17. C. Sugarman, note 13.

18. Compare C. Thakur, A. Jha, "Influence of Milk, Yoghurt and Calcium on Cholesterol-Induced Atherosclerosis in Rabbits," *Atherosclerosis* 39:211–15 (1981); G. Mann, "A Factor in Yoghurt Which Lowers Cholesterolemia in Man," *Ibid.* 26:335–40

(1977); E. Hussi, et al., "Lack of Serum Cholesterol-Lowering Effect of Skimmed Milk and Butter Milk Under Controlled Conditions," *Ibid.* 39:267–72 (1981); W. MacLean, et al., "Wheat Based Diets," *American Journal of Diseases of Childhood* 131:1119–21 (1977).

19. D. Davies, note 2; "Immunologic Assessment of Cow's Milk Allergy," *Nutrition Reviews* 39(3):122–23 (1981); J. Annand, note 12. But see M. Gibney, et al., "Antibodies to Heated Milk Protein in Coronary Heart Disease," *Atherosclerosis* 37:151–55 (1980).

20. "Enzyme in Homogenized Milk Said to Damage Arteries," *Vegetarian Times* (March 1984), page 14. But see P. Rank, note 6.

21. See Chapters 17–18.

22. R. Hur, *Food Reform* (Austin, Tex.: Heidelberg Publishers, 1975), page 109.

23. H. Valkenburg, "Osteoarthritis in Some Developing Countries," *Journal of Rheumatology* 10 (supp. 10):20–22 (1983).

24. See Chapter 10.

25. "Riddle of the Joints," NOVA, Public Broadcasting System (December 8, 1987).

26. L. Power, "Exploring Link Between Diet, Arthritis," *Los Angeles Times* (May 6, 1986), Part V, page 3.

27. R. Panush, et al., "Food-Induced (Allergic) Arthritis: Inflammatory Arthritis Exacerbated by Milk," *Arthritis and Rheumatism* 29(2):220–26 (1986); A. Parke, G. Hughes, "Rheumatoid Arthritis and Food: A Case Study," *British Medical Journal* 282:2027–29 (1981).

28. C. Lucas, L. Power, "Dietary Fat Aggravates Rheumatoid Arthritis," *Clinical Research* 29(4):754A (1981).

29. R. Beasley, et al., "Low Prevalence of Rheumatoid Arthritis in Chinese," *Journal of Rheumatology* 10 (supp. 10):11–15 (1983).

30. P. Beighton, et al., "Rheumatoid Arthritis in a Rural South African Negro Population," *Annals of the Rheumatic Diseases* 34:136–41 (1975); L. Solomon, "Rheumatic Disorders in the South African Negro. Part I. Rheumatoid Arthritis and Ankylosing Spondylitis," *South African Medical Journal* 49:1292 (1975).

31. C. Dong, J. Banks, *New Hope for the Arthritic* (New York: Ballantine Books, 1975).

32. N. Svartz, "The Primary Cause of Rheumatoid Arthritis is an Infection—The Infectious Agent Exists in Milk," *Acta Medica Scandinavica* 192:231–39 (1972).

33. C. Welsh, et al., "Early Rheumatoid-Like Synovial Lesions in Rabbits Drinking Cow's Milk," *Int. Archs. Allergy Appl. Immun.* 78:145–60 (1985); C. Welsh, et al., "Comparison of the Arthritogenic Properties of Dietary Cow's Milk, Egg Albumin, and Soya Milk in Experimental Animals," *ibid.* 80:192–99 (1986).

34. P. Butcher, "Milk Consumption and Multiple Sclerosis—An Etiological Hypothesis," *Medical Hypotheses* 19:169–78 (1986).

35. H. Sherman, E. Hawley, "Calcium and Phosphorus Metabolism in Childhood," *J. Biol. Chem.* 53:375 (1922).
36. P. Butcher, note 34.
37. D. Hegsted, "Balance Studies with Macro-Elements," in Advisory Board on Quartermaster Research and Development Committee on Foods, *Methods for Evaluation of Nutritional Adequacy and Status* (Washington D.C.: National Academy of Sciences—National Research Council 1954), pages 103–10.
38. J. McDougall, "Can Diet Help Multiple Sclerosis?", *Vegetarian Times* (June 1985), page 52, citing B. Agranoff, *Lancet* 2:1061 (1974), and R. Baker, *Lancet* 1:26 (1963).
39. R. Swank, "Multiple Sclerosis: Twenty Years on a Low Fat Diet," *Archives of Neurology* 23:460 (1970).

Chapter 22
MINERALS: YOU DON'T HAVE TO CHOOSE
BETWEEN ANEMIA AND CARDIAC ARREST

1. D. Hegsted, "Balance Studies with Macro-Elements," in Advisory Board on Quartermaster Research and Development Committee on Foods, *Methods for Evaluation of Nutritional Adequacy and Status* (Washington D.C.: National Academy of Sciences—National Research Council 1954), pages 105, 108.
2. See M. Abdulla, et al., "Nutrient Intake and Health Status of Vegans. Chemical Analyses of Diets Using the Duplicate Portion Sampling Technique," *American Journal of Clinical Nutrition* 34:2464–77 (1981); L. Kramer, et al., "Mineral and Trace Element Content of Vegetarian Diets," *Federation Proceedings* 40:882 (1981); and various studies cited in A. Kurtha, F. Ellis, "The Nutritional, Clinical and Economic Aspects of Vegan Diets," *Plant Foods for Human Nutrition* 2:13–22 (1970).
3. U.S. Department of Health and Human Services, *Vital and Health Statistics. Dietary Intake Source Data: United States, 1976–80*, DHHS Publication No. (PHS) 83–1681 (Hyattsville, Md.: National Center for Health Statistics 1983). For lacto-ovo-vegetarians, these relative percentages are reversed. Their diets contain twice as much calcium and only slightly more iron than the ordinary mixed American diet. See text at notes 32–37.
4. The Royal College of Physicians of London, *Medical Aspects of Dietary Fibre* (London: Pitman Medical, 1980), page 146.
5. See R. Schwartz, et al., "Apparent Absorption and Retention of Ca, Cu, Mg, Mn, and Zn from a Diet Containing Bran," *American Journal of Clinical Nutrition* 43:444–55 (1986), in which phytate provided by ordinary foods impaired mineral absorption after 1 week but not after 4 weeks. See also the Royal College of Physicians, note 4, pages 144–58.

6. H. Sandstead, et al., "Influence of Dietary Fiber on Trace Element Balance," *American Journal of Clinical Nutrition* 31:S180–84 (1978).
7. See notes 22, 24–26.
8. R. McCance, E. Glaser, "The Energy Value of Oatmeal and the Digestibility and Absorption of Its Proteins, Fat and Calcium," *British Journal of Nutrition* 2:221–28 (1948); R. Ballentine, *Diet and Nutrition* (Honesdale, Pa.: Himalayan International Institute, 1982), page 71.
9. A. Walker, B. Walker, "Effect of Wholemeal and White Bread on Iron Absorption," *British Medical Journal* 2:771–72 (1977).
10. J. Kelsay, et al., "Impact of Variation in Carbohydrate Intake on Mineral Utilization by Vegetarians," *American Journal of Clinical Nutrition* 48:875–79 (1988).
11. R. Burk, N. Solomons, "Trace Elements and Vitamins and Bio-Availability as Related to Wheat and Wheat Foods," *American Journal of Clinical Nutrition* 41:1091–1102 (1985).
12. Royal College of Physicians, note 4, page 150; R. Ballentine, note 8, page 250; C. Prosser, F. Brown, *Comparative Animal Physiology* (Philadelphia: W. B. Saunders Co. 1961), page 128.
13. O. Malm, "Calcium Requirement and Adaptation in Adult Men," *Scandinavian Journal of Clinical and Laboratory Investigation* 10 (supp.36) (1958). The reason a few of the men never succeeded in adapting to the low-calcium diet may have been that its protein content was too high (over 100 grams/day). See text at note 19.
14. A. Helman, I. Darnton-Hill, "Vitamin and Iron Status in *New* Vegetarians," *American Journal of Clinical Nutrition* 45:785–89 (1987).
15. E. Ernst, et al., "Blood Rheology in Vegetarians," *British Journal of Nutrition* 56:555–60 (1986).
16. R. Stevens, et al., "Body Iron Stores and the Risk of Cancer," *New England Journal of Medicine* 319:1047–52 (1988).
17. C. Kies, et al., "Zinc Utilization by Omnivores and Vegetarians," *Federation Proceedings* 40:855 (1981). An investigation of the 2 groups on their normal diets revealed no significant differences either in their zinc intakes or in their blood zinc levels. Compare M. Brune, et al., "Iron Absorption: No Intestinal Adaptation to a High-Phytate Diet," *American Journal of Clinical Nutrition* 49:542–45 (1988); and J. Kelsay, et al., note 10.
18. D. Beitz, R. Hansen, *Animal Products in Human Nutrition* (New York: Academic Press, 1982), page 266.
19. H. Sandstead, et al., "Influence of Dietary N on Requirements for Zn, Cu, Fe, Ca, P, and Mg," *Federation Proceedings* 40:885 (1981).
20. See L. Allen, "Calcium Bio-Availability and Absorption: A Review," *American Journal of Clinical Nutrition* 35:783–808 (1982); and Chapter 11.
21. Food and Nutrition Board Committee on Dietary Allowances,

Recommended Dietary Allowances (Washington, D.C.: National Academy of Sciences, 1980), page 129.

22. L. Schroeder, et al., "The Utilization of Calcium in Soybean Products and Other Commercial Sources," *Journal of Nutrition* 32:413–22 (1946); W. Adolph, S. Chen, "The Utilization of Calcium in Soy Bean Diets," *Journal of Nutrition* 5:379–85 (1932); D. Miller, P. Mumford, "The Nutritive Value of Western Vegan and Vegetarian Diets," *Plant Foods for Human Nutrition* 2:201–13 (1972).

23. C. Jacobs, J. Dwyer, "Vegetarian Children: Appropriate and Inappropriate Diets," *American Journal of Clinical Nutrition* 48:811–18 (1988).

24. See G. Ellis, V. Montegriffo, "Veganism, Clinical Findings and Investigations," *American Journal of Clinical Nutrition* 23:244–55 (1970); M. Abdulla, et al., note 2; and studies cited in notes 25 and 26.

25. N. Levin, et al., "Mineral Intake and Blood Levels in Vegetarians," *Israel Journal of Medical Sciences* 22:105–08 (1986).

26. B. Anderson, et al., "The Iron and Zinc Status of Long-Term Vegetarian Women," *American Journal of Clinical Nutrition* 34:1042–48 (1981).

27. U.S. Department of Health and Human Services, *Vital and Health Statistics. Hematological and Nutritional Biochemistry Reference Data for Persons 6 Months - 74 Years of Age: United States, 1976–80*, DHHS Publication No. (PHS) 83–1682 (Hyattsville, Md.: National Center for Health Statistics 1982), pages 88, 115.

28. B. Worthington-Roberts, et al., "Iron Status of Premenopausal Women in a University Community and Its Relationship to Habitual Dietary Sources of Protein," *American Journal of Clinical Nutrition* 47:275–79 (1988).

29. T. Sanders, et al., "Haematological Studies on Vegans," *British Journal of Nutrition* 40:9–15 (1978).

30. See notes 32–36.

31. S. Faelten, et al., *The Complete Book of Minerals for Health* (Emmaus, Pa.: Rodale Press, 1981), page 478.

32. L. Kramer, et al., "Mineral and Trace Element Content of Vegetarian Diets," *Federation Proceedings* 40:882 (1981); L. Kramer, et al., "Mineral and Trace Element Content of Vegetarian Diets," *Journal of the American College of Nutrition* 3:3–11 (1984).

33. U.S. Department of Health and Human Services, note 3, page 20.

34. See studies cited in A. Kurtha, et al., note 2.

35. L. Kramer, et al., note 32 (second cite).

36. U.S. Department of Health and Human Services, note 3, page 24.

37. In the Canadian study (note 26), the vegetarians had followed their diets an average of 19 years; their protein intake averaged 58 grams a day; and their vitamin C intake averaged 166 mg/day—nearly twice that of American meat-eating women in the same age group. (See D.H.H.S., note 3, page 38.)

38. R. Ballentine, note 8, page 257.

39. Food and Nutrition Board Committee on Dietary Allowances, note 21, pages 137–41.

40. M. Krause, L. Mahan, *Food, Nutrition, and Diet Therapy* (Philadelphia: W.B. Saunders Co., 1984), page 591; W. Mertz, "The new RDAs: Estimated Adequate and Safe Intake of Trace Elements and Calculation of Available Iron," *Journal of the American Dietetic Association* 76:128–33 (1980).

41. L. Hallberg, L. Rossander, "Absorption of Iron from Western-Type Lunch and Dinner Meals," *American Journal of Clincal Nutrition* 35:502–09 (1982); M. Gillooly, et al., "The Effects of Organic Acids, Phytates and Polyphenols on the Absorption of Iron from Vegetables," *British Journal of Nutrition* 49:331–41 (1983); T. Morck, et al., "Inhibition of Food Iron Absorption by Coffee," *American Journal of Clinical Nutrition* 37:416–20 (1983). Spinach alone may not impair iron absorption; but when eaten along with a high-fiber diet, it does have this effect. J. Kelsay, E. Prather, "Mineral Balances of Human Subjects Consuming Spinach in a Low-Fiber Diet and in a Diet Containing Fruits and Vegetables," *American Journal of Clinical Nutrition* 38:12–19 (1983).

42. J. Kelsay, et al., "Effect of Fiber from Fruits and Vegetables on Metabolic Responses of Human Subjects. II. Calcium, Magnesium, Iron, and Silicon Balances," *American Journal of Clinical Nutrition* 32:1876–80 (1979). See J. Cook, et al., note 43.

43. J. Cook, et al., "Effect of Fiber on Non-Heme Iron Absorption," *Gastroenterology* 85:1354–58 (1983).

44. L. Hallberg, et al., note 41.

45. V. Young, M. Janghorbani, "Soy Proteins in Human Diets in Relation to Bio-Availability of Iron and Zinc: A Brief Overview," *Cereal Chemistry* 58:12 (1981). The bio-availability of iron from soy has varied considerably in different studies, for reasons which have yet to be agreed upon. But the presence or absence of absorption-enhancing factors like vitamin C is clearly one of them.

46. T. Morck, et al., note 41.

47. E. Morris, "Effects of Dietary Fiber on Bio-Availability of Minerals," *Nutrition and Vegetarianism* (Chapel Hill, No. Car.: Health Sciences Consortium 1981), page 168. Iron-fortified foods aren't recommended either, because iron bio-availability is very low from this source. See L. Hallberg, et al., "Low Availability of Carbonyl Iron in Man: Studies on Iron Fortification of Wheat Flour," *American Journal of Clinical Nutrition* 43:59–67 (1986).

48. L. Kramer, et al., note 32. (second cite).

49. See notes 24–26.

50. L. Kramer, et al., note 32. (second cite).

51. H. Sandstead, et al., note 19.

52. J. Pohit, B. Pal, "Zinc Content of the Diets of the Sedentary

Bengalees," *International Journal for Vitamin and Nutrition Research* 55:223–25 (1985).

53. C. Swanson, et al., "Bio-Availability of Dietary Zinc: Studies in Pregnant and Non-Pregnant Women," *Federation Proceedings* 40:840 (1981).

54. J. King, et al., "Effect of Vegetarianism on the Zinc Status of Pregnant Women," *American Journal of Clinical Nutrition* 34:1049–55 (1981).

55. F. Hytten, "Do Pregnant Women Need Zinc Supplements?", *British Journal of Obstetrics and Gynaecology* 92:873–74 (1985).

Chapter 23
VITAMINS AND MINERALS WITHOUT PILLS

1. Quoted in D. Georgakas, *The Methuselah Factors* (New York: Simon and Schuster, 1980) at page 197.

2. J. Shriver, "As Vitamin Sales Pep Up, So Do Worries on Overuse," *Los Angeles Times* (March 23, 1986), Part IV, page 1; V. Stults, "Nutritional Hazards," in H. Roberts, ed., *Food Safety* (New York: John Wiley & Sons, 1981), pages 82–87, 111–13; "Getting Sick On Vitamins," *Newsweek on Health* (fall 1986), page 5.

3. M. Read, D. Thomas, "Nutrient and Food Supplement Practices of Lacto-Ovo-Vegetarians," *Journal of the American Dietetic Association* 82:401–04 (1983).

4. See, e.g., A. Kurtha, F. Ellis, "The Nutritional, Clinical and Economic Aspects of Vegan Diets," *Plant Foods for Human Nutrition* 2:13–22 (1970).

5. A. Immerman, "Vitamin B12 Status on a Vegetarian Diet," *World Review of Nutrition and Dietetics* 37:38–54 (1981).

6. J. Bergan, P. Brown, "Nutritional Status of 'New' Vegetarians," *Journal of the American Dietetic Association* 76:151–55 (1980); V. Herbert, "Nutritional Requirements for Vitamin B12 and Folic Acid," *American Journal of Clinical Nutrition* 21(7):743–52 (1968).

7. M. Albert, et al., "Vitamin B12 Synthesis by Human Small Intestinal Bacteria," *Nature* 283:781–82 (1980).

8. *Ibid.*

9. R. Ballentine, *Diet and Nutrition* (Honesdale, Pa.: Himalayan International Institute, 1982), pages 185–86.

10. A. Immerman, note 5; "Vegetarian Diet and Vitamin B12 Deficiency," *Nutrition Reviews* 36(8):243–44 (1978); A. Dong, S. Scott, "Serum Vitamin B12 and Blood Cell Values in Vegetarians," *Annals of Nutrition and Metabolism* 26:209–16 (1982); T. Sanders, F. Ellis, "Haematological Studies on Vegans," *British Journal of Nutrition* 40:9–15 (1978).

11. See studies discussed in A. Immerman, note 5. The author distinguishes each of these cases and demonstrates there is no

reliable evidence that veganism results in a clinical deficiency of vitamin B12. But see V. Herbert, note 13.

12. F. Ellis, V. Montegriffo, "The Health of Vegans," *Plant Foods for Human Nutrition* 2:93–103 (1971); A. Kurtha, et al., note 4; T. Sanders, et al., note 10.

13. V. Herbert, "Vitamin B-12: Plant Sources, Requirements and Assay," *American Journal of Clinical Nutrition* 48:852–58 (1988).

14. *Ibid.*

15. K. Rohatgi, et al., "Effect of Germination on Vitamin B12 Values of Pulses (Leguminous Seeds)," *Journal of Nutrition* 56:403–08 (1955); P. Burkholder, "Vitamins in Dehydrated Seeds and Sprouts," *Science* 97:562–64 (1943).

16. *Ibid*; see V. Kulvinskas, *Sprout for the Love of Everybody* (Wethersfield, Conn.: Omangod Press, 1978).

17. G. Briggs, D. Calloway, *Nutrition and Physical Fitness* (University of California at Berkeley: 1979), page 286.

18. See Chapter 13 and W. Crook, *The Yeast Connection* (Jackson, Tenn.: Professional Books, 1985).

19. V. Herbert, note 13.

20. J. Kirschmann, L. Dunne, *Nutrition Almanac* (New York: McGraw Hill Book Co., 1984), pages 263, 272–73.

21. G. Briggs, et al., note 17.

22. See, e.g., M. Abdulla, et al., "Nutrient Intake and Health Status of Vegans. Chemical Analyses of Diets Using the Duplicate Portion Sampling Technique," *American Journal of Clinical Nutrition* 34:2464–77 (1981); M. Abdulla, et al., "Nutrient Intake and Health Status of Lacto-Vegetarians. Chemical Analyses of Diets Using the Duplicate Portion Sampling Technique," *American Journal of Clinical Nutrition* 40:325–38 (1984); A. Kurtha, F. Ellis, note 4; E. Carlson, et al., "A Comparative Evaluation of Vegan, Vegetarian and Omnivore Diets," *Journal of Plant Foods* 6:89–100 (1985); D. Miller, P. Mumford, "The Nutritive Value of Vegan and Vegetarian Diets," *Plant Foods for Human Nutrition* 2:201–13 (1972).

23. M. Abdulla, et al., note 22 (two studies).

24. Iodine deficiency results in goiter, or thyroid enlargement, which is prevented by only 50–75 mcg of the mineral daily. Food and Nutrition Board Committee on Dietary Allowances, *Recommended Dietary Allowances* (Washington, D.C.: National Academy of Sciences 1980), page 148.

25. T. Shultz, J. Leklem, "Selenium Status of Vegetarians, Non-Vegetarians and Hormone-Dependent Cancer Subjects," *American Journal of Clinical Nutrition* 37:114–18 (1983).

26. B. Debski, et al., "Selenium Content and Glutathione Peroxidase Activity of Milk from Vegetarian and Non-Vegetarian Women," *Journal of Nutrition* 119:215–20 (1989).

27. L. Cohen, "Diet and Cancer," *Scientific American* 257(5):42–48 (1987).

28. T. Shultz, et al., note 25. The cancer patients were 16 omnivorous women diagnosed as presently having or previously having had hormone-dependent malignancies. All had been in remission for at least 6 months.
29. E. Carlson, et al., note 22.
30. R. Ballentine, note 9, pages 175–76.
31. See D. Miller, et al., note 22; and studies cited in A. Kurtha, et al., note 4.
32. See D. Lawson, et al., "Relative Contributions of Diet and Sunlight to Vitamin D State in the Elderly," *British Medical Journal* 2:303–05 (1979).
33. *Ibid.*; M. Poskitt, et al., "Diet, Sunlight, and 25-Hydroxy Vitamin D in Healthy Children and Adults," *British Medical Journal* 1:221–23 (1979).
34. D. Fraser, "The Physiological Economy of Vitamin D," *Lancet* (April 30, 1983), pages 969–72.
35. M. Holick, "Photosynthesis of Vitamin D in the Skin: Effect of Environmental and Life-Style Variables," *Federation Proceedings* 46:1876–82 (1987).
36. D. Lawson, et al., note 32; D. Fraser, note 34; D. Corless, et al., "Response of Plasma-25-Hydroxyvitamin D to Ultraviolet Irradiation in Long-Stay Geriatric Patients," *Lancet* (September 23, 1978), pages 649–51.
37. J. Dwyer, et al., "Risk of Nutritional Rickets Among Vegetarian Children," *American Journal of Diseases of Childhood* 133:134–40 (1979).
38. M. Holick, note 35.
39. A. Norman, ed., *Vitamin D: Molecular Biology and Clinical Nutrition* (N.Y.: Marcel Dekker, Inc., 1980), page 526.
40. "The Ultimate Seafood: A Plunge Into Sea Vegetable Cookery," *Vegetarian Times* (February 1985), page 44.
41. "Do Chlorophyll and Spirulina Offer Any Health Benefits?", *University of California, Berkeley Wellness Letter* (May 1988), page 8.
42. *Vegetarian Times* (July 1987), page 25.
43. D. Howard, *The Spirulina Diet* (Secaucus, N.J.: Lyle Stuart Inc., 1982).
44. C. Adams, *Nutritive Value of American Foods in Common Units*, Agriculture Handbook No. 456 (Washington, D.C.: USDA 1975).
45. "B Vitamins in Sprouted Cereal Grains," *Nutrition Reviews* 15:356 (1943); V. Kulvinskas, note 16, pages 26–33, 50–56.
46. See V. Kulvinskas, note 16.
47. J. Kirschmann, note 20, pages 235, 245; J. Nelson, "Wheat: Its Processing and Utilization," *American Journal of Clinical Nutrition* 41:1070–76 (1985).
48. Milk contains .1 mg of iron per 8-ounce serving, while tofu contains 4.3 mg. C. Adams, *Nutritive Value of American Foods in Common Units*, Agriculture Handbook No. 456 (Washington, D.C.: USDA 1975).

Chapter 24
RAISING A HEALTHY CHILD ON GRAINS AND GREENS

1. E. Widdowson, R. McCance, "Studies on the Nutritive Value of Bread and on the Effects of Variations in the Extraction Rate of Flour on the Growth of Undernourished Children," *Medical Research Council Special Report Series* No. 287 (London: Her Majesty's Stationery Office 1954).
2. C. Paterson, "Calcium Requirements in Man: A Critical Review," *Postgraduate Medical Journal* 54:244–48 (1978).
3. The daily requirement for protein for a 44-pound child is only 16 grams (12.2 grams of milk protein, with a safety factor added in). See B. Torun, et al., "Protein Requirements of Preschool Children: Obligatory Nitrogen Losses and Nitrogen Balance Measurements Using Cow's Milk," *Archivos Latino-Americanos de Nutricion* 31(3):571–85 (1981). This amount of protein is supplied by 3 whole wheat English muffins.
4. R. McCance, E. Widdowson, "Mineral Metabolism in Healthy Adults on White and Brown Bread Dietaries," *Journal of Physiology* 101:44–85 (1942).
5. *Natural Foods Guide*, excerpted from *Whole Foods Magazine* (Berkeley, CA: And/Or Press, 1979), pages 97–98; L. Hallberg, et al., "Low Bio-Availability of Carbonyl Iron in Man: Studies on Iron Fortification of Wheat Flour," *American Journal of Clinical Nutrition* 43:59–67 (1986).
6. I. Vyhmeister, et al., "Safe Vegetarian Diets for Children," *Pediatric Clinics of North America* 24(1):203–210 (1977).
7. See Chapter 23.
8. "Vegetarian Diet and Vitamin B12 Deficiency," *Nutrition Reviews* 36(8):243–44 (1978); letter to the editor by P. Fleiss, et al., *New England Journal of Medicine* 299(23):1319 (1978).
9. C. Jacobs, J. Dwyer, "Vegetarian Children: Appropriate and Inappropriate Diets," *American Journal of Clinical Nutrition* 48:811–18 (1988).
10. J. Carter, et al., "Preeclampsia and Reproductive Performance in a Community of Vegans," *Southern Medical Journal* 80(6):692–97 (1987); J. O'Connell, et al., "Growth of Vegetarian Children: The Farm Study," *Pediatrics* 84(3):475–81 (1989).
11. T. Sanders, F. Ellis, "Haematological Studies on Vegans," *British Journal of Nutrition* 40:9–15 (1978).
12. T. Sanders, et al., "Studies of Vegans: The Fatty Acid Composition of Plasma Choline Phosphoglycerides, Erythrocytes, Adipose Tissue, and Breast Milk, and Some Indicators of Susceptibility to Ischemic Heart Disease in Vegans and Omnivore Controls," *American Journal of Clinical Nutrition* 31:805–13 (1978).
13. T. Sanders, "Growth and Development of British Vegan Children," *American Journal of Clinical Nutrition* 48:822–25 (1988). See also T. Sanders, "An Anthropometric and Dietary Assessment of the Nutritional Status of Vegan Preschool Children," *Journal of Human Nutrition* 35:349–57 (1981).

370   *Ellen Hodgson Brown*

14. J. Dwyer, et al., "Nutritional Status of Vegetarian Children," *American Journal of Clinical Nutrition* 35:204–16 (1982).
15. See U.S. Department of Health and Human Services, *Vital and Health Statistics. Dietary Intake Source Data: United States, 1976–80,* DHHS Publication No. (PHS) 83–1681 (Hyattsville, Md.: National Center for Health Statistics 1983), page 24.
16. J. Dwyer, et al., "Mental Age and I.Q. of Predominantly Vegetarian Children," *Journal of the American Dietetic Association* 76:142–47 (1980). Not that meat necessarily impairs intelligence. More likely, the vegetarian children came from parents of above-average intelligence.
17. E. Shinwell, R. Gorodischer, "Totally Vegetarian Diets and Infant Nutrition," *Pediatrics* 70(4):582–86 (1982).
18. Royal College of Physicians of London, *Medical Aspects of Dietary Fibre* (London: Pitman Medical 1980), pages 148–49.
19. J. Reinhold, et al., "Availability of Zinc in Leavened and Unleavened Wholemeal Wheaten Breads as Measured by Solubility and Uptake by Rat Intestine in Vitro," *Journal of Nutrition* 104:976–82 (1974). Rickets is also common in Iran, where a similar unleavened flat bread is the principal food. *Ibid.*
20. Royal College of Physicians, note 18.
21. J. Pietrek, et al., "Prevention of Vitamin-D Deficiency in Asians," *Lancet* (May 29, 1976), pages 1145–48.
22. A. Shah, S. Seshadri, "Anemia in Relation to Dietary Iron Deficiency, Iron Availability and Parasitic Infection," *Nutrition Research* 5:341–47 (1985). Most of the nonanemic children in this study drank milk with their meals. Compared to meat and Vitamin C, milk inhibits iron absorption; but compared to tea, it seems to enhance it.
23. T. Sanders, "Vegetarianism: Dietetic and Medical Aspects," *Journal of Plant Foods* 5:3–14 (1983).
24. J. Hebert, "Relationship of Vegetarianism to Child Growth in South India," *American Journal of Clinical Nutrition* 42:1246–54 (1985).
25. M. Higginbottom, et al., "A Syndrome of Methylmalonic Aciduria, Homocystinuria, Megaloblastic Anemia and Neurologic Abnormalities in a Vitamin B12-Deficient Breast-Fed Infant of a Strict Vegetarian," *New England Journal of Medicine* 299(7): 317–23 (1978); "Vitamin B12 Deficiency in the Breast-Fed Infant of a Strict Vegetarian," *Nutrition Reviews* 37(5): 142–44 (1979).
26. A. Immerman, "Vitamin B12 Status on a Vegetarian Diet," *World Review of Nutrition and Dietetics* 37:38–54 (1981).
27. M. Higginbottom, et al., note 25.
28. A. Immerman, note 26. See also note 8.
29. See, e.g., E. Shinwell, et al., note 17.
30. See Chapter 22.
31. F. Oski, "Is Bovine Milk a Health Hazard?", *Pediatrics* 75 (Suppl):182–86 (1985). See also the Swiss Pediatric Associa-

tion's response in "Health Hazards of Cow's Milk," *Pediatrics* 76(6):1021–23 (1985), which includes a reply by Dr. Oski.

32. R. Hunter, "Iron Nutrition in Infancy," in *Report of the 62nd Ross Conference in Pediatric Research* (Columbus, Ohio: 1970), page 22.

33. F. Oski, note 31, citing WHO Tech. Rpt., Series #580, *Control of Nutritional Anemia with Special Reference to Iron Deficiency* (Geneva 1975). But see note 22.

34. J. Wilson, et al., "Studies on Iron Metabolism: V. Further Observations on Cow's Milk-Induced Gastrointestinal Bleeding in Infants with Iron-Deficiency Anemia," *Journal of Pediatrics* 84:335 (1974).

35. F. Oski, note 31.

36. See R. Williams, *Nutrition Against Disease* (New York: Pitman Publishing Corp. 1971), pages 271–73.

37. W. MacLean, et al., "Wheat-Based Diets: Effect of Short-Term Consumption on Serum Cholesterol and Triglyceride Levels in Infants," *American Journal of Diseases of Childhood* 131:1119–21 (1977).

38. B. Lindquist, "Recent Views on Infant Nutrition," *Paediatrician* 8(1):37–47 (1970).

39. L. Lotzof, "Dairy Produce and Coronary Artery Disease," *Medical Journal of Australia* 1(26):1317 (1973).

40. B. Lindquist, note 38.

41. C. Jacobs, et al., note 9.

42. *Ibid.*

Chapter 25
VEGAN SOLUTIONS TO THE FOOD CRISIS

1. See "Sensible Eating," *British Medical Journal* (July 9, 1977), page 80.

2. F. Lappé, *Diet for a Small Planet* (New York: Ballantine Books, 1975), page 9.

3. S. Vaghefi, et al., "Lysine Supplementation of Wheat Proteins: A Review," *American Journal of Clinical Nutrition* 27:1231–46 (1974); "FYI," *Vegetarian Times* (August 1988), page 8.

4. W. Shurtleff, A. Aoyagi, *The Book of Tofu* (Brookline, Mass.: Autumn Press, Inc. 1975), page 17.

5. R. Hur, *Food Reform* (Austin, Tex.: Heidelberg Publishers, 1975), page 183; see Chapter 5.

6. Joint FAO/WHO Ad Hoc Expert Committee, *Energy and Protein Requirements*, Techn. Rpt. No. 522 (Geneva: World Health Organization 1973); R. Hur, note 5, page 182; see Chapters 2, 5.

7. D. Georgakas, *The Methuselah Factors* (New York: Simon and Schuster, 1980), page 198.

8. R. Hur, note 5, pages 181–82.

9. *Ibid.*, pages 186, 188.

10. K. Mellanby, *Can Britain Feed Itself?* (London: Merlin Press, 1977).
11. "Sensible Eating," *British Medical Journal* (July 9, 1977), page 80; F. Lappé, J. Collins, *Food First: Beyond the Myth of Scarcity* (New York: Ballantine Books, 1977), page 13.
12. R. Hur, note 5, pages 184–85; V. Kulvinskas, *Sprout for the Love of Every Body* (Wethersfield, Conn.: Omangod Press, 1978); S. Vaghefi, et al., note 3; E. Irving, "Agency Links Vitamin A Use with Saving Lives," *Front Lines* (December 1987), page 3, quoting Dr. Frances Davidson.
13. A. Walker, B. Walker, "Recommended Dietary Allowances and Third World Populations," *American Journal of Clinical Nutrition* 34:2319–21 (1981).
14. S. Darke, et al., "Frequency Distributions of Mean Daily Intakes of Food Energy and Selected Nutrients Obtained During Nutrition Surveys of Different Groups of People in Great Britain Between 1968 and 1971," *British Journal of Nutrition* 44:243–52 (1971).
15. A. Walker, et al., note 13.
16. See L. Jacobs, *Free Our Public Lands!*, (Cottonwood, Ariz.: P.O. Box 2203), pages 2–4, 29.
17. H. Dregne, "Desertification of Arid Lands," *Economic Geography* 53(4):325 (1977).
18. F. Lappé, et al., note 11, pages 44–48.
19. L. Jacobs, note 16, pages 2–4, 12, 16, 29; D. Ferguson, N. Ferguson, *Sacred Cows at the Public Trough* (Bend, Ore.: Maverick Publications, 1983).
20. Two percent of our annual per capita beef intake is about 25 ounces. (See note 16 and Chapter 1.)
21. W. Root, R. de Rochemont, *Eating in America: A History* (New York: Ecco Press 1976), page 205.

Index